A HISTORY OI

MW00987266

Why do we sing and what first drove early humans to sing? How might they have sung, and how might those styles have survived to the present day? This history addresses these questions and many more, examining singing as a historical and cross-cultural phenomenon. It explores the evolution of singing in a global context – from Neanderthal man to Auto-tune via the infinite varieties of world music from Orient to Occident, classical music from medieval to the avant-garde, and popular music from vaudeville to rock and beyond. Considering singing as a universal human activity, the book provides an in-depth perspective on singing from many cultures and periods: Western and non-Western, prehistoric to present. Written in a lively and entertaining style, the history contains a comprehensive reference section for those who wish to explore the topic further, and will appeal to an international readership of singers, students and scholars.

JOHN POTTER is a singer and writer. He was for many years a member of the Hilliard Ensemble and he has an eclectic discography of some 150 titles which include five gold discs and several Grammy nominations, and music ranging from Leonin to Led Zeppelin. He currently maintains a portfolio of freelance performance projects and also coaches vocal ensembles and choirs all over the world. He spent twelve years as a lecturer at the University of York and is now an independent performer and scholar, researching all aspects of the voice. He is the editor of *The Cambridge Companion to Singing* (2000), author of *Vocal Authority* (1998) and *Tenor: History of a Voice* (2009), and has contributed to several Cambridge Histories of Music.

NEIL SORRELL is Senior Lecturer in Music at the University of York. He specialises in Asian music and has written, broadcast and lectured extensively on Indian and Javanese music. He is the author (with the great sarangi player, Pandit Ram Narayan) of *Indian Music in Performance: A Practical Introduction* (1980) and is a recipient of the 1999 Hafiz Ali Khan Award, an international award in recognition of contributions to Indian classical music. He co-founded and directed the English Gamelan Orchestra, the first group of British musicians dedicated to the study, composition and performance of music for the Javanese gamelan. He has composed several pieces for the gamelan, and is the author of *A Guide to the Gamelan* (second edition 2000).

A HISTORY OF SINGING

JOHN POTTER AND NEIL SORRELL

CAMBRIDGE
UNIVERSITY PRESS

CAMBRIDGE
UNIVERSITY PRESS

University Printing House, Cambridge CB2 8BS, United Kingdom

Cambridge University Press is part of the University of Cambridge.

It furthers the University's mission by disseminating knowledge in the pursuit of education, learning and research at the highest international levels of excellence.

www.cambridge.org
Information on this title: www.cambridge.org/9781107630093

© John Potter and Neil Sorrell 2012

First published 2012
Paperback edition first published 2014

A catalogue record for this publication is available from the British Library

ISBN 978-0-521-81705-9 Hardback
ISBN 978-1-107-63009-3 Paperback

Contents

Acknowledgements

We would like to thank the staff at Cambridge University Press for being so patient, especially Jodie Barnes and Rebecca Taylor, commissioning editors Penny Souster and Vicki Cooper, and our assiduous copy editor Hilary Scannell. Among the many people whose advice we have sought we should particularly like to thank Alan Bilgora, Tim Day, Liz Haddon, Larry Josefovitz, Daniel Lasker, David Lefkowitz, Chris Macklin, Ned Potter and Penny Potter. Parts of chapters 5 and 7 have drawn on John Potter's 'Beggar at the Door: the Rise and Fall of Portamento in Singing', *Music & Letters* 87: 4 (2006).

Introduction

The original idea for this book was for a single-authored volume by a singer, giving a broad historical overview of singing in a global context. One of the anonymous readers of the proposal for Cambridge University Press gently suggested that this might be rather a lot for one person to undertake, and sure enough, several missed deadlines later the project morphed into a book with two authors: one a specialist in Western singing and the other in non-Western music.

The first thing we should say is that it is *a* history of singing, not *the* history. This is not just because trying to write a comprehensive history of all the singing in the world really would, even if possible, require a vast team and not just two authors, but also because there is no way of knowing exactly what the history is. The chapter on origins makes it clear that the when, as well as the why and what, of the origins of singing cannot be established with any certainty. There is also a danger of getting bogged down in the question of what singing actually is. A great deal of vocal tract activity, often a long way from bel canto or crooning, is accepted as singing even if actual pitches are not always discernible. Inuit 'throat singing', the whispered songs of Burundi and even the singing of Tom Waits all rely on timbre and rhythm rather than pitch and tune yet are readily classified as singing.[1] Laurence Picken, a biologist as well as a distinguished musicologist, wrote 'This is indeed song: the fundamental frequency of phonation generated by the larynx is varied systematically. Song is nothing else.'[2] While we have a scientific description of singing we must distinguish between 'song' as physical act and 'singing' as meaningful human activity.

---

[1] Jonathan Stock's transcription of a Burundi whispered praise song notates the voice on an unpitched single line, with the explanation 'rhythm only'; see his *World Sound Matters* (London: Schott Educational Publications, 1996): 57–9.
[2] From the foreword to Peter Fletcher, *World Musics in Context: a Comprehensive Survey of the World's Major Musical Cultures* (Oxford University Press, 2001): 10.

Still, it would be impossible to write a history of singing without including some history of songs and singers.

Regarding how to approach even a small sample from the bewilderingly diverse music cultures of the world, the question inevitably arises not only of how the strands may be brought together but also of how perceptive and informed the resulting accounts may be. Sources will vary hugely in nature and validity. Writings in the English language inevitably predominate, meaning that much of the information has been documented by 'outsiders' who, nevertheless, for the most part strive to convey as closely as possible the 'insider' terminology, perception and, above all, evaluation of what the music means. This can bring to the history all sorts of legends and beliefs which do not accord with other available facts; but they must nonetheless be admitted and appreciated as they are what 'insiders' believe and therefore help to shape their perception of music and its meaning. Because of this need to elevate the 'insider' view, the 'outsider' researcher shrank away from the temptation to impose his or her views and attempted instead to become an idealised conduit through which ideas might flow directly from their source into publication. The data could be challenged even then and the whole methodology brought into question through the realisation that the researcher was not a neutral conduit but more of a filter.

Perhaps we are turning full circle to the first half of the twentieth century, an era when Western scholars followed the obvious path of comparing what they discovered with what they already knew: an approach disparagingly known as comparative musicology. It is very hard to put all pre-conceived ideas out of our heads and pretend that unfamiliar music is not somehow being evaluated and understood in terms of what we already know and think of as music. In so doing we are seeking out points of reference, the universals which are a major impetus behind cross-cultural research. If there are no universals then it becomes impossible for one culture to hear another culture's music as music. We even go outside our species and find song among the birds and whales. At the same time the warm embrace of such perceptions leads to obstructive fallacies, perhaps the most familiar of which is the notion of music as a universal language. Picken made the connection from this misconception to much broader methodological concerns: 'That which would begin to make sense of "ethnomusicology" as a scientific discipline is a primary recognition and acceptance of the "otherness" of music, as compared with language.'[3]

---

[3] Ibid.: 26.

While music is not the same as language in the first place, and therefore cannot be adequately compared to it, the analogy throws up at least one useful notion. Language is universal (as is music) but languages are mostly mutually unintelligible, so the process of translation is necessary. The fallacy also rests on the assumption that music needs no such process, implying an instant understanding. We may enjoy listening to a poem or watching a drama entirely in a foreign language we do not understand, revelling in the sounds and soaking up the special atmosphere, and this is really how we listen to so much 'World Music' (a poor term largely replacing the old-fashioned – and even worse – 'exotic'). So the ways in which we approach foreign cultures – and what our responses are – must be an abiding concern, which extends to the ways in which these cultures are presented. The reader should be aware of the dynamics and potential for partial understanding and even misinformation.

Laurence Picken set out an analytical framework, admitting both insider and outsider views, and issued a warning which we do well to heed:

Reading ethnomusicological writings of the last decade, a biologist is at times saddened to witness the attempt to comprehend, and give definitive, all-embracing description, to complex ritual processes. Our minds are not equipped so to do; our most useful intellectual attribute is that of analytical discrimination. Comprehensive description, whether diachronic or synchronic, eludes us. The modern abusive use of the term 'reductionist' is symptomatic of the age. At times it seems to be used almost as if any analytical approach to any aspect of culture is to be regarded as 'racist'.[4]

The reference to diachronic or synchronic description also appears to jeopardise the attempt to trace a history, and the thrust of Picken's remarks is not only to sound a note of caution but may also seem to paint us into a corner. Ethnomusicology is not lacking in ambition and even seems to be trying to do everything. An ethnomusicologist is often perceived to be someone studying music outside the Western classical tradition and having some knowledge of all such music. How this dauntingly extensive knowledge is obtained is to be left open, though if it is to be acquired at all it must be primarily of a secondary nature, relying on the work of others rather than on one's own primary research (usually through fieldwork). To paraphrase Wittgenstein: whereof one has not undertaken fieldwork, thereof one must be silent. The reliance on fieldwork lies at the heart of ethnomusicology, directing its fundamental research methodology, but it presents a contradiction when attempting a wide survey, such

---

[4] Ibid.: 23.

as the one for which Picken wrote his trenchant foreword, or this one. The contradiction emerges whenever the scope of the research becomes over-ambitious and the critical reception is correspondingly unforgiving.

A good example is the Cantometrics project of the 1960s, devised by the great folk-song collector Alan Lomax (1915–2002). Despite the controversy surrounding the project it was a notable attempt to help us understand and classify the wealth of singing styles around the world by correlating singing styles with social and cultural data. It was never really put to extensive use, yet its contribution to our understanding of what singing is, how it varies and how it can sound remarkably similar in cultures separated by thousands of miles should not be ignored and for this reason at least a brief discussion of Cantometrics must have its place in a history of singing. Lomax asked some original and important questions; the fact that he could not be expected to find all the answers should not lead to the outright dismissal of his controversial theories. He was in many ways ahead of his time in realising, by the 1950s, that staff notation was inadequate to capture the essence of folk song as it could not express the texture and gestures that are essential to the singing style, and certainly could not give any clue as to the music's social function.

On a field trip to Spain in 1953 (and later in Italy) Lomax perceived a relationship between the singers' high-pitched, strained and emotional sound and the high degree of sexual prohibition (specifically of female pre-marital intercourse). In more permissive areas the singing tended to be lower, softer and more relaxed. These observations led not only to the whole idea of Cantometrics but also perhaps to its most notorious aspect. They are also held up as an example of the flaws in the project, most notably the danger of generalisation. Vocal tension is hard to determine simply by listening and on that basis the hardest criterion on which to reach a consensus. One would, moreover, expect singing style to reflect more than just one aspect of a culture.

Lomax formulated and applied the aims and methods of Cantometrics in the 1960s in collaboration with Victor Grauer, a composer and musicologist, at Columbia University (New York).[5] Cantometrics was a statistical method to study the performance style of singing rather than the

---

[5] Lomax met Grauer in 1960 during a visit to Wesleyan University, Connecticut, where Grauer was working on an MA under the supervision of the distinguished anthropologist and ethnomusicologist David MacAllester (Gage Averill in Ronald D. Cohen (ed.), *Alan Lomax: Selected Writings 1934–1997* (New York and London: Routledge, 2003): 237). Work began in earnest on the generously funded Cantometrics project the following year. Grauer is still helping to keep some interest in it alive today, largely via blogs.

actual songs. It was nothing if not hugely ambitious, and its pretensions were bound to attract a proportionate amount of criticism. Cantometrics attempted to establish something universal, an attempt which was attractive both to music lovers and scholars, as the universality of music and the ability to appreciate so much across such divergent cultures is almost an anchor for the study of music. At the same time it is fraught with problems as so much of what might be glibly termed 'universal' is no such thing and a search for the universal may be no more than an attempt to force irreconcilable variants together under a single world view. To give Lomax and Grauer credit for a pioneering achievement, Cantometrics did seek a better understanding of music and its social function – a quest which has never ceased to be the cornerstone of ethnomusicology. Cantometrics must be treated as a heuristic, rather than a purely objective method. In its very broad-based comparisons it compelled a union, not entirely comfortable, between specialists and generalists. It rested on a set of premises: how people sing is influenced by the dominant values of their society and affected by modes of subsistence, political and class structures, sexual mores, treatment of children, and so on; the singing varies according to social structure, so solo and unison singing go with social cohesion and centralisation, while more varied group singing without a leader goes with individualistic societies and egalitarian groups; the distribution of vocal styles relates to the distribution of societies, so when dissimilar societies resemble each other according to these criteria their singing styles will also resemble each other; this will permit such groups to be placed into much larger regional groupings.

Part of the criticism of the methodology involved in Cantometrics was that the investigation relied on decontextualised recordings and the sample of ten songs per culture was deemed too small to be reliable; yet the real question was not the size but whether the sample was representative. Lomax relied to some extent on the collectors themselves to choose representative selections, according to their expertise and experience, which could vary from one collector to the next. While not generally adopted by ethnomusicologists Cantometrics has by no means fallen into complete obscurity or survived merely as a historical aberration.[6] Statistical analysis is problematic and perhaps less appealing to ethnomusicologists than to scientists. Yet it is precisely the lack of scientific objectivity and rigour,

---

[6] Gage Averill pointed out, however, that of 'the many obituaries and tributes that followed Alan Lomax's death in 2002, few even mentioned Cantometrics, the centrepiece of his academic project' (in Cohen, *Alan Lomax*: 234).

as well as a reliance on hypothetical conclusions, that led to the rejection of Cantometrics within the humanities. A different explanation was offered by Grauer: simply that Lomax was not an academic and resisted any temptation to become one, but in so doing isolated himself not only from an influential army of arbiters of intellectual worth but also from a potential body of graduate students who could carry on and champion his work.[7] Worse still, Lomax failed to make his database readily available, thus denying even those wishing to adopt Cantometrics any real means of doing so.[8] Unsurprisingly, therefore, Cantometrics has fallen to scientists to attempt a greater degree of scientific objectivity and rigour, finding a new lease of life in the work of the evolutionary biologist Armand Leroi (at Imperial College, London), in collaboration with Brian Eno and the Alan Lomax Foundation of New York. With more sophisticated technology and a sample of something in the order of twenty times the already large collections of songs available to Lomax almost fifty years ago the research should lead to a revaluation of the original project, even if only through taking it as a starting point and inspiration.

Cantometric theory would also be very difficult to apply to Western classical singing (the necessary fieldwork would mean acquiring a great deal of personal information which singers might be reluctant to give) and theories or histories of vocal development within Western music are thin on the ground. Pop singing has only come within range of musicologists and analysts within the last thirty years or so, and the rush to invest pop musicology with academic credibility has sometimes caused considerable obfuscation, much to the amusement of those rock singers inclined to read the literature. The questions raised by obscure pop lyrics, for example, could often be solved by picking up the phone to the singer; rather than resort to this simple short cut we can opt for lyrical analysis, a version of the 'lit crit game' which often tells us more about the writer than the written about. It is not surprising that the legitimisation of pop music over the course of the twentieth century has produced a legitimising literature, and pop musicology now has distinguished authorities of its own to call upon; but for many years musicologists would look outside music for points of reference, conceptual frameworks or even suitable vocabulary.

The last quarter of the twentieth century in particular saw numbers of academics drawing on Roland Barthes's eloquent essay 'The Grain of the Voice' in an attempt to understand how pop singing worked. In

---

[7] Grauer quoted by Averill in ibid.: 243.   [8] Ibid.: 244.

geno-song and pheno-song, Barthes's terms borrowed from the semioti-
cian Julia Kristeva, many commentators found a way of explaining the
process by which pop singers communicate meaning. Barthes's 'grain'
was the point at which voice and language meet. Geno-song is the area
of vocality which presents the meaning – the sensual, physical pleasure
that excites the neural pathways; pheno-song is the supporting technical
process which enables this to happen. Some singers have a gift for geno-
song, others merely go through the motions and we only hear pheno-
song. Ironically, Barthes was talking about classical singing, and he cited
Charles Panzéra and Dietrich Fischer-Dieskau as examples of the respective modes. In the singing of the latter Barthes hears only 'the lungs, never
the tongue, the glottis, the teeth, the mucous membranes, the nose',[9]
whereas Panzéra expressed the truth of language. Barthes asked if he was
alone in perceiving this, and the answer was a resounding 'no' from many
musicologists, who recognised Barthes's seductive terms not in classical
singers, but in pop singers.

Few of those who drew on Barthes were singers themselves, and those
who were often found it difficult to understand how the musical taste of
a French philosopher could have such an impact on musicology. Barthes
learned his singing from his armchair, and his writings on the subject are
purely subjective. It is quite possible to listen to his two singers and come
to the opposite conclusion about their deployment of his two modes.
Taste is time specific – Panzéra is of a previous generation to Fischer-
Dieskau, and represents the kind of singing Barthes would have heard in
his formative years. Fischer-Dieskau is the new singing – Elvis Presley to
Panzéra's Sinatra, or John Lennon to his Elvis. Had he been born a generation later Barthes would have thought rather differently. In another
irony, Barthes derived his theory from his listening yet ignored the creative subjectivity with which listeners complete a performance in their
own heads. The result has been a lot of intellectual endeavour based on
a speculative theory which singers have very little time for. The fact that
classical singing has largely ignored Barthes is something of a relief (the
prospect of conservatoire courses in geno-song is not a happy one), but
there have been attempts to produce perfect singers. In some classical

---

[9] Roland Barthes, 'Le grain de la Voix', *Musique en jeu* 9 (1972), trans. Stephen Heath, in *Image,
Music, Text* (London: Fontana, 1977): 183–4. Barthes elaborated on his love for Panzéra's voice in
The Responsibility of Forms: Critical Essays on Music, Art and Representation (New York: Hill and
Wang, 1985; Berkeley: University of California Press, 1992). The relevant section is reprinted as
'Music, Voice, Language', in Martin Clayton (ed.), *Music, Words and Voice: a Reader* (Manchester
University Press, 2008): 79–84.

singing studios computers are used to enable students to copy successful models, and pop music entrepreneurs are able to create boy and girl
bands more or less to order. In our survey of singing we have generally
steered clear of why singing works in the way that it does, believing that
it is the listeners' prerogative to decide that for themselves. In any culture
or genre, the most creative singers will always have something that no
one else has, and if there was a secret to perfect performance we certainly
would not want to reveal it.

Mindful of the problems facing anyone wishing to write – or read –
what purports to be a comprehensive survey or post-Cantometrics
research model, we can only attempt presentations of varying magnitude
and depth from selected traditions and world cultures, accepting that
the proportion of the impossible 'everything' they occupy must be tiny.
Because preferences, quirks and individual expertise are unlikely of themselves to produce enough material, other strategies need to be adopted.
Commencing an incomparably more wide-ranging and single-authored
book, Peter Fletcher remarked: 'Generalist books usually contain a distil-
lation of the specialist work of others',[10] which will of course apply (to a
lesser extent) to this book, especially in those pages that venture beyond
the European art tradition. As already argued, the question of how far
beyond and exactly where is deeply problematic. The aim is to touch upon
issues from less familiar traditions in various parts of the world, which
may help the lay reader to form a historical image or series of contrasting
images to inflect and enrich those already acquired from the process of
enculturation.

Western classical singing does loom rather large in this context, in
part because its history (and even, to some extent, its prehistory) can be
deduced from written sources over a period of some two thousand years.
We have not attempted to construct a grand theory of singing that might
draw together the various global strands, but have broadly tried to explain
our own specialist areas as we understand them (some chapters are individually authored, others are collaborations). We have conceived the book
in three broad categories, two of which are necessarily silent and therefore
somewhat speculative as they pre-date the recording watershed. The first
of these, on mythology and muses, offers some thoughts on the possible
origins of singing as a human activity; the second section, on historical
voices, looks at the evolution of Western classical singing up to the end of
the nineteenth century; the third part, on recorded voices, continues the

---

[10] Fletcher, *World Musics in Context*: v.

more recent history of the Western classical tradition, but in the context of other sorts of singing that we can hear on record: singing from non-Western cultures (especially the Indian subcontinent) and the evolution of singing in popular music. In the final section we take two slices across the planet, on latitudes 42 degrees north and 22 degrees south, not with a view to joining vocal dots, but rather the reverse: to give an idea of the extraordinary diversity of vocal activity we humans get up to. More slices would reveal an almost unimaginable variety of singing, confirming the impossibility of the task. We have tried to interrupt the narrative with only a minimum of footnotes, but all our sources are documented in the final sources and references section. This not only explains where we got it all from, but also includes other material that we may not have used but which readers might find helpful. We are very conscious of the fact that this is a small book on a big topic, so we have tried to give readers the possibility of exploring further if they wish.

PART I

Imagined voices

CHAPTER I

Origins, myths and muses

A history is usually expected to be chronological and to start at the beginning. Searching for the origins of singing in turn raises the question of the impulse to sing, as without that there would have been no origin. Scientists and musicologists have offered various theories to address the questions of when and how, while different peoples around the world assume a plethora of reasons for singing and the inspiration behind what is sung, be they from mythological muses (often divine inspiration, typically conveyed in dreams) or the mundane ones around them (non-human, such as birds, as well as human teachers). Tracing a path through all this in order to offer a cohesive account is no easy task, since theories conflict and even the results of scientific research remain perforce speculative. Instead, a far more selective and concise discussion is proposed of the impulses to sing, which may help us to understand how singing manifested itself and why both impulses and manifestations may have stood the test of time (a very long period of time at that). Thus 'why' and 'what' are more fruitful lines of enquiry concerning the origins of singing than 'when' or 'where'.

With an evanescent activity such as singing, which leaves no fossils or other tangible or visible evidence (and later notations convey the song rather than the singing), it is not only impossible to say exactly when or where the beginning was but also what was (and, we may venture, still is) meant by the term 'singing':

All over the world, from the Eskimo to the Fuegians, from the Lapps to the Bushmen, people sing and shout and bleat with voices wild or monotonous; they scream and mumble, nasalize and yodel; they squeak and howl; they rattle, clapper, and drum. Their tonal range is limited, their intervals are foreign, their forms short-winded, their inventive capacities, it seems, rather deficient, their traditional shackles all powerful. Is it permissible to call these noises music, if the word denotes the sacred art of Bach and of Mozart?[1]

---

[1] Curt Sachs, *The Rise of Music in the Ancient World, East and West* (New York: Norton, 1943): 210.

The usefulness of this quotation, allowing for its outdated terms, is that it puts singing in its widest possible context. Despite its appallingly biased comparisons, resting on a European classical yardstick of excellence, it does raise the question of what singing is. Sachs may have overlooked the contradiction between 'sing' in the first sentence and 'noises' in the last, and his summary rather questions the nature of music than of singing. The point is that, whether or not we like the sound it makes, we are able to recognise singing in its widest manifestations and when problematic distinctions between singing, speech or plain noise occur they are just as likely to do so within our culture as when we are confronted with an unfamiliar one. (Some would more readily apply 'shout and bleat with voices wild or monotonous; they scream and mumble …' to a Wagnerian singer than to a Fuegian or Bushman. And might not, say, the vocal display of an auctioneer be interpreted by perhaps even the very same Fuegians or Bushmen as singing?) We have no great difficulty in using the word singing to cover a huge variety of vocal sounds, even if we do not know whether the culture from which they emanate would classify them as singing. A classic mistake in this respect is to think of the Muslim call to prayer or Koranic recitation as singing, which on one empirical level they might be considered, whereas they are emphatically separated from what is usually understood by the word in actual Muslim theory. This raises a doubt whether our clear sense of distinction between speech and singing is universal, or whether it should be more securely proposed as culturally determined. When equating speech with human language, we freely extend the term singing beyond our own species: to birds, whales, gibbons and so on (and in so doing run the risk of anthropocentric perception); occasionally 'singing' is also applied to inanimate objects, for example the 'singing bowls' of Tibet.

Whatever singing was among our prehistoric ancestors we can be fairly sure that it would not have been what is today understood by singing: a tuneful and pleasant vocalisation of discrete pitches. At the same time it is at least tempting to think that vestiges of the earliest singing survive around the world today, not only in so-called primitive societies but also in advanced industrialised ones. In the tendency to look for survivals of the oldest singing styles in 'primitive' music it is all too easy to assume that the more primitive the culture the less likely it is to change. If we accept that some cultures change quickly, others hardly at all, we should equally agree that, as Sachs points out, 'rigid, immutable cultures do not exist'.[2]

---

[2] Ibid.: 4.

Even if we accept that the more primitive the culture the less it is likely to change, whether this permits the assumption that what we hear now is much like what was sung thousands, even tens of thousands of years, ago is another matter. It is no less fanciful to imagine that the whole history of singing can take place within an individual's lifetime, from infant babblings through the myriad of vocal sounds made through life, be they related to recognised language and music systems or not. Bruno Nettl suggested much the same thing, while advancing his own theory on the origin of music from an undifferentiated method of communication which was neither speech nor music but possessed pitch (not fixed), stress (irregular patterns) and duration (relative, not consistently demarcated): from which developed language (acquiring vowels and consonants) and music (acquiring fixed pitch). This describes, to a certain extent, the development from infancy through childhood to adulthood.

WHAT MAKES US SING?

Most humans sing, whether or not they think they can, and most either want to or are expected to on many occasions. When people sing it is easy to say why, but it is less easy to give reasons for the impulse to sing across history and cultures. Professional singers will have no difficulty as the activity brings them a livelihood and, one presumes, not only pleasure but compulsion: they sing because they have to. In fact, the necessity of singing is common throughout the world as it is part of rituals which could not take place without it, and participation may be expected from all, removing our distinction between singers and non-singers, as well as professionals and amateurs. Perhaps the most succinct reason for singing came from Anthony Seeger's study of an Amazonian people (the Suyá Indians of the northern Mato Grosso, Brazil): 'The Suyá sang because they were happy; singing made them happy.'[3] This is probably the most obvious reason and even the most widespread. While the 'feel-good factor' may be at the top of the long list of reasons why people sing, a warning must be added that music cannot be reduced to some kind of guilty pleasure we can do without or should even avoid, and its close relationship to emotion goes far further than merely serving to cheer us up. As Steven Mithen put it 'We don't have emotions for free or for fun.'[4]

---

[3] Anthony Seeger, *Why Suyá Sing: a Musical Anthropology of an Amazonian People* (Cambridge University Press, 1987): xvii.
[4] Steven Mithen, *The Singing Neanderthals: the Origins of Music, Language, Mind and Body* (London: Weidenfeld and Nicolson, 2005): 25.

Nor can we claim that singing arose purely as emotional expression, as the current spectrum of uses testifies. Calls and other signals function best as a kind of singing (or shouting with modulated tones) because they carry over large spaces better than speech. Not far removed from the sheer pleasure of singing is the uplifting, even ecstatic, sensation from using the voice in religious worship, which may even point towards the very origins of singing, as exhortations to sing in praise of God abound in the Bible, along with the ancient chants and mantras of the Hindus. In *zikr* (remembrance of Allah) the repetitive, rhythmic chanting of the Sufi mystics is an aid to memory and concentration, and ultimately to union with Allah. (It is hardly surprising that belief systems based on the divine creation of life also tend to believe that music is a divine gift, most directly put to use in singing, and that it affirms most strongly the connection between mortal and deity.) A more obvious connection with the pleasure principle lies in the use of music, especially singing (as it contains sexuality in its very sound), to attract a mate, which in turn connects it to the fundamental imperatives of survival.

The simple idea that singing is beneficial is too well established to need much emphasis, but the nature of the benefit merits a brief discussion. Of course singing enhances musicality and may even assist with concentration and learning in general, as well as developing self-awareness and confidence. The social aspects of singing lie at the heart of why it is so fundamental to human experience. For the earlier notion (from the Suyá) that we sing because we are happy we might substitute the even more fundamental idea that we sing because we must. Seeger explores a paradox here. 'No genetic imperative for singing has been discovered in human beings, although highly structured sounds are produced by members of every society.'[5] Yet he also reports the Suyá as saying 'when we stop singing, we will really be finished'.[6] So, while there may be nothing to make us sing, once we do we will not want to stop and may indeed fear doing so. The primacy of singing in music making could be moved a step closer to its necessity to human existence. Singing results from breathing (and the breath activates a process within our bodies, rather than passing through a wind instrument) which is not only essential to our physical survival but also to our spiritual being. Words such as *ātman* (Sanskrit), *anima* and *spiritus* (Latin) conjoin a sense of spirit and breath. Music must breathe whether it is sung or not, and 'spiritual' is a much-used word in connection with the art.

---

[5] Seeger, *Why Suyá Sing*: xv.   [6] Ibid.: xix.

While singing in groups for ritually prescribed reasons as well as the sheer pleasure of it is found all over the world, music does not always have to be a shared activity and mode of communication. Both children and adults often sing to themselves, oblivious of anyone who may be listening. Musicians especially (though there is no reason to suggest that it does not apply to anyone) are likely to sing to themselves internally, so that no one else can hear and the individual activity remains private, even in a crowd. The lonely shepherd or cattle herder may use singing (often instrumental music too) as personal comfort and entertainment, though another motivation may be the rather more mundane need for practice, an activity usually conducted alone. Albert Lord cited the example (from Montenegro) of the *guslar* (epic singer) Šećo Kolić who combined tending sheep (alone) with the practice necessary to maintain his status as a *guslar*.[7] Music thus functions rather differently from language as communication: thinking words to oneself is an everyday activity, but saying them out loud when alone is much less common and is generally regarded as strange behaviour, whereas singing out loud when alone is seen as perfectly normal and even as a sign of mental health. Whether we sing as readily when no one else is listening as when we are in front of an audience or part of a group, singing in either case is an affirmation of individual/group identity. Singing sends out the signal 'Here I am. Listen to me' (and, in group contexts, 'Here we are. Listen to us') even if, paradoxically, no one is actually listening. At least the singer is, and in many societies a strongly held belief is that an unseen deity is always listening, so that the song can be about praising and connecting with the deity as well as individual or group identity.

There are of course many other reasons for singing than just to be or become happy, but perhaps it is a case of when happy we break into song; when sad we prefer to listen to someone else singing. When we break into song we are most likely to sing a well-known number, as when we choose to listen to someone else. In other words, we sing what we know and also look for consolation there. Singing when sad is common, and yet more so is singing to express sadness. Fear can be another common emotion expressed or overcome/fought against through singing. In all cases singing can be said to help share and ritualise emotions, thereby enabling people to deal with them. Keening and other funeral laments are a good example, and a localised example would be the end of Schoenberg's *A Survivor from Warsaw*, where bursting into song is shown to help the

---

[7] Albert B. Lord, *The Singer of Tales* (Cambridge, MA: Harvard University Press, 1960): 21.

group defy their oppressors and more readily accept the ordeal that is to come. A similarly poignant example was the singer-songwriter, actor, dancer, anti-Apartheid activist and African National Congress (ANC) member Vuyisile Mini, who sang freedom songs (including some of his own compositions) on his way to the gallows (in 1964). The event was movingly related by Ben Turok (himself in prison at the time) in *Sechaba*, the official ANC journal:

The last evening was devastatingly sad as the heroic occupants of the death cells communicated to the prison in gentle melancholy song that their end was near … It was late at night when the singing ceased, and the prison fell into uneasy silence. I was already awake when the singing began again in the early morning. Once again the excruciatingly beautiful music floated through the barred windows, echoing round the brick exercise yard, losing itself in the vast prison yards.

And then, unexpectedly, the voice of Vuyisile Mini came roaring down the hushed passages. Evidently standing on a stool, with his face reaching up to a barred vent in his cell, his unmistakable bass voice was enunciating his final message in Xhosa to the world he was leaving. In a voice charged with emotion but stubbornly defiant he spoke of the struggle waged by the African National Congress and of his absolute conviction of the victory to come. And then it was Khayinga's turn, followed by Mkaba, as they too defied all prison rules to shout out their valedictions. Soon after, I heard the door of their cell being opened. Murmuring voices reached my straining ears, and then the three martyrs broke into a final poignant melody which seemed to fill the whole prison with sound and then gradually faded away into the distant depths of the condemned section.[8]

The point about such a long example, apart from the sad beauty of its expression, is that it demonstrates that singing is not only a life-affirming activity but can also prepare us in a unique way for death. Mini was showing his defiance to the last and strengthening himself, while performing his swan song. What that did to his own spirits we have the right only to guess, but another important aspect is that voices, especially iconic ones such as obviously possessed by Mini, inspire others, almost as if they are singing themselves. Only a few would have heard the actual sound on that day; the rest of us must imagine it, and the effect may not be significantly diminished through the silence. Song and the act of singing have been more than just a soundtrack to revolution since long before 'La Marseillaise', and recent examples are plentiful. As with the French

[8] *South African History Online* website, accessed 1 February 2011. The role of music and musicians in the South African freedom struggle, including the most famous of South African singers, the late Miriam Makeba, is explored in Lee Hirsch's 2002 documentary *Amandla! A Revolution in Four Part Harmony*.

example, the song 'Nkosi Sikeleli Africa' became the national anthem of post-revolution South Africa, 'We shall overcome' is linked to the civil rights movement in the USA, and so on. Such songs are not only stirring as pieces of music but the act of singing them makes an important statement of identity and purpose. In the words of the famous singer and social activist Harry Belafonte 'if you sang the songs of the people the people would remember who they are and what they have to do. In song the human soul is in harmony with itself.'[9]

Rigid distinctions between happy and sad singing are actually more difficult to sustain than we may imagine and we may easily misunderstand the emotional message of singing from another culture. For example, we rather simplistically expect a wedding to be happy and a funeral to be sad, despite possibly having attended such ceremonies where exactly the reverse was true. Women frequently cry and sing sad songs at their wedding and the tears do not come primarily from happy, overflowing emotions. The wedding may be forced or they may just be lamenting the fact that they will be leaving the security of their own family and home for an unfamiliar, uncertain future. Fletcher cited examples from China, Ethiopia, Russia and the Balkans.[10]

Leaving aside instances of solitary singing discussed earlier, music and language have a primary function of shared activity and means of reaching out to other human beings, expressing trust and support. Group music-making helps to create empathy: if everyone sings the same thing in a way they cease to be individuals, and momentarily losing the sense of self can be deeply therapeutic (or socially and politically problematic). We might balk at the notion that music can do the same as language and just as easily be used to express distance and hostility, as our expectation is that it will be an essentially pleasurable and beneficial activity, yet music is also used as a stylised means of criticism and disparagement, when plain words could be dangerous, so that one may sing what cannot be spoken. The point is that the singing is a means of ritualising the criticism or insult, thereby helping prevent it from turning nasty. The Inuit have competitions to sing insult songs. 'In a similar vein, South Asian [specifically Gujarati] wedding singers are careful to ensure that insults contained in *fatana* [insult songs sung during the ceremony] are ritual, not real.'[11] More

[9] Harry Belafonte broadcast in 'Playing Rosa's Tune – Music of the Civil Rights Struggle', BBC Radio 4, 31 January 2006.
[10] Peter Fletcher, *World Musics in Context: a Comprehensive Survey of the World's Major Musical Cultures* (Oxford University Press, 2001): 359.
[11] Viv Edwards and Thomas J. Sienkewicz, *Oral Cultures Past and Present: Rappin' and Homer* (Oxford: Basil Blackwell, 1990): 130.

unequivocally malevolent functions include military music, developing from sounds to instil fear in the enemy, as well as to embolden their opponents, and singing for political and revolutionary purposes. Song brought down Apartheid as the trumpet destroyed the walls of Jericho. The *toyi-toyi* chant and dance, resembling a charge, was also a frightening and effective weapon used in the struggle. More sanitised nowadays, and almost a form of entertainment, is the Maori *haka*, not unlike *toyi-toyi* both in form and intent (although its familiar aggressive function is by no means its only one). It has found worldwide fame through its adoption by the All Blacks rugby team who perform it before the start of a match. Nor has it stayed the same within that context. In time for their grand slam tour of the British Isles in 2005, the All Blacks modified the aggressive chant to include the controversial throat-slitting gesture at the end, an excess which led to calls for the *haka* to be abandoned altogether.[12]

Singing can even become the lethal weapon itself in some forms of witchcraft, to the extent of bestowing the power to sing an enemy to death. This might provoke ironic thoughts about the experience of listening to some opera or pop singers, or more amateurish efforts at karaoke. Despite this moment of frivolity, the destructive power of singing should not be hard to comprehend in our culture. The Sirens of Greek mythology used their singing indirectly: not as an ugly weapon that could kill in itself but as a beautifully seductive means to lure sailors to their death through shipwreck on lurking rocks. In the same way the Lorelei of the Rhine lured passing fishermen to their death on the rock with her singing. What these two tales have in common, apart from their European origins, is something that resonates through history and cultures, and even sacred texts: male fear of female power used through guile and seduction, resulting in loss of power, even death. A misogynist analysis would unbalance the argument, as women can obviously be charmed by male voices. Perhaps it is different as male superior physical strength and control of power give more obvious and direct means to bring about the destruction of women, whether or not seduction (possibly using singing) plays a part in the process. The message of the Sirens and the Lorelei could be interpreted as an example of male foolishness in allowing the seduction through singing

[12] How the opponents coped with the All Blacks and their aggressive overture usually aroused interest. Wales, in 2008, famously met loud chanting with silence, and stylised movements with stoic immobility, to the extent that the referee had to stir the players from their statuesque poses to start the game (this can be viewed at http://news.bbc.co.uk/sport1/hi/rugby_union/7745706. stm). One may wonder why the Welsh, so famed for their rousing singing, did not use that means to counter, even drown out, the New Zealanders. Fifteen men on the pitch and their thousands of supporters in Cardiff's Millennium Stadium could surely have managed that …

to work. (Wise Odysseus knew as much by taking drastic precautions to ensure that he and his men would not succumb to such a trick.)

Such colourful and revealing stories aside, the overriding concern is with music as a force for well-being, which appears to be universal and includes the use of music to heal or to relieve stress. The notion that well-being through communal music-making might have had its origins in the struggle for survival is most intriguing. The logic is that communal singing, dancing and music-making express shared concerns and mutual dependence, necessary when the community is engaged in the shared activities of hunting and gathering and, more recently, agriculture. While in themselves not part of the actual work that ensures survival, the music and dance reaffirm the social structures on which they depend and renew in a pleasurable, recreational way the bonds of trust and support that ensure that the work continues efficiently and fruitfully. To take part is to show one's willingness to participate in this shared enterprise and to pledge cooperation in more arduous, even dangerous, tasks. This is a variant of the familiar adage 'a family that plays together stays together', so a community that sings together sticks together when life-supporting activities are required and crises occur. Perhaps the further we are removed from ancient agricultural methods and other ways of gathering food the less likely is this simple proposition to occur to us; we are left with the pleasure and sense of community without being sure – or even aware – of exactly what other benefits might accrue.

A POSSIBLE GENESIS

To put a date on the beginning of singing is obviously too much to ask but Frayer and Nicolay suggest that we can go back 1.5 million years, when it appears that the respiratory and nasal systems of hominids developed into what they are now.[13] Not only does this indicate a very long history but it also forces huge leaps in time, as the gap is enormous between the sounds of prehistory and the development of *sapiens* singing styles and yet more recent developments about which it is possible to offer definite information. Theories as to what happened in the beginning inevitably conflict as they are based on anthropological constructions and myths, as well as scientific research. All offer tantalising, even entertaining, insights

---

[13] David W. Frayer and Chris Nicolay, 'Fossil Evidence for the Origin of Speech Sounds', in Nils Wallin, Björn Merker and Steven Brown (eds.), *The Origins of Music* (Cambridge, MA: Massachusetts Institute of Technology, 2000): 232.

even if it proves difficult to find common ground and rather easier to find examples of blatant conflict.

Before we turn to the work of scientists, we should note that musicians themselves (from Wagner and before) theorised about the origins of singing. With the development of scholarly disciplines the investigation moved into more organised schools of thought. Curt Sachs, one of the greatest pioneers of what was known as comparative musicology – and now as ethnomusicology – produced a considerable body of influential work on singing in a global context, long before the fashionable (and unforgivably problematic) phrase 'World Music' came into being.[14] His forthright views attacked musicians, anthropologists, biologists and archaeologists alike. He challenged the belief (from Jean-Jacques Rousseau, Herbert Spencer, Richard Wagner and others) that music descended from spoken language, maintaining that it would not have grown from one root and indirectly posing the question: what language?[15] A later work developed many of the themes and also showed a radically different perception of world music from that to which we are accustomed nowadays, as the emphasis is firmly on a history of European music, with cursory examinations of 'the primitives' and, as a 'civilising' counterweight, 'the Orient', which nevertheless suffered from inertia compared to the rapidly developing Western art music.[16] The latter book certainly gets off to an audacious start:

> Mythology is wrong … And wrong, so far, are all the many theories presented on a more or less scientific basis – the theories that man has imitated the warbling of birds, that he wanted to please the opposite sex, that his singing derived from drawn-out signalling shouts, that he arrived at music via some co-ördinated [*sic*], rhythmical teamwork, and other speculative hypotheses.[17]

Thus both mythology and science, from Charles Darwin down, are dealt an unequivocal blow. The problem for Sachs lies in the fact that we cannot unearth the origins of singing through archaeology, and the 'living fossil' approach through postulation of ancient survivals in secluded, primitive tribes employing Stone Age technologies is also problematic. A less controversial axiom – and certainly one to endorse in this book – is: 'Music began with singing.'[18] This is likely to be widely accepted as

---

[14] The coining of the term is often erroneously given as 1987 in Islington (London), whereas it was being used officially in at least one US university teaching programme (for example at Wesleyan University, Connecticut) a quarter of a century before then. We find it also in the title of Curt Sachs's 1956 publication *A Short History of World Music* (2nd edn, London: Dennis Dobson).
[15] Sachs, *The Rise of Music*: 19–20.
[16] Sachs, *A Short History*, 8.
[17] Ibid.: 1.   [18] Ibid.: 4.

it is common to find singing at the forefront, possibly the only form of music-making, and very rare (in fact no example springs to mind) to find the situation reversed in favour of instrumental music. It may even strike many as a statement which is not only highly plausible but even obvious, yet again it is impossible to be certain. Sachs used the term 'voice masks' to describe the modifications, such as drums and trumpets held close to the mouth, used by 'primitive' singers to veil their voices.[19] The German phrase 'kein Blatt vor den Mund nehmen' (literally 'to take no leaf against the mouth') is an idiomatic way of describing plain speaking, and refers to this erstwhile practice of veiling the voice.[20] This indicates not only an ancient precursor of kazoos and electronic manipulation of the voice but also provides a very interesting angle on the relationship of voices and instruments.

Sachs's theory is that the first singers sought shape and order and found two contrasting means of expression: the logogenic (word-born) in which the words are the sole focus of attention and the music a 'simple, monotonous singsong'; and the pathogenic (passion-born) which is more interested in strong emotions than words.[21] Logogenic melodies, of which, for some unexplained reason, he found the earliest examples 'in Patagonia, Ceylon and elsewhere',[22] have a very limited range, while the pathogenic style 'leaps noisily up to the top and staggers to the bottom in wild and rumbling cataracts of shouts and wails, in which, in the process of growing organization, some definite intervals, as octave, fifths and fourths, or even thirds, become accented footholds'.[23] Despite Sachs's rejection of any emphasis on sexual selection, it is difficult not to think of an almost Darwinian agenda in this analysis. Indeed, despite denying a simple progression from simple and primitive to complicated and civilised, Sachs did write of 'a long evolution'[24] of logogenic music, as it gradually added notes to its original two, so that a kind of merger with pathogenic music resulted and, in fact, a third style, called melogenic, emerged, in which the melodic line was the main concern, beyond just the words or unbridled emotions.[25] Later, he suggested that the term logogenic might be abandoned, as many such melodies used nonsense syllables and were thus not word born.[26]

---

[19] Sachs, *The Rise of Music*: 23.
[20] Curt Sachs, *The Wellsprings of Music* (The Hague: Martinus Nijhoff, 1962): 84.
[21] Sachs, *A Short History*: 4.
[22] Ibid.   [23] Ibid.: 5.
[24] Ibid.: 4.   [25] Ibid.: 5.
[26] Sachs, *The Wellsprings*: 70.

Here he appears to have anticipated relevant scientific research. For example, Dean Falk draws attention to the significant difference between singing with words and without (for example to 'la'): the former involves the left hemisphere of the brain (the one associated with language) and the latter depends more on the right.[27] Instead of the logogenic type Sachs proposed horizontal melodies (and tumbling melodies for the pathogenic type).[28] In all types the intervals depend on the motor type of the singer, so that tribes who dance in wide steps and leaps sing in wider intervals, and women often both sing and dance in narrower steps than do men.[29] Generalising about the nature of 'primitive' singing is as problematic as the use of the word primitive itself. In Sachs's generation it was still common to use the word and find as many universals as possible. Before him, for example, Richard Wallaschek had reported the prevalent belief that primitive singing tends to be pitched very high, with frequent use of falsetto.[30]

Children's singing, even in Europe, seems to follow the same evolutionary principle outlined above and resembles the primitive styles in which tiny patterns of just a few notes are repeated over and over again, to which Sachs added the word 'alas'.[31] A rather fanciful interpretation could be constructed from this process, pointing towards a cyclic historiography in which the history of singing is repeated over and over again within the individual life cycle (as proposed near the start of this chapter). As the child proceeds in a 'forwards' evolution, so the adult, to some extent, goes into reverse, because the vocal activity so common around the world, referred to as IDS (infant-directed speech), is an empathetic imitation of the infant's sounds and this adult regression is permitted – actually expected – in this context. Steven Mithen went as far as to propose that it comes closest to the precursor of language and music.[32] A saving grace to what Sachs perceived as a regrettable way of singing was afforded by the common practice of varying it through call and response procedures.[33]

Another sophistication was the construction of two consecutive and balancing phrases: another familiar procedure, often called question and answer. Finally, when more than one singer sang the same melody without the discipline expected in the modern world, a kind of 'pseudo-unison'

---

[27] Dean Falk, 'Hominid Brain Evolution and the Origins of Music', in *The Origins of Music*: 204–5.
[28] Sachs, *The Wellsprings*: 70. [29] Sachs, *A Short History*: 5.
[30] Richard Wallaschek, *Primitive Music* (New York: Da Capo Press, 1970. First published London: Longmans Green & Co., 1893): 75–7.
[31] Sachs, *A Short History*: 5. [32] Mithen, *The Singing Neanderthals*: 275.
[33] Sachs, *A Short History*: 5.

arose, in which the singers managed the same melodic outline but not quite together.[34] This is known as heterophony, which, elsewhere, Sachs describes as 'a wilfully inexact unison'.[35] Sachs grudgingly conceded that the primitives were also able to construct something as advanced as canon, though it arose from the seemingly negative surrender to impatience: the singers simply did not wait their turn but entered before the leader had finished.[36] We cannot leave this topic without at least a brief clarification of the word 'heterophony', which remains one of the most misunderstood terms in music. To paraphrase Derek Bailey[37] on the even wider term 'improvisation' it is perhaps the most practised and yet least understood type of concerted, stratified music. Other types of polyphony may lay as much or greater claim to that description, except that they will be less misunderstood. For example, Bruno Nettl described singing in parallel intervals as 'probably the most common type of polyphony in the world'.[38] Singing in octaves does not count (and we refer to it as unison anyway). The parallel fifth is the most commonly used interval. It is next in the harmonic series after the octave. Apart from its prevalence in many parts of Africa and in the organum of medieval Europe it survives in Icelandic *tvisongur* and in the choral singing of parts of the Caucasus. Parallel thirds are also common and can lead to the mistaken assumption that, because they sound so much like the European music with which we are so familiar, their use in Africa or the South Pacific must be due to European influence. Parallel seconds are also encountered in many regions, notably in some East European and Balkan folk music. The trouble with the term heterophony, on the other hand, is that it has to do service for so many different methods of stratification and lumping them together under this term is clumsy and misleading. In the psalm singing of the Hebrides we can hear the congregation approximating to the melody set by the leader and it sounds untogether and almost wild, yet mysterious and endlessly fascinating. This may serve as a good example of a primitive and chaotic form of polyphony, as heterophony is often described. Yet the 'blurred unisons' of Mahler's *Song of the Earth* (a good sub-title for this book!) can hardly be described as accidental, chaotic or unsophisticated. The same applies to the concept of accompaniment in Indian music. In North Indian classical singing what happens is not what we understand as, say, the piano accompaniment to a

---

[34] Ibid.: 6.   [35] Ibid.: 10.   [36] Ibid.: 6.

[37] Derek Bailey, *Improvisation: Its Nature and Practice in Music* (Ashbourne: Moorland Publishing, 1980): 1.

[38] Sachs, *A Short History*: 81.

Schubert *Lied*, but a shadowing of the singer by one or more instruments, resulting in a heterophonic time lapse, as well as paraphrases and extensions of what the singer has just sung – again, anything but primitive or chaotic. Still less arbitrary or uncivilised are the other types lumped together under the term heterophony, when it is defined as different versions of the same melody performed simultaneously. This happens in, for example, most gamelan music, though to a lesser extent than often implied by attaching the heterophony label to the whole system. In any case, the resultant polyphony cannot be described as primitive or inferior (and indeed Debussy provocatively asserted that it was superior to that of the revered Palestrina).

Sachs never quite abandoned his comparative musicologist persona. The problem lies not with all those people around the world being deemed unworthy of what he called the 'sacred art' (of the music of Bach and Mozart) but with those who decree what music is, and judge all manifestations by restricted and culturally specific criteria. So it is with singing. Our expectation is that it is a pleasing, melodious sound, overlooking the unpleasant excesses of the wild operatic vibrato or the anti-establishment vocal mannerisms in some pop music. But the criteria which might sit happily with Western music do not apply universally; they must not be reduced to what the West has and the rest of the world has not, which will smack both of complacency and arrogance. To paraphrase Hamlet, there are more vocal sounds, colours, effects and utterly virtuosic feats on earth than are dreamt of in our philosophy. The West's recent 'discovery' of 'extended vocal techniques' merely goes to serve the old adage that there is nothing new under the sun, and what we try to do in the search for newness has already been done far better somewhere else on the planet. Sachs implied as much in discussing what he called 'vocal mannerisms', which he described as 'the hardest and most neglected branch of our studies'.[39] And to reverse his invidious comparisons above, the sound of Western bel canto can sound as ludicrous, comical and ultimately unrefined to the so-called 'primitives' as their singing may to us. One overriding message of this book, or any study of singing in a global context, is that there is no such thing as a 'natural voice' – or, rather, a natural voice is what is natural to the singer producing it and how that singer's culture perceives it. In some ways, Sachs's arguments could imply that the most natural voice is what harks back to the ancient logogenic, pathogenic and melogenic categories; but further development of that idea would be the pursuit of a red herring.

---

[39] Sachs, *The Wellsprings*: 85.

Sachs himself burst another bubble in refuting a notion that is still, unfortunately, bandied about today: 'Music is not the universal language.'[40] In the same way, the activity called singing may be universal, as is language, but its sounds, devices, uses, intentions and comprehensibility are not (as with language). Indeed, one of the fundamental paradoxes is that singing is the most universal musical activity yet the hardest to adjust to from one culture to another. The use of a foreign language is the least of the concerns: it has much more to do with the different way in which the voice is used. Unfamiliar singing styles are far more likely to arouse mirth or alienation than the sounds of unfamiliar instruments. Perhaps this is like saying that a person's face will excite stronger reactions than his or her clothes, as our instincts incline more to the person than to impersonal accretions, like clothes – or musical instruments. An instrument can be borrowed; a voice cannot be used by anyone else. The degree of personal ownership of a voice, and of individual identification with it, is illustrated by an experience during a field trip in the Indian state of Rajasthan in 1976. The eminent folklorist Komal Kothari told the author that some of the singers were refusing to be recorded because they were afraid the microphone would steal their voices.

UNTANGLING UNIVERSALS

So the problem in clinging to the notion of music as universal language lies not as much with the universality of music as with music described as a language, thereby conflating two words and even overlooking an oxymoron. We should not forget that in the Tower of Babel story God's intention was to prevent universality (of language). So it came to pass, and the question remains whether the same was also meant to apply to music or whether music is there to remedy the problem. Whatever speculation comes to mind, the problem of universality is obviously one that remains close to the question of the origins of music (and singing) as two chapters in a scientifically orientated symposium[41] are devoted to it. Bruno Nettl stated that 'all societies have vocal music' and such universality almost, but not quite, applies to instrumental music.[42]

---

[40] Ibid.: 219.
[41] Nils L. Wallin, Björn Merker and Steven Brown (eds.), *The Origins of Music* (Cambridge, MA: Massachusetts Institute of Technology, 2000).
[42] Bruno Nettl, 'An Ethnomusicologist Contemplates Universals in Musical Sound and Musical Culture' in *The Origins of Music*: 468.

The obvious reason for the distinction is that we all have a voice but instruments have to be made, posing questions of available materials and technologies that do not apply to the voice. In a hark back to Sachs, Nettl also postulated 'the world's simplest music' as a universal, arguing that songs of short phrases, few pitches and a restricted range, with repetition, form part of the repertoire of most societies.[43] He went as far as to suggest that these may be 'a credible remnant of the world's earliest music'.[44] The use of such songs in social contexts (we see it in, for example, children's games and football chants) and in obsolete rituals suggests that these are old material to which has been added more complex music.[45] In his tentative analysis Nettl considered the many objections, conceding that some of these simple traits are found in complex music and that such constructions of universality are based on selective criteria from one particular culture.[46] Moreover, the notion that monophonic singing to discrete pitches is the oldest kind must be challenged with the more plausible idea that the earliest singers moved 'glissando-like through the voice's range' with 'only very vaguely defined relationships among the voices'.[47] This implies that the 'glissando-like' way of singing could be the 'natural' way to sing. At least it warns us not to think of singing always as a matter of precisely defined pitches and intervals. The first sound we make is crying, then babbling, gurgling and other such sounds which have neither language nor discrete pitches, yet are a sonic expression of feelings as strong as if they were articulated with definite words and notes. (Crying is certainly an expression of feelings through sound.) Later an awareness of precisely defined pitches and intervals leads to an ability to reproduce them through singing, and instruments are generally designed also to reproduce them. Yet what Nettl is reminding us is that singing never relied solely on such clear steps but also glided through a wide range in a way that no instrument can. After all, the voice does not have fingers, and does not need them.

François-Bernard Mâche proposed some universal features, among which is the uniquely human pentatonic polyphony on a drone, of which he cited examples from Vietnam, Niger, Taiwan, Albania, India and Indonesia. Given the extreme unlikelihood that such similarities arose from cultural contact, we are led to seek the explanation in the common origin of humans. (Polygenesis rather than diffusion.) Mâche examined similarities between bird song and human song but questioned the central

---

[43] Ibid.: 468–9.   [44] Ibid.: 471.
[45] Ibid.: 469.   [46] Ibid.: 470.   [47] Ibid.: 471.

aesthetic distinction by pointing out that notions of concerts and listening to music for aesthetic enjoyment are by no means universal. As an example he stated that the Toraja of Sulawesi (in Indonesia) have no lullabies, wedding songs or dirges and 'never make music for the sole pleasure of singing or listening' but only during ceremonies in large, polyphonic choirs.[48]

BIRDS AND BEASTS AS SINGERS

In the scientific quest for the origin of music a consideration of our link to non-humans assumes some importance. It is not only because we anthropomorphise so much but more because we have strong genetic links with certain other species, so what they do is historicised into what we used to do. A favourite example is mating calls, leading to the theory (for which there is much obvious and irrefutable evidence on a daily basis) that singing is an important way of attracting the opposite sex. (Funnily enough, at the height of Beatle mania, what seemed to drive the hysterical girls in the audience to almost complete loss of control were the singers' falsetto whoops rather than their normal singing with words.) Dean Falk argued that because humans are closely related evolutionarily to gorillas and chimpanzees the communication systems of those animals are especially relevant in the search for the origins of music, hence singing.[49] He cited an example, offering the term 'gorillian chants', of male gorillas vocalising together, which 'perhaps foreshadows human singing without words'.[50] At an earlier stage of research into the origins of music, Marius Schneider stated: 'Vocal imitation is the strongest form of mystic participation in the surrounding world.'[51]

Despite Sachs's rebuttal quoted earlier, birds never seem far from ideas about human singing. The question is not as much whether humans perceive bird sounds as music, even if birds are capable of producing pitches similar to the pentatonic scale and of transposition, as how bird song might be a direct influence on human singing. Since birds have been around for longer than humans it seems inevitable that our distant ancestors would have admitted such an influence. No other species outside our own gives humans as much auditory pleasure and in many societies birds

---

[48] François-Bernard Mâche, 'The Necessity of and Problems with a Universal Musicology', in *The Origins of Music*: 475–8.

[49] Falk, 'Hominid Brain Evolution': 209.

[50] Ibid.: 210.

[51] Marius Schneider, 'Primitive Music', in Egon Wellesz (ed.), *New Oxford History of Music*, vol. I (Oxford University Press, 1957): 10.

are caged for their singing. Too many composers to mention, from well
before Vivaldi, through Beethoven to Messiaen, have imitated birdsong.
That is within the confines of the Western art music tradition; when we
look further afield the examples of avian inspiration proliferate and vary
quite dramatically, from the classical tradition of Iran to the Kaluli people
of Papua New Guinea.[52] So around the world birds may be regarded as a
species that makes and inspires music, and birds may even be considered
in some measure to be our teachers. At the same time, we have the propensity to make any sound we like 'musical'. It can be from other species,
from nature – where the Aeolian harp derives from the breath of the wind
passing through wires, in a way mimicking our breath and vocal cords –
and from human artefacts not specifically designed to be musical instruments (for example, steam engines and the clickety-clack of the wheels
rushing along the tracks). On the vexed issue of bird and animal 'song'
and the perception of it as music, Peter Slater offered several qualifications to remind us of the central point that it is humans who make the
connection and relate what they hear to their ideas of music, which in any
case has not been universally defined.[53]

A SCIENTIFIC APPROACH

To what extent can scientific research offer hard evidence concerning
when, how and why singing began? A clear schism lies between Sachs's
rejection of a route to the origins of music and singing through archaeology and Steven Mithen's avoidance of a discussion of Sachs's dated
notions in his masterly exposition of a proto-music;[54] yet there is an
element of circularity as Mithen developed the proposition of the ethnomusicologist and social anthropologist John Blacking that there was a
musical mode of thought and action that pre-dated language.[55] Beyond
the generation of Blacking (albeit at least a whole generation after Sachs)
Mithen was able to meld the range of disciplines needed to tackle this
problem, such as ethnomusicology, anthropology, archaeology, neurology
and palaeontology. Still, the inevitable sense of speculation remains and
Mithen started from the beguiling premise that 'without music, the prehistoric past is just too quiet to be believed'.[56]

[52] Steven Feld, *Sound and Sentiment: Birds, Weeping, Poetics, and Song in Kaluli Expression*
(University of Pennsylvania Press, 1982, 1990).
[53] Peter Slater, 'Birdsong Repertoires: Their Origins and Use', in *The Origins of Music*: 60.
[54] Mithen, *The Singing Neanderthals*.
[55] Ibid.: 5.   [56] Ibid.: 4.

To paraphrase his argument, we can safely assume that the prehistoric past had a great deal of movement as, for one thing, survival depended on vigorous physical activity such as hunting. We know that music and movement are connected in activities such as dance, and 'song itself is no more than a product of movement, made by the various parts of the vocal tract reaching from the diaphragm to the lips'.[57] The close association of music and movement is conveyed in such everyday phrases as 'song and dance' and 'all singing, all dancing' as is the frequent occurrence of entertainment provided by singing and dancing girls and women. Work songs, by their very nature, involve movement: the singing alleviates the tedious repetition and signals that the work is eased through sharing. Lullabies also tend to involve movement, when the mother combines gentle singing with rocking movements to soothe the baby. We commonly see it also in pop concerts, where the audience, whether or not they are singing along, sway together and swing their arms above their heads. Writing about mother–infant interaction, at the very start of music learning, Ellen Dissanayake wrote: 'I consider it essential that we incorporate movement (or kinesics) with song as integral to our thinking about the evolutionary origin of music', citing cultures (Australian Aboriginal, Andamanese) where, to this day, dance and singing are inextricably linked.[58]

To avoid mixing the word 'language' into the origins of music, Mithen coined acronyms to describe the precursor to both language and music, derived from 'holistic, multi-modal, manipulative, and musical'.[59] Holistic means not comprising segmented elements; manipulative means influencing emotional states, thence behaviour; multi-modal refers to sound and movement; musical means sound in time, in some way rhythmically and melodically organised, so we are close to the modern understanding of music as rhythm and melody, sound and movement, which manipulate the emotions. From these words Mithen created 'Hmmmm', which invites the confused reaction that the Neanderthals were humming rather than singing, and Mithen actually presented a section entitled '"Hmmmmm"-ing Neanderthals',[60] albeit not in quite the same sense. 'Hmmmm' became 'Hmmmmm' with a fifth 'm' coming from the addition of 'mimetic',[61] which drew on the neuroscientist Merlin Donald's[62] distinction between

---

[57] Ibid.: 15.
[58] Ellen Dissanayake, 'Antecedents of the Temporal Arts in Early Mother-Infant Interaction', in *The Origins of Music*: 397.
[59] Mithen, *The Singing Neanderthals*: 138.
[60] Ibid.: 233–5.   [61] Ibid.: 172.
[62] Merlin Donald, *Origins of the Modern Mind* (Cambridge, MA: Harvard University Press, 1991).

mimesis, mimicry and imitation. Mimicry attempts exact duplication while imitation accepts more approximation. Mimesis might involve both mimicry and imitation but also involves sound symbolism and gesture and is the 'invention of intentional representations'.[63] Laurence Picken conflated mimesis and imitation to offer another interpretation:

> It was the Greeks for whom *mousikē* was not *technē* ('craft'), but *mimēsis* ('imitation'), as were poetry and sculpture also. In music we are imitating – but what? Perhaps: remembered musical gestures in the first, meaningful sung melodies, addressed to us by our mothers, before we were capable of speech, before we had knowledge of words.[64]

Mimesis as 'invention of intentional representations' could open up a huge vista of theatrical and ritual creativity around the world. While Mithen did not believe that the early humans were capable of sophisticated types of mimesis,[65] modern occurrences include sago fertility rituals in Papua New Guinea where the dancers identify with the cassowary bird and act out the representation and, in the realm of singing, Indonesian *wayang* (shadow plays) where the *dhalang* (puppeteer) changes his voice to speak the words of a god without actually knowing what the god sounded like. A less indirect or extreme example is from the same region, where the performers in the Balinese *kecak* (nicknamed 'monkey chorus' for its modern entertainment value, as opposed to the trance dances from which it originated) obviously know what monkeys sound like.

Mithen's theories invite the sceptical, somewhat facile, reaction of a slightly contracted 'Hmm', and knowledge of whether 'singing' existed in prehistoric times and what it would have been like will probably have to remain fixed in the realms of speculation. If 'Hmmmmm' did exist it would, according to Mithen, have had a history of more than two million years,[66] earning it something of a record in the history of singing, with its demise a mere 28,000 years ago. Part of Mithen's thesis is that the Neanderthals may well have been better, or at least more versatile, singers than us, because pre-language singing demanded a greater range of sounds and effects to communicate emotion and meaning than singing to words, where the words obviously do a large part of the job.[67] Allowing

---

[63] Donald, *Origins of the Modern Mind*, quoted in Mithen, *The Singing Neanderthals*: 167.
[64] In Fletcher, *World Musics in Context*: 29.
[65] Mithen, *The Singing Neanderthals*: 169.
[66] Ibid.: 268.
[67] This counter-evolutionary analysis may not be as far-fetched as it seems, given the boundless admiration heaped by artists such as Picasso and Werner Herzog on prehistoric cave paintings. Although the Chauvet cave in southern France (containing the oldest paintings yet discovered)

for relatively big leaps through pre-history, from the disappearance of the Neanderthals to the late Stone Age, we are still impeded by the long silence that is the entire history of singing up to a mere century ago. We thus have no evidence of what singing was or sounded like to compare with the cave paintings of Lascaux, although their indication of a sophisticated artistic life can only fuel the notion that the people who made the cave paintings would have indulged in other artistic activities such as singing, perhaps mirroring the visual imitations of wild life with vocal ones, as well as using their voices for communication and bonding with their fellows. Mithen pointed out that some caves chosen for painting also possessed marked acoustic properties and added: 'So whereas we now visit painted caves in a hushed reverence, they probably once reverberated with the sounds of pipes, stalagmite xylophones, singing and dancing.'[68]

MYTHOLOGICAL CONCLUSIONS

Let us conclude this broad survey more or less where it began. The whole chapter has inevitably spent most of its time in the mists of speculation, exploring a kind of history in reverse, applied retrospectively: attempts to interpret the inaccessible past through the more recent, more accessible past, thereby risking an anachronistic construction. Musicological theories and even those which are genuinely scientific cannot tell us exactly how, when and why singing began, and still less what it was and what it sounded like. Birds as survivals from the dinosaur age and 'primitive' societies as extensions of much earlier traditions may give us clues and point towards a relatively firm basis. In apparent opposition are folk beliefs and mythologies that may not necessarily offer an explanation for the very origins of singing but do propose a colourful diversity of beliefs as to where particular songs came from. A common one is that they came from dreams, be that a reference to the 'Dreaming' or 'Dreamtime' of the Australian Aborigines (not quite dreaming in our sense but a mythical time of creator ancestors and supernatural beings, creation itself, a beginning without end) or to the dreams we all have. The unconscious can easily be related to divine intercession, so inspiration is often explained in

---

is closed to the public (like Lascaux) it is not 'silent' in the way that prehistoric singing must unfortunately remain to us, and some idea of its magnificence can be seen in Herzog's 3D documentary film *Cave of Forgotten Dreams* (2010). Part of the documentary concerns the discovery of bone flutes and what appears to be a tuning to the familiar pentatonic scale, which may tell us about what singing could have entailed.

[68] Ibid.: 270.

those terms. More mundane reasons are given: music can be a commodity, so songs can be created and traded in much the same way as anything else placed on the market.

It may also be admitted that songs simply came from other people: accretions from neighbouring cultures and, widely, in the 'covers' of popular music. Diasporas of songs and singing styles are so common that they can almost be thought of as the norm. What was once brought by armies, ships and traders is now more rapidly brought by recordings and the internet. A seemingly isolated people, the Amazonian Suyá, actually rely on external sources: 'all songs were said to come from outside Suyá society'.[69] The very old songs were given mythical origins, where men turning into animals (a deer, a pig) sang songs incorporated into ceremonies (for that animal). This kind of transformation is different from among many other South American Indian groups, where songs were taught by culture heroes or spirits. New songs were taught by witches (of either gender) and persons said to be without a spirit, referring to those upon whom witches had taken revenge. The removal of the spirit could, as expected, be the process of death, but the spirit could also be removed to plants or animals and so the person might continue to live. Thus the feared and reviled witches (sometimes killed in retaliation) were depended upon for the creation of new songs.[70] The Suyá also offer an example which must be one of the strangest reasons for a song's origin: learnt from a woman with a penis growing on her right thigh.[71] If nothing else this underlines the widespread belief that the creation of songs is a special activity and that musicians can be a strange breed. To end the chapter there would be sensationalist and bewildering. Yet the whole subject of why and when we began to sing and what may have inspired us to do so is the most intriguing with which we have to deal. Theories and myths, both in huge varieties and often in direct conflict, may not give us precise answers but at least they show how central these questions are to human identity, experience and understanding.

[69] Seeger, *Why Suyá Sing*: 52.
[70] Ibid.: 53–4.   [71] Ibid.: 58.

PART II

Historical voices

CHAPTER 2

The genesis of the Western tradition

At the beginning of the third millennium, the variety of singing accorded the highest status in countries within the Western sphere of influence remains that employed by opera singers. Historically, opera is a European phenomenon which has taken root in most of the former colonies of the old British, French and Spanish empires as well as continuing to flourish in all of the individual countries of Europe itself. The singing has transcended national boundaries but retained its essential European-ness in a world teeming with other vocal varieties. The high status of opera in most world capitals generally ensures a well-organised infrastructure and the genre is traditionally supported by similarly well-funded national pedagogical institutions. No other variety of singing has embedded itself in the various national musical psyches to such an extent, though many countries have a form of national music that may have a wider appeal and much rock music comes close to the status of classical music in its seriousness of purpose.

The origins of this success can be traced back over several millennia. Many of the great world singing traditions share a common ancestry, which is hinted at in tomb paintings and inscriptions across a band of latitude north of the equator and south of the Tropic of Cancer. We know almost nothing about the nature of these types of singing but they are assumed to be monophonic – that is to say the essence of the music was conceived as pertaining to the sounds produced by one single instrument or voice without harmony as we would now understand it. The music was not written down, but was probably generated by a mixture of improvisation, memory and formulaic repetition and very much defined by the individual poet-singer who uttered it. Singing in the context of religious rituals may well have required chanting by groups of people singing the same material simultaneously. This mode of singing was a crucial part of Christian rituals as the religious sect transformed itself from a branch of Judaism to a supranational religious and administrative structure. The extent and complexity of the ritual chants and the new church's perceived need for a unified corpus of music eventually made it impossible for singers to rely on memory to maintain the tradition, and at some point in the middle of the first millennium CE chant began to be written down. The manuscripts thus generated were initially an aid to memory and a means of storing a vast amount of material, but the act of writing music enabled developments that have no parallel in any other music, eventually leading to the separation of performer and composer into two distinct creative entities. At about the same time as music writing emerged, and for reasons which are still not understood, singers began to devise ways of combining voices, and an increasingly complex polyphonic tradition began to develop. The church was a powerful means of disseminating developments in singing, and the learning of the chant corpus required an institutional pedagogy which developed its own criteria for good singing. The integration of church and state also meant considerable blurring of the distinction between sacred and secular, and the patronage of courts and their chapels in time permitted the development of professional singers.

Secular music has a history that is probably equally complex but because so much of it was not written down it has a very long prehistory which we cannot access in any detail. Since classical times singing was to be heard in theatres and this tradition continued in both religious and secular theatre into the Renaissance. The conjunction of theatrical music-making with virtuosic professional singers led to large-scale events which we should now think of as opera from the end of the sixteenth century onwards. Over the next two hundred years or so the singing freed itself of its institutional constraints and reached a peak of creative and technical development. So successful were singers across national boundaries that schools were developed to maintain the supply of good performers. Largely as a consequence of this, the rampant individualism of the greatest singers began to be curtailed, at the same time as composers and conductors began to assert their authority over what they considered to be composers' (rather than performers') music.

By the end of the nineteenth century the age of creative singing had come to an end. The first half of the twentieth century, aided by recording (which over the course of the century would become the main mode of performance), was an age of retrenchment, when dedicated music colleges produced highly skilled singers whose art was largely confined to interpreting music created for them by composers, while maintaining a carefully crafted legato-orientated sound based on nineteenth-century ideals. Many of the traditional hallmarks of the old singing were still to be heard in jazz singing, which still found room for improvisation, portamento and rubato, among other traditional devices, with a much less categorical division of labour between composer or arranger and performer. As the century progressed, and especially after World War II, 'classical' singers began to pay much greater attention to the text, which led to a more intellectual approach from many singers, especially in the song repertoire which towards the end of the century was almost exclusively confined to recorded performances or musical college syllabuses; old music was revisited by the early music movement, and the avant-garde began to explore ways of vocalising that would not have been recognised as singing at all in previous eras.

ORAL TRADITION IN THE ANCIENT WORLD

The oldest records of what might have been singing are almost as old as civilisation itself. We will probably never come very close to knowing the true nature and function of singing in the thousands of years that precede written reference to it. We can imagine a role for singers in ritual and magic, and in something like work songs perhaps, based on evidence from cave drawings and inscriptions on figurines and pots, but the formal contexts and any sense of what the singing meant to those who heard it are lost to us (see chapter 1 above). We do not *know* that mothers sang to their children (however reasonable the assumption may seem), or when what we think of as a folk tradition may have evolved. The European singing that we are familiar with today had a very long gestation period which saw contexts and functions change almost imperceptibly over many hundreds of years. The music (and singing) that we now take for granted appeared relatively recently, and is in part a product of the increasingly rapid pace of change since the seventeenth century.

The earliest clues to actual music-making are to be found in depictions of what are assumed to be musical events in ancient Egyptian and Mesopotamian inscriptions, and in the Old Testament. We can identify three broad categories of song: functional music designed for specific social contexts (such as work songs or courtly entertainment), ritual or magic song (for mourning, making rain or improving crop yields, for example) and praise singing in honour of a god, ruler or dignitary. A further subdivision is distinguishable, that between what we might think of as solo singing, and what we might think of as choral, performed by groups of people. These basic modes and functions of singing have been

continually refreshed over the course of Western history: work songs probably have an unbroken history and can still be heard in rural Europe and
America. Singing still fulfils a vital function in much Christian liturgy,
and the praise song can still be heard in national anthems and certain
varieties of rap.

Vocal history from the twentieth century onwards can increasingly be
written in terms of what can be heard, and in the third millennium CE it
may well come to be considered an absurdity to write musical history in
terms of what can be seen and read. Before about 1900 we are dependent
on silent written evidence which becomes increasingly sparse the further
back we go, so that by the time we reach the end of the first millennium there is very little evidence of any sort at all. But we know from the
archaeological record that singing evolved as urban societies themselves
developed during at least two millennia BCE, and that the earliest written
evidence represents a change in the nature of oral culture as much as the
beginnings of a literary one.

Some of the earliest records of singing are the royal hymns from late
third-millennium-BCE Sumer, which survive in the form of inscribed clay
tablets. These hymns constitute a distinctive genre of praise song, and
are likely to represent a much older oral tradition (as is suggested by the
survival of the earliest known harps, which pre-date the Sumerian praise
hymns by about five hundred years). The so-called Culgi (or Shulgi)
hymns of the Sumerian King Culgi of Ur (2094–2047 BCE) are typical of
a certain sort of praise hymn; the so-called Culgi Hymn B is a list of the
king's own achievements expressed in the very extravagant language of a
great warrior. Among his many talents, however, is a gift for music, and
his egotistical ramblings on the topic open a window on what appears to
have been a thriving (but largely unknowable) musical culture. Having
expounded his prowess on many sorts of instruments he goes on to refer
to what are clearly praise singers:

Furthermore no one will assert under oath that to this day there is any mention
in my inscriptions of a single city that I have not devastated, or wall that I have
not demolished, or land that I have not made tremble like a reed hut, or praise
that I have not completely verified. Why should a singer put them in hymns? An
eminent example deserves eternal fame. What is the use of writing lies without
truth? For me, the king, the singer has recorded my exploits in songs about the
strength of the protective deity of my power; my songs are unforgettable, and
my words shall not fall into oblivion.[1]

---

[1] From Culgi Hymn B, *The Electronic Text Corpus of Sumerian Literature* lines 320–36 (http://etcsl.
orinst.ox.ac.uk/index.html#), the ETCSL project, Oriental Institute, University of Oxford, 2006.

The extensive Sumerian corpus also contains drinking songs, work songs (cow herders are referred to frequently) and a genre of laments both for people and for the fall of great cities. The influence of Mesopotamian music on the exiled Jews is thought to account for the flourishing of Temple music, which ended with the Roman destruction of the Temple in Jerusalem in 70 CE, after which the Jewish diaspora maintained a link with its ancient roots by sustaining a ritual singing tradition in communities dispersed throughout the northern hemisphere. The evidence for similar repertoires in third-millennium Egypt at about the same time is the more compelling because inscriptions are often accompanied by paintings. Harpists are depicted in tombs dating from the Old Kingdom (*c.*2686 – 2181 BCE) and they are often in the company of what appear to be singers, though there are very few pictures of ancient Egyptians with their mouths open. There is no notation but the presence of text suggests an oral performance of some sort. This may not have sounded very different from speech: there are words that are translated as 'singer' and 'song', but little that suggests that 'singing' is objectively conceptualised as a vocal act. Whatever the performer needed to enhance his recitation was inherent in the text or in his own rhetorical skills, which are now lost to us. Egyptologists have identified performative acts such as funeral laments, love songs and herding songs, banqueting and religious singing which took place in different contexts. Some examples (the so-called Herdsman's Song, for example) are found in several different tombs, suggesting a common appreciation of specific songs. In these ancient records we also see glimpses of a division of function by gender. In both Mesopotamia and Egypt praise-singing is a male prerogative, whereas the vocalised rituals of mourning are for women only. Egyptian tomb paintings also show what appear to be groups of women singing at banquets (an early example of choral singing, perhaps), whereas solo singers with harp appear to be male.[2]

Memories are long in proto-literate societies, but the extreme length of many early epics makes simple rote reproduction very unlikely. The 'singer' referred to by Culgi is likely to have embodied his songs in very specific ways. If we think of the act of singing as somehow representing the person, then a precursor of this would perhaps imply more fundamental embodiment, a synthesis of song, performer and text. This could be achieved by contriving formal structures within which there was space

---

[2] See Albert B. Lord, *The Singer Resumes the Tale*, ed. Mary Louise Lord (Ithaca: Cornell University Press, 1995): 2 n2 for a brief overview of the gender question.

for improvisation or spontaneous recomposition. This technique, known as formulaic oral transmission, was first explored by Milman Parry in connection with the works of Homer, and later refined by his student Albert Lord and others. The basic principle is that young aspiring singers learn from listening to practising performers; they may remember isolated phrases but more importantly they also remember key elements such as categories of event, genealogies, forms of address or phrases appropriate to particular actions. The singer does not need to memorise vast amounts of text or music, but learns how to create narrative by inserting relevant details into the appropriate formal structure.[3] Linguistic analysis supports the theory for texts, and it is a reasonable assumption that a similar creative process could have been applied to the music (although the attempts to do this with later music have not met with universal agreement). The Parry–Lord research on twentieth-century performances of Balkan epics suggested that similar processes were still at work in the present. Freely improvised song is less likely; listeners need some sort of recurring structural device to give the brain time to interpret what is heard, and performers need a sense of form within which they can display the rhetorical means to keep listeners' attention.

Epic stories, part entertainment, part attempts to explain both present and the past, are found in all pre-literate cultures; that is to say they appear as fully formed literature at the time when they are written down. Literacy marks a fundamental change in the nature of textual and musical transmission: instead of oral narratives being re-created to order, written versions become permanent. The need for permanency is determined by cultural factors: what is to be communicated eventually becomes too much or too complicated for a purely oral transmission. Writing may have developed as an aspect of record-keeping in more complex societies, and as societies became increasingly adept at accounting it was probably a small step to fix official documents of all kinds, including lineages and histories that legitimised the kingdom, tribe or clan. Musical notation develops much later than writing but for similar reasons, as an aid to memory and in order to transmit and store musical information accurately: to make things permanent. Eventually it would permit different creative processes which would come to be thought of as composition; in fact it would make possible the concept of composition as a reflective

---

[3] Parry described a formula as 'a group of words which is regularly employed under the same metrical conditions to express a given essential idea'. Albert Lord, *The Singer of Tales* (Cambridge, MA: Harvard University Press, 1960; repr. 1981): 30.

act of creation as opposed to the instant creation that formulaic transmission enabled. It also implies potential performance by someone who is not himself the originator of the work (or part of its living tradition) as well as offering huge potential as a pedagogical tool.

The earliest notation systems (dating from roughly the time of the Culgi hymns) appear to be aids for remembering accompaniment to singing. This suggests that the singing itself was still able to be relatively free, but that the accompanying was more formalised. In modern societies the essence of the music is often considered to reside in the score itself; in oral or proto-literate societies the music resides in the person. Teaching a chant to a novice singer is not simply pedagogy for its own sake, but is actually transferring immediately useable knowledge directly from one person to another. The earliest examples of notation aid this process, but they do not represent the music itself. In the future, musicians would become conscious of a broad division between written, fixed, composed music, and that which was not written; the latter might be improvised, less permanent and perhaps of less cultural value in a society where literacy was equated with power and control.[4]

ORAL TRADITION IN ANCIENT GREECE

There was a rich musical culture in the Hellenistic world in the first millennium BCE. Like many Babylonian epics, the *Iliad* and the *Odyssey* are literary representations of a world several centuries before writing began. They reveal a culture of song encompassing love songs, praise songs, wedding songs, harvest songs and laments of various sorts. Several famous performers are referred to by name; in the *Odyssey* the singer Demodocus is fêted by King Alcinous, who tells him:

It was either the Muse, the child of Zeus, who taught you, or Apollo. You sing the sufferings of the Achaeans extraordinarily well, all that they did and suffered and laboured, almost as though you had been there yourself, or had heard it from a witness. But now you change your theme, and sing the making of the wooden horse ... If you can narrate all that in the proper way, I

[4] This distinction has been central to the development of music in European culture. Although secular Greek notation systems survived into the Christian era they were never applied to Gregorian chant. The early church condemned secular music as frivolous, and when neumatic notation appeared it was applied solely to religious texts. Over several hundred years the written became associated with the religious, and the oral with secular music. The distinction blurred somewhat with the invention of printing, but the process of defining music in terms of what can be definitive continues to the present day with the recording technologies of the twentieth and twenty-first centuries.

shall not hesitate in saying to all men how generously the god has endowed you with divine song.[5]

The singer Phemius, pleading for his life at the feet of Odysseus, reminds him of the connection between singing and the divine:

It will bring harm to you later, if you kill a singer, one who sings for gods and men. I am self-taught, and a god has breathed all kinds of melodies into my mind. I could sing beside you as though to a god.[6]

Singers are mediators between gods and men, they shape events; there is a real sense of the power of performance to move people. These two singers were involved in traditional private, courtly performances, but from the fifth century BCE onwards there are signs of public performances at festivals and competitions; in the theatre there were choruses, boys and men singing in octaves. Clarity and purity were valued, and singing was distinguished from speaking by precise pitching. Notated vocal music survives from the fifth or fourth centuries BCE; the tradition remained an oral one, however, notation seemingly only used for harmonic analysis, pedagogical purposes and as an aid to memory.

CHRISTIANITY: A RELIGION OF THE VOICE

Two linked events early in the first millennium were to have profound effects on singing in the West: the foundation of Christian sects shortly after the death of Christ, and the subsequent legitimisation of Christianity as the official religion of the Roman Empire in 312. Although the latter was in many ways a pragmatic recognition by Constantine of the strength and efficiency of Christian administrative structures, it contributed to a revolution in the way music was conceived. The ancient world had been pantheistic and increasingly secular as its values began to dissipate, and the monotheistic world that sought to replace it was driven by a religion of the word. The church associated instrumental music with dance, entertainment and the excesses of the pagan world, and its own music became increasingly defined in terms of singing. The evidence for early Christian music-making is sparse. There are references to the singing of hymns and psalms, a tradition carried over from Judaism, of which the first Christians were a sub-sect. Early twentieth-century chant scholarship assumed a

[5] Andrew Barker, *Greek Musical Writings*. Vol. 1: *The Musician and his Art* (Cambridge University Press, 1984): 29.
[6] Ibid.: 31.

Jewish origin for actual chants, but the influence from Judaism is likely to have been one of function rather than substance; the devotional repetition of a body of religious texts was retained from Judaic tradition but the psalms themselves would been sung either in vernacular languages or, as the sect progressed within Roman society, in Latin. The likelihood is that hymns and psalms were newly composed to reflect the requirements of the new sect.

The fragmented post-Roman world saw the beginnings of monasticism in which both choral and solo singing were to coalesce as Gregorian chant. The extent to which psalms were actually vocalised in late antiquity has been the subject of much debate; the desert monasticism which was the channel through which learning and literacy survived the vicissitudes of post-Roman upheaval was fragmented and often very personal. Psalms may have been 'recited' silently by individual anchorites, and there is evidence for the mantra-like repetition of phrases, a meditative 'ruminating' on a text which would have produced something like a rumbling or droning sound rather than what we would think of as singing. A lasting influence of Judaism was an assumption of gender difference in music as the framework for worship became more formalised. Christian communities evolved with distinctly gendered singing traditions; both used the growing corpus of chant as a basis for their worship but the Pauline strictures against women in church resulted in a separate and an impoverished women's musical tradition for the whole of the medieval period, despite the remarkably creative efforts of certain individuals such as Hildegard von Bingen.[7]

There is continuing debate over whether Gregory I or Gregory II was the pope responsible for compiling a book of chants that came to be associated with his name, but it is clear that papal leadership ensured the primacy of a Roman chant tradition among the hundreds of local variants. The rise of the Carolingian empire under Charlemagne in the eighth century saw a northward shift in musical culture as the emperor of the Franks sought to consolidate his power through association with the old Roman centre. In 785–6 Pope Hadrian I presented Charlemagne with a Sacramentary (a book of Propers sung by the officiating priest), an event which began the modification of the northern Gallic tradition and which

---

[7] References to singing in the medieval period almost always imply males. As Joseph Dyer notes, singing by women is often equated with weakness or with children, and even the sympathetic reference to women's singing by the fourteenth-century Arnulf of St Ghislain may not be free from irony. See Joseph Dyer, 'The Voice in the Middle Ages', in John Potter (ed.), *The Cambridge Companion to Singing* (Cambridge University Press, 2000): 166.

in turn was re-exported back to Rome generations later. The Sacramentary would have had no music as notation had not yet been developed, and it would have been useless without the specialist singers that were sent to interpret it. The evolving chant tradition eventually grew into the twin repertoires required for the rituals of Mass and the Office (the series of eight services celebrated each day). These required music of two sorts: the 'Ordinary', which remained the same, and the 'Propers', which were specific to each day. With the exception of the Credo (which did not feature in the liturgy until the eleventh century) the fixed movements of the Mass (Kyrie, Gloria, Sanctus and Agnus Dei) were in place by about 700, at which time, as James McKinnon put it, 'The intellectual elite of Europe was engaged for a goodly part of the day, seven days a week, three hundred and sixty five days a year, from childhood till death, in the singing of gregorian chant.'[8]

At this stage it was still a purely oral tradition, with the music-making shared between the *schola* or monkish choir and cantors, increasingly virtuosic soloists with their own individual repertoires. Exactly how the monks retained such a vast corpus of music in their heads is still a matter for conjecture. The work of Leo Treitler and Helmut Hucke demonstrated the possible connection between formulaic learning, memorisation and notation; the difficulty for us today is in understanding the function of literacy within an oral tradition. Our formal learning is almost entirely dependent on literacy, and we tend to think of performances accomplished by written and oral learning as two entirely different processes; we also tend to make rather categorical distinctions between the permanence of the written and the supposedly ephemeral nature of the unwritten.

The concept of improvisation that is implied by aspects of oral performance is also problematic: where the permanence of the written is the norm, improvisation is not thought to carry the same cultural weight; it needs a leap of the imagination for us to conceive of one of the most significant European musical achievements as being semi-improvised, or to imagine a musical culture where there was no real boundary between composition and improvisation. This perception may change with the increasing cultural and commercial legitimisation of jazz and popular musics generally, where the basic creative impulse is essentially an oral/aural one, with notation often used in a very rudimentary form (if at all) and only as a reminder before pieces are committed to memory. Oral

[8] James McKinnon, 'The Emergence of Gregorian Chant in the Carolingian Era', in James McKinnon (ed.), *Antiquity and the Middle Ages: from Ancient Greece to the 15th Century* (London: Macmillan, 1990): 89.

culture flourishes in modern societies, but probably in a very different form from its medieval equivalent (we first experience music aurally and orally, and many people spend much of their time listening to recordings of music which has never been notated in a conventional way).

ORAL VERSUS WRITTEN SOURCES

Helmuth Hucke, following Treitler's work on the Homeric formulaic transmission of chant, first conclusively demonstrated that the chant notation that survives from the ninth century – neumes with no staves, indicating approximate pitches and no rhythm – represents an oral performance practice rather than what we would think of as a score. The music is encoded by a scribal notator, to provide models for the application of formulaic compositional rules. This results in a mixture of recurring patterns which are more or less fixed, and more free-flowing passages where the singer can interpolate his own improvisations. So what is written down may be an example of what the notator actually heard (or sang himself, perhaps), or simply a hypothetical example to generate further ideas. The early chant books are too small to have been read from in a dark monastic church; they are intended as reference materials to be used for teaching oral performance, or perhaps for the monks to consult before a service to remind themselves of previous renderings. Gregorian melodies often seem curiously wayward to modern ears and lacking a sense of compositional logic; this is perhaps a consequence of the creative and somewhat aleatoric nature of music that may have come into existence as transcribed improvisations, with very loose formal structures allowing the whim of the performer to have full expression.

All the singing referred to so far has been monophonic; that is to say it was essentially melodic, with no harmony. Late twentieth-century performance practice has sometimes included drones beneath the melody where there is a modal consistency that would support their use. This is unlikely to have happened in the first millennium; drones were traditionally associated with bagpipes and dance music, which would not commend them to the church, and there is no reference to vocal drones in the surviving literature.[9] At some point during the second half of the first millennium, however, the genesis of harmonic music-making occurred,

---

[9] Guido d'Arezzo does allow for a variety of *organum* in which the lower of two voices repeats the same note, but this is quite different in function from a sustained drone. See his *Micrologus* in *Hucbald, Guido and John on Music: Three Medieval Treatises*, trans. Warren Babb and Claude Palisca (ed.), (New Haven: Yale University Press, 1978): 81 (example 18).

possibly taking the form of a second part shadowing the chant original at a consistent interval, perhaps a fourth or fifth ('harmonic' in the sense of more than one voice sounding simultaneously; the perception of the music may well have remained linear until the fifteenth century when composer-singers became more aware of the expressive possibilities of dissonance).

By the mid to late ninth century the technique was sufficiently familiar to be codified in a number of pedagogical works, the most celebrated of which is the anonymous *Musica Enchiriadis*. This handbook aimed to teach the rudiments of singing (for that is what music was) to young monks, and after some basic instruction in notation gives exercises or examples of how to create diaphony or *organum*. It does not represent the birth of polyphony, but the inscribing of a process that had probably been going on for many generations. We have no idea of how the process originated, but it is likely to have been in a male establishment rather than a female one because of the greater range available in choirs of boys and men: the simple contrast of high and low, and its potential for serendipitous notes in between, would have been less obvious in choirs of nuns (both *Musica Enchiriadis* and Hucbald of St Amand's slightly later *De Harmonica Institutione* speak of men and boys singing polyphony).[10] Although the principle of *organum* singing is based on parallel movement, by the time of the ninth-century treatises there is already an awareness of consonance and dissonance. Much of the basic instruction gives formulae for avoiding dissonant combinations (especially the tritone), an indication that singers now have to acknowledge a vertical element within the fundamentally linear performance implied by chant. The formulae for the avoidance of dissonance by contrary motion are the first signs of singerly creativity being applied to polyphony.

Notation becomes more sophisticated as theorists struggle to define precise pitches, with total enlightenment ultimately provided by the staff notation developed for his new Antiphoner by Guido of Arezzo around 1025 (though he may not have actually invented the idea). This was another revolutionary change for singers: once notation could encode actual pitches the notes could be sung at sight, reducing the lifetime process of learning the chant repertoire to almost no time at all. Guido also introduced a *solfège* system based on the hymn 'Ut queant laxis', which conveniently starts each new line a step higher than the previous one. The

---

[10] *Musica Enchiriadis*, trans. Raymond Erickson (New Haven: Yale University Press 1995): 23; *De Harmonica Institutione*, in *Hucbald, Guido and John on Music*: 19.

syllables sung to this ascending sequence give the note names, enabling singers to remember the pitches that they could now see. The idea of seeing an exact pitch was revolutionary and must have been a significant aid to memorisation. The developments associated with Guido did not mean that singers started to perform from manuscripts; the new notation was initially a means of learning music more efficiently and memorising it more speedily.

The writings of many of the theorists towards the end of the first millennium are eminently practical; their main goal is the improvement of the chant and its singers, and their careful instructions are sometimes very revealing. Guido in his *Micrologus* (a book of instructions for boy trebles) explains how to shape musical melodic lines: one can rhythmicise the chant in the manner of poetry, giving appropriate accents; the ends of phrases should be slowed down to prepare for breathing space (and changing the spacing of the neumes will indicate this); the qualities of the neumes should be observed, such as those that mean delay (*morula*) or trembling (*tremula*); often notes 'liquesce' so that 'the interval from one note to another is begun with a smooth glide and does not appear to have a stopping place en route'.[11] These seem to be early references to what we think of as rubato, vibrato and portamento, and suggest that such effects are extremely ancient. As with the *organum* exercises, the writings do not imply a read performance but an oral one enabled by written instructions, giving singers the means to be spontaneously creative within certain limits. The *De Musica* of the otherwise unknown John (possibly of Afflighem) dates from around 1100 and is heavily indebted to *Micrologus*, quoting substantial parts of it. John's treatise is more informal, with asides that give us glimpses of performance practice. In an extraordinary passage on the difference between theoretical and practical music-making he gives his young charges permission to be as creative as possible:

[T]he musician [i.e. theorist] and singer differ not a little from one another. Whereas the musician always proceeds correctly and by calculation, the singer holds the right road intermittently, merely though habit. To whom then should I better compare the singer than to a drunken man who does indeed get home but does not in the least know by what path he returns?[12]

---

[11] *Hucbald, Guido and John on Music*: 72. A full description of the complexities of neumatic notation and other significant aspects of Gregorian chant such as modes and modal rhythm is beyond the scope of this chapter; see G. Cattin, *Music of the Middle Ages I* (Cambridge University Press, 1984) for a concise overview.
[12] *De Musica* in *Hucbald, Guido and John on Music*: 105. The 'drunken man' analogy will be familiar to anyone involved in improvised music.

John acknowledges the importance of musical writing and precepts but admits that completely illiterate 'jongleurs and actors' are quite capable of coming up with very good tunes; later, he even suggests that the creator of chants should turn his attention to secular song. He also confirms a relationship between singing and speech, the various pauses interpolated at appropriate points being analogous to punctuation marks. As one would expect, there are copious instructions on how to interpret existing chants and how to create new ones, and John also reveals the problems associated with staffless neumes and the advantages of Guido's new system. He points out that with lines to indicate exact intervals, once the pitches are learned it is impossible to forget them, so there will be no more chaotic choir practices when singers come together from different pedagogical traditions:

For one says, 'Master Trudo taught me this way'; another rejoins, 'but I learned thus from Master Albinus'; and to this a third remarks, 'Master Solomon certainly sings far differently.' ... rarely do three men agree about one chant, far less a thousand. Naturally, since everyone prefers his own teacher, there arise as many variations in chanting as there are teachers in the world.[13]

It is the daily routine singing of monophonic chant that represents the essence of music for John and his intended readership, but his brief chapter on *organum* hints at a new sophistication in the construction of polyphony, which is by now entrenched in the singing tradition. John acknowledges a wider range of intervals, encouraging a move away from strictly parallel voices, and introduces a crucial element of compositional choice. With John's treatise we see that the musical process is changing as singers begin to be aware of the creative possibilities of notation, although we still do not fully understand how the singers used the written page.

THE SOUND OF MEDIEVAL SINGING

So far we have looked mainly at *what* singers sang as opposed to *how*. The *what* is closely bound up with literacy, so we can see it with increasing clarity from the twelfth century onwards, but the *how* relies on conjecture based largely on common sense and extrapolation from the small number of references to singers and singing, most of which are ambiguous at best. We can also take into account the context of the singing and the nature of the 'performance'. Monks were not trained in singing in an abstract or objective sense, and nor were they selected on the basis of vocal ability; their life's work was rendering the chant, personifying

[13] *Ibid.*: 147.

rather than interpreting it perhaps. One might argue that the chant performed *them*, rather than the other way round. The sound of a monastic choir was determined by the individuals who contributed to it, and
who perhaps understood chant singing as something closer to meditation
than 'performance'. There is not much evidence of projection, although in
larger establishments the singing would certainly have been coloured by
the acoustics. Reverberation has become almost fetishised in the modern
performance and consumption of music, and it is tempting to imagine
the monks revelling in the depth of sound produced by their voices in
the building. We do not know if they did this, and looking at the iconography we may feel that the minds of the monks were probably not focused
on their acoustic environment; there are many pictures of singing monks
huddled together as though depending on each other for support; they
hardly seem to open their mouths, confirming later authorities' observa-
tion that the mouth should be open no further than a finger's width. We
can be a little less tentative in the case of solo singing: some of the solo
chants are extremely virtuosic, and in a musical culture where the singer
is creating the chant from source material and a set of rules it is much
easier to imagine a sense of self-belief among the soloists as opposed to
a more modest belief in the hereafter assumed by the choir. Soloists are
much more likely to have felt engaged by the acoustic, especially in the
twelfth-century polyphonic repertoire, but unfortunately for us there are
very few pictures of soloists singing either polyphony or chant.

The larynxes of these singers would have been no different from those
of modern singers, but the sound that they made is likely to have been very
different from that of third-millennium choirs. We get a sense of the individuality of singers as early as the seventh-century Isidore of Seville, who
characterises voices as pertaining to a number of categories ranging from
sweet (*suavis*) to hard (*dura*) and harsh (*aspera*). His ideal voice is not too
delicate (*subtilis*) because it would then sound too much like a sick person
or a woman, or even a stringed instrument; for perfection a voice must be
high, sweet and clear (*alta, suavis et clara*).[14] The same individuality is still
present six hundred years later in the writings of Jerome of Moravia, who
also understands something of vocal registers. A vocal register is the vocal
tract position used for a set of notes. Most people (male and female) are
conscious of having at least two: a chest or modal register and a falsetto.
'Head voice' is sometimes experienced as a transitional placing between
chest and falsetto. Jerome identifies three of them: the chest, the throat

---

[14] Translation in Joseph Dyer, 'The Voice in the Middle Ages': 166–7 and 255 (n6).

and the head; he appears to say that singers should maintain the integrity of each register, which would have meant that singers would sound quite different depending on which part of their voice they were using.[15]

It is not until the fifteenth century, with the *De modo bene cantandi* of Conrad von Zabern that we get a clearer picture of what medieval choirs may have sounded like. Conrad was a priest who devoted much of his life to the improvement of chanting in southern Germany. As early as the ninth century John the Deacon had criticised singers north of the Alps in general and German singers in particular, a complaint perhaps dating from the attempts of Charlemagne to introduce Roman chants to the north a hundred years before. These attempts seem not to have been entirely successful, with the German singers finding it difficult to meld the Italian style with their own. Conrad castigates monks for their tuning and for bawling, for singing through the nose, distorting vowels or aspirating between the notes of melismas; singers should move people to devotion by their deportment and the joy with which they interpret the chant. Most interestingly, he clarifies Jerome's apparent insistence on the separation of registers, and admonishes singers for attempting to make a uniform sound throughout their range. He believes that the voice works best when singing comfortably within a register and cautions singers against trying to extend the register beyond its natural tessitura. In this way, he says, singers will achieve the refinement and control appropriate to good chant singing. The fact that two major sources agree on the distinctness of registers suggests that the monastic choir would have had three perceivably different colours corresponding to the top, middle and bottom of the singers' ranges. This exploitation of the unique characteristics of each register when combined with the speech-like individuality of each voice, would have produced a vibrant, colourful heterophony that was probably nothing like the blended uniformity that we expect today.

NOTRE DAME AND AFTER: THE SPECIALISED SOLOIST

In the second half of the twelfth century the cathedral of Notre Dame de Paris transformed itself from a Romanesque basilica into the Gothic cathedral that still stands today. Although there were centres of musical creativity all over Europe (many of them, such as Winchester and Bologna,

---

[15] There are various ways of interpreting Jerome's descriptions. See ibid.: 169 and Carol MacClintock, *Readings in the History of Music in Performance* (Bloomington: Indiana University Press, 1979): 6–7 for slightly different translations. There is an extended analysis of other aspects of Jerome's treatise in Timothy McGee, *The Sound of Medieval Song* (Oxford: Clarendon Press, 1998): 62–70.

with large churches or cathedrals) Paris was the hub of an intellectual and artistic reawakening that accompanied a period of relative prosperity and peace. We know the names of many clerics and poets from the period, but although poets may lay claim to authorship it is rare for musicians to be identified with specific pieces of music. Two of the earliest names associated with actual music are the Parisians Leonin and Perotin. We know of them only because some one hundred years after they flourished an anonymous cleric (possibly from Bury St Edmunds) tells of a *Magnus Liber Organi* (a great book of *organa*) that Leonin put together, containing two-voice extended *organum* pieces (without the accompanying chants, which would have been sung from memory) for the significant festivals of the church's year. He goes on to say that Leonin's presumed successor, Perotin, edited or arranged the pieces and provided new *organa* (several of which he identifies) in three and four voices. Copies of the *Magnus Liber* survive, and they do indeed contain the pieces specified in Anonymous iv (as our scribal source is known) which makes them the earliest known polyphonic works to which we can attach a name with any certainty. The *Magnus Liber* is an extraordinary achievement, but precisely what it means has been the subject of a scholarly debate which is not yet resolved. If it is typical of the music books of great establishments then it is also a testament to what has been lost to history. Leonin and Perotin were certainly not composers in the modern sense and may have been singers, scribes, editors or compilers or a combination of all or any of these. The *Magnus Liber* is not what we would think of as a score (though in many ways the manuscripts look like one). It represents a record of a performance practice that we will never fully access, the encoding in written form of a set of models or formulae perhaps, or transcriptions of possible performances. A written record of an oral practice will always be inadequate without some sort of description of its use.

The *Magnus Liber* certainly reveals a picture (if a rather blurred one) of a sophisticated vocal culture driven by virtuosity and exuberant vocalism. From a vocal point of view, the music is broadly of two varieties; the first of these is a note-against-note or *discant* style, in which the voices may be freely composed with similar characteristics, with between one and three notes occurring over a single note; the other basic style is what was originally known as *organum purum* in which a tenor line would be created using an existing chant slowed down so that one note may occupy the equivalent of several pages in a modern edition. Over this foundation another voice would weave elaborate melismas. For the first time we begin to see hints of rhythmic organisation, with the introduction of a number of rhythmic modes, which correspond approximately to poetic metre. The extent to which the singers applied the modes is debatable (there are references to irregularities in performance) but what is clear is that there were two types of solo singer, who had skills that were different both from each other and from those of the choral establishment or *schola*. The lower line was held by the tenorista, while singers of the upper parts (up to three additional voices) were known as machicoti. The tenorista seems to have done the vocally impossible: hold the same note for page after page without breathing, and it was assumed for many years that these lines were sung by the choir. It is likely, however, that far from being a subsidiary voice, the tenorista was a specialist singer with skills or knowledge that the machicotus may not have had. The tenorista is in effect singing an unmeasured line: he would need to be sufficiently familiar with the source material to be able to hold his part without forgetting where he was within the totality of the chant; he would need to know where to change words, and he would need to know where to breathe in relation to what was going on above him. Singing in such a sustained and stylised way may have resulted in a rather instrumental sound and perhaps set the tone for future generations of singers who would be quite capable of interpreting an untexted line in an appropriate way. Modern singers tend to find the sustained singing of one note extremely taxing, and it is likely that the tenorista possessed a particular talent or technique for doing this comfortably. Interestingly, the terms used for the upper voices change over time, but as late as the sixteenth century there are still references to tenoristae, whose skills were clearly appreciated as much as those required for the more soloistic lines.[16]

The machicoti are easier for a modern singer to understand: the soaring lines that they were asked to sing still hold a powerful attraction for modern early music tenors. If the tenorista relied to some extent on arcane knowledge of chant (and was an older person, perhaps?), the machicotus was light of voice and fleet of brain, able to make artistic decisions on the hoof about how to differentiate between measured and unmeasured passages, when to pause, when to add a new melodic cell, which cadential formula to apply. He is working with the habits and customs of memory, but probably has a sophisticated understanding of notation as a performance tool, which enables him to refine his performance as he goes along, to revisit figures that he has seen, as opposed to those that are instinctive vocal gestures born of habit. For the first time we get a feeling that these may have been singers with whom we might have been able to have

---

[16] For more on the tenorista see John Potter, *Tenor: History of a Voice* (New Haven: Yale University Press, 2009): 4–8 and pp. 64–5 below.

a conversation. They were also professionals: the Notre Dame account books show how much was paid to each singer. This is no longer music solely in the service of God, but something that musicians do because they are good at it and can make a living from it.

As performance and composition evolved beyond *organum* more elaborate forms began to take shape. The Notre Dame repertoire includes examples of *conductus*, a form of non-liturgical song probably originating in southern France, which marks a major leap forward in compositional and performance technique. Like *organum* the process was horizontally conceived, but unlike the earliest polyphony it did not use a pre-existing chant; a new tenor line was composed which might be used on its own or with up to four other voices. Exactly how this worked in practice is difficult to determine as the surviving manuscripts look very much like finished compositions, with an elegant sense of structure that seems to imply a written genre. It is perhaps with the arrival of *conductus* that singerly creativity began to give ground to composerly constructivism. By the middle of the thirteenth century the *conductus* had itself been largely replaced by the motet, a yet more sophisticated form which would become the generic non-liturgical form for at least two hundred years. Motets might have separate texts for each voice (which need not even be in the same language). A pre-existing tenor would normally be used but this need not be chant, or even sacred music of any sort: by the middle of the thirteenth century vernacular texts were more common than Latin ones.

There is a delightful informality about the texts set by composers of the earliest motets, a self-conscious cleverness that rejoices in secularity and is often quite personal. Many of the pieces appear to be composed by students, and the vernacular tenor may reference communities, friends and the mutual and enjoyment of music and literature, while the Latin *contratenor* (an additional tenor line written 'against' the tenor part) will keep the music morally on track with a few words about the Blessed Virgin Mary. The conviviality visible in these motets is another glimpse of a musical world that has some reference to our own; the context may be different but the human interaction has a timelessness that we can identify with. There is a similarly recognisable sense of actuality in the late thirteenth-century *Cronica* of Salimbene de Adam, who describes the activities of Vita of Lucca, a singer and composer who entranced his listeners. He would often write new tunes to tenors composed by his friends and fellow Franciscans. Of a piece written by one brother Henry of Pisa, Salimbene observes:

the counter-tune ... was written by Brother Vita of the Order of Minor Friars from Lucca, the best singer in the world in his day in both kinds of song, namely liturgical and extra-liturgical. He had a voice that was graceful or subtle, and delightful to hear.[17]

Brother Vita would have dialogues with nightingales and everyone would be silent when he sang. One nun was so moved that she jumped out of a window in order to listen to him, breaking her leg in the process. There is also the suggestion that what would later be called chamber singing was different from that required for church: 'his voice was better suited to a room than to a choir', says Salimbene, who clearly values what Vita does with his voice as much if not more than the music itself.[18]

Although singers were increasingly able to feel a sense of their own worth, their lives were entirely at the mercy of the feudal system in which economic and cultural value were conditioned by personal loyalty and service. There was no sense of nationality as we might understand it (the only over-arching authority common to all was the church itself) and we cannot discern anything resembling national styles. What we do see is the rise to prominence of ruling dynasties in various European centres. As France faltered in the mire of the Hundred Years War, the cultural centre of northern Europe shifted to the court of Burgundy, which from the accession of Philip the Bold in 1364 began a period of expansion and prosperity that lasted for more than a hundred years. The Burgundian court and its satellite outposts were typical of princely establishments throughout Europe, differing from most only in conspicuous artistic consumption. The dukes of Valois were formidable patrons of the arts, and made it their business to attract the finest musicians available. Philip's preferred instrument was the harp, and he spent substantial sums on instrumentalists for ceremonial occasions and courtly entertainment. Among the singers he sponsored there were several famous women, who probably performed monophonic songs. In their day singers such as Jeanne la Page and Aiglautine de Tournay may have been as famous as their male counterparts, but left no written music for historians and musicologists to pore over.[19] Although Philip did not establish his own personal chapel until relatively late in his reign, when he did so he procured musicians from outside Burgundy itself, eventually acquiring singers from the papal court at Avignon.

Courts were mobile, and singers were expected to travel; the provision of a horse was very much the equivalent of a company car, and it was

---

[17] Salimbene de Adam, *Cronica*, trans. Alberto Gallo, in *Music of the Middle Ages*, vol. II (Cambridge University Press, 1985): 130–2.

[18] Ibid.: 131.

[19] See Craig Wright, *Music at the Court of Burgundy* (Henryville, PA: Institute of Medieval Music, 1979): 28.

the responsibility of the feudal lord to provide musicians with lodging, clothing, food and drink as well as incidental expenses. This drain on courtly finances was reduced by the practice of granting benefices (the income from church sinecures) to favoured singers. The number of singers employed by the courts was variable, Philip's chapel reaching as many as twenty-eight in 1404, but lesser establishments such as that of John of Brittany could muster only eight. The implications for performance practice are not entirely clear, but the possibilities must have ranged from one voice to a part to several singers per line. There were also boys' voices available; the singer and composer Jean Tapissier was given the task of looking after four choirboys on behalf of Philip's successor, John the Fearless. He was required to teach them to sing and was responsible for their accommodation and general welfare, as well as ensuring that they appeared for functions throughout the dukedom and beyond as needed.

These singers were skilled readers of notation and when hired would often bring new music with them, disseminating the Franco-Flemish repertoire well beyond Burgundy. Secular, notated, polyphony was increasingly valued as a sophisticated alternative to monophonic song, and books of rondeaux, ballades and virelais were part of the musicians' baggage. These three interrelated *formes fixes* had their origins in twelfth-century France, and may have evolved out of the attempt of poet-singers to formalise poetic structures and relate the musical form more closely to the poetic structure in order to make songs easier to memorise. Between the twelfth and fifteenth centuries the forms change and overlap, but from a singer's point of view the ballade eventually takes on the form AAB, the virelai a more elaborate ABBA, and the rondeau AAABAB (although how often the songs were performed in their fully formed versions is open to question). On the cusp of the change to more complex forms is Adam de la Halle, whose chansons look back to an older, monophonic tradition, and whose motets foreshadow the complexities of the *Ars Nova*. He was one of the first singer-composer-poets to have a concept of aspects of his work surviving beyond his own lifetime, and may even have overseen the manuscript collection of his work.[20] The historical significance of this is considerable, in that it suggests an awareness of a potential future for music which exists in written form and will still exist when its creators are no longer around to perform it. In time this will lead to a fundamental change in the nature of singing as performers become interpreters rather than creators, a process that would reach its most complete realisation in the twentieth century.

[20] See Mary O'Neill, *Courtly Love Songs of Medieval France* (Oxford University Press, 2006): 181–2.

SECULAR MONOPHONY: FROM ORAL TRADITION
TO POETIC LYRIC

The church so dominated the musical and literary world that secular music is barely visible during the first millennium. The little that the church allows us to see is further reduced by the inevitable gaps in the historical record that affect all music. Oral epics created in a similar fashion to the Homeric model appear to have flourished among the north European tribes in the period following the disintegration of Roman society. As with the Greek poems, the likelihood is that the Icelandic and Saxon epics were written down many generations after they were first created. The manuscript of the Anglo-Saxon *Beowulf*, the story of an epic struggle between the eponymous hero and the monster Grendel, dates from the eleventh century and recalls events from five hundred years before; it could date from almost any time between the fifth and tenth centuries.[21] Harps ring out, accompanying the singing of histories and myths, as they had in the ninth century *Widsith* (also of uncertain date), whose eponymous hero calls himself a gleoman. The poem represents not Widsith's song but the context in which it happens. The gleoman announces himself in the courtly mead hall with hints at the generosity of previous patrons:

> And so I can sing and tell a tale,
> declare to the company in the mead-hall
> how noble rulers rewarded me with gifts

and he goes on to list his travels, a fabulous itinerary of most of the known world, legitimising his status as a praise-singer of vast experience. Then he and his companion Scilling, a fellow musician who is possibly his harpist, sing the praises of Queen Ealhhild, daughter of Eadwine:

> Then Scilling and I with our clear voices,
> before our glorious lord, struck up our song;
> sung to the harp, it rang out loudly.

We do not know what he actually sang, but this was apparently a typical evening's work for a wandering minstrel:

> Wandering like this, driven by chance
> minstrels travel through many lands;
> they state their needs, say words of thanks,
> always, south or north, they find some man
> well-versed in songs, generous in gifts,

---

[21] British Library, Cotton Vitellius A. xv.

who wishes to raise his renown with his men,
to do great things, until everything passes,
light and life together; he who wins fame
has lasting glory under the heavens.[22]

The roles of these minstrels are much like those of the Sumerian praise-singer, though their achievements lack the wider compass of Culgi. Such narratives are very specific to the societies that generated them and are essentially feudal, reinforcing a sense of cultural identity based on dynastic history at a times of social instability; those that survive into the age of literacy are likely to be only a small fraction of the original repertoires and were probably recontextualised into a literary tradition for their poetic worth or antiquarian value. A twelfth-century northern French tradition of *chanson de geste* or *cantus gestualis* is recorded by Johannes de Grocheo, who notes that these are songs recounting noble deeds, the lives of saints or the exploits of Charlemagne; the third category was presumably once somewhat larger when the Holy Roman Emperor was still in people's memories. Some one hundred *chansons de geste* remain, none complete – many of the missing elements presumably being those improvised by the performer. In Italy we also find *materia di Francia*, stories of Charlemagne alongside Arthurian legends and chivalrous tales from the thirteenth century onwards, several hundred years after the time the events are supposed to have happened.[23]

In contrast to these vernacular works there was a late flowering of Latin lyrics from the sixth century onwards; the strict metre and rhyme suggests a literary genre rather than an oral one, although little is known about the elusive *vagantes* or wandering scholars, displaced clerics perhaps, whose exquisite verses tell of love, life and loss, often displaying a sense of humour that tends toward the scatological. The scholar's lyric reaches its most eloquent expression in the collection known as the *Carmina Burana* manuscript, originating (probably) in the Bavarian monastery of Benedicktbeuern some time in the thirteenth century. We know that the poems were intended to be sung (some of them have staffless neumes as a reminder) and many of the tunes can be reconstructed from other manuscripts (thirteen of them survive in Notre Dame sources, for example). The collection is hugely varied: sacred songs and plays, songs of

---

[22] Trans. Jørn Olav Løset.
[23] See James Haar, *Essays on Italian Poetry and Music in the Renaissance 1350–1600* (Berkeley: University of California Press, 1986), especially chapter 4, '*Improvvisatori* and their relationship to Sixteenth Century Music' for a fuller account of the *cantastorie* and the role of improvised singing in an increasingly literate world.

love, sex, gambling, eating, drinking and riotous behaviour generally. The Benedicktbeuern manuscript also contains almost fifty songs in Bavarian dialect, many of which are based on *Minnesänger* lyrics, love songs created by the German successors to the troubadours.

With the appearance of secular lyrics in vernacular languages we can see the beginnings of what we now recognise as a separate genre from religious music, which continued to be sung in Latin. Troubadour song originated in the first quarter of the twelfth century in what is now southern France. The language of the troubadours was *occitan*, or the *langue d'oc* (as opposed to the *langue d'oïl*, a reference to the respective words for 'yes' in southern and northern France); their songs are almost all love songs, and although the first known troubadour was Duke William IX of Aquitaine the singers were drawn from all levels of society. The genre was essentially a courtly one, however, since princely households were the only places outside the church where literary culture could flourish, though the performers' status was a hybrid one. Whatever the reason they took to the road, their music could be expected to assure them of a place in courtly entertainment. The end of the twelfth century and the first quarter of the next saw the height of the troubadour art, with more than two dozen named composers among the hundreds of anonymous singer-poets. The north of France had its own tradition, which flourished in the thirteenth century, a similar genre of aristocratic monophonic song known as *trouvère* poetry (in French, or the *langue d'oïl*). Although we now make convenient distinctions between the 'national' styles of France, Provence and Germany, such an atomised view would not have been typical of the time. The much-travelled Holy Roman Emperor Otto IV, for example, was familiar with many of the great singer-poet-composers of his time including the troubadours Bertran de Born and Guiraut de Bornelh as well as the legendary minnesinger Walter von der Vogelweide, and was a friend of Richard the Lionheart (himself a troubadour).

Spain, too, had its *cantigas de gesta*, but the most famous surviving repertoire of the period is the collection of songs known as the *Cantigas de Santa Maria*. This was assembled under the auspices of the Spanish King Alfonso the Wise in the second half of the thirteenth century and contains more than four hundred songs, mostly in a verse-refrain form, telling of miraculous interventions by the Virgin Mary, often in the most bizarre circumstances. The collection is profusely illustrated, suggesting an infinite number of performance possibilities, with bowed and plucked strings and a variety of wind and percussion. Exactly how these instruments were deployed is not known, but the array of instruments suggests a colourful palette, perhaps doubling the vocal line or alternating with it. The integration of the Spanish peninsula's substantial Jewish and Muslim communities was unique in Europe, and Alfonso employed Moorish and Jewish musicians at court. The likelihood is that the singing of the *cantigas* would have had a distinctly North African Mediterranean flavour, something of which may survive in the Muslim singing of present-day Morocco.

In the British Isles, which were an outpost of French culture from the eleventh century onwards, it is harder to discern signs of vernacular song. The oldest surviving songs in the English language are attributed to the sometime crusader and eventual hermit Godric, who apparently received a troped Kyrie and a number of short songs in praise of the Virgin and St Nicolas from his dead sister Burgwen in a dream. Godric had led a full life before devoting himself to contemplation in his cell by the River Wear, into which he was occasionally lowered in a barrel when overly secular thoughts got the better of him. Of similar antiquity is the manuscript containing the so-called Cambridge Songs, a collection (mostly without music) probably acquired by a monk of St Augustine's Canterbury while visiting Germany.

The various genres of European secular song have a number of characteristics in common. Even if the songs are written down they are likely to have had an improvised element and to have been performed from memory (the manuscript being essentially a method of storage). The manuscripts may be records of actual performances (as opposed to prescriptions for future ones); they are normally strophic, whether an epic narrative (which might be very long indeed), a crucifixion lament or a simple love song. During the thirteenth century poet-composers began to explore more formal structures, which eventually coalesced into the three *formes fixes* which in time became the favoured structures for both monophonic and polyphonic song. Less formal varieties of singing (which in the twentieth century would become known as 'popular' music) are almost invisible to the written record. Vincenzo Giustiniani's *Discorso sopra la musica*, dating from about 1628, contains the thoughts of a nobleman and dilettante who wrote on a number of different topics towards the end of his life. For completeness he mentions in passing several sorts of vocal activity which common sense suggests had been part of everyday life for hundreds of years: the singing of lullabies to children (and animals), songs to ease the sufferings of the sick, work

songs by field workers, sailors and porters, spice-crushers, children singing in the dark to lessen their fears, drinking songs and 'crazy songs' to
lessen the boredom of long journeys on horseback.[24] These are timeless
manifestations of singing which form the background to the evolution
of singing as a performance art.

[24] Vincenzo Giustiniani, *Discorso sopra la musica*, trans. Carol MacClintock (Middleton, WI:
American Institute of Musicology, 1962): 74–6.

CHAPTER 3

The emerging soloist and the primacy of text

The evidential fog that engulfs much of music in the early medieval period begins to lift a little as we get into the fourteenth century. For the first time we can see significant evidence of secular polyphonic song. We know from the iconography of the period that singing was a sociable activity; men and women are depicted singing and playing together, often outside and in mixed vocal and instrumental groups. What they sang is still a matter for speculation as there is nothing that links any illustration to specific pieces of music (or music to specific instruments). The relationship between composer and performer was still very little like our modern concept of clearly defined roles: a competent musician was expected to compose, sing, play and probably write poetry and dance too, and would have made very little distinction between any of these activities, which were subsumed within much looser concepts of poet, musician or courtier. We know the names of some who were singers, sometimes because they themselves appear in song texts or have some sort of singerly diminutive attached to their name, and increasingly because they figure in account books: singers are making money from their craft. Many more we know and value as composers, something that would have been incomprehensible to a fourteenth-century musician. It is an inevitable fact of survival that manuscripts remain, ghosts of music as act, but performers and performances of the act do not. It is significant that musicians are increasingly willing to be identified with their compositions, and this is the very beginning of a centuries-long process that will eventually lead to music history being written in terms of composers and 'their' works. In the late medieval period, however, this was not the case, and those whom scribes identify as composers are likely to have been better known to their contemporaries as doers or makers of music in a much wider sense.

Singers travelled widely, moving from post to post, often head-hunted by rival courts or loaned to friendly ones. Many, now forgotten, were as famous as the composers we still remember. Reinhard Strohm considers

Jean Cordier to be 'perhaps the most famous singer of his time'.[1] A friend of Jacob Obrecht, Cordier began his singing career as a clerk in Bruges in 1460. He went on to sing for the Medici court in Florence where he must have sung Dufay, and where Lorenzo de Medici admired his improvising to the *lira da braccio*. His career took him to the Sforzas in Milan (where he probably sang Josquin) and the Hapsburg and papal courts, before his death in Bruges in 1501. His improvising skills may have been as important as his ability to sing polyphony or to the lute.

More successful still was Pietro de Burzeris, known as Pietrobono, born in Ferrara around 1417. Lewis Lockwood perfectly encapsulated Pietro's problem with posterity:

[O]f Pietrobono not a note of written music is preserved, yet he is beyond doubt one of the most important figures of all fifteenth-century music, certainly in Italy. Only the tendency of modern historiography to base its views entirely on written sources, rather than on these in relation to the larger landscape from which they emerge, could prevent us from seeing Pietrobono, in his domain, as a figure comparable to the greatest polyphonic masters of the period.[2]

What did he sing, and how? His reputation as a singer of tales and as an improvising polyphonist was unsurpassed; he was courted by the leading families of the day and among the medals struck in his honour is one comparing him to Orpheus. He is often referred to in connection with his *tenorista*; it is unusual for performers of the period to have their own personal backing musicians, and this may have added both to Pietrobono's performance possibilities and to his cachet as a musician. Contemporary notated two-part polyphony invariably has a relatively simple lower part, which would enable the singer to concentrate on the upper part if he was accompanying himself. Freed of the need to hold down his own bass lines, Pietrobono would be able to display much greater virtuosity whether singing or playing. The *tenorista* would also have enabled him to perform improvised polyphony in up to three parts, a skill that is now completely lost. There is evidence of an improvised epic tradition in Italy, perhaps related to the French *chansons de geste* (or indeed the formulaic epic on the other side of the Adriatic observed by Parry and Lord), so Pietrobono may have been a creator of oral epic. He may have declaimed poetry according to one of the fixed forms; he may have had a repertoire of stock tunes on which he could busk, and with his *tenorista* he could

---

[1] Reinhard Strohm, *Music in Late Medieval Bruges* (Oxford: Clarendon Press, 1990): 37.
[2] Lewis Lockwood, *Music in Renaissance Ferrara 1400–1505* (Cambridge, MA: Harvard University Press, 1992): 98.

have sung and played in three- or four-part harmony, or invented virtuosic tropes over plainsong tenors. Whatever he did, he impressed like no other; as James Haar reminds us, 'part of the essence of *aria* was melody, but much of it was style, personal and untranscribable'.[3] Pietrobono and his contemporaries were charismatic singers with reputations equivalent to today's pop musicians.

POLYPHONIC SONG

The chief employers of singers were religious establishments and the courts of the many European city states, the latter also often doubling as the former. The music – ranging from chant to Mass movements and motets or chansons – became ever more complex. The texts for the Mass were of two kinds: the Propers, which were specific to each day of the year, and the Ordinary, a framework of texts repeated at each service. The Gloria and Credo sections of the Mass Ordinary, the two most substantial parts of the Mass, offered composers the chance to show how they could sustain longer swathes of music, but it was the first and last of the polyphonic sections that offered the singers the chance for performative self-indulgence. The fashion for interpolating into the Kyrie additional texts for specific occasions often meant that this opening movement, in essence a simple tripartite repetition of a single line of text, could become a substantial prelude to the Gloria which immediately follows it. The terms 'movement' and 'prelude' are, of course, used figuratively in this context: the Mass sections were not movements in the sense that a symphony would later have movements; although there may be unifying elements each section had a specific function embedded in a liturgical context and these would not have been perceived as parts of a musical whole. It is often the practice for modern performers to present the sections of medieval and Renaissance Masses consecutively, which gives a misleading impression of the nature of these compositions. At the end of the Mass the Agnus Dei became the most abstractly expressive movement in almost all Mass settings from the fourteenth century onwards.

The earliest surviving manuscript of a complete set of Ordinaries is preserved in the library of Tournai cathedral. Its Agnus Dei is quite different in conception from the other movements, being based on a secular chanson tenor and having a new trope embedded in the upper parts. It

---

[3] James Haar, *Essays on Italian Poetry and Music in the Renaissance 1350–1600* (Berkeley: University of California Press, 1986):83.

would become the custom to add an extra voice in this final movement, often another bass. In the slightly later Machaut Mass (the first set of Ordinaries known to be by a single composer) we see evidence of a new sensuality that would be a major feature of Mass settings until the seventeenth century. The rhythmic conceits and vocal cleverness of imitative counterpoint found in the fourteenth-century pieces are in part a product of the confidence composers felt in their mastery of more complex notation. By the following century this vocal and compositional dexterity had given way to something altogether more sensuous. The new expressiveness may have been inspired by the polyphonic chanson, where love and life were celebrated in a reflective and overtly communicative way. The expressiveness works by the mutual interaction of the voices, which do not compete against each other but are mutually dependent for emotive 'affects' to work. The music is still conceived linearly and yet composers clearly have an ear for vertical alignment, and it is often the apparently serendipitous conjunction of independent voices that creates specific moments of great expressive potential.

OCKEGHEM AND JOSQUIN: COMPOSING SINGERS

Masses were still composed using either plainchant or popular songs as the framework on which to weave the polyphony. One tune which captured the imagination of some two dozen composers was 'L'homme armé':

> L'homme, l'homme, l'homme armé,
> L'homme armé doibt on doubter,
> On a fait partout crier,
> Que chascun se viengne armer
> D'un haubregon de fer.
> L'homme, l'homme, l'homme armé,
> L'homme armé doibt on doubter.
>
> The man, the man, the armed man,
> The armed man should be feared.
> It has been proclaimed everywhere
> That everyone shall arm himself
> With a coat of iron mail.
> The man, the man, the armed man,
> The armed man should be feared.

The origins of the tune are uncertain (a call to a new crusade, a symbol of the Order of the Golden Fleece, the name of a tavern?) but it was surely its melodic and structural characteristics that commended it to composers;

it is elegant and memorable, easily recognisable within the polyphonic texture by listeners outside it. It is simple enough to generate canons and imitation, and a modern analysis would point to the chordal implications inherent in the tripartite melodic structure, offering potential for rich polyphonic textures to be heard vertically. It has a range of an octave and one note, which gives singers plenty of opportunity to exploit their own ranges, and the middle section settles in a high tessitura which gives the chance for voices to soar.

One of the most eloquent examples (and possibly one of the earliest) of its use in a Mass is by Johannes Ockeghem. The Agnus Dei, as we would expect, is the sensual climax of the Mass, here given added poignancy by the irony of the armed man metaphorically pleading for peace through the simultaneous performance of the *Dona nobis pacem* (give us peace). Ockeghem adds an extra bass, immediately lowering the overall tessitura of the piece, but still retaining a relatively high tenor line. Ockeghem duly delivers the *Dona nobis* with snaking lines that collide with each other, break apart and rejoin carrying the singers ever upwards in a phrase that seems as though it will have no end. One can only guess what listeners made of this texture, with its prolonged tension and ultimate relaxation, but for singers of today the performance of this piece is a supremely satisfying example of the intimate relationship between composer and performers, and of the possibilities that exist for creative interaction between the singers themselves.[4] It is essentially singers' music, the intricacies of the counterpoint only really perceivable from within, in the act of creating the music in the moment. It is Ockeghem's remarkable achievement to be celebrated today by musicologists for his ingenuity and by singers for his sensuality. Ockeghem would have sung this music himself, having almost certainly begun his musical life as a choirboy in Antwerp in 1443 and gone on as an adult to sing at the French court, ending his career as treasurer of St Martin de Tours. Almost all composers of sacred music were lay clerics or chaplains who were hired in the first instance because they were the best singers their patron could afford. This synergy is the single most important factor determining the nature of Franco-Flemish polyphony, and it is still what makes it moving to sing.

Ockeghem's fame and influence was extensive. Erasmus, in a Latin tribute set to music by the otherwise unknown Johannes Lupi, referred

---

[4] See John Potter, *Vocal Authority* (Cambridge University Press, 1998): 178–82 for a brief analysis of a modern performance of the Agnus Dei from Antoine Brumel's *Missa Victimae Paschali*, which attempts to explain how this works in practice.

to his golden voice and his life was celebrated in a number of moving laments after his death in 1497. There is an inevitable formality about the poetic eulogies that mark the passing of great figures of the period, but the laments by singer-composers for their fellow musicians often seem to be a direct connection with people of the past, sometimes giving us a very personal glimpse of one singer seen through the eyes of his contemporaries, students or successors. Josquin's *Déploration sur la Mort d'Ockeghem* is a setting of Jean Molinet's poem 'Nymphes des Bois', in which he constructs a lament in the style of Ockeghem around the chant Gradual from the Mass for the Dead, *Requiem aeternam*. The second part summons up the names of four of the great musician's younger contemporaries, including Josquin himself:

> Accoutrez vous d'habits de deuil,
> Josquin, Piersson, Brumel, Compère,
> Et pleurez grosses larmes d'œil.
> Perdu avez votre bon père.
>
> Clothe yourselves in mourning,
> Josquin, Pierre de la Rue, Brumel, Compère,
> And weep great tears from your eyes,
> You have lost your good father.

Josquin and the other three great figures of fifteenth-century music were singers as well as composers; all had known Ockeghem personally and probably sung his music.

THE WRITTEN AND THE SUNG: INTABULATION

In chapter 2 it was suggested that the written evidence of early polyphony did not represent instructions for a performance, but perhaps an acknowledgement of possibilities for performance. The written notes were part of the information that would be needed by a singer, who would provide the rest from his repertoire of formulaic knowledge and improvisation. We will never know exactly how the written and the oral meshed together in the thirteenth century, and the same is still true two hundred years later. Notation had become more sophisticated: singers were used to coping with information about rhythmic proportions and elaborate polyphony: we can tell that from the manuscripts. For singers of today the modern editions of Franco-Flemish polyphony look very like modern scores; they seem, musicologically speaking, complete and performable. We are still not certain about the extent to which the complexities of notation – and the composerly control that it potentially enables – may have eroded those more improvised elements that the individual singer might be expected to add to the creation of the piece. It seems unlikely that singers would give up the chance to 'improve' on what they saw in front of them, though the evidence either way is inconclusive. Sources are scarce until the sixteenth century when numerous treatises appear with instructions for singers to embellish their lines. This tradition may well have been in place for many generations, a survival of thirteenth-century improvisatory practices perhaps, but the rash of treatises from the second quarter of the sixteenth century could suggest that pedagogues were responding to a tradition which may have been in decline.

We can glean some information from instrumental manuscripts which survive from the mid-fourteenth century onwards. As there was very little dedicated instrumental music, organists and lutenists would transcribe vocal music, reducing the original set of individual parts to a short score written in tablature (similar to the chord charts used by modern guitarists). This not only made the music readable from a single copy, but it told the player exactly which notes to play. A vocal manuscript contains only the notes which the composer wrote, whereas by telling us all the notes that were intended to be played, tablature can give us valuable clues about performance practice. The oldest surviving example is the so-called Robertsbridge Codex; this includes two motets from the *Roman de Fauvel*, which the intabulator has ornamented by breaking longer notes down into shorter ones, often displacing the rhythm, and adding turns and trill-like figures. There are many more notes than in the original compositions, and this suggests that instrumentalists at least were still expanding and elaborating the original written material. The Buxheimer Orgelbuch of around a hundred years later is considerably more comprehensive, confirming the practice of intabulation to be widespread across all musical genres from motets to chansons. Almost all intabulations feature a recomposed upper part, corresponding to the highest vocal line in the original. Many of the ornaments are clearly idiomatic for the fingers rather than the voice (lute intabulations feature a characteristic turn or flourish that enables a non-sustaining instrument to fill in a long note, for example) but singers may well have done something very similar. If the custom of adding improvised notes to the manuscript source survived from the oral tradition of earlier centuries we would not expect to find evidence in the score: singers would be quite capable of spontaneously personalising the music.

FROM POLYPHONIST TO SOLOIST: THE RISE OF THE VIRTUOSO

By the sixteenth century this practice was the most common way that new music was disseminated from the formality of the cathedral and chapel to the multifarious domestic environments where musicians performed whatever they could with whatever resources were to hand. In a culture where kings deferred to popes, the differences between what we now think of as sacred and secular were much less clear cut, and it was normal for music which first appeared in one context to be plundered for use elsewhere. Secular texts and tunes had long been incorporated into religious music in the multi-texted fourteenth-century motet and parody Mass; the process also happened in reverse, with Mass movements transcribed for domestic or courtly instrumental performance. Many composers published only sacred polyphony, but that does not mean that their works were only sung in church by choirs. Their original manuscript or print was the source material from which the subsequent life of the music could develop, often over a period of several generations. There are many intabulated collections which imply participation by singers. The Adrian Denns collection from 1594 has separately notated parts for two singers and lute, and a manuscript in the British Library dating from about the same time omits the highest voice.[5] The missing line was clearly intended to be sung – perhaps from memory and in a similarly elaborated way. We can only speculate about what the singers actually did, but the task of the singer is still twofold: to be creative with the notes and clear with the text. If you are singing with a lute or vihuela which has intabulated all the parts, you can focus on both of these elements, adding notes where appropriate but (just as importantly) leaving them out so that you can create a more coherent reading of the text; the solo singer need not be troubled with the endless repetitions that a polyphonic singer is obliged to make in order to sustain the musical line. In creating solo song out of polyphony singers took another step towards mastering the sophisticated vocal logic that connects text declamation with virtuosic display.

There is an analogy with jazz: in the twenty-first century it is perfectly possible to create composed (as opposed to improvised) jazz, but almost all sung jazz allows for the possibility of vocal inflections that

---

[5] Adrian Denns, *Florilegium omnis fere generis cantionum suavissimarum ad testudinis tabulaturam accommodatarum longe iucundissimo* (Cologne, 1594); BL Add. MS 31992; see also BL Add. MS 29246-7.

do not appear in the score. These correspond to the graces that an early sixteenth-century singer might add to a performance, small ornamental figures that personalise the music as in the Robertsbridge and Buxheimer sources. Jazz has a spectrum of ornamentation that ranges from virtuosic embellishment to free improvisation, and this range of vocal behaviours was also available as sixteenth-century singers began to acquire the taste for virtuosic vocalism as an end in itself. It is only our own more recent notions of the primacy of the score that lead us to assume that the written notes somehow represent a performance practice: it may be that this was never the case in any sort of vocal music until composers and conductors insisted on their ownership of the music within the last century and a half. If we disregard this idea, it is only a small step to dispensing with modern notions of accuracy, rhythm and the function of notation itself.

We can guess, then, that in addition to singing sacred polyphony in churches and chapels, sixteenth-century singers were able to secularise the repertoire by creating ornamented and improvised solo song. By mid-century we also get considerable help from the flood of instructional handbooks that appear, and they confirm that the ornamental singing style was applied across the board: you just could not stop singers doing it. In Adrian Petit Coclico's *Compendium Musices* of 1552 we have instructions for young singers written by a musician who claimed to have been a student of Josquin Desprez (Josquin died in 1521 when Coclico would have been just into his twenties, so the dates work although no other evidence has been found to link the two). Whether or not Coclico was taught by the most famous composer of the age, his writings do give us clues as to the performance of sacred polyphony (Coclico is addressing choirboys, and presumably remembering his own experience). As we would expect from our knowledge of the intabulation repertoires, stepwise movement is elaborated by curling turns, and leaps of a fifth can be filled in with scales. Coclico had a culinary turn of phrase, and describes his models as meat seasoned with salt and mustard. The importance of his examples is that they are models – they are not prescriptive but just possible ways of ornamenting – and they are ornamental rather than structural so that the original shape provided by the composer is preserved. The basic principle is one of division or diminution, so a simple three-note ascending or descending figure may be amplified into one containing three or four times as many notes.

Although he was of Flemish origin Coclico spent most of his life in Germany. His *Compendium* was published in Nuremberg and he seems to have had little experience of Italian singing, commending the

Netherlanders and the French as being the best exponents of the art. His writings, together with the intabulations of the German organists in the Buxheimer vein, suggest that in northern and central Europe ornamental performance was the norm, and he was not expounding anything new. He studied at the University of Wittenberg, where he would have encountered his younger contemporary Hermann Finck who taught there from 1554. In 1556 Finck published his *Practica Musica* for the benefit of his students, giving over the final part of his treatise to vocal performance. He, too, gives examples of how to perform divisions, which he calls *coloraturae* of the throat. He also refers to song 'embellished by roaring and screaming' and the 'deplorable sight' of otherwise excellent singers distorting their faces and bellowing; there was clearly more than one way to sing.[6] These complaints are typical of singing treatises of the period: some singers were clearly effortful and over the top in the way they presented themselves. Divisions require a particular technique, and from the increasing use of the word *gorgia* (literally 'throat') to describe the singing it is clear that this is something different from sustained melismatic singing or delivering a text. Some overdo it, making a sound that to many commentators sounds like the bleating of a goat or sheep. Similar comments surface towards the end of the century with the reiterated single note ornament known as a *trillo*. We also begin to discern at this time the notion of taste: there is a proper way to do things that is artistic, elegant and subtle, and shows what you can do without actually needing to show off too much.

Ornamental singing flourished in much of Europe but it was in Italy that a distinctive class of virtuosi developed. The necessary conditions in which music and the arts can grow are broadly the same in all cultures: peace and prosperity within a social system that can sustain both creators and consumers. The Italian city states, some of which were very small indeed, were in some respects miniature versions of European capital cities, with all the cultural competition that such societies thrived on. The patchwork of principalities had more of everything – war and disease as well as high art – and it is probably these wider cultural considerations that ensured artistic survival even in the most catastrophic of times. Most of the treatises that appear from mid-century onwards were published in Italy, and in them we get a much fuller picture of what singers got up to. Often singing is mentioned in passing in more substantial works of

---

[6] Carol MacClintock, *Readings in the History of Music in Performance* (Bloomington: Indiana University Press, 1979): 62.

musical scholarship and theory. Gioseffe Zarlino's *Istitutioni Harmoniche*, published in Venice in 1558, contains several references to vocal performance. Zarlino had been an organist and singer at the cathedral in Chioggia before becoming a student of Willaert in Venice. He was director of music at St Mark's from 1565 until his death in 1590, so had enormous knowledge of things vocal. He is writing primarily for composers, but they need to know the kind of barbarisms that singers are likely to inflict on their music; many will undermine the composition by indulging in 'certain divisions that are so savage and so inappropriate that they not only annoy the hearer but are ridden with thousands of errors, such as many dissonances, consecutive unisons, octaves, fifths, and other similar progressions absolutely intolerable in composition' and some singers in church or chamber will use 'such crude tones and grotesque gestures that they appear to be apes'. [7]

Nicola Vicentino's *L'Antica Musica Ridotta alla moderna Prattica* (*Ancient Music Adapted for Modern Practice*) published in Rome in 1555 is one of the earliest and most comprehensive musical manuals of the period, and it is bursting with the writer's excitement at the possibilities, both theoretical and practical, of the musical arts. Unusually, Vicentino does not seem to have been a performer himself, but a composer and theorist who enjoyed the patronage of the Este court at Ferrara, a centre of musical dynamism comparable to Vienna at the time of Schoenberg and Webern. His main interest was tuning and temperament and he devised a microtonal keyboard not primarily as a performance instrument but as a means of teaching singers to perform his microtonal madrigals. The madrigals are a challenge to modern singers: read as conventional part writing they appear to be relatively simple, but when the composer's microtonal chromatic modifications are taken into account they take on colours that are startlingly unfamiliar in an age of equal temperament. Tuning is fiercely difficult, and like Stockhausen's *Stimmung*, requires sustained and detailed work for singers to become acclimatised to the genre (see p. 238 below).

Vicentino also gives detailed instructions in compositional method, but as a byproduct of this we also get insights into key aspects of performance practice. He tells us how to improvise over plainchant, which confirms that this oral practice from several hundred years earlier was still current in sixteenth-century Italy. He complains that some singers introduce rapid, extensive and graceless divisions into their improvised

[7] Gioseffe Zarlino, *The Art of Counterpoint: Part Three of Le Istitutioni Harmoniche*, 1558, trans. Guy Marco and Claude Palisca (New York: Norton, 1968): 110, 111.

chant polyphony, another early reference to the singerly excess that would drive many pedagogues to put pen to paper in the future. In his more general remarks he explains that good singers will have their own repertoires of *gorgie*, divisions sung with a throat technique, which they can match to the style of the composition. He advocates changes in dynamics and tempo according to the passions expressed in the poetry, comparing singers with orators in their power to move listeners.

Vicentino is one of a number of sources to point out that although church singers sang rather loudly (to fill a large acoustic, presumably) the best singing in courtly circles was soft, and this is crucial for the understanding of throat technique. Consider the dynamic range of the lute. Almost all singers would have accompanied themselves at some point, and as we have seen from the intabulation repertoire the lute (or its Spanish equivalent, the vihuela) was the accompanying instrument of choice. Modern singers find it almost impossible to sing quietly enough to balance with the instrument (recordings even out the balance artificially), and one way to begin to access a Renaissance technique is to reduce your volume until it matches the lute. Once you achieve this, several things about technique become clear: the sound you make is much more like your spoken voice (you will sound less like a generic soprano or tenor) so the enunciation of the text is much easier, and you discover that the voice is much more agile at low volume levels. The operation of the vocal tract is conditioned by the volume of air that passes through it. We know nothing about Renaissance singers' breathing technique, but we do know that loud singing needs lots of air which does not last very long, and quieter singing uses less air which therefore lasts longer. The secret of throat technique is to do it quietly: it is the bellowers who end up sounding like farmyard animals. Vocal agility can be a gift or it can be learned, and there are many examples of singers (both now and in the Renaissance) with a natural coloratura. As would later be the case with Cathy Berberian's dental trill (see p. 235 below), it may have been hearing a performer with a unique natural talent that encouraged imitators who could only find the solution by study and practice. It is something modern singers can easily experiment with (though few do), as the best sixteenth-century advice seems to have been to try it until it works.

In addition to works of scholarship such as those of Zarlino and Vicentino the century saw an increasing number of instruction books with a more practical intent.[8] Many were written by instrumentalists, often

---

[8] There is a list of pedagogical sources in Ernest Ferand, 'Didactic Embellishment Literature in the Late Renaissance: a Survey of Sources', in Jan LaRue (ed.), *Aspects of Medieval and Renaissance Music: a*

acknowledging that players should aspire to the artistry of singers. Some were designed for serious students, but most were probably intended for courtly 'amateurs', gentlemen (or women) singers who could aspire to virtuosity but would not dream of getting paid for it. Many of them offered instruction for learning to sing 'without a master'. Giovanni Maffei's 1562 letter to his patron Giovanni da Capua, the Count of Alta Villa, explains the whole process in considerable detail. Maffei was the count's physician and court musician, and the letter seems to have been written in response to his patron's enquiries about the voice, and in particular how to make divisions. He begins by attempting to describe how the voice works (as a doctor he has some understanding of the physiognomy), and he goes on to explain that all voices need lungs and a throat; so insects have no throats and therefore no voice, and dolphins, dogfish and whales are similarly disadvantaged because they have no lungs. He eventually arrives at a number of rules and examples for good singing, before concluding with a selection of recipes for throat lozenges. Several of the rules are concerned with deportment and presentation. He advises conserving the breath, and opening the mouth no wider than in conversation. Singers should practise a lot and listen to other singers. Then he gives examples of divisions, including a madrigal with ornaments in all four parts. His models are conservative – perhaps because the count did not have a natural facility – but he does remark that as well as the standard voice types there are singers who can manage divisions that cross from one range to another, perhaps referring to virtuoso basses such as Giulio Cesare Brancaccio who could extend their voices upwards by using falsetto. The advice on deportment (that features in several other manuals too) is a reminder that people would not have experienced this sort of singing unless they were connected to a court and only then as a special event, so it was important for singers to present themselves properly.

Towards the end of the century the number of instruction manuals increases dramatically, and it is clear that the most virtuosic singers in the public eye were generating scores of imitators, and several singers and players offered to explain how to do it. The Venetian Girolamo dalla Casa published *Il Vero Modo di Diminuir* in 1584 for the benefit of the dilettante keyboard, viol, wind player or singer. Dalla Casa was, as all singers were, a composer, but his fame rested mostly on his playing of the cornetto, the instrument which was said to most resemble

Birthday Offering to Gustave Reese (Oxford University Press, 1967) and discussion of the most useful ones in Howard Mayer Brown, *Embellishing 16th-Century Music* (Oxford University Press, 1976).

the human voice. He gives examples of madrigals by Willaert, Lassus, Cipriano and many others with ornamented top lines to be sung to lute accompaniment, and a version of Cipriano da Rore's 'A la Dolc'Ombra' with divisions in all of the voices. These are more elaborate than Maffei's and for the first time we can see that singers are becoming aware of the importance of the final cadence as the last chance to show what they can do – a hint of the cadenzas of the future.

The following year another Venetian, Giovanni Bassano, published his *Ricercate, Passaggi et cadentie*. Bassano, too, was a virtuoso cornettist, and taught singing at the seminary of San Marco. In 1591 he published a wide-ranging collection of motets, madrigals and chansons (including many set by dalla Casa) arranged for virtuoso soloist. The 1585 handbook is for singers and players, and consists of twenty pages of diminution exercises with only a brief introductory text. The exercises are repetitive with many small variations which give the student a chance to visualise figures that may have been impossible to grasp in detail from listening to a high velocity performance; they would be perfect teaching material to enable a student to cope with his later, more extensive publication.

Two significant singers published handbooks and arrangements in the 1590s. Like Bassano, the falsettist Giovanni Luca Conforti published a book of exercises followed by a later volume of real music. Conforti sang in the papal choir, among other appointments, and was renowned for his graceful and speedy ornamentation. His *Breve et Facile Maniera … per cantare …* of 1593 reckons to teach singers the basics in two or three months. In his 1601 *Salmi passaggiati* he refers back to the handbook and says that you could take examples from it or invent even better ones for yourself. Giovanni Battista Bovicelli published his *Regole, passaggi di musica, madrigali et motetti passeggiati* with instructions for applying improvised formulae to madrigals and motets by Palestrina, Cipriano and Victoria, among others, with the soprano lines so heavily ornamented that many of the pieces seem like recompositions. The act of reading these publications requires a leap of the imagination to comprehend fully what they actually meant for musicians and cognoscenti of the time. The writers are trying to capture and interpret the essence of an aural/oral phenomenon: their paradigms are improvisations. The original madrigal or motet exists on paper, but the divisions are ephemeral, fleeting wisps of vocal magic summoned up on the spot by the best virtuosi and never heard the same way again. Those who best cultivated this art learned at the feet of past masters and had no need of a book. The painstaking exercises of Bassano and others are the evidence we have, but they are poor examples of what the practice sounded like at its brilliant best.

The madrigal in its sixteenth-century incarnation proved to be the seedbed for a type of virtuoso singer that had probably not been heard before. Madrigal prints were attempts by composers and printers to reach the widest possible audience. To make sure that the books would appeal to as many singers as possible all parts were underlaid with text, even though performance by any combination of voices and instruments was possible, especially as they were conceived primarily for use at home. This flexibility of use is more obvious in the English madrigal books which often bear the rubric 'apt for voices or viols' and other instruments. Solo singing with instruments was just one of the possibilities that the part books offered. It was also possible to reduce the score to a single sung line and one accompanying instrument. The intabulations by Willaert of Verdelot's madrigals published in 1536 are among the earliest printed examples of a song-plus-accompaniment derived from polyphonic madrigals, but as we have seen, the madrigal books were plundered for similar uses throughout the century in just the same way as the sacred polyphonic repertoire was converted by singing lutenists into solo song. As the century drew to a close the virtuosity of singers knew no bounds, and the division school improvisers may have been some of the most virtuosic performers in history.

REVELATION VERSUS ROULADES: VIRTUOSITY AND THE PRIMACY OF TEXT

If it is the case that one of the essential functions of a singer is to communicate words, then it was inevitable that there would be a reaction to the displays of what seemed to the arbiters of aristocratic taste to be increasingly pointless virtuosity.[9] Almost all the later treatises complain that singers cannot restrain themselves and cannot help slipping into vulgarity. Giulio Caccini duly attempted to provide a counterbalance to what he considered the tasteless excesses of his fellow singers. Caccini was a highly successful lutenist, singer and composer at the Medici court in Florence from the 1560s onwards. His *Nuove Musiche* of 1602 is a collection of twenty-three songs with a substantial introduction and instructions for their performance.[10] It is, in the evolving tradition of commentaries on singing, of a pessimistic bent (Caccini's chief aim being to rein in the

[9] For a theory which suggests that the efficacious delivery of text is the key driving force behind changes in singing style and technique see Potter, *Vocal Authority*, especially chapter 10, 'Towards a Theory of Vocal Style'.

[10] Giulio Caccini, *Le Nuove Musiche* (Florence, 1602); ed. and trans. H. Wiley Hitchcock (Madison, WI: A-R Editions, 1970).

vocal incontinence that has overtaken his contemporaries) but in reading it we can make informed guesses about what that singing might have been like (as opposed to what Caccini would have liked it to be). In the context of the history of singing this is one of the first examples of a composer seeking to impose his will on the music: Caccini's composer self is sensitive to the text, which he has taken care to set in an appropriate manner. He does not want his carefully crafted songs 'improved' by singerly creativity, and gives examples of the kinds of ornamentation that he claims will enhance the meaning of the text and not destroy it. He does find room for melismatic divisions but they are always on words which give the singer opportunities for particular kinds of expression; this is especially effective when combined with *sprezzatura*, a word with aristocratic overtones which implies a carefully structured 'neglect' of the tempo. So, for example, in his 'Dolcissimo Sospiro' there is a repeated falling ornament on 'sospiro' (sigh) which the singer can play with, and a longer roulade with divisions on 'amante' (lover), which enables the singer to express the thought as well as just the word.

Caccini's songs are designed for small rooms with singers probably accompanying themselves on a large lute. In keeping with the new monodic thinking he provides bass lines only, leaving the performer to expand these at will. Singing over an instrument which is improvising harmony from a bass line is an invitation to improvisation, and Caccini was probably not successful in his attempts to persuade singers to stop showing off. He was, though, in demonstrating composerly concern for singerly excess, ahead of his time (his sentiments would have resonated with Rossini more than two centuries later). The stage works of his contemporaries required the opposite of his introverted subtlety, and as theatrical works became more common and more elaborate so the singing became similarly more complex and larger. The freedom to ornament was if anything given impetus by the restraint required for recitative, an entirely new way of declaiming text as a form of heightened speech, extending the rhetorical techniques of oratory into singing. The new style was a byproduct of the stage works that we now think of as opera, and was developed by Caccini, Peri, Monteverdi and others as a means of carrying the narrative forward and developing action between characters. In the hands of a sensitive composer passages in recitative almost wrote themselves by following the speech patterns and inflections of the spoken language.

In conventional music history Caccini is seen as one of the markers of a move to a vertical, baroque style in which the words are clear, as opposed to the linear polyphony of earlier periods where the part-writing obscures the text. The new style is particularly associated with dramatic music – the evolution of the narrative voice of recitative was one of the devices that enabled opera to evolve beyond the *intermedi* entertainments that had been a common feature in Italian theatre for around a hundred years. For singers life went on as usual: by the beginning of the seventeenth century spectacular vocalism had been a fact of Italian musical life for many generations. Singers had long ago learned to cope with sacred and secular styles; adding recitative to their repertoire would not have taxed them very much since the application of rhetoric and oratory was what they already did when it was necessary.

The renewed emphasis on secular music gave many more opportunities to women singers. Much of the evidence from earlier in the period is inevitably male-orientated: men ran the religious establishment, and although we are now seeing evidence of Renaissance convents with thriving musical communities, women would have to wait until the late twentieth century before the church began to consider equal rights for women musicians. The balance between oral and written, secular and sacred traditions, also tended to work in favour of men: women were denied posts in cathedral and court chapel choirs but surely sang secular music elsewhere, most of which has gone unrecorded (Boccaccio's fourteenth-century *Decameron* being an early exception). Something of a revolution in the status of women singers took place at the Este court in Ferrara during the second half of the sixteenth century. Duke Alfonso had always maintained a musical court; invitations to his *musica secreta* or private elite musical establishment were highly sought after. On his marriage to his third wife, the fifteen-year-old Margherita Gonzaga, he brought to the court to amuse her three ladies in waiting selected primarily for their singing ability. This in itself was not new – in highly cultured establishments courtiers were often favoured for their musical talents – but the three ladies of Ferrara, Laura Peverara, Anna Guarini and Livia d'Arco, were among the most talented singers of their generation and were from outside the customary court circle. As the *concerto delle donne* they were at the heart of the Ferrarese avant-garde and began a tradition of quasi-professional singing that inspired imitators in many other Italian courts. The high profile of these virtuosic soloists and ensemble singers paved the way for many female singers from outside aristocratic circles to make careers solely on the basis of their performing ability. All were composers and multi-instrumentalists and in the early years of the next century Francesca Caccini (daughter of Giulio), Barbara Strozzi, Anna Rienzi and others would go on to achieve international reputations.

There were star male singers too, such as the basses Brancaccio and Palantrotti and the tenor Francesco Rasi. Rasi was also a gentleman 'amateur' rather than a paid professional and appeared in all the first operas by Peri, Caccini, Cavalieri, Monteverdi and Gagliano before his career was interrupted in 1609 when he murdered his step-mother's servant. He escaped being hung, drawn and quartered thanks to the protection of the Gonzagas, and the sentence was eventually commuted in 1620. He travelled widely between Italian courts and as far north as the Low Countries, and died in 1621 at the age of forty-seven. His life was celebrated by the poets Soranzo and Chiabrera among others, and his status must have been comparable to that of Pietrobono more than a hundred and fifty years earlier. Some compositions survive but his opera does not and there are no great works to interest musicologists, so his reputation is lost to history (unlike Francesca Caccini, whose surviving opera has ensured her posthumous reputation). Many of Rasi's songs hint at his virtuosity (as does the aria 'Possente spirto' in Monteverdi's *Orfeo* which still taxes the most gifted tenors today).

Despite Caccini's *Nuove Musiche*, division manuals continued to be published – audiences went home from the opera wanting to sing like Rasi or Monteverdi's Arianna, Virginia Andreini. If singers were aware that they were entering a new 'baroque' era it was likely to be because of the scale and popularity of the new stage genres – court opera at first and public opera from 1637. Caccini talks of imitating the idea behind the words, but Francesco Rognoni, in his *Selva di varii passaggi* of 1620, finesses this further while at the same time justifying tasteful virtuosity. The voice, he says, expresses the concept of the soul ('il concetto dell'anima') rather than simply the word itself. Singing can express something that the words themselves can only hint at, which is what happens in opera arias. In the early seventeenth century singers were just as virtuosic as they had always been but they had the possibility of deploying their skills with more sophistication, and this they would continue to do for many generations. Many were tasteful and restrained; if the increasing distress of the commentators is to be believed, most probably were not.

ITALIAN SINGING EXPORTED

Italian singing began its conquest of Europe when singers such as Rasi and Francesca Caccini were offered engagements north of the Alps. But although musical news travelled fast the new singing did not supplant the various northern styles until much later. Caccini's work was known in England soon after its publication and there was a tradition of employing Italian musicians at the English court, but as the florid Italian style was reaching its peak of velocity and virtuosity, the English aristocracy was concerned with a much more poetic music. The first English lute song prints appeared in 1597, and for about twenty years dominated the musical landscape, before the Italian style caught up with them and many found new expression as continuo songs surviving only in manuscripts. There was a similar tradition of *airs de cour* in France; both genres focused exclusively on poetic song rather than vocal display. The songs were strophic, and often with texts by leading poets of the day. We know remarkably little about how the songs were performed, but as with the intabulation tradition, the singers would have had to balance to the lute and we can imagine a kind of rhetorical musical speech (in the accent of the singer). John Dowland was the most prominent among many English composers, and probably sang his music to his own accompaniment. In 1609 he published a translation of an early sixteenth-century singing treatise by the German Andreas Vogelsang (or as he preferred to be known, Andreas Ornithoparcus). The *Micrologus* is a substantial work of musical scholarship, comparable to Thomas Morley's *Plaine and Easie Introduction to Practicall Musicke* of 1597 and the final chapter contains rules for singing (mainly of church music).[11] This is a very different world from the high velocity Italian virtuosi or even the German mid-century commentators: for Vogelsang singing is much simpler than that expounded by Coclico and Finck thirty or forty years later. By 1609 much of the work was inapplicable to music in Reformation England, but presumably Dowland considered this older way of looking at the world more appropriate for his restrained and elegant songs. Vogelsang had a somewhat jaundiced view of singing in Germany (they howl like wolves and bellow and bray in church) and his instructions are very straightforward: know the music, present it properly, sing in time and in tune and do not distort the words (as in *aremus* – let us plough – for *oremus* – let us pray). Do not bray like an ass (God is not deaf) and do not make mad faces. His remarks on vowels suggest that he prefers the high form of the language rather than dialect, and perhaps this resonated with Dowland, who would have heard a variety of accents among musicians. Dowland must have known his market, and although his songs were embraced by

[11] John Dowland, *Andreas Ornithoparcus His Micrologus or Introduction: Containing the Art of Singing* (1609) (Whitefish, MT: Kessinger Publishing, 2010); Thomas Morley, *A Plain and Easy Introduction to Practical Music* (London: 1597), ed. Alec Harman (London: Dent, 1962).

musicians of the younger generation we can imagine him finding anything beyond modest ornamentation distasteful.

Caccini and Dowland were concerned with using the delicacy of
refined singing to express the poetic text with clarity and elegance. They
did not engage with the sound of language itself; ultimately it is the
singing alone which would convince listeners. The modifications that
singers need to make in order to turn a spoken language into singing are
obviously dependent on the nature of the spoken vernacular. The 'pure'
vowels of Italian facilitate very efficient use of the acoustics of the vocal
tract, a fact which makes it a relatively natural-seeming process to turn
speech into song. It may also be easier to maintain a semblance of textual
cohesion during a melisma if the vowel sustaining the pitches remains
close to the spoken paradigm, as it tends to do in Italian. Consonants
ideally need to be liquid sounding so that they do not disrupt the airflow.
For the other major languages of Europe these processes were problematic, and the task of creating sustainable sung pitches without losing the
essence of the spoken text is at the heart of national differences in singing style which begin to be increasingly visible as solo singing develops
across the continent ('national' used here as a linguistic identity: there
were no nation states yet). German, French and English singers all had
to make significant modifications in vowel structure to create effective
solo performances: English singers had to negotiate diphthongs, and
both German and French were characterised by guttural consonants,
to which the French added the problem of nasality. The identification
of language with national culture may also have conditioned the nature
of the sung language, especially in France and Germany: as Italian singing became increasingly dominant all over Europe singers had to decide
how far to compromise their own language in order to sound fashionably
Italianate. The problems of French singers getting to grips with the sung
version of their own language surface in Bénigne de Bacilly's *Remarques
Curieuses sur l'Art de Bien Chanter* which went into four editions between
1668 and 1681 and remained influential for many years afterwards. The
Remarques are our main source of information about the application of
French *agréments* to *airs de cour*, strophic songs not unlike English lute
songs often intended for the *haute-contre*, the uniquely French high tenor.
These small and elegant ornaments are directly related to linguistic and
poetic stress, and there is a clear understanding among modern performers about how to apply them according to Bacilly's rules. He was not
unaware of Italian style (his teacher, Pierre de Nyert, was an italophile)
but his main concern was the proper articulation of the French language.

The virtuosic display found in Italian handbooks is conspicuous by its absence (although absence from Bacilly's treatise does not necessarily mean absence from the singers he is addressing).[12]

Although it is possible to trace a line of development broadly focusing on Italy, the localised nature of any performance must have meant an unknowable plurality of practice. In England, for example, repertoire and styles from all over Europe were on offer to those who wished to keep up with vocal fashion. In 1610 Dowland's son Robert published *A Musicall Banquet* containing 'delicious airs' from England, France, Spain and Italy, including three of his father's songs alongside pieces by Caccini, Guillaume Tessier, Pierre Guédron and others. Three years later the appearance of *Prime Musiche Nuove* by Angelo Notari, an Italian musician at the English court, confirms that virtuoso singing was being actively cultivated in England (the collection even includes a division version of Cipriano's 'Ben qui si mostra' for tenor-bass). Michael Praetorius was the first German authority to refer to the 'new' Italian singing, and he references both Caccini and Bovicelli in his remarks on teaching choirboys in the third volume of his *Syntagma Musicum* of 1619. Although his sources are exclusively Italian, the vocal techniques he describes are not so different from those known in Germany for many years, given added spice by rhetorical names from the *Nuove Musiche*. One stylistic quirk that Praetorius got from Caccini is the practice of starting a piece on a different note from that printed (something that modern singers are reluctant to do). Some start on the printed pitch, he says, but others start a tone below and glide up to it, while others begin up to a fourth below. The French would take a bit of persuading to commit to Italian display, and in 1636 Marin Mersenne was berating his French compatriots in the vocal section of his *Harmonie Universelle* for not being as effusive and passionate as the Italians. He suggested a cocktail of Italian experiences from Sylvestro Ganassi's *Fontegara*, a hundred-year-old treatise on virtuoso recorder playing, to the more current *Nuove Musiche* of Caccini. Instruction in diminution was available almost everywhere for those brave enough to try it, and as the seventeenth century progressed, whatever attempts were made to rein them in, there would always be singers prepared to push the boundaries of extravagant vocalism.

---

[12] See John Potter, *Tenor: History of a Voice* (New Haven: Yale University Press, 2009) for the problems of French tenors.

CHAPTER 4

The age of the virtuoso

Seventeenth-century singers lived and worked in a continuing present, and the historical baggage they carried with them probably extended only to re-used music from a generation or two earlier and memories of more recent legendary local performances. The works that music historians see as significant landmarks such as *Euridice, Orfeo* and the other early *favole in musica* would have been just larger-scale realisations of the kinds of theatrical creations that were part of an Italian singer's normal working life. The reimagining of polyphony as solo song had been part of the singer's skill set for perhaps a hundred years before composers began to write what we now recognise as monodies. There may perhaps have been a sense of liberation at not having to go through the process of converting polyphony into solo song, but from a technical point of view the vocal delivery cannot have been very different. Singers always had to be aware of the verticality of harmony, or they would have got lost when extemporising. They were also aware of having a special obligation towards the poetic text, and this would have been enhanced by their experience of the more declamatory recitative. There was plenty of instruction available about how to deliver texts or high-speed ornaments, but the detail of how these things were really achieved is not yet visible in the surviving sources. The seventeenth century saw the triumph of the virtuoso and virtuosa, but the art was not just in the velocity of the divisions. This becomes more evident towards the end of the century, when we have the reflections of older singers looking back at the singing of their youth, and we are able to fill in some of the gaps with evidence of devices such as portamento, *messa di voce* and rubato. None of these (and many other subtle additions to the stylistic repertoire) has an identifiable point of origin: our sources are always conservative and retrospective, leaving us to speculate.

For many male singers life would have begun in a church choir, where as trebles they would have learned the trade. When their voices broke they might hope to continue as adult singers, and the best of them might seek service with the local aristocratic family where they would be hired in a general capacity but with an eye to improving their social standing through music-making. One of Caccini's non-musical assets was that he was said to be green fingered with a particular talent for pruning fruit trees. Female court singers would similarly be expected to do the domestic bidding of the duchess or whoever was the next rank up in the social hierarchy. At the courts of Italian city states male and female singers mixed freely, and the conjunction of men and women singing secular music together in the lavish entertainments promoted by their masters provided the ideal environment for the development of large-scale theatrical works.

Elsewhere in Europe aristocratic courts would also hire courtiers for their musical expertise and also promoted increasingly large-scale theatrical events, but these tended to involve the active participation of courtiers with a broader range of skills, especially dance. In England, for example, the expertise for the creation of large dramatic works existed in much the same way as it did in Italy; there were multi-talented designers such as Inigo Jones and plenty of singers and composers with an interest in theatre, but their collective creative energies went into the masque, a collaborative enterprise that was generated in the first instance by poets and playwrights in which the whole court would take part. The British Isles also suffered from a lack of artistic competition, the royal court in London being the only one to compare with noble establishments on the European mainland. The French court preferred more participatory social music-making, focusing on dance. Francesco Cavalli's productions in Paris in the early 1660s included ballets by Lully in which the king and queen danced. In such circumstances large-scale productions with a clear division between performers and audience, an elaborate narrative structure and specialised roles for highly skilled singers took much longer to coalesce into opera.

The high points of any Italian singer's career would be the court spectaculars staged by their patron to mark significant political events. One of the most extravagant of the age took place in Florence in 1589 at the dynastic marriage of Ferdinando de Medici and Christine of Lorraine in Florence. The wedding celebrations lasted over a month and included mock naval battles, animal baiting, parades, jousting and even an aristocratic game of football. For musicians the main events were the *intermedi* (interludes) between the acts of Girolamo Bargagli's play *La Pellegrina*, staged in the Teatro Mediceo degli Uffizi. Conspicuous display being very much the point of the exercise, a souvenir book and prints were produced to commemorate the performance, so we have an official eye-witness account of the whole event from the courtier Bastiano de Rossi. Composer and singer Emilio Cavalieri was responsible for organising the event, which brought together musicians, poets, actors, painters, costume and set designers, engineers and creative thinkers from all over Italy. Far more elaborate than the first operas would be, it represents the peak of the performing arts at the end of the sixteenth century, and from a vocal point of view it confirms what we can imagine from the pedagogical writings of about the same time. Male and female singers made equally spectacular contributions to the occasion. There were three main female soloists: Vittoria Archilei, a star singer at court and wife of composer Antonio Archilei, Giulio Caccini's first wife Lucia, and a pupil of the Archileis known only as Margherita (who may subsequently have become Caccini's second wife). There was a host of composers, including Caccini, Marenzio, Malvezzi, Archilei, Peri and Cavalieri himself, all of whom also performed on stage either singing, playing or both at the same time.

The first *intermedio* opened with Vittoria Archilei, 'the Euterpe of our age' as Peri called her, descending from the heavens on a cloud, accompanying herself on a chitarrone, scattering diminutions on the noble assembly below her. Over the next seven hours landscapes dissolved and re-formed, dragons roared, the chimneys of Pisa belched smoke and perfume, souls were devoured and gods and goddesses flew across the sky to the accompaniment of some of the finest musicians to be found. Jacopo Peri performed his 'Dunque fra torbid'onde' from a ship, firing off divisions which were echoed by two other singers before he leapt into the oscillating wave machine (flinging his chitarrone to safety on the way, one hopes). The singing included polyphony in up to thirty parts and could never have been less than spectacular amid such wonders, the extravagantly costumed performers often accompanying themselves on harps, lutes and strings of various sorts. Although the production was repeated during the course of the celebrations, the concept would never be repeated on such a lavish scale. You had to be there: Rossi's *Descrizione* was not so much a souvenir of the occasion as a means of flaunting the wonders you missed if you were not.

The singing perfectly expressed this sense of the moment – everything happening for the first and last time. As Peri further said of Vittoria Archilei's 'long windings of the voice', her singing revealed 'those elegances and graces that cannot be written, or, if written, cannot be learned from writing'.[1] Each vocal event was unlike any other and had to make

---

[1] From the preface to *Euridice* quoted in Oliver Strunk, *Source Readings in Music History* (London: Faber, 1952; repr. 1981): 15.

maximum impact – like some of the best jazz solos, if you can transcribe it you have probably not been listening hard enough. It is no wonder that cognoscenti such as Luigi Zenobi railed at both the poseurs who tried too hard and the equally ignorant audiences who fell for their rolling eyes, angry ranting and tasteless ornaments: courtly singing was an extravagance born of ingenuity and taste which all involved recognised when they heard it.

CASTRATO: AN ARTIFICIAL VOICE FOR VOCAL ARTIFICE

The *intermedi* cast also featured at least three castrati: Onofrio Gualfreducci (a former member of the Sistine Chapel choir) and Pierino Palibotri and Niccolò Bartolini (who had both studied with Caccini). Although the most successful singers were still sopranos or tenors of the calibre of Archilei or Peri, there is increasing evidence of this new breed of singer in the second half of the century. Castration eliminates or arrests many of the effects of puberty, so that boys retain their pre-pubescent voice into adulthood.[2] The larynx remains of childlike size and flexibility, though it does continue to develop – soprano castrati would often sink into a lower tessitura as they got older. The body of the castrato, deprived of sufficient testosterone, would develop elongated limbs and a much larger rib-cage and lungs than normal; these were generally big, impressive men by the time they reached adulthood. The resulting male soprano would therefore have huge breath capacity, powering a small, flexible larynx. Such a physical make-up was perfect for the division repertoire: castrati could create extended runs of very fast notes without needing to pause for breath, or could linger far longer on sustained notes than a soprano or tenor. Their increased lung capacity would have made it far easier for them to control the flow of air, giving them a much wider dynamic range than unmutilated singers. The argument has often been advanced that castration was an expedient to get round St Paul's ancient proscription of women uttering in church, but why it was considered justifiable when the church had apparently managed quite well with boys or falsettists in the past is still a mystery. Although the practice became identified with Italy the evidence for an Italian origin is slight, but the sound and artistry of these mutilated singers was such that the Italian church and aristocracy that employed them felt that the

---

[2] Some males, due to certain endocrinological conditions, retain their child's voice into adulthood. There are many examples in the twenty-first century of male sopranos who come close to replicating the castrato condition, so that it could be argued that the earliest 'castrati' in Europe were not castrated at all (there is no evidence either way; see Alexandros Constansis, *Hybrid Vocal Personae*, unpublished doctoral thesis, University of York, 2009).

musical end justified the means. In the magical world of opera, the earliest libretti of which concerned themselves with gods and men, they also had the advantage of androgyny.

Guglielmo Gonzaga was among the first to employ castrati at the Mantuan court, probably from 1555 onwards (he certainly had three by 1565). They were rare then and not procurable from within Italy, and in the following decades the duke sent his agents to Spain and France to try to maintain a supply. Guglielmo seems to have employed his as much for secular music as in his chapel; castrati from Spain were to be found in the Sistine Chapel in the last quarter of the century but the supply was by no means assured. By 1607 there was something of a shortage of castrati in Mantua, and Francesco Gonzaga had to borrow one from the establishment of his brother Ferdinando for the first performance of Monteverdi's *Orfeo*. Giovanni Gualberto Magli was despatched from Pisa to sing La Musica and probably Proserpina and Speranza as well. Curiously, despite being a pupil of Caccini (and therefore accustomed to monody, presumably) he seems to have found the music difficult to learn. He eventually impressed, but Rasi the tenor was clearly the star of the show. As opera evolved over the course of the century, however, the power, agility and often the sheer magical eloquence of castrati came to dominate the casting, and tenors in particular were eclipsed by male sopranos who could perform as either gender.

TRAINING AND PEDAGOGY: THE LONG TAIL OF RENAISSANCE TECHNIQUES

By 1600 enough castrati were sufficiently successful in Italy for the phenomenon not to excite comment beyond descriptions of their vocal qualities. The question of how they came to the condition was rarely asked, and the number of botched operations (or voices that failed to bloom following surgery) is unknown. Since the process was illegal there is very little evidence of the early life of these mutilated boys, especially in the seventeenth century. The fate of unwanted children was often to end up on the street, or if surplus to aristocratic requirements in an age of unreliable birth control, in an orphanage. These were usually religious foundations, often attached to monasteries, and since the liturgy necessarily required musical instruction many came to specialise in musical pedagogy. These *conservatori* are the first institutions devoted to music (the forerunners of today's conservatories) and by the eighteenth century the richest establishments in Naples, Rome or Bologna could attract teachers of the highest reputation. Sexes were segregated: Venice became famous for its *ospedali* which catered only for women, and Naples was associated with the education of boys, especially castrati. Young castrati were educated separately from the other boys, and given a rigorous training in vocal and instrumental technique.

Thanks to a number of later eye-witness accounts we have a good idea of what a musical education for young children typically consisted of. Charles Burney arrived in Naples in October 1770, determined to research the *conservatori* and especially the education of castrati for the *History* that he would publish twelve years later. He was received by Niccolò Piccini, whose comic opera *Gelosia per Gelosia* was playing to packed houses at the Teatro de' Fiorentini, and who informed him that there were over four hundred scholars in the three schools, each of which was run by a composer and a singing teacher. Burney visits the San Onofrio *conservatorio* (where Piccini had studied in his youth) and finds a cacophony of some thirty or forty boys in a dormitory where the beds double as seats for the seven or eight harpsichords, and violinists and keyboard players are all practising different pieces at the same time. In another room are wind instruments, with the lucky cellists having one to themselves; trumpeters and horn players are supposed to be in the attics but scream away on the stairs. Also upstairs are sixteen young castrati, kept warm in case a chill should compromise their future careers, and expected to study from before daybreak until eight in the evening. San Onofrio does not castrate the boys inhouse for fear of death or excommunication: they arrive intact for an audition, go home to their parents and some reappear mysteriously transformed. Burney is shocked by the cruelty of it, and the waste – finding that the church choirs are made up of 'the refuse of the opera house'.[3] The *conservatori* would take boys between the ages of eight and twenty; the seventeen-year-old Irish tenor-to-be Michael Kelly came to Naples in 1779 with a view to studying with Fedele Fenaroli at the *conservatorio* Santa Maria di Loreto. Kelly's experience was similar to Burney's:

in the great schoolroom … there were some singing, others playing upon the violin hautboy, clarionet, horn, trumpet … each different music and in different keys. The noise was horrible; and in the midst of this terrific Babel, the boy who studied composition was expected to perform his task and harmonize a melody given him by his master. I left the place in disgust …[4]

[3] Charles Burney, *The Present State of Music in France and Italy* (London, 1771; facs. Elibron Classics, 2005): 303–4.
[4] *Solo Recital: the Reminiscences of Michael Kelly*, ed. Herbert van Thal (London: Folio Society, 1972): 39.

Kelly did study briefly with Fenaroli but was allowed to go home at night and excused wearing the uniform. A chance meeting with Giuseppe Aprile led to his being taken on by the great castrato as a student, a form of apprenticeship that eventually enabled him to perform successfully all over Europe.[5]

Earlier in the century the composer and singing teacher Nicola Porpora had taught at all three of the Naples *conservatori*. Porpora was born in Naples in 1686 and died there in 1768, having had a European career to rival that of Handel, and having taught some of the most famous singers of the eighteenth century. The teaching he received after enrolling at the Conservatorio dei Poveri di Gesù Cristo in 1696 (and passed on as a student teacher from 1699 onwards) would have been along the lines of that espoused by Pier Francesco Tosi (whose teachings are discussed below); his private pupils included two of the greatest castrati, Farinelli and Caffarelli, and he later taught the soprano Regina Mingotti and the young Haydn, who became his valet and accompanist. Porpora then is a central figure in the transmission of pedagogical ideas, crucially linking the end of the seventeenth century with the classical period. The French historian Fétis later claimed that Porpora gave Caffarelli a single page of exercises, which once mastered, over a period of five years or so, equipped him to sing anything.[6] Whether this was or was not the case, the story illustrates the very small amount of pedagogical material used by teachers of the time, and the importance of individual personal instruction from the master. Many castrati founded schools of their own, or took on private pupils as apprentices. Antonio Pistocchi founded a famous school in Bologna in 1706, and taught the castrato Antonio Bernacchi who went on to teach the castrati Senesino and Carestini and the tenors Panzacchi and Raaff, ensuring that the techniques of the age of Scarlatti were still being used at the time of Mozart.

The triumph of Italian singing as practised by castrati eventually created a demand for pedagogical works in all the centres of European culture so that potential amateurs and singing teachers could initiate themselves into the latest technical and stylistic secrets. The pedagogical literature of the eighteenth century is much more comprehensive than anything we have seen so far, and fortunately for us consists of a good deal more than one page of exercises. Of course, it has never been possible

---

[5] He later created the role of Don Basilio for Mozart. See John Potter, *Tenor: History of a Voice* (New Haven: Yale University Press, 2009): 33–4.

[6] François-Joseph Fétis, *Biographie Universelle des Musiciens et Bibliographie Générale de la Musique* (Paris: Firmin-Didot, 1870).

to learn singing from a book (most treatises on the subject acknowledge this, and so do most performers – an exception being the German soprano Gertrude Mara who claimed to have learned much from Tosi's *Opinioni*).[7] Any text from the pre-gramophone era has to be read with a certain discretion: very few authors put pen to paper to celebrate the state of the art; almost all of them are unhappy with the way things currently are, and look back fondly to a time (not usually specified) when they were better. Books on singing tend to be written at periods when tastes are changing, and usually by people who have a vested interest in the status quo and who are often not themselves currently successful as performers. For the historian this presents interesting problems of interpretation: the historical reality may be revealed by what the author complains about, rather than by what he is proposing as a solution (something that bedevilled the late twentieth-century movement for 'historically informed performance', which often conflated the intentions of the composer or author with historic actuality).

The earliest comprehensive singing treatise is by the castrato composer and singer Pier Francesco Tosi, who published his *Opinioni de' cantori antichi e moderni* in Bologna in 1723. Bologna, along with Naples, Ferrara and Rome, was one of the great centres of Italian vocal culture, and Tosi was a product of an environment in which castrato teaching was passed from generation to generation by some of the finest singers of the day. He was not himself a superstar, but was sufficiently successful to have performed throughout Europe as a chamber singer, having begun his career (like so many *musici* or *evirati*, as they were called) in church choirs. Almost as important as his own experience as a performer was the fact that his travels on behalf of the Elector Palatine took him into the best society, where he was able to observe some of the greatest performers of the time. Tosi first visited London in 1692 (he would have been in his late thirties) and promoted a small series of concerts as a performer, teacher and composer. It is possible that as a new and exciting male soprano in London he may have been known to Henry Purcell though there is no evidence of this, London's obsession with castrati dating from a generation or so later. He seems to have returned many times over the next twenty years, his charm and erudite conversation endearing him to his patrons, who included the Earl of Peterborough to whom the book is dedicated. Tosi died in Faenza in 1732, having left London for the last time around 1727.

---

[7] Isabelle Emerson, *Five Centuries of Women Singers* (Westport: Praeger, 2005): 84.

By this time, thanks to the success of Handel and the imported star singers required for his Italian operas, the capital was in the grip of a fascination with virtuosic singing that has continued to this day. The most successful singers would also be engaged to sing for society hostesses (a practice that continued well into the twentieth century) and the resulting mix of amateur and professional music-making contributed to the ready demand for singing teachers and books about singing. In 1743 the composer John Galliard published his translation of Tosi's *Opinioni* as *Observations on the Florid Song* for the benefit of 'persons of eminence, rank and quality', describing it as 'useful for all performers, instrumental as well as vocal'.[8] Tosi's Italian original had been aimed at singers and teachers with some knowledge of the vocal arts (when he talks about soprani he means adolescent castrati), and he saw his task as codifying existing good practice, maintaining the standards that he had grown up with and which were being eroded by the younger generation. Like most such treatises it is a conservative document (he sees himself as being in the tradition of Zarlino), reminding his readers what good singing is supposed to be like. It represents our best window on the singing of the seventeenth century (bearing in mind that Tosi had been singing since he was a treble in the 1660s). Galliard's audience is different, perhaps society amateurs (of both sexes) and their teachers, and he provides helpful footnotes for his more general readership who may not have had professional aspirations but were swept along by the dynamic mid-eighteenth-century vocal culture. There had been a community of Italian performers and teachers in London since the late sixteenth century (and possibly even earlier) and the respect that these musicians commanded must also have registered with Galliard. Needless to say, twenty years after the original publication the feared vocal apocalypse had not yet happened, so Tosi's writings were still relevant in the London of the later Handel (and as we shall see below, continued to be read in much of Europe into the next century).

The teaching of singing was directly related to the nature of composition and the role of the composer; all composers were performers of some sort, and many performers were more than capable composers. This blurring of roles made the compositional process one of mutual creativity; it was not the composer's task to conceive of a complete work which the performer would then attempt to reproduce or interpret. The music itself did not exist on paper in the same way that a modern score

[8] John Galliard, *Observations on the Florid Song* by Pier Francesco Tosi (London, 1743; facs. London: Reeves, 1967): preface p. iii.

can be said to represent the intentions of the composer; indeed, the composer's intentions were probably much less important to performers than demonstrating their own vocal and artistic prowess. The realisation of a performance was a collaborative process, with the composer generating ideas which the performer would then elaborate within accepted parameters, producing a unique performance for a given occasion. The composer was a provider of source material for the singers who actually created the music, and, in effect, owned it. If a singer did not like a particular aria he or she would have no qualms about asking for it to be rewritten or substituting another piece altogether. As Giambattista Mancini put it, in a vocal score 'we get only the conception of a simple melody which shows just enough musical phrasing to allow the talented interpreter full liberty to embellish as he desires and conceives'.[9] Although it was acknowledged that some composers were capable of producing extraordinary work (Handel, Hasse, Mozart and Haydn were obvious examples) it was performers whom audiences came to see and whose fame generated the increasingly substantial sums involved in the musical economy. If the composer got it right, there would be sufficient creative room for the singer to bring a piece to fruition in a way that would reflect well on both the composer and his performers.

The challenge for singers was to elaborate on the score in a way which showed sensitivity to the original material while at the same time demonstrating the performer's unique talents as a creative artist. Knowledge of repertoire was a secondary consideration (the concept of a repertoire of pieces as opposed to a repertoire of vocal devices was unknown at this time). What was most important was the additional and unique material that the singer would add to the composer's blueprint. Singers needed a technique that would enable them to bring their own creativity to any given piece of music. From the audience's point of view the singing was far more important than the music; it was the singer who moved listeners, not the composer. To do this, the singer needed to be in complete control of his or her instrument, and to have a repertoire of models or formulae from which new material could be derived instantaneously mid-performance.

From Tosi we learn far more detail about this process than from any previously published singing manual. The virtuosity of the sixteenth century has matured into a complex art that required intensive study. The essentials were taught within a very simple framework based on two sorts

---

[9] Giambattista Mancini, *Pensieri e Riflessioni Pratiche sopra il Canto Figurato* (Vienna, 1774), trans. Pietro Buzzi, *Practical Reflections on the Figurative Art of Singing* (Boston, 1912): 49.

of exercise known as *solfeggi* (or *solfège*) and *vocalizzi* (or *vocalises*). Tosi
tells us that *solfeggi*, the singing of solfa letter names in order to develop
sight reading and a sense of pitch, would normally be taught by 'a master
of lower rank'. He did not provide examples of *solfeggi* or *vocalizzi* as he
expected teachers to devise their own, based on the problems and aspirations of the individual student. This must have been the practice since his
youth, and it probably remained so for the rest of the century and beyond
(Aprile sent Michael Kelly to the otherwise unknown Signor Lanza to
learn the basics). These were often simple exercises taken slowly, so that
the teacher could analyse faults and correct basic mistakes. The singer
would learn good posture, the correct mouth position (slightly smiling) and proper vowel formation. Once he had mastered these the singer
would move on to *vocalizzi*, wordless exercises of increasing complexity
using open vowel sounds. These could become miniature songs in themselves and more generic versions of such exercises would feature in singing
handbooks until late in the nineteenth century. *Vocalizzi* would enable
the student to master the two pillars of baroque vocal technique, *messa di
voce* and portamento. *Messa di voce* consisted of a held note begun piano,
followed by a crescendo to forte and a corresponding diminuendo back
to nothing. This apparently simple exercise was not only considered to
be in exquisite taste, but it actually enabled the student to develop control of both his larynx and his breathing. Its origins are unknown, but it
may have developed from the *esclamazione*, an accent followed by a rapid
diminuendo and longer crescendo found in Caccini and earlier authorities. Tosi complains that people are forgetting how to do it, but fifty years
or so later Giambattista Mancini, singing master at the imperial court in
Vienna (and also a castrato), devotes several pages to the technique in his
Pensieri e Riflessioni Pratiche sopra il Canto Figurato, and it is a regular feature of most didactic works up to the twentieth century. Slow scales on
different vowels with a *messa di voce* on each note would have contributed
to a well-developed musculature over a period of time, and the exercise
partially explains the frustrating lack of information on breathing technique in early treatises (which often only say that you need good lungs or
to take a deep breath). For a modern singer well-supported and controlled
breathing is fundamental to a sound technique; for an eighteenth-century
singer the mastery of *messa di voce* enabled precisely that. Portamento is
something that both Tosi and Mancini take for granted; Tosi describes
it as 'to glide with the vowels, and to drag the voice gently from the
high to the lower notes'; for Mancini it means 'the gliding of the voice'.
Once they have understood these basic techniques, students are ready for

ornamentation lessons. These begin with the appoggiatura, or replacement of a written note with a higher one, and progress through the many types of trill (Mancini quotes Tosi's eight varieties with approval) to the complex passagework required for improvised elaboration and cadenzas. These should be done as spontaneously as possible and not become stale with overuse.

From the start the singer would be aware of having two overlapping registers, called *voce di petto* or chest voice and *voce di testa*, a term translated as head voice or falsetto. A key element in all singing is the unifying of these two dispositions of the voice. Tosi says the singer should:

unite the feigned and the natural voice, that they may not be distinguished; for if they do not perfectly unite, the voice will be of diverse registers, and must consequently lose its beauty.[10]

Mancini confirms this:

The great art of the singer consists in acquiring the ability to render imperceptibly to the ear, the passing from the one register to the other. In other words, to unite the two, so as to have perfect quality of voice throughout the whole range, each tone being on a level with your best and purest tone.[11]

Both Tosi and Mancini observe that exceptionally, some sopranos may sing entirely in chest voice, but that in men such a thing is almost unknown. The joining of registers was taught by specially devised *solfeggi* and *vocalizzi* that would concentrate on the area around the 'break' between them. This would enable an evenness of tone throughout the range and was to become especially important in the development of the tenor voice as tenors exploited their upper registers from the late eighteenth century onwards.

These basic techniques were the foundation of castrato technique, and absorbed patiently over a number of years they could produce remarkable results. We cannot know what they sounded like, but we can read descriptions of castrati performances by people for whom words are barely adequate to describe what they are hearing. Mancini's description of the legendary Farinelli sums up the perfection that could be achieved:

The valiant and noble-hearted ... Farinello, who besides possessing all the graces and embellishments of the art of singing, possessed the *messa di voce* to perfection; which in the opinion of most critics was what made him famous and immortal ... His voice was considered perfect, beautiful and sonorous in its quality and unparalleled in range. It was perfect from the lowest note to the

---

[10] Tosi, *Observations*: 23.   [11] Mancini, *Pensieri*: 59.

highest. A like voice was never given to us to hear. He was also gifted with a very keen and inventive mind which, developed and educated in a proper way, enabled him to exercise such originality and feats of his own in singing, that he was impossible of imitation. The perfect art of holding the breath, and retaking it with such cleanness, so as not to allow anyone to know when he was breathing, started and ended with him. The perfect intonation, the unfolding, the extending and expanding of the voice, his portamento, the perfect union of registers, the sparkling agility, and the perfect trill were all in him in the same degree of perfection. In every style of singing he was perfect, and to such a degree as to make himself inimitable.[12]

Farinelli, born Carlo Broschi, was in his day the most famous singer Europe had ever known. Burney was almost unable to contain his delight at spending a day at the almost complete Farinelli *palazzo* just outside Bologna, where he and Farinelli were joined at dinner by the distinguished antiquarian, teacher and composer Padre Martini for stories and gossip. Farinelli tells him of his studies in Naples with Porpora, his famous contest with the trumpeter in Rome when he was only seventeen, visits to Vienna where the Holy Roman Emperor Charles VI revolutionised his singing by telling him that less is more (it is not enough to be supernatural, 'if you wish to reach the heart, you must take a more plain and simple road', to delight as well as astonish),[13] the ecstasy, rapture and enchantment of the English audiences he seduced (he has a picture on his wall of an English chimney-sweep urchin playing with a cat), having to sight read Handel before the king with the music in the wrong clefs, gossip about Cuzzoni and Faustina, and his on-stage embrace by Senesino, so overcome by Farinelli's singing that he had to stop and give him a hug. Farinelli's house was a regular meeting place for musicians passing through the north of Italy; the young Mozart, whom Burney met a few days after his Farinelli experience, had also been a guest there some months earlier.

FROM *PRIMO UOMO* TO PRIMA DONNA

Both the teaching and the success of the castrati eventually had an effect on the technique of unmutilated voices as sopranos in particular tried to match the virtuosity of their male equivalents. The blurring of gender roles had a particularly deleterious effect on the evolution of the tenor (sidelined into walk-on parts in *opera seria* for much of the eighteenth century) but women singers continued to make their mark and could even be interchangeable with castrati, this sometimes resulting in a female role being played either by a male soprano or a female one. Such

---

[12] Ibid.: 121–2.   [13] Burney, *Present State*: 208.

was the case with Handel's *Radamisto*, first performed in London in April 1720 and revived in December of that year and again in 1728. Revival in the case of baroque opera means reconceiving the piece for a different cast, and since the music was tailored by the composer to match the abilities of specific singers this could often mean substantial rewriting. Negotiations between singers and theatres could be complex and protracted, and the Royal Academy was unable to secure the services of the alto castrato Senesino (probably Handel's first choice for the title role) until the end of the year. Instead of the lesser-known soprano castrato Benedetto Baldassari Handel gave the leading male role to the soprano Margherita Durastanti. For the December revival he recast Senesino as Radamisto and Durastanti sang the prima donna role of Zenobia. Handel had first worked with Durastanti in Italy in 1709 and he must have appreciated her versatility and temperament. Within two years, however, she was succeeded as prima donna by Francesca Cuzzoni, whose rivalry with Faustina Bordoni came to a head during a performance of Bononcini's *Astianatte* in 1727 with the pair and their supporters fighting it out 'until they had left sanguinary marks of their hostility on each other's faces'.[14] Mancini was as ecstatic about Cuzzoni as he had been about Farinelli, and evokes a vivid picture of her singing:

This woman possessed all the necessary requisites to be truly great. She had sufficient agility and art of guiding the voice to sustain, reinforce and diminish it to that degree which made her deserve the title 'professor'. When singing a melodic song, she knew how to adorn and embellish it with such varied 'gruppettos' and passages without marring the melody; now blending, then vibrated with trills and mordents; now 'staccato' then sustained, and then loose runs in a redoubled style, soaring with a portamento from chest tone to a high head tone … She left aside the usual and common, and made her singing rare and wonderful.[15]

He was even more impressed with Bordoni, who at the time of writing was living quietly in Venice with her husband the composer Hasse, 'taking a well-deserved rest'. Bordoni had all the requirements of the perfect virtuosa, and:

Beside these gifts, she had a quick and ready trill and mordent and also perfect intonation. She was a master in the unfolding and sustaining of the voice, and the fine art of holding and retaking of the breath, and all these gifts were a sublime quality in her, acquired through assiduous study with which she cultivated all the natural dispositions. Thus she was enabled to perform everything with ease and that perfection required by the rules of art.[16]

---

[14] Ellen Clayton, *Queens of Song: Being Memoirs of Some of the Most Celebrated Female Vocalists* (New York: Harper Brothers, 1865; facs. Whitefish, MT: Kessinger Publishing, 2005): 56.

[15] Mancini, *Pensieri*: 39–40. [16] Ibid.: 38.

All three of these women had reputations to match those of their castrato rivals; all were thought to bring their art to a kind of perfection, each in her own way: Durastanti for her adaptable technique and musicianship, Cuzzoni for her speed and staccato, Faustina for her sustained subtleties of breathing and colour. Tosi thought Cuzzoni and Bordoni between them helped 'to keep up the tottering profession from falling into ruin' and fantasised about the two being combined into one glorious vocal creature.[17] The existence of such a creature would, of course, have deprived the public of the chance to appreciate two great but separate talents. With each excited description we gain more knowledge of how great singers were received, some understanding of what they did, and if we are lucky a little more insight into how they did it. To understand the latter we are dependent on the treatises, especially where these can be given legitimacy by connection with known performers or composers.

TOSI'S EUROPEAN REACH

Just as Galliard's translation of Tosi was the first serious book on singing to appear in English, so Johann Agricola's translation and commentary of 1757 was the first important German singing treatise. Agricola, a former pupil of J. S. Bach, updated Tosi with copious annotations, reinterpreting his writings for a later, German generation brought up on Hasse, Graun and C. P. E. Bach. As we have seen, the principles that Tosi espoused also appear in Mancini's *Pensieri e Riflessioni Pratiche sopra il Canto Figurato* (1777), and Johann Adam Hiller incorporates much of Tosi's pedagogy in his *Anweisung zum musikalisch-zierlichen Gesang* (1774/80). This is a remarkable dissemination of ideas that had their origin in the previous century. Tastes change, as the musical examples in Galliard, Agricola and Hiller clearly show, but the currency of Tosi's writings (over several generations and countries) suggests that the essence of good singing changed very little between the end of the seventeenth century and the beginning of the nineteenth. In these later treatises we get further insight into the very distinctive stylistic devices such as portamento and rubato that had probably been current for many generations but are only just beginning to be explained in print. Agricola's references include the flute player Quantz, a keen observer of singing whose treatise is likely to have been known by Agricola's German readers. Quantz enjoys portamento and says

---

[17] Tosi, *Observations*: 171.

a singer must understand 'das Tragen der Stimme (porter la voix)' and that 'a good portamento' is preferable to too many ornaments.[18] Agricola gives musical examples which do not quite tally with Galliard's, but he does describe 'slurring' ('an imitation of a certain slippery smoothness') and legato ('which consists of allowing the preceding note to sound until the following begins, so that there is no gap between them').

Johann Adam Hiller published his *Anweisung* in two parts, the first appearing in 1774, and the second (*Anweisung zum musikalisch-zierlichen Gesange*) in 1780. His writings complement Agricola's updating of Tosi and Mancini's *Pensieri e Riflessioni* of 1774, both of which he draws on at length. Hiller was an indefatigable enthusiast for the improvement of German singing when he was not composing *Singspiele*. He founded a music school open to both sexes (a true reformer, he thought it unfair that women should be penalised for historic religious reasons) and by his *Anweisung* hoped to bring Italian enlightenment to the Germans. There are substantial sections on tuning, declamation and ornamentation. The latter he divides into essential figures such as trills and appoggiaturas which must be correctly applied, and arbitrary or improvised ornaments such as divisions or *passaggi* which are at the performer's discretion.

Hiller's composer contemporaries, Agricola, C. P. E. Bach and Quantz, were fastidious in their application of appoggiaturas and the like, and expected either to indicate them in the score or for singers to know precisely when to apply them where they were not indicated. These grace notes obviously have their origins in improvised figures, and singers were sometimes much less rigorous than composers would like them to be. Tosi, who had been a singer first and foremost, and whose success as a teacher depended on his reputation as a performer, had insisted on the singer's right to almost complete freedom to ornament within the bounds of that elusive set of criteria called 'taste'. In trying to rein in Tosi's freedoms Hiller is very precise in his descriptions; one has the sense that both Hiller and Agricola, effectively two generations on from Tosi's 1723 publication, knew that Tosi's basic principles enshrined the true art, but felt that excessive freedom simply led to abuse and declining standards. Hiller's substantial preface credits Mancini and Burney as his main historical sources (Burney's three exploratory journals were published in German translation in 1772–3). Hiller had met Burney in Leipzig in 1772, and was as impressed by his hospitality as he was depressed by the singing

---

[18] Johann Joachim Quantz, *On Playing the Flute* (1752); trans. Edward R. Reilly (2nd edn, London: Faber, 2001): 300–1.

he heard (although Burney had enjoyed his earlier experiences of Italian opera in Germany).

The instructions for improvised *passaggi* and cadenzas are designed to show German singers how to sound Italian, and there is much good advice on how to make ornaments work (or to change or omit them if they do not suit the individual singer's vocal disposition). There are exercises for portamento, which clarify Tosi's thoughts on the subject, singers are urged to use rubato and *messa di voce*, and we get a picture of elegant sliding with occasional fireworks just such as Tosi might have experienced. For modern singers this is a real challenge, suggesting as it does that there has been little discernible change in basic singing style for more than a hundred years. Tosi's writings could be applied to Purcell, Agricola's to Bach, and Hiller's to Haydn and Mozart – they are all remarkably similar. Hiller's final chapter, 'On arbitrary variation of the aria', notes that singers should always be aware of where the beat is, and that they need a knowledge of harmony. They need to understand the composer's structure so that they can improvise over it. It should sound easy, masking the often extreme difficulty; be inventive: don't sing anything twice. These could be instructions from a jazz tutor. He follows this with two extraordinary examples, one German and sacred, the other Italian and secular, in which he writes complete arias with an ornamented version on a second stave above the original. These are priceless models which – in their refined Haydnesque complexity – would not be predictable from simply reading the foregoing text.

There is no evidence that Hiller ever met Mozart, though they did have mutual acquaintances and Hiller performed the *Requiem* in Leipzig after the composer's widow brought him a manuscript copy in 1792. But Hiller's examples of how to perform arias are a reminder that underlying all these pedagogical sources are performance practices that require far more imaginative interpretation than modern singers are generally prepared to make, especially with canonised figures such as Mozart, Haydn and Beethoven. Mozart's letters tell us a great deal about his experiences with singers: frustration at his first encounter as a fourteen-year-old with the tenor Guglielmo d'Ettore who did not take him seriously, reassurance from the ageing but awkward Anton Raaff, for whom he wanted his music to fit like a suit, falling in love with Aloysia Weber, sister of Constanza whom he subsequently married. He wrote seven or eight concert arias for Aloysia, and she sang in several of the operas. She was not of international reputation (she may not have been a great actress), but a study of 'Non sò d'onde viene', the first concert aria the twenty-two-year-old composer wrote for her, suggests that she must have been quite a virtuosa. We do not know what the singer would have added to it in performance, but Mozart wrote several versions of it so there was obviously nothing sacrosanct about the original version. The application of Hiller-like embellishments would certainly be in the spirit that Mozart would have expected.

The influence of Porpora, to whom both Hiller and Farinelli owed so much, is still visible in London at the turn of the century (several of the singers Mozart encountered had learned with him), and is evidence of a pedagogical continuity. In Domenico Corri's *Singers' Preceptor* of 1810 we find more clues about basic concepts. Corri was born in Rome in 1746 and began his musical education with lessons in violin and in solfa. He studied with Porpora for five years before moving to London, where like many of his Italian contemporaries he found congenial work in English society as a harpsichordist, composer and singing teacher. Part of his manual takes the form of a socratic dialogue between master and student, emphasising the importance of long and patient study of *messa di voce*, text articulation, ornamentation, rubato and portamento. Of these the fundamental exercise is in *messa di voce* which Corri describes as 'the soul of music' and to which he devotes two pages of examples. He also writes in some detail about the virtues of *solfeggio* exercises that we have read about but not seen in the writings of Tosi and Michael Kelly. Citing Porpora, Corri advocates basic interval training on the vowel 'a' before embarking on the complexities of solfa exercises so that the student's ear becomes attuned to intervals without having to think about note names. He confirms that in quick passages one might retain the solfa name that starts the phrase rather than articulate individual solfa syllables on each note. He asks for a *messa di voce* on any note of significant duration, which gives us a picture of subtle shaping of every single note.

Corri's advocacy of paralinguistic or onomatopoeic sighs and sobs seems startlingly similar to the descriptions of Renaissance singers of several hundred years earlier, and he envisages the art of speech and the art of singing unified in musical rhetoric. Portamento, for example, is a stylised means of re-creating an expressive aspect of speech that would be missing if notes were simply joined without such an effect. For many hundreds of years commentators on singing had referred to the primacy of text articulation; to modern singers this sits rather uneasily with vocal virtuosity (especially with seventeenth-century throat technique).

The twin demands of virtuosity and textual clarity may have caused considerable tension as the eighteenth century progressed, necessitating more elaborate ways of reconciling the two. Corri's association of portamento with the enunciation of words hints at a sophisticated deployment of the effect, enabling syllables to be joined in an expressive manner that assists in the delivery of the words, leaving melismatic passages to take care of themselves. The vagueness of his definition also suggests that by the early nineteenth century expressive sliding is so much a part of artistic singing as to be taken for granted, and that singers do it in a very individual way which makes it impossible to define except in very general terms:

> *Portamento di voce* is the perfection of vocal music; it consists in the swell and dying of the voice, the sliding and blending one note to another with delicacy and expression – and expression comprehends every charm which music can produce; the *Portamento di voce* may justly be compared to the highest degree of refinement in elegant pronunciation in speaking. Endeavour to attain this high qualification of the *portamento*, and ... deliver your words with energy and emphasis, articulate them distinctly ...[19]

Corri is conservative when it comes to ornamentation, approaching the subject more as a composer; he would like to see more respect for the notes on the page. He gives only a page of 'Passages', none of which is very elaborate, and his cadenza examples come after his summing up and conclusions, which suggests that he intends the amateur to reflect before risking anything overly virtuosic.

The Italian influence on English singing surfaces again with the publication in 1833 of Nicola Vaccai's bilingual *Metodo Pratico di Canto Italiano* or *Practical Method of Italian Singing*.[20] Vaccai already had a considerable reputation as a composer and teacher both in Italy and Paris when in 1832 he visited London, where his charm, like that of Tosi and Corri before him, soon found him a ready niche in bourgeois drawing-rooms. His treatise is short, practical and wastes very few words. He realised that wealthy amateurs would be easily bored by hours of *solfeggi*, and devised a series of tuneful exercises that would entertain his pupils as well as educate them in basic singing technique and the Italian language. Vaccai seems to have been the first to use words rather than solfa syllables for basic exercises. His manual consists of fifteen lessons, each containing exercises composed to texts by Metastasio, some of which are prefaced by interpretative rubrics. In the first lesson Vaccai explains the nature of

[19] Domenico Corri, *Singers' Preceptor* ('Dialogue between master and scholar'), in *Domenico Corri's Treatises on Singing*, ed. Richard Maunder (New York: Garland, 1995), 3–4.
[20] Nicola Vaccai, *Metodo Pratico di Canto Italiano per Camera in 15 Lezioni e un'Appendice* (1833), ed. Michael Aspinall (Turin: Giancarlo Zedde, 1999).

legato by replacing the conventional syllabification with an orthography of his own which implies that the vowel is maintained for the longest possible time before the change of note. In the phrase 'Manca sollecita' the conventional way to underlay the syllables would be 'Man-ca sol-le-ci-ta'; Vaccai suggests 'Ma-nca so-lle-ci-ta'.

This pedagogical shortcut using real language rather than solfa was quite revolutionary in its day, and it may explain part of the attraction that the book still has for singers (it has remained continuously in print): it is almost impossible to imagine today's singing students spending several hours each day singing what are in effect nonsense syllables. The first five of the sixteen lessons into which the book is divided are about getting smoothly from one note to another. Vaccai then deals with various basic ornaments and concludes with a short lesson on recitative and a final summative aria exercise not unlike Hiller's models. There appear to be no exercises for *messa di voce*, but the first lesson is preceded by a note on the compass of the voice together with a printed scale with what looks like a *messa di voce* on each note (omitted from the 1975 English edition by John Glenn Paton). His lesson on the trill is also very perfunctory compared with those of Mancini and others, which perhaps implies that the book is intended to be used in conjunction with a teacher. He does make a distinction between legato and portamento, giving us an insight into the nature of this elusive technique:

On the Glide or Manner of Carrying the Voice: by carrying the voice from one note to another, it is not meant that you should drag or drawl the voice through all the intermediate intervals, an abuse that is frequently committed but it means to unite perfectly the one note with the other. When once the pupil understands thoroughly how to unite the syllables, as pointed out in the first Lesson, he will more easily learn the manner of carrying the voice as here intended: of this however as before observed nothing but the voice of an able master can give a perfectly clear notion. There are two ways of carrying the voice. The first is, by anticipating as it were almost insensibly with the vowel of the preceding syllable the note you are about to take, as shown in the first example. In phrases requiring much grace and expression it produces a very good effect: the abuse of it however is to be carefully avoided as it leads to mannerism and monotony. The other method which is less in use is by deferring or postponing as it were almost insensibly the note you are going to take and pronouncing the syllable that belongs to it with the note you are leaving as pointed out in the second example.[21]

For Vaccai the generalised meaning has now given way to two specific varieties, one more common (and perhaps considered more tasteful) than

---

[21] Ibid.: 32.

the other. He still uses the Galliard/Tosi term 'glide', and he is clear that excessive use of intervening pitches is undesirable. The reader can have no idea of how much of the intervening pitched material would be audible and Vaccai is aware of this: the only way to be sure is to listen to someone who knows how to do it. From the earliest mention of portamento-like effects almost all references tend to be couched in terms of taste and accompanied by a warning against excessive use. We are unlikely ever to understand all the subtle intricacies of eighteenth-century taste but we can make a number of observations about the ideological background of those who write about it. Most of the sources (including all of those quoted so far) were teachers rather than successful performers and perhaps more significantly they have all seen themselves primarily as composers. Composition, performance and pedagogy are each driven by different ideological, social and musical criteria. Of the three, composition and pedagogy are inevitably more rule bound, with the performer's role ultimately more creative and less predictable than either of the other two (and perhaps even perceived as threatening by composers and teachers); all are seeking to control 'their' materials as far as convention will allow.

The master–apprentice model continued to be the norm for all aspiring singers in England until well into the nineteenth century, in contrast to mainland Europe where there were institutional changes that fundamentally altered the way singing was taught. The system of apprenticeship that had grown up in the seventeenth century had involved singers attaching themselves to a master for many years. Teaching was on a one-to-one basis and learning was primarily by example, with each student treated as an individual. Since (as far as we can tell) singing before the nineteenth century probably used a higher larynx position than singers do today, it is likely that individual singers were able to bring something of the uniqueness of their speech to their singing voices. This tendency was encouraged by the oral tradition within which seventeenth- and eighteenth-century teachers worked. The wave of encyclopaedist fervour that swept France in the wake of the Revolution was characterised by an almost missionary attitude to pedagogy and the arts. The new climate opened up singing as a potential profession to a much wider cross-section of society. The founding of the Paris Conservatoire in 1795 was not a revolutionary change in the nature of musical teaching in learning, but did represent a formalised and state-controlled version of the private *conservatori* that had produced so many Italian singers earlier in the century. The Conservatoire commissioned its own teaching materials to ensure that the new era was built on the foundations of the old. The volumes published throughout the new century are often extremely detailed works of reference and many would have been used as a resource, either in a one-to-one situation or in a class. Whenever possible, distinguished Italian teachers would be brought in, including castrati, despite the historic French aversion to them and the pre-Revolutionary decadence that such singers increasingly represented.

Girolamo Crescentini was Napoleon's favourite singer, and he appointed him singing teacher to the imperial family in 1805. One of the last star castrati, Crescentini wrote a bilingual French and Italian book of exercises for the Conservatoire in 1811, followed by a volume of *vocalises*. Crescentini's main aim was to keep alive the tradition of embellishment supported by meticulous and imperceptible breathing. Like many castrato treatises, the Italian version assumes the student will be in the presence of the master to help him through the *vocalises*, and it gives a set of twelve basic rules illustrated by six basic examples of how to interpret them. The French translation seems to take account of the fact that the student may not be very knowledgeable and includes a footnote to explain that *vocalises* are sung on A without solmisation or words, something that a singer versed in the old Italian tradition would not need to be told. The *vocalises*, which are annotated with varied attacks and *messa di voce*, are all marked *sempre legato*, the first one also qualified by a slur and *e portando la voce* (which may be implied for all the exercises). They are clearly intended to teach and test traditional techniques; there are long held notes on which a *messa di voce* would be essential, scales which cross register breaks and arpeggiated figures that achieve the same effect by leap. Crescentini's rules stress colour and expression, energy and suppleness, variety in execution and, most importantly, he urges his students to aim to touch the hearts of his listeners, however good or bad their voices may be. His passionate creativity is inspirational and a perfect paradigm for teachers to present to their students but it is very much a product of an age that was already receding from view, to be replaced by the more powerful and dynamic singing that we begin to see espoused in later French treatises. Two other great castrati published treatises at the turn of the century, Aprile's 1795 volume and Rauzzini's of 1812. The basic two-hundred-year-old tenets are still being taught, but against an increasing sense of loss.

There has been much lamenting of the demise of these extraordinary singers, and in the twentieth century many publications appeared claiming to reveal the secrets of their lost techniques. The best castrati were undoubtedly capable of vocal feats that it is impossible to replicate today, but the pedagogical literature of the later nineteenth century suggests that the core skills which their physical condition facilitated were not so much actually lost as metamorphosed into the more powerful and richly coloured technique that was required by composers whose music was not predicated primarily on vocal virtuosity. The decision by Rossini to write more ornamentation into his scores in order to rein in the embellishment that his singers would otherwise have added is symptomatic of the period. Once ornamentation became a function of the composition (as opposed to the performance itself) it could be quantified and reproduced on an institutional scale. The more realistic plots of composers such as Donizetti, Verdi and Puccini called for new colours in the voice, not simply impressive singing (which might distract from the action). This did not mean the end of virtuosic singing but performers became more disciplined in their application of ornaments; without the direct experience of castrato teachers, singers began to explore the capacity of the 'natural' voice in ways that had hitherto not been imaginable. The new singing, while acknowledging traditional principles, owed as much to those who had not themselves been taught by castrati.

THE COMPOSER AS SINGER

For most of the nineteenth century it would still be the singers who called the shots, and composers would still construct an aria around the talents of the singers, just as Mozart had done. Berlioz's satirical complaint could have been written by any composer of the period about any of its singers:

A score must continually be fitted, recast, patched up, lengthened or shortened to put it into a state (and what a state!) in which it can be performed by the artists to whom it is delivered. One singer finds his part too high, another too low, this one has too much to sing, that one not enough. The tenor wants every phrase to end with *i*, the baritone wants *a*. One singer finds an accompaniment bothersome, his rival complains of a chord that rubs him the wrong way. One aria is too slow for the *prima donna*, another too fast for the tenor. In short, if a wretched composer took it upon himself to write the scale of C in the middle register, to a slow tempo and without accompaniment, he would not be sure of finding singers who would sing it *without making changes*. Most would still insist that the scale *does not fit their voice*, not having been composed expressly for them.[22]

The relationship between singers and composers was a great deal more complicated than this rant implies and in many instances there was a kind of synergy between the two. The first musical experience of many

---

[22] Hector Berlioz, *The Art of Music and Other Essays (A Travers Chants)*, trans. and ed. Elizabeth Csicsery-Rónay (Bloomington: Indiana University Press, 1994): 58. The original appeared in *Débats* 6 February 1853.

composers was as a boy singer either in church choirs or on the stage, their crucial first awareness of their musical talent revealed through singing. As we have seen, it would have been unthinkable for a sixteenth-century musician not to sing, play and compose, and probably teach as well, and only posthumously do musicians become dedicated composers. The success of public opera from the mid-seventeenth century was a factor in the increasing professionalism of music, and musicians were better able to create careers based on economic opportunity. The Venetian Francesco Cavalli, for example, was famous as a boy soprano before he joined the choir of San Marco, and subsequently gained a reputation as a fine tenor. The choir at San Marco was full of singers who also composed, and the most successful would go on to write for the burgeoning theatres and well-endowed churches, gaining status as well as salary; large-scale works require many singers and players but (usually) only one composer. Alessandro Scarlatti was the son of the tenor Pietro Scarlata, grew up surrounded by singers but became obsessed by opera as a genre. Cavalli and Scarlatti both wrote music that comfortably fits the voice, and one can imagine them singing the music at least in their heads. Neither Handel nor Mozart was a child singer (though Mozart did have lessons from the castrato Manzuoli when he was in London in 1764–5) and their relationships with singers in adulthood were perhaps more objective, often seeming to challenge rather than simply give opportunities.

Rossini, however, most vocal of composers, had the strongest links with singers throughout his life. As a treble he had been taught by the tenor Matteo Babbini and was destined for a career as a singer (his treble voice was so beautiful that an uncle advised castration, to ensure a career as a *primo uomo*).[23] He subsequently married Isabella Colbran, one of the most successful singers of the day, and maintained a serious interest in singing teaching throughout his life. He published a book of *gorgheggi e solfeggi* while in Paris in 1827 and many subsequent manuals refer students to the 'exercises of Rossini'. He was appointed *Consulente onorario perpetuo* to the Liceo Musicale in Bologna in 1839 (despite his reservations about the conservatoire system) and those singers to whom he was close (Domenico Donzelli, Giovanni Battista Rubini, Maria Malibran, among many others) ensured that the principles of Rossini were transmitted through their own pupils. Donizetti and Bellini were similarly grounded in singing: Bellini is said to have sung his first aria at the age of

[23] Edmond Michotte, *Richard Wagner's Visit to Rossini (Paris 1860)* and *An Evening at Rossini's at Beau-Sejour (Passy) in 1858*, trans. and ed. Herbert Weinstock (University of Chicago Press, 1968): 109.

eighteen months, and (somewhat later) studied the theory of singing with Crescentini (who also taught Isabella Colbran) and was an inspiration to the young Rubini; as a youth, Donizetti was influenced by some of the finest Italian tenors, including Domenico Viganoni, Andrea Nozzari, Donzelli and Rubini, and became the teacher and confidant of Gilbert-Louis Duprez and Adolphe Nourrit. Many of these singers were themselves composers, and appreciated the lengths that composers had to go to in order to get the best out of their performers. As in Handel or Mozart's day, extensive rewriting could occur between performances if there had been a change of cast (as, for example, when Meyerbeer rewrote the tenor role in *Le Prophète*, having replaced the ageing Gilbert-Louis Duprez with the younger but less capable Gustave Roger).

Very few composers complain that singers do not ornament enough, and Rossini was one of the first to realise that if you want to keep the respect of your singers but at the same time give them plenty of opportunities to show off, you have to write complex music that will allow them to impress without feeling the need to recompose the piece. Times were changing, and so too was the singing, with increasing evidence of new techniques. For the first time in countless generations new thinking would be applied to the singing itself, eventually bringing to an end hundreds of years of creative virtuosity and replacing it with interpretative artistry.

CHAPTER 5

The nineteenth-century revolution

The hundred years from the end of the eighteenth century to the end of the nineteenth century saw more identifiable changes in singing than any earlier comparable period. There are, of course, purely vocal reasons for any sort of change – a new generation of singers will have new composers to negotiate with, older singers retire and new stars rise. But underlying and fuelling this perennial evolution were social and political upheavals, especially in Italy and France, that affected the whole of Europe. Italian singing continued to be exported to the rest of Europe and increasingly to the Americas during the first quarter of a century or so, but then in a relatively short space of time the centre of gravity passed from Naples, Rome, Milan and Bologna to Paris, London and St Petersburg, with Paris at the centre of creative endeavour. The French capital was prone to social and political upheaval, one of the consequences of which was frequent bouts of renewal and regeneration in its artistic life. It was also within easy reach of London and several other major north European cities, which if you were a singer made it a logical place to establish a career. Promoters, composers and performers were irresistibly drawn to its opera houses and concert halls.

It was possible for anyone with enough capital to set up an opera house and post-Revolution Paris had at least three at any one time, whose names and sites seemed to change as often as their casts. The Académie royale de musique was the national house, L'Opéra, which put on grand opera; the Opéra-Comique did not necessarily put on comic opera, but the Théâtre italien was dedicated to Italian language productions and it was there that Rossini had his greatest triumphs after moving to the city in 1823. Big names at the opera meant fashionable soirées, which successful singers would be paid to attend. Pedagogy became increasingly institutionalised, more complicated and in some respects unable to keep up with new demands composers were putting on singers. There were new voices – increasingly French or German – for new roles, and by the end of the century the role itself would be transferable between singers without rewriting for the individual performer. The age of the castrato was drawing to a close: the *primo uomo* was being supplanted by the prima donna, and the age of grand opera was about to begin. After centuries of fruitful collaboration between singers and composers, singers were about to lose the right to improvise, and composers would no longer tailor their music to the precise requirements of performers: singers would become interpreters of whatever the composer or conductor required of them.

Women singers have historically not had the same opportunities as men, but by the end of the eighteenth century there was sufficient demand from composers and promoters to generate significant careers for female sopranos and, increasingly, mezzo-sopranos and contraltos – there could be more to singing than speed of execution and stratospheric tessitura. Some learned from established teachers, others sprang from nowhere and many were controversial. Some made society marriages and continued their careers in the drawing-room rather than on the stage (Henrietta Sontag was obliged to relinquish the stage before the Sardinian court would approve her marriage to the diplomat Count Carlo Rossi) but for most the stage was no bar to a successful career: Mrs Arne, Mrs Cibber, Madame Mara, Mrs Crouch, Mrs Billington, Malibran and Viardot – a host of women continued to have successful careers while known by their husband's names. The list of divas able to command high fees in Europe at the beginning of the nineteenth century was impressive: Mara, Banti, Billington, Grassini, Catalani, all of whom were skilled negotiators and set records for high fees. They were not all the products of diligent study and grooming.

Details of the early life of Brigida Banti are sketchy, but she was rumoured to have been a street singer before being discovered in a Parisian café. Illiterate and unable to read music, she had an intuitive musicianship and a formidable memory which enabled her to remember any tune after only one or two hearings. She was notoriously immune to the potential benefits of pedagogy, had little time for the niceties of bourgeois drawing-rooms and was said to drink a bottle of wine a day. In these circumstances her vocal charisma must have been extraordinary; by all accounts she had a powerful voice with an easy coloratura. It was for Banti that Haydn wrote his *Scena di Berenice*; this was first given in 1795 at Haydn's benefit concert in London, which earned him a princely 4,000 gulden (only in England could such a thing happen, he said). Michael Kelly recounts that at Banti's own benefit in 1802 the crowd stampeded, carrying Signor Banti to the very edge of the pit and losing the night's takings in the process. Kelly had been impressed when he first heard her in Venice, and sang with her in twenty performances of Gluck's *Alceste* at the Haymarket in London in 1796; he found her acting sublime and her singing charming. Her greatest fan was Lord Mount Edgcumbe, dilettante, observer of the opera scene and amateur composer. He wrote his opera *Zenobia* for her 1800 benefit concert, and in his *Reminiscences* we glimpse the changing times. Mount Edgcumbe was a connoisseur of singing and singers (he believed the castrato Pacchierotti to be an almost perfect paradigm). The *primo uomo* in *Zenobia* was scheduled to be the castrato Agrippino Roselli. Roselli turned out not to be up to it and was persuaded to hand over the role to the tenor Giuseppe Viganoni. That is the last we hear of Roselli or any other castrato on the London stage until the valedictory performances of Velluti twenty-five years later. In 1802 Banti returned to Italy where she died in 1806; she left her larynx (said to be unusually large) to the city of Bologna (which has since mislaid it).

Banti was succeeded as prima donna in London first by Elizabeth Billington and then by Angelica Catalani, both of whom had developed their voices after impressing as child singers and made their adult professional debuts while still in their teens. Catalani was also possessed of a huge voice (Queen Charlotte had to put cotton wool in her ears) and was among the last of the great divas to have grown up in competition with castrati. She sang with both Luigi Marchesi and Girolamo Crescentini and had a phenomenal coloratura which many complained she used to excess. Spohr thought she had no soul, as did Stendhal ('God somehow forgot to place a heart within reasonable proximity of this divine larynx')[1]. Mount Edgcumbe thought her 'capable of exertions supernatural' and admired her greatly despite her wilfulness and lack of taste. He also realised that the age of spectacular castrato-inspired vocalism was fast coming to an end, and that she was 'the last great singer to be heard in this country whose name is likely to be recorded in musical annals'.[2] She died of cholera in 1849, not long after hearing the young Jenny Lind, to whom she gave her blessing.

While these high-flying nightingales were captivating audiences everywhere another kind of voice was emerging, less virtuosic perhaps, lower and less perfect, unpredictable in inspiration, but above all dramatic. Lord

[1] Stendhal (Henri Beyle), *The Life of Rossini*, trans. Richard Coe (2nd edn, London: Calder, 1985): 337.
[2] Richard Mount Edgcumbe, *Musical Reminiscences of the Earl of Mount Edgcumbe: Containing an Account of the Italian Opera in England from 1773 to 1834* (London, 1834; rpr. New York: Da Capo Press, 1973): 108.

Mount Edgcumbe felt that Giuditta Pasta was a better actress than Banti and a more powerful singer than Velluti. Both Chorley and Stendhal agree that her ornamentation was graceful and unrivalled, Pasta being one of very few singers who would experiment at great length to find the perfect ornament and then retain it rather than spontaneously recompose. Mount Edgcumbe thought her typical of the current generation of singers who were too loud for drawing-rooms:

the modern music spoils the singers for concerts, especially in private houses. The constantly singing concerted pieces adapted only for the theatre gives them the habit of so forcing their voices that they know not how to moderate them to the small space of an ordinary room ... The ear is often absolutely pained by their loudness.[3]

Chorley's recollections of her are extraordinary in their bleak assessment of the elements of her talent, compared with the magic of the complete Pasta experience. 'The ninety-nine requisites of a singer ... had been denied to her': her voice was uneven and some notes were never ever in tune; she was a poor musician and a slow reader. And yet none of this mattered because 'Though I knew it was coming, when the passion broke out, or when the phrase was sung, it seemed as if they were something new, electrical, immediate.'[4] He loved the grandeur of her style, her taste, courage and timing, and the veracity of her recitative. Between 1819 and 1835 she became every composer's favourite soprano, creating roles for Rossini, Donizetti, Pacini and Meyerbeer among many others.

From 1830 onwards she was most famously associated with Bellini, who wrote fiercely difficult roles for her in *Il Pirata*, *La Sonnambula* and *Norma*. Coping with the technical and dramatic requirements of Norma took its toll on her will to sustain such intense artistry, and she retired from the stage in 1835 to live the next thirty years in her villa on Lago di Como, the most successful soprano in the world. She could not resist returning for an occasional farewell performance, and Chorley's famous and moving account of an ill-judged return to London at the age of fifty-two captures her attempt to relive the final *scena* from *Anna Bolena*, composed for her by Donizetti twenty years before:

Her voice, which at its best had required ceaseless watching and practice, had long ago been given up by her. Its state of utter ruin on the night in question passes description ... A more painful and disastrous spectacle could hardly be looked on.

---

[3] Mount Edgcumbe, *Musical Reminiscences*: 170.
[4] Henry Chorley, *Thirty Years' Musical Recollections* (New York: Vienna House, 1972): 89.

There was ridicule from sections of the audience, but not from one who might be considered Pasta's successor, Pauline Viardot, then in her prime and hearing Pasta for the only time in her life:

Dismal as was the spectacle, broken, hoarse, and destroyed as was the voice, the great style of the singer spoke to the great singer ... Later she attempted the final mad scene of the opera – that most complicated and brilliant among the mad scenes on the modern musical stage, with its two cantabile movements, its snatches of recitative, and its bravura of despair, which may be appealed to as an example of vocal display, till then unparagoned, when turned to the account of frenzy, not frivolity – perhaps as such commissioned by the superb creative artist. By that time, tired, unprepared, in ruin as she was, she had rallied a little. When, on Ann Boleyn's hearing the coronation music for her rival, the heroine searches for her own crown upon her brow, Madame Pasta wildly turned in the direction of the festive sounds, the old irresistible charm broke out; nay, even the final song, with its roulades, and its scales of shakes ascending by a semitone, the consummate vocalist and tragedian, able to combine form with meaning – the moment of the situation with such personal and musical display as form an integral part of the operatic art – was indicated: at least to the apprehension of a younger artist. 'You are right' was Madame Viardot's quick and heartfelt response (her eyes full of tears) to a friend beside her...'It is like the *Cenacolo* of da Vinci at Milan – a wreck of a picture, but the picture is the greatest picture in he world.'[5]

Although she always sang soprano roles, accounts of Pasta's range suggest that she may have been a mezzo who also had top notes. This may offer a clue both to the dramatic intensity of her singing and to her relatively early retirement: projecting a low voice higher can access a wider range of tone colours, but the tension created by routinely singing outside her comfortable tessitura would in the end have tired her musculature beyond help. A similar fate may have befallen Pauline Viardot, also a mezzo who retired early, and like Pasta a new breed of thinking singer. Daughter of one of Rossini's favourite tenors and sister of Malibran, Pauline Garcia grew up in the lyric theatre but intending at first to become a pianist. She studied piano with Liszt and composition with Reicha, was fluent in several languages and was the intellectual equal of any of the philosophers who flocked to her soirées. She had been well-drilled by her father in what would become during her lifetime the black arts of improvisation, but it was her dramatic intelligence that appealed to composers and audiences. She could manage the florid repertoire of Rossini, Bellini and Donizetti but there were others (such as the highly competitive Grisi) who were perhaps yet more effortless and spectacular. Her real forte lay

---

[5] Ibid.: 92–3.

in exploring the new drama of composers such as Halévy and Meyerbeer, and the theatrical, vocal and musical insight she could bring to bear on the actual compositions. This was not the same thing as a baroque or classical composer fitting the music around the performer's predilections, but more a process of consultation at times akin to co-composing. She had close working relationships with Gounod, Berlioz and Massenet, and became a pivotal figure in the evolution of the mezzo-soprano. Meyerbeer completely reconceived *Le Prophète* around the talents of Viardot, focusing on the role of the mother Fidès rather than John of Leiden when it became obvious that Gilbert-Louis Duprez was too old for the role. She sang the role more than two hundred times all over Europe, and her performance opened the way for more complex female roles that were less dependent on the old virtuosity. She also reinvented old music, triumphing spectacularly in Berlioz's restoration of Gluck's *Orphée* (though even here she could not resist some spontaneous recomposing).[6]

THE RISING MALE

Male voices also became more prominent with the decline of the castrati. Lully and others had used basses (or *basse-taille*, more like a modern baritone) in preference to castrati for more noble roles, but elsewhere the evolution of the bass voice went into reverse after promising developments in the early seventeenth century, as had been the case with the tenor. Virtuosic tenor-basses of the calibre of Brancaccio were obviously rare, and with castrati able to play either gender both tenors and basses were reduced to stock characters with little opportunity to exploit their own vocal potential. Exceptionally, Buononcini and Handel wrote substantial bass arias for the basses Giuseppe Boschi and Antonio Montagnana, whose colour, virtuosity and power he obviously appreciated. Burney thought 'Handel's genius and fire never shone brighter than in the bass songs which he composed for Boschi and Montagnana: as their voices were sufficiently powerful to penetrate through a multiplicity of instrumental parts, he set every engine at work in the orchestra to enrich the harmony and enliven the movement.'[7]

Mozart worked with some of the most famous basses of the era (bass at this time generally meaning a generic low voice, often corresponding to

---

[6] 'Gluck's Orphée', in Hector Berlioz, *The Art of Music and other Essays (A Travers Chants)* trans. Elizabeth Csicsery-Rónay (Bloomington: Indiana University Press, 1994): 71.

[7] Charles Burney, *A General History of Music*, vol. IV (London, 1979; facs. *Eighteenth Century Collections Online*): 261.

what we now think of as a baritone). Ludwig Fischer was his first Osmin in *Die Entführung aus dem Serail* and Mozart thought him irreplaceable despite his getting disastrously lost in the closing trio during the second performance, leaving the tenor Adamberger to pick up the pieces. The composer wrote of allowing Fischer's 'beautiful deep notes to glow' and mentions the curious fact that the Archbishop of Vienna thought he was too low for a bass.[8] Mozart was also impressed by Francesco Benucci, for whom he wrote Figaro in *Le Nozze di Figaro* in 1786 and who sang Leporello in the Viennese performance of *Don Giovanni* two years later. These were much more than *buffo* blusterers, as Mozart's music for them confirms; but the core *basso buffo* repertoire required volume, flexibility and talent as an actor rather than a dazzling vocal technique; however entertaining most of them were it was rare for basses to be commended for the quality of their singing. In these circumstances it was sometimes difficult even for successful basses to maintain a career. George Hogarth laments the fact that 'in tyrants, old men, or rough and harsh characters, the bass voice could be appropriately introduced: but it would seem that nothing more was required from the performance than force and energy'.[9] Lord Mount Edgcumbe mentions in passing the otherwise unknown Morelli, apparently a powerful Italian bass and skilled actor who played opposite Nancy Storace in Paisiello's *Gli Schiave per Amore* in London in 1787, but who 'having been a running footman to Lord Cowper in Florence … could not be a great musician'.[10] This might have been for reasons of snobbery, of course, and careers could be made by the enterprising; the Viennese bass Josef Staudigl had sung as a treble and as a teenager intended to become a monk, before escaping to study medicine in Vienna in 1827. Poverty drove him to join the opera chorus at the Kärnertor as a young bass, and he began a career which eventually saw him singing Mozart and Meyerbeer in London and the first performance of Mendelssohn's *Elijah* in Birmingham. Chorley was impressed by his two-octave range and the nobility of his voice, 'equal, rich, sonorous, in no common degree', though he thought him a complete disaster in Italian roles.[11]

During the first quarter of the new century we begin to see more of a distinction between basses, who tend to be old, authoritative and

---

[8] Mozart to his father 26 September 1781, *The Letters of Mozart and His Family*, ed. Emily Anderson, 3rd edn rev. Stanley Sadie and Fiona Smart (London: Macmillan, 1985): 768–9.

[9] George Hogarth, *Memoirs of the Opera*, vol. I (London: Richard Bentley, 1851; repr. New York: Da Capo, 1972): 342.

[10] Ibid.: 57.   [11] Chorley, *Recollections*: 133, 191.

deep-voiced, and baritones who could be subtler, younger and higher,
with the bass-baritone having something of the old tenor-bass potential. Louis Lablache, perhaps the most famous bass of the first half of
the century, was educated as a treble at the Conservatorio della Pietà in
Naples, where he would have learned the style and technique still being
used by castrati. This stood him in good stead when his voice broke,
and having made his adult debut as a *buffo* his study was rewarded with
a contract as a *basso cantante* in Palermo. He sang Rossini, Mercadante
and Meyerbeer at La Scala from 1821 to 1828 and made a brilliant début
in London in 1830, when Mount Edgcumbe thought his one of the
deepest voices he had ever heard. Both he and Henry Chorley were
impressed with the sheer size of the man (Chorley reckoned his foot was
the size of a child's boat).[12] It was his supreme versatility that appealed
to Rossini, Donizetti, Bellini and Meyerbeer, his comic genius as well
as his ability to move audiences as a tragic actor. His contemporary
Antonio Tamburini also impressed the Londoners, especially when he
and Lablache appeared together as members of the so-called Puritani
Quartet with soprano Giulia Grisi and the tenors Mario or Rubini.
Tamburini ('a brilliant bass singer and actor combining more attractive qualities than any other (save Lablache)', thought Chorley)[13] created
roles for Donizetti and Bellini (Riccardo in *I Puritani* to Lablache's
Giorgio, and Ernesto in *Il Pirata*) and commuted between London and
Paris. These were lyrical singers, part of a post-castrato blossoming of
the bass, and although Lablache in particular was on the cusp of a new
age, having had works written for him by the young Verdi and Wagner,
his *Méthode Complète du Chant* of 1840 is a classic traditional singing
treatise which makes no concessions to basses at all.[14] The newer generation of baritones would have to cope with Verdi, whose key male roles
became identified with the brilliant upper fifth of the baritone range.
Unlike Wagner, who was almost obsessed with singers and singing,
Verdi had little interest in singing for its own sake, only what it could
achieve in the service of the drama.

Even more than basses and baritones, tenors profited from the demise
of the castrati. Handel and Mozart had written memorably for tenor.

---

[12] Ibid.: 12.   [13] Ibid.: 34.

[14] Louis Lablache, *Méthode Complète du Chant* (Paris, 1840). In the late 1830s Wagner had offered
Lablache the aria 'Norma il predisse' for insertion into Bellini's *Norma* (which the singer
declined); in 1847 he created the role of Massimiliano in Verdi's *I Masnadieri*. An English translation of his *Méthode* was published in New York in 1873 (*Lablache's Abridged Method of Singing*,
Cincinnati, OH: John Church, 1873).

Handel was able to call on the best Italian tenors, Francesco Borosini, Annibale Pio Fabri and Giovanni Battista Pinacci, for the King's Theatre, and British tenors Alexander Gordon, Thomas Lowe and John Beard in both opera and the new genre of oratorio.[15] Mozart could depend on Valentin Adamberger and Anton Raaff, both of whom were firm friends, the elder statesman Raaff often smoothing the way for the impetuous young composer. None of these men sounded like our modern idea of a tenor: the smooth joining of registers is characteristic of all singing teaching of the period, and would have affected the tenor voice more than any other. By uniting the chest voice and the falsetto, tenors were able to extend their ranges into the soprano register. Haydn expected Karl Friberth to be able to manage a top D as well as a baritonal bottom A in the same aria, and the upward extension reached its peak in the top F that Bellini wrote for Giovanni Battista Rubini in the third act of *I Puritani*. During the first quarter of the nineteenth century, however, we find a more robust breed of tenor emerging, and instead of switching to falsetto at the 'break' (around E or F in most tenors) the more adventurous risk-takers would continue upwards in chest voice to A or even higher. This new masculinity was part of a dramatic realignment of voices that would see the tenor become the romantic lead, finally displacing the castrato *primo uomo*. The bigger sound probably began with Domenico Donzelli, who had been a student of Eliodoro Bianchi (significantly, perhaps, a tenor rather than a castrato). Donzelli sang the florid Rossini repertoire very successfully, but became more at home in the heavier Donizetti and Bellini roles from about the 1820s onwards as his voice became deeper and richer (possibly as a result of singing with a lower larynx position). Perhaps the most celebrated single note in the whole of history was the top C which the French tenor Gilbert-Louis Duprez let fly in Rossini's *Guillaume Tell* at the Paris Opéra in 1837. Rossini hated it, but it caused a sensation and once unleashed there was no going back: within a very short time the tenor falsetto had almost vanished, to be replaced by an extended chest register. Some very fine tenors, such as the intelligent and elegant Adolphe Nourrit, were unable to stay the course, though the old virtuosity still had its adherents in Rubini and Mario.

Seven years before Duprez's ear-splitting revelation Giovanni Battista Velluti had retired from the stage. The great castrato must have cut a solitary figure in the latter part of his career, being one of the last successful

---

[15] See John Potter, 'The Tenor–castrato Connection', *Early Music* 35:1 (2007).

survivors of a practice that produced the most extraordinary music by the cruellest means. His appearance in London in 1825 for Meyerbeer's *Il Crociato in Egitto* (the last opera to include a castrato role) was an extraordinary event, the first time anyone had heard a castrato for a quarter of a century. He had arrived earlier in the season and met with abuse from audiences, and there was much agonising over whether the Meyerbeer première should go ahead. Mount Edgcumbe, helpless admirer of Pacchierotti and all that was good and great about the art of the castrato, wrote of the occasion:

At the moment he was expected to appear, the most profound silence reigned in one of the most crowded audiences I ever saw, broken on his advancing by loud applauses of encouragement. The first note he uttered gave a shock of surprise, almost of disgust, to the inexperienced ears, but his performance was listened to with attention and great applause throughout, with but few audible expressions of disapprobation speedily suppressed.[16]

Mount Edgcumbe's further musings on Velluti's performance are a vivid and sad evocation by one who was there. It was, ultimately, a triumph, as Meyerbeer wrote to the critic Francesco Pezzi two weeks later:

During the evening's performance [Velluti] had to struggle against strong opposition. This opposition was not directed at his talent but rather at his person because a portion of his audience considered it improper and immoral to allow a castrato to appear on the stage. Velluti remained calm and did not let himself be shaken by the murmurs and whistles. He gloriously won over all of his critics and created a sensation.[17]

Almost unnoticed on such a fateful occasion, another tiny piece of history was unfolding. The role of Felicia was played by the seventeen-year-old mezzo-soprano Maria Garcia, whose brief and fantastic career as Maria Malibran would excite the whole of Europe before her death after a riding accident eleven years later. Maria's younger sister Pauline (later Pauline Viardot) would also become one of the great divas of the age, and her brother Manuel would become its foremost singing teacher. Maria's contract had been negotiated by their father Manuel del Populo Vincente Rodriguez Garcia, favourite tenor of Rossini (for whom he had composed the role of Almaviva (*Il Barbiere di Siviglia*) in 1815). The ambitious father and daughter insisted on replacing an aria with one by Garcia himself, designed to show off her virtuosity. Thus the Garcia dynasty, which would

---

[16] Mount Edgcumbe, *Musical Reminiscences*: 162.
[17] Letter of 10 July 1825 in Heinz and Gudrun Becker, *Giacomo Meyerbeer: a Life in Letters* (London: Christopher Helm, 1983): 38–9.

stretch into the twentieth century, witnessed the end of the castrati while still themselves a part of that world of extraordinary vocal display.

Watching this performance was seventeen-year-old musician *manqué* Henry Chorley, who would become the music and literature critic of the *Athenaeum* in five years' time, and who is one of our main sources of insight, information and gossip about singers of the period. It would be impossible to document all of the successful singers of the times (the various attempts at categorising them seem quaintly unhistoric), and we will never know what any of these singers sounded like; but by looking at the critical response to a small number of highly acclaimed performers we can get a sense at least of the effect the singing had on listeners. Chorley devotes the first sub-chapter of his *Recollections* to Malibran, and was still trying to make sense of the impact she had on him more than twenty-five years after her tragically early death. Almost all of Chorley's comments can be corroborated from other sources; the impression we get from him is that of a trustworthy if rather biased witness determined to give a true account. He knows how difficult it is: 'we know past ecstasies, dreams, terrors, by heart: yet may fail, by any exercise of ingenuity, to convey an idea of them to others'.[18] Malibran had had a tough schooling at the hands of her father, and had hardened into a tenacious and 'fearlessly original' mezzo-soprano with a compass of more than two and half octaves. Significantly, her father's training in improvised agility had given her 'the power and science of a composer', but 'she was found unequal, bizarre and fatiguing by many of our opera loungers', says Chorley. Her performances in English were something wondrous, 'her vehemence in *La Sonnambula* too nearly trenched on frenzy to be true', despite the fact that she did not have 'a voice of first-rate quality' and was not 'a creative dramatic artist'. Malibran is often compared with Maria Callas, an imperfect diamond with the capacity to electrify audiences by an inspired vocal gesture. Like so many great artists she was a one-off, transcending whatever her listeners were used to. As Chorley poetically put it, 'she passed over the stage like a meteor, as an apparition of wonder, rather than as one who, on her departure, left her mantle behind her for others to take up and wear'.

The end of the castrati did not mean the end of creative extravagance. What was preserved in the larynx of the castrato was the voice of youth, and it is no coincidence that the female coloratura sopranos who superseded them started very young. From what we know of the Renaissance period there seems to have been little distinction between

---

[18] Chorley, *Recollections*: 6; subsequent quotes referring to Malibran are from pp. 6–10.

a mature child's voice and that of a young adult. Francesca Caccini may have sung in Peri's *Euridice* at the age of thirteen and many of her contemporaries were married as teenagers. Nancy Storace, Mara, Malibran and Patti were child stars who maintained their success into adulthood, Laure Cinti-Damoreau was only fourteen when she made her Paris début. Very few divas were more than sixteen or seventeen when they launched their careers (Cuzzoni and Bordoni were a relatively ancient eighteen and nineteen on their respective débuts). Our modern assumption about the sound of the castrato voice, perhaps born of the experience of generations of church-educated trebles, is that it was a boy's voice projected into adulthood; yet the androgynous sound that so bewitched audiences might better be thought of as more of an ungendered child's voice. The sound of the youthful nineteenth-century female soprano, especially the lighter ones such as Sontag, Lind and Patti, may have touched the same nerve as that of their mutilated male predecessors.

NEW TIMES, NEW TEACHING: GARCIA AND THE CONSERVATOIRE

Despite changes in voices and compositional styles many aspects of singing teaching continued to be much the same as they had been for generations, but applied with more rigour. Music was still being created for specific singers but the number of revivals was reaching a critical point where singers could learn existing roles in addition to generic techniques. The creative balance of power between singers and composers was gradually shifting in favour of the latter, but as yet there was little reduction in ornamental opportunity, much though composers might have wished for it. Singers were still well versed in the art of agility, whether they came through the new conservatories or studied at the feet of a master, or were natural talents with no training at all. The gradual emancipation of the *seria* and *buffa* genres in the writing of Rossini, Meyerbeer, Bellini and Donizetti gave singers more opportunities to impress as actors while continuing to astonish audiences with their virtuosity. If there was a Golden Age of singing it was probably between Rossini's arrival in Paris, when audiences paid to hear singing at its brilliant best, and the advent of a different kind of music drama later in the century when audiences expected to appreciate the interpretation of roles. The concept of singing as a partnership between performer and composer, the singer adding a decorative overlay to the composer's model, which had been central to the development of Western classical music for more than three hundred years, would finally end with the reimagining of singing that came with Verdi, Wagner and later with Strauss and Puccini. Sadly, the peak was probably reached just before the invention of recording, and we missed hearing some of the greatest singers of all time by only a generation or two.

A study of the vast amount of pedagogical material produced in this period suggests that the new singing (or singings, perhaps) did not immediately replace the old, but existed alongside it for many years; it also featured many of the same characteristics, changing only in certain very specific areas. The elder Manuel Garcia wrote a short treatise and set of exercises published after his death in a bilingual French/Italian edition that looks remarkably like an eighteenth-century manual; there is a set of rules *à la* Crescentini followed by 339 increasingly difficult exercises. Garcia settled in Paris, where his school produced many successful singers including not only opera stars such as the tenor Adolphe Nourrit, but also his son, Manuel Patricio Rodriguez. The elder Garcia had been taught by Ansani, who in turn had been a pupil of Porpora, so his background was one of castrato principles without actually having been taught by one. His prefatory material mentions all the traditional principles including *messa di voce*, portamento and the joining of registers, and his first exercises are designed to practise all three at the same time. There are further portamento exercises over a leap of an octave in which the singer passes 'rapidement par toutes les distances intermediaires'. There is also the customary mixture of long notes alternating with virtuosic scale passages, and many examples of the kinds of formulae that singers can apply to cadences, suggesting that the old art is by no means dead.

Much more comprehensive information about singing in mid-century France is given in the treatises of Garcia's son and his two near contemporaries Garaudé and Panofka, and their writings and students continued to be influential for several generations. Heinrich Panofka, a composer, critic and violinist, moved to Paris in 1834 and during the next few years became so enamoured of the singing he heard there that he was inspired to study the technique of soloists such as Lind and Lablache as well as the current pedagogical literature. His *L'Art de Chanter* and its accompanying *Vade-Mecum du Chanteur*, published for the Conservatoire in 1854, brought him fame beyond France and is brief but scientific and accurate (especially when one considers that he had never been a professional singer himself). There are drawings of the vocal tract and lungs and accurate descriptions of vocal function, together with a list of publications on the physiology of the voice. He understands traditional technique: there are exercises for the joining of registers, legato singing, various sorts of attack, and portamento. The agility exercises are more like routines to get the musculature working rather than models for improvisation.

Alexis de Garaudé was a composer and singing teacher who had been a pupil of Crescentini and taught at the Conservatoire from 1816 to 1841. He produced a great deal of pedagogical writing from 1809 onwards, some of which continued to be reprinted into the twentieth century. The second edition of his *Méthode Complète de chant* of 1841 represents his life's work as teacher and observer of singers. His manuals were already in use in Milan and Naples, obviating the need for a bilingual edition. Garaudé's and Garcia's are among the first treatises to be informed by science; they are also (with Fétis's summative publication of 1870) by far the most comprehensive manuals published before the twentieth century. Garaudé understands something of the science of vocal acoustics; his description of the elements involved from the diaphragm to the vocal tract is physiologically accurate (though some of his terms, such as the labelling of chest sounds as 'laryngeal' and head voice as 'pharyngeal', are misleading). History has treated Garcia rather more favourably; he not only taught an extraordinary number of famous singers but he lived to see his 101st birthday in 1906 (Garaudé died in 1852), spending the last fifty years of his life as a professor at the Royal Academy of Music in London.

Garaudé observes that voices vary according to sex and individuals. He considers how students should practise, advising them to stop at the first signs of tiredness – half an hour once or twice a day in the first months then up to four hours in three or four daily bursts. This should enable an adequate technique to be acquired in a few years. A good ear and proper intonation are achieved by *solfège* and good breathing is the key to expressive singing (*à la* Crescentini). Garcia's writing are detailed and comprehensive, giving us a picture not only of singing in the 1840s, but of the tradition on which that art was built (a point which the author himself makes in the introduction to his first French edition, where he locates himself in the tradition of Porpora, Tosi, Mancini and Agricola among others). He was born in Catalonia in 1805, one of three children born to Manuel del Populo Vincente Rodriguez Garcia and soprano Joaquina Sitchès (who fell in love with the elder Garcia while watching him sing, Sterling Mackinlay tells us, when they were both under contract to the opera in Madrid). There were three Garcia children, and they were all taught singing by Garcia senior from an early age, and all became fabulously successful musicians. Maria Malibran and Pauline Viardot, the two sisters, were among the most famous divas of the nineteenth century.

After various musical excursions to Mexico and the USA the family finally settled in Paris in 1829/30, where the younger Garcia started teaching at his father's singing school. He took over the responsibility for the teaching of his sisters after their father died in 1832, and became the most successful singing teacher of the century. After the 1848 revolution Garcia moved to London where he was attached to the nascent Royal Academy of Music for the remaining fifty-three years of his life. His reputation during his lifetime was colossal: the list of his pupils amounts to a *Who's Who* of nineteenth-century singing, including Julius Stockhausen, Jenny Lind, Mathilde Marchesi, Johanna Wagner (the composer's niece) and dozens of others employed in opera houses all over Europe and the USA. He was credited with the invention of the laryngoscope, the device for looking down throats still used by doctors today, which he perfected to enable him to see his own vocal folds in action. He was the first teacher to have direct experience of laryngeal function, both as a surgeon (he had been attached to the Napoleonic army as a field surgeon, which had enabled him to experiment with human and animal larynxes) and as an observer of the phenomenon of live vocalisation.

While he was still at the Paris Conservatoire, the younger Garcia published his *Traité complet de l'art du chant* in two parts in 1840 and 1847. The first English version of his writings for the benefit of English college students appeared in 1857 and was reprinted in 1870 and again during the First World War. The small changes that are evident in the various editions (both in English and French) reflect simplifications and clarifications of key concepts, and changes in musical taste rather than any significant development in technique: his published writings on *messa di voce,* portamento, rubato and the basic techniques are essentially the same in 1915 as in 1841. Garcia also survived well into the age of the gramophone (he was still teaching when the first recordings became available in the decade before his death), so he had ample opportunity to revise his work in the light of this technological innovation should he have thought it necessary. The fact that Garcia approved his English students using the translation of his treatise (even if he did not himself translate it) means that our understanding today need not be filtered through possible misunderstandings of the original French: the 1857 English version is grandly titled *Garcia's New Treatise on the Art of Singing. A Compendious Method of Instruction with Examples and Exercises for the Cultivation of the Voice;* along the top is flagged 'As used at the Royal Academy of Music, Royal College of Music, Guildhall School of Music and all the Principal Colleges in the United Kingdom'.

This version of the treatise is also divided into two parts, the first being an overview of basic technical rules, and the second amplifying specific details in the context of musical examples by Mozart, Rossini and others. The English version is missing the complete arias that appear in the French editions but otherwise follows the originals quite closely. Garcia begins by describing the principles of phonation, including one of the earliest examples of a discussion of timbre. He explains registers (he recognises three: the chest, falsetto – later changed to 'medium' in his 1894 *Hints on Singing* – and head). There is an assumption that the student will already have studied *solfeggio* (the intended readership is students at music college) and will also need to learn the piano and understand harmony. The reason for the latter is that:

> it is only by the knowledge of harmony that a singer is able to vary his songs extemporaneously – whether for the purpose of enlivening the effect, or of skilfully passing over a difficult passage, when, through temporary illness, a voice loses some of its notes. This often happens with opera singers, and proves the artist's proficiency.[19]

This is eighteenth-century artistry embellished with nineteenth-century pragmatism, and shows that singers are still happily ornamenting their way out of trouble when they need to. In the same paragraph Garcia outlines what the teaching might be expected to achieve: the equalisation of tone, firming up of unsteadiness, correct intonation, and an increase in the compass and agility, all of which require 'well-directed and persevering study'. After his preliminary explanations he ends Part I with more than two hundred exercises in aspects of vocal agility. These can only be done with the aid of a teacher, and he gives advice about practice time: five or six minutes, repeated several times during the day to start with, extending to not more than half an hour after a few weeks and half an hour up to four times a day after six months. He gives precise instructions on how the exercises are to be carried out, beginning each day with slow, sustained notes. *Messa di voce* appears only after the 167th exercise, as Garcia explains in great detail how to practise this, linking vocal onset with regulating the airflow, which he thinks would be too tiring unless the student was already quite experienced. With Garcia's remarks the point of *messa di voce* suddenly comes into focus, and we can finally understand how such an apparently simple exercise can have been the basis of a complete phonatory technique for more than two hundred years.

---

[19] Manuel Garcia, *Garcia's New Treatise on the Art of Singing* (London, n.d.): 6..

Part II includes detailed instruction on breathing, and Garcia puts into writing the kind of hints that teachers must have given for generations: the only way to breathe in the middle of a long run, for example, is to miss out bits of it. There are also clear examples of how rubato works, Garcia citing both his own father and Paganini as being masters of freely 'abandoning themselves to their inspiration' while the orchestra kept time beneath their rhythmic alterations'.[20] He deals with portamento in both parts. Half of chapter 7 of Part I is given over to 'Gliding or slurring (*con portamento*)', which suggests that all three terms (which we have encountered before and been unable to distinguish satisfactorily from each other) are to some extent interchangeable by this time. All of the main sources quoted so far have made a distinction between legato – basic joined-up singing – and alternative ways of linking notes expressively; Garcia also defines legato, as Hiller and Vaccai did before him, making it clear that:

To sing legato means to pass from one sound to another in a neat, sudden, and smooth manner, without interrupting the flow of voice; yet not allowing it to drag or slur over any intermediate sound … As an example of this we may instance the organ and other wind instruments, which connect sounds together without either *portamento* or break.[21]

If Garcia had read the treatises of the authors he looks back to, then he must have been aware of the inadequacies of previous explanations; his organ analogy is as explicit as it is possible to be without actually hearing it, and he specifically says that legato singing does not involve portamento, which he defines thus: 'To slur is to conduct the voice from one note to another through all intermediate sounds.'[22] On the face of it, this interpretation seems excessively chromatic compared with that of Vaccai, who expressly said that singers should not 'drag or drawl the voice through all the intermediate intervals, an abuse that is frequently committed'.[23] But perhaps Garcia actually sheds light on what Vaccai means: it is possible that both teachers are making a similar point in different ways and that the difference between them is one of degree rather than perception. Garcia goes on to say:

The time occupied by a slur should be taken from the last portion of the note quitted; and its rapidity will depend on the kind of expression required by any passage in which it occurs. This dragging of the notes will assist in equalising the registers, timbre and power of the voice.[24]

[20] Garcia, *New Treatise*: 51.   [21] Ibid.: 10.   [22] Ibid.

[23] Nicola Vaccai, *Metodo Pratico di Canto Italiano per Carvera in 15 Lezioni e un'Appendice* (1833) trans. and ed. Michael Aspinall (Turin: Giancarlo Zedde, 1999): 32.

[24] Garcia, *New Treatise*: 10.

Garcia then says that it is very difficult to determine when portamento should be used but that it will always work 'whenever, in passionate passages, the voice drags itself on under the influence of a strong
or tender sentiment', supporting his words with a quotation from Act
I, scene 2 from *Don Giovanni*. This confirms Corri's remarks linking
portamento use with text declamation; what he seems to be hinting at
is what we might think of as emotional management. It is some half a
century before concepts of verismo give singers and composers permission to behave in a pseudo-realistic way, but the vocal wherewithal to
do this is already in place. Garcia's final example is of how *not* to do it,
part of an aria from Meyerbeer's *Robert le Diable* in which every note is
slurred and 'the melody becomes nauseously languid'.[25] This dismissive
epithet is a pejorative equivalent of 'dragging', a term used by many writers (including Garcia, as we have seen) and which clearly implies some
sort of tempo manipulation. For most singers and writers on the topic
today portamento is expressed as a pitch inflection and little attention is
given to the rhythmic implications. Changes in micro-tempo – rhythmic
inflections within syllables and words – are often what distinguish one
performance from another; the most communicative performances are
often subtly nuanced, enabling the singer to create an illusion of spoken
communication within the singing line. The 'dragging' element of portamento is therefore likely to be just as important as the nuancing of the
pitch; the singer has control of both pitch and rhythm for the time it
takes to express a word or phrase. Because it involves micro-changes in
the rhythmic structure it is impossible to notate conventionally, which
perhaps accounts for some of the mystery surrounding its use; in the
twenty-first century we do not have to analyse portamento in real time
and can call on printed spectrograms and notation programs which
enable us to transcribe vocal movements in minute detail. Garcia and
his predecessors were limited to the written word and the conventions of
nineteenth-century notation. It is relatively easy to show when to use a
portamento – a slur is perfectly adequate – and one can describe to some
extent the pitch change element; the rhythmic aspect, however, would be
impossible to notate both because the notation would be absurdly complex and because it presumably varied from singer to singer and from
performance to performance. It is not surprising that so many writers
conclude their explanations by urging their readers to go and hear it for
themselves as it can only be captured very generally in print.

[25] Ibid.: 53.

Both Garaudé and Garcia discuss a new and more powerful way of singing that involves lowering the larynx, a technique that may have assisted Gilbert-Louis Duprez on his way to his famous top C, the *ut de poitrine*. Garaudé mentions in a footnote that a surgeon at Lyon has discovered a new type of voice called *sombre*, brought onto the lyric scene a few years ago by an unidentified *chanteur célèbre* (presumably Gilbert-Louis Duprez). This new sound world is accessed by 'tenant le menton un peu abaissé' (holding the chin a little lower). He says Garcia (*père*) and Rubini can mix it in effectively (*sombrée mixte*) but others risk loss of agility, tiredness and permanent damage. He considers it more violent than the 'natural voice' and advises singers to steer clear of it. He also observes, possibly for the first time in a didactic work, that some tenors are capable of singing the upper head voice range entirely in the *voix de poitrine*, although the exercises he gives take no account of this, taking tenors up to high D in head voice. He has several pages of exercises for each voice to join the chest, medium and head registers in the traditional way.

Garcia's writings on timbre are much more positive, and reveal a true understanding of the enormous potential that laryngeal manipulation has for singers who exploit the timbral possibilities of the different registers. The French editions of his treatise contain substantial footnotes in which he tried to explain the complexities of modifying the shape of the vocal tract to access both 'clear' and 'sombre' timbres. The English edition is more succinct:

> the varieties of *timbre* will correspond to the multitudinous mechanical changes of which the vocal tube is susceptible. We shall understand these movements of the pharynx, if we consider it as a deep and highly elastic pipe, beginning below at the larynx, forming a curve at the arch of the palate, and ending above at the mouth; a tube, which, when at its shortest dimensions, forms only a slight curve, and, at its longest, nearly a right angle, the larynx in the first case rising towards the soft palate, dropping to meet it; whereas in the second case, the larynx drops and the soft palate rises, thus making the distance between them greater. The short and gently curved shape produces the bright timbre, while the sombre is caused by the lengthened and strongly curved form.[26]

He understands the basic acoustic phenomena and he realises that the low larynx position somehow leads to increased vocal efficiency. He sees huge advantages in the new technique, especially for male voices, reducing the need for falsetto at the top, facilitating the joining of registers and accessing a much wider range of tone colours. In essence what Garcia is talking about is the basis of modern classical singing. Modern science

[26] Ibid.: 5.

can now account for his astonishment at the gains in acoustic efficiency: we now know that by increasing the length of the vocal tract singers gain access to extra resonance. The acoustic space in the pharynx contains a number of formants which in effect multiply the frequencies and create resonance; the so-called singers' formant is an extra resonance in a frequency range which enables voices to carry over a symphony orchestra with no extra effort.[27]

In the tradition of Hiller, Corri and others, Garcia provides musical examples by Cimarosa, Crescentini, Morlacchi and Rossini which show the difference between what appears in the score and what singers should actually sing. Garcia's annotations are minutely detailed, and by studying them we can imagine singing in the generation or two before we can actually hear recordings. The most striking thing is the glorious rhetorical extravagance – in an age in which so many commentators value simplicity and restraint. All of the models have a great deal of rewriting, which is something we could probably predict from the kinds of exercises in any treatise of the period, but the paralinguistic elements which are usually taken for granted are here illustrated in melodramatic detail. Not only is each emotional nuance described, but also the means of realising it vocally: energetic portamenti, changes of tempo, inhaled and exhaled sobbing, gasping, laughing, 'outbursts of the soul'. If this represents nineteenth-century restraint, one can only wonder at what a castrato would have done with Cimarosa a hundred years before.

TECHNIQUE AND STYLE POST-GARCIA

Garcia's lasting fame has been due to the resonance that much of his teaching had for singers in the twentieth century. He has had his detractors (especially over the so-called *coup de glotte* or vocal onset that was misunderstood by many not taught by him) and his true position in the pedagogical pantheon is not easy to determine. His seminal publications came at a time of perceived and actual change in important aspects of singing, and his writings and teaching were a crucial link between the old virtuosity of the past and the (relatively) restrained dramatic efficiency of the future. Although he came to symbolise the state of the art, we should remember that many of his fellow Conservatoire pedagogues would have taught a similar regime even if their publications are not so meticulously

[27] On the singer's formant see Johan Sundberg, *The Science of the Singing Voice* (Dekalb, IL: Northen Illinois University Press, 1987): 123–4.

detailed. Gilbert-Louis Duprez and Laure Cinti-Damoreau were examples of highly successful stars who taught at the Conservatoire. Duprez's *L'Art du Chant* of 1846[28] is quite a radical departure, and as befits the first tenor to return to earth from previously unrecorded heights, recognises two distinct styles, those of strength and agility. For all Duprez's modernity, agility is still important, and he gives helpful examples of famous singers' (often very elaborate) cadenzas.

Laure Cinti-Damoreau, who created the leading soprano roles in all Rossini's Paris operas, joined the staff in 1833 and continued to teach there until 1856; she must have known Garcia well (as a sixteen-year-old she had sung in Garcia *père's Caliph of Baghdad*). The exercises in her *Méthode de Chant Composée pour ses Classes du Conservatoire* of 1849 address many of the traditional devices and techniques that Garcia deals with, but its function as a publication is rather different.[29] Apart from the introductory remarks addressed to her students there is very little comment or instruction: the book is (as its title suggests) a resource designed to be used in her classes, with instruction given by the teacher. Cinti-Damoreau was, of course, famous for her coloratura, and it was the secrets of her agility that the committee of the Conservatoire hoped she would impart to the students. The final section of her treatise is devoted to specimen cadenzas from specific operas, and her teaching must have focused on these as the ultimate goal for her pupils. Garcia, however, explained the process, and in the second half of the century the explications of a vocal scientist came to be valued more than the exercises of a successful practitioner.

Garcia's pupils included some of the most famous singers of the nineteenth century, and although we can trace a line of succession through those of his students who became teachers themselves (especially in the students of Mathilde Marchesi), when we try to hear the evidence of his teaching in the recordings made by his students, so individual are all the first singers to record that it is impossible to identify traits in any of them as being specifically Garcian.[30] Mathilde Marchesi (*née* Graumann) was

[28] Gilbert-Louis Duprez, *L'Art du Chant* (Paris, 1846).
[29] Laure Cinti-Damoreau, *Méthode de Chant* (Paris, 1849); repr. as Laure-Cinthie Damoreau, *Classic Bel Canto Technique* (New York: Dover, 1997).
[30] Philip Miller, in his introduction to the reprint of Mathilde Marchesi's *Method* (New York: Dover, 1970) and Henry Pleasants in *The Great Singers* (London: Victor Gollancz, 1967): 272 claim to detect similarities of technique in the recordings of Melba, Calvé and Eames, but evenness of tone, easy agility and precise tuning are to be found in many of the first singers to record, including the students of other noted nineteenth-century teachers such as Lamperti and Delle Sedie. George Bernard Shaw was among those unconvinced either by Garcia's teaching or traces of its survival in his students; see his *Music in London*, vol. II (London: Constable, 1932): 226.

a German mezzo-soprano who came late to singing and found her true métier to be in teaching rather than performing. She is only known to have appeared in one opera but toured extensively with a concert repertoire, often with her husband, tenor Salvatore Marchesi. In terms of status, she was probably the most authoritative teacher after Garcia and was an indefatigable promoter of his methods. She taught only women in her Parisian school, including Nellie Melba, Emma Calvé and Emma Eames, who all had successful careers on both sides of the Atlantic. Her *Theoretical and Practical Vocal Method*,[31] like Cinti-Damoreau's, has very little in the way of instruction, and is designed to be used with a teacher (as well as to impress those not fortunate enough to study with her). Both handbooks have *messa di voce* and portamento exercises though Marchesi has a very limited selection of agility exercises, possibly because she herself had very limited experience of the stage, or perhaps because she was more in tune with the changing times. Jenny Lind studied for an intensive ten months with Garcia in 1841–2, during which he cured her of stamina problems resulting from a lack of serious training. Many years later one Professor Bystrom, involved in the setting up of the Stockholm Conservatorium in 1868, asked her advice about teaching. In her reply Lind played down Garcia's influence ('I have taught myself to sing, Garcia could only teach me a few things')[32] but wrote a few pages describing her method, describing portamento, trilling and the importance of a sound breathing technique.

Although both portamento and agility are still dealt with in most treatises, we can detect an increasing ambivalence towards portamento as well as the usual hostility to excessive ornament. But these are only two of the symptoms of change that overtook many aspects of singing during the century. The tenor voice changed out of all recognition, as the old castrato-based teaching gave way to tenors taught by other tenors who were beginning to discover the power that could be unleashed by continuing upwards in chest voice the upper part of their range for which they would traditionally have used falsetto. Baritones began to explore the upper limits of the non-tenorial bass voice, and singing became louder and less refined in all voices as performers sacrificed agility and elegance to the power and richness of tone that could be achieved by lowering the larynx. The proliferation of opera houses, concert halls and conservatories

[31] Mathilde Marchesi, *Bel Canto: a Theoretical and Practical Vocal Method* (New York: Dover, 1970).
[32] V. M. Holmstrom, 'Jenny Lind's Singing Method', *The Musical Quarterly* 3:4 (1917): 548. Lind's letters 1841–2 are considerably more enthusiastic; see Sterling Mackinlay, *Garcia the Centenarian and his Times* (London, 1908): 139–55.

(not to mention the vast numbers of drawing-rooms that contained a piano) perhaps meant more singers of a certain standard and less individuality; orchestras became larger and instruments louder and more efficient. Not everyone liked it; Berlioz, journalist and often caustic observer of the musical scene mid-century, blames the public ('sharks that follow ships and are caught by fishermen: both the bait and the hook'), the size and acoustic deficiencies of theatres (box office is everything), modern orchestration (especially Rossini's use of percussive effects), rising pitch and tessitura, and the tendency of singers to bawl ('volume has become the primary aim. To obtain it nuances must be left out').[33] Berlioz frequently complained about the sheer noise made by orchestras mid-century, and Rossini's orchestration was hardly subtle.

Yet the didactic literature taken as a whole retains many of the concepts that would be familiar to a singer of the seventeenth century. These writings are inevitably conservative and are unlikely to reflect the actual state of singing with 100 per cent accuracy: almost all writers refer to the 'old Italian school' and are likely at least to pay lip service to its most treasured tenets as a matter of principle. The school became 'old' in the sense of redundant when composers from Rossini onwards expected to hear much more of what they wrote in their scores and a lot less of singers' attempts to improve them (though how successful Rossini was in attempting to give singers less room for ornamental manoeuvre is a matter for debate: Austin Caswell has shown that in ornamenting Bellini Laure Cinti-Damoreau would add more *fioriture* to passages that were already complex, and fewer to simpler sections).[34] But once ownership of the music passed to the composer, the entire pedagogical edifice was living on borrowed time. Cadenzas in music that required them remained improvised though reduced in scale and length, but the new dramaturgy had little use for ornament for its own sake.

Wagner himself and Rossini before him still considered agility training essential if singers were to have complete control of their voices, but both were in agreement that singers needed to be curbed. Verdi too wanted as little creativity as he could get away with, though as Will Crutchfield has shown he very rarely got only what was in his scores.[35] Their reasons

[33] His essay, originally published in *Débats*, 6 February 1853 on the occasion of a performance of Verdi's *Luisa Miller*, is translated as 'The Current State of the Art of Singing', in Berlioz, *The Art of Music*: 58–68.

[34] Austin Caswell, 'Mme Cinti-Damoreau and the Embellishment of Italian Opera in Paris: 1820–1845', *Journal of the American Musicological Society*, 28 (1975): 459–92.

[35] Will Crutchfield, 'Vocal Ornamentation in Verdi: the Phonographic Evidence', *19th-Century Music* 7:1(1983): 3–54.

were slightly different: Rossini was acutely aware that the demise of the castrati, especially as teachers, had changed the nature of virtuosic singing for the worse. The first performances of his operas had been created by some of the greatest virtuosi and the composer was happy to leave ornamentation to these supreme experts. As performances multiplied and singing declined (Rossini cites the replacement of the old private academies by institutional conservatories as another major cause) he came to loathe second-rate singers swamping his music with what he considered to be tasteless divisions. For Rossini it was largely a matter of taste and judgment: the singing he describes as 'bel canto' would be recognisable by Tosi or any of the old castrato teachers and studying its method would inevitably create singers of incredible virtuosity; but they had to know when to stop. Wagner, in his famous (though possibly fictional) encounter with Rossini in 1860, showed a similar hatred of virtuosity for its own sake, but his objections were determined by his vision of opera in which all of the arts were in the service of the drama. The future of music would ideally dispense with the librettist, and with the very idea of the composer 'illustrating' the text; the formal set pieces of *opera seria* and *opera buffa* would be replaced by a dramaturgical logic; dramatic declamation would in time replace pointless virtuosity. Wagner spoke with incredulity of:

those bravura arias, those insipid duets fatally manufactured on the same model, how many other hors d'oeuvres that interrupt the stage action without reason! Then the septets![36]

in which characters would set aside their roles and all stand in a line across the stage to sing the same thing. In future singers would be known for the skill with which they characterised their roles rather than merely for their ability to get round the notes.

Merely standing on stage to sing and then either leaving or remaining to stand around without movement or any other sign of genuine dramatic engagement with the action could no longer be tolerated.

WAGNER'S VOCAL VISION

As far as Wagner's legacy to singing is concerned, a polarity may be perceived between the hypothesis that his art, taken to its logical conclusions, could result in an opera in which the role of singing would be drastically altered, even minimal, and the rather less fanciful reality now that

---

[36] Edmond Michotte, *Richard Wagner's Visit to Rossini (Paris 1860)*, trans. Herbert Weinstock (University of Chicago Press, 1968): 57.

the Wagnerian volcano has surely ceased its major eruptions. There are many myths surrounding Wagner's use of the voice, mostly concerning the strains on the singers (considered potentially fatal after the death of Schnorr von Carolsfeld, the first Tristan). The major roles make enormous demands with a very physical preparation. Within minutes of appearing for the first time in the *Ring* cycle Brünnhilde must change from a high soprano to a mezzo. For long stretches, she (and other characters) must remain silent (though still, of course, acting) only then to launch into some very demanding singing, without much chance to warm up. It is in such matters of control and pacing that the real challenge lies, rather than the misconception that Wagner's orchestra is too loud for his singers. His vision was not immediately apparent to Wagner's first performers. The first performance (in Magdeburg, 1836) of one of the early operas *Das Liebesverbot* was a disaster, and the work was later disowned by its composer. Drawing on Wagner's reminiscences in his autobiography *Mein Leben*, Robert Gutman gives the following account of that first night: 'The leading tenor [Freimüller], as his memory failed, hid behind an enormous feather boa and came up with bits and pieces of Auber and Hérold to fill the gaps.'[37] Gutman blames lack of rehearsal time, forced by the bankruptcy of the company. The second night was even worse than the first, with hardly anyone turning up to see the opera. The behaviour among the singers was even more lurid, with the husband of the leading soprano (Karoline Pollert) attacking and wounding the second tenor (Schreiber) backstage, suspecting him of being his wife's lover. 'As the victim fled, dripping blood, she, racing in to stop the fracas, also received her husband's hand and immediately succumbed to convulsions.'[38]

It was a singer none the less whom Wagner credited for his true artistic awakening: Wilhelmine Schröder-Devrient, the daughter of the baritone Friedrich Schröder and Germany's greatest tragedienne Sophie Bürger Schröder. Brought up as a child of the theatre (as a fifteen-year-old she played Ophelia among many other stage roles) she made her singing debut in Vienna at the age of sixteen, playing Pamina in Mozart's *Die Zauberflöte*. Her voice was impressive, but never having had the full pedagogical rigour applied to it she often struggled in the more florid Bellini and Donizetti roles. It was her performance as Leonore in Beethoven's *Fidelio* that established her reputation as a dramatic soprano, and so impressed the sixteen-year-old Wagner in 1829; she stood out from other

---

[37] Robert Gutman, *Richard Wagner: the Man, His Mind and His Music* (London: Penguin Books, 1971): 91.
[38] Ibid.: 91–2.

singers by achieving what was to become the central ideal of Wagnerian singing: the matching of vocal prowess with equal dramatic skill, making her a genuine singing actress. Henry Chorley saw both her and Malibran as Leonore, and 'the Spaniard threw more horror into the scene in the vault than her predecessor, but the German is before me when, in the introduction to the Chorus of Prisoners, as they creep out of their cells, she questioned one ghastly face after another, with the heart-piercing wistfulness of hope long deferred'.[39]

Wagner's first success, *Rienzi* (1842), had her singing the part of Adriano, with another icon of early Wagnerian singing, Joseph Tichatschek, in the title role. As her career advanced, the flaws in her vocal technique became more apparent and even her acting skills were thought to have lapsed into exaggeration, so her creation of three major Wagnerian roles (Adriano in *Rienzi*, Senta in *Der fliegende Holländer* and Venus in *Tannhäuser*) actually came during her period of relative decline. At the time of the ill-fated *Das Liebesverbot*, Wagner seemed, uncharacteristically, almost ashamed of his German-ness and instead espoused the traditional Italian way of doing things. He had been inspired by hearing Schröder-Devrient in Bellini's *Montecchi e Capuleti* (in 1834) and noted that what had saved her voice from ruin was the study of Italian vocal technique.[40] His admiration of Bellini and Italian vocal technique endured, as did that of Wilhelmine Schröder-Devrient, though their relationship was stormy. She lived a full life, with three marriages and many lovers, and rehearsals were never easy; her calling in of a loan she made to Wagner to enable the publication of his operas almost forced him into bankruptcy. But he never forgot the debt he owed to her art, his appreciation expressed as late as the 1870s more than ten years after her death, in essays such as 'Über die Bestimmung der Oper' ('On the Destiny of Opera') of 1871, and more especially in 'Über Schauspieler und Sänger' ('On Actors and Singers') of 1872, actually dedicated to her memory. In this essay Wagner gave a moving and detailed critical evaluation of her art:

Concerning this artist I have again and again been asked if her *voice* was really so remarkable, since we glorified her as a singer – the voice being all folk seem to think about in such a case. It constantly annoyed me to answer this question, for I revolted against the thought of the great tragedian being thrown into one bevy with the female castrati of our Opera. Were it asked once more to-day, I should answer somewhat as follows: – No! She had no 'voice' at all; but she

[39] Chorley, *Recollections*: 9.
[40] Ernest Newman, *Wagner as Man and Artist* (2nd edn, London: Victor Gollancz, 1924; repr. 1963): 189.

knew how to use her breath so beautifully, and to let a true womanly soul stream forth in such wondrous sounds, that we never thought of either voice or singing! Moreover, she had the gift of teaching a composer how to compose, to be worth the pains of such a woman's 'singing': this she did through that 'example' afore-said, which she, the mime, gave this time to the dramatist, and which, among all to whom she gave it, has been followed by *myself* alone.[41]

Wilhelmine Schröder-Devrient's special balance of singing and acting put her in a class of her own and she must be viewed as something of an exception. From time to time composers have been drawn to charismatic performers for whom acting was of equal importance to singing; Virginia Adreini singing Monteverdi's Arianna, and Mrs Cibber singing Handel's 'He was despised' were perhaps the historical precedents for Schröder-Devrient.

Schröder-Devrient's colleague at the Dresden Hofoper was Joseph Tichatschek. He had studied in Vienna with Ciccimarra and developed a voice noted for its beauty and ability to sing both lyric and dramatic tenor parts. Paving the way for the Wagner Heldentenor (a term closely associated with Wagner, though not actually used by him), Tichatschek created the title role not only of *Rienzi* but also of *Tannhäuser* (1845) and later added the part of Lohengrin to his repertoire. Wagner admired his glorious voice and musicianship but had strong reservations about his dramatic range. Thus he was clearly something of an opposite of Schröder-Devrient and had his own uniqueness in a technique which enabled him to produce the traditional ideal of fine singing. Among the major singers associated with the living Wagner only Tichatschek seems to have pos-sessed the consistent ability to produce the much-vaunted true legato. He was not much of an actor, however, though by all accounts uncommonly genial. Berlioz writes revealingly of his experience with 'the famous tenor' in Dresden on the occasion of a performance of his *Requiem*:

Tichatschek ... has a pure and charming voice which in the theatre, under the stimulus of dramatic action, takes on uncommon warmth and energy. His style is simple and tasteful; he is a most accomplished musician and reader. He at once agreed to sing the solo in the Sanctus without having seen it, and with-out frowning or making excuses or generally acting the god. He could, as so many do in such circumstances, have accepted the Sanctus on condition that he be allowed to throw in some pet cavatina to ensure a personal success, but he refrained. What about that![42]

[41] Richard Wagner, *Actors and Singers*, trans. William Ashton Ellis (Lincoln: University of Nebraska Press, 1995): 219.
[42] David Cairns (ed.), *The Memoirs of Hector Berlioz* ((London: Victor Gollancz, 1969): 301.

The male singer closest to Wagner's heart and in his way on a par with Wilhelmine Schröder-Devrient was Ludwig Schnorr von Carolsfeld. He sang many Wagnerian roles (including Erik, in *Der fliegende Holländer*, Tannhäuser and Lohengrin) but is forever associated with Tristan. Schnorr and his wife Malvina Garrigues took the title roles in the famous Munich première (1865) of *Tristan und Isolde*, conducted by Hans von Bülow. Wagner's original choices for the roles were Albert Niemann and Luise Dustmann-Meyer but after numerous changes of plan, including where the opera was actually to be staged, and the initial refusal by the Schnorr couple to take part (fearing the exceptional demands of the roles) but especially on hearing Ludwig Schnorr as Lohengrin, Wagner settled on the historic casting. The fears of the couple turned out to be justified. The strain singing Tristan imposed on Ludwig, especially in the third act where the hero sings some of Wagner's most impassioned and technically demanding music while lying on his deathbed, led to a feverish chill which in turn developed into something fatal (possibly gout spreading to the brain, or typhoid). In his own delirium and on his own deathbed this first interpreter of Tristan is reputed to have burst into song, calling the name not of Isolde but of Wagner. For his part Wagner was deeply affected, both at the loss of a young man for whom he had a genuine affection but also of a singer whose artistry he greatly valued. He was also keenly aware of the part he had played in bringing about the tragic loss. Although conceding that Schnorr was not the equal of Tichatschek in terms of vocal ability Wagner considered him vastly superior in dramatic power and performing intelligence. In her turn Malvina was devastated by Schnorr's death, and subsequently abandoned her career, which had been built on a solid technique nurtured by the younger Manuel Garcia.[43]

In his study of the difficult early history of *Tristan und Isolde* and its singers, William Ashbrook points out that the Schnorrs had strong lower registers: Malvina was as much mezzo as soprano and Ludwig was often described in reviews as *baritonartig*. 'This baritonal foundation is a point of resemblance between Schnorr and a number of later Wagnerian tenors.[44] Not only does this affect our perception of the roles in themselves and of the true nature of Wagnerian singing, but it also touches on the relationship of the title roles to other parts in the work:

To consider the implications of Wagner's casting of the first *Tristan* performances is to find several ways in which later traditions of performance differ. The most

[43] For a fuller account of the Wagner–Schnorr relationship see John Potter, *Tenor: History of a Voice* (New Haven: Yale University Press, 2009): 62–6.
[44] William Ashbrook, 'The First Singers of *Tristan und Isolde*', *The Opera Quarterly* 3:4 (1985/6): 14.

striking of these are the use of a high soprano, rather than a mezzo-soprano, for Brangäne, and a baritone rather than a bass for King Marke.[45]

In both cases Wagner seemed to have wanted to suggest that the characters were much more youthful than is commonly supposed.[46]

Although radical and disruptive in many ways, *Tristan und Isolde* did not alter Wagner's fundamental beliefs in what constituted good singing, expressed in various ways and at various points throughout his career. That he regarded singing as central to his art and not some kind of add-on to a protracted symphony is proved by his concept of *melos*, which he defined as a *singing* (our emphasis) style, guiding the tempo and shaping the melodic phrases, through rubato and accent.[47] The two main tensions seem to be between singing versus acting and singing versus orchestral music. The mistake can lie simply in removing singing from each, making Wagner's art acting and declamation with an orchestral underpinning. Wagner had much to say on these topics and also on singing as singing. If he attached so much significance for his own work to the skills of Wilhelmine Schröder-Devrient it is clear that the balance of singing and acting was crucial, and in many ways it determined the whole history of Wagnerian singing. In *Actors and Singers* Wagner used the term *Mime* to signify both the actor and the singer, indicating that this balance should in fact be a unity. To bring about opera's 'entire new-birth' singers would have to be taken back 'to the starting-point of their so degenerated art, to where we find them acting still as players'. The mixture of 'our own stage-singer' with the Italian opera singer had led to 'the senseless opera-screaming (*Opernsingerei*) of to-day'.[48]

The importance Wagner attached to beautiful, well-trained voices meant that if forced to choose between a singer of intelligence and poor voice and one of less intelligence but better voice he would be inclined to pick the latter. An understanding and clear enunciation of the text did not mean declamation rather than singing. Wagner took pains to notate the details and to rehearse the singers in their realisation, in an effort to secure both clear enunciation and beauty of sound. Entirely typically, he saw himself as some kind of liberator, even redeemer, in this case of singers. If Michotte's account of the meeting with Rossini in 1860 is to be believed, Wagner told the veteran master of Italian opera:

As for the singers, whose resistance you raised to me as an objection, they will have to submit, to accept a situation that, what is more, will elevate them. When

---

[45] Ibid.: 20.   [46] Ibid.: 21–2.

[47] Christopher Fifield, 'Conducting Wagner: The Search for Melos', in Barry Millington and Stewart Spencer (eds.), *Wagner in Performance* (New Haven and London: Yale University Press, 1992): 1

[48] Wagner, *Actors and Singers*: 201.

they have understood that the lyric drama in its new form will furnish them, not, it is true, with the elements of easy success owing either to the strength of their lungs or to the advantages of a charming voice – they will understand that nevertheless the art demands a much higher mission from them. Forced to stop isolating themselves inside the personal limitations of their role, they will identify themselves with both the philosophic and the esthetic spirit dominating the work. They will live, if I may express myself this way, in an atmosphere in which – *everything contributing to the whole* – nothing should remain secondary. Further, broken of the habit of ephemeral success through fleeting virtuosity, delivered from the torment of having to expand their voices on insipid words lined up in banal rhymes – they will understand how it will have become possible for them to surround their names with a more glorious and durable aureole when they will be incarnating the characters they represent by complete penetration – from the psychological and human point of view – of their *raison d'être* in the drama; when they will base themselves on deepened studies of the ideas, customs, character of the period in which the action occurs; when they will join irreproachable diction to the prestige of masterly declamation, full of truth and nobility.[49]

Beyond all these precedents Wagner sought to reinvent the opera singer, in a new relationship to his reinvented orchestra – ideally invisible, as at Bayreuth, where hiding the orchestra would not only change its sound but also its role and inevitably impact on the sound and role of the singers, placing them visually even more at the centre of the drama without fear of being drowned by the orchestra. Singing standards and technique had been at the forefront of opera's development and the orchestra now had to catch up and create a new relationship:

The Opera has given us singers, *i.e.* vocal virtuosi on the stage, and in the orchestra a gradually increasing tale of instrumentalists to accompany the singing of those virtuosi: with the growth of the orchestra's skill and importance there consequently arose the critical axiom, that of these two factors the orchestra should properly supply the "pedestal," the singer the "statue," and that it was wrong to wish to set the pedestal upon the stage, the statue in the orchestra, as happened when the latter took too prominent a part. This comparison itself betrays the whole misconstitution of the operatic genre: for there to be any talk of statues and pedestals, one at most can think of the icy rhetoric of French Tragédie, or the no less cold Italian-operatic vocalism of castrati of the eighteenth century; but when one comes to living Drama all analogy with sculpture ceases, for its mother-element is only to be sought in Music, out of which alone was born the Tragic Artwork.[50]

---

[49] Quoted in Michotte, *Wagner's Visit*: 66–7. There is one small point where Wagner may have overlooked a crucial feature of at least the *Ring* dramas: the singers could hardly study the period in which the action occurs, as the essence of myth is that it is timeless.
[50] Wagner, *Actors and Singers*: 198.

Even though the innovative design of the Bayreuth *Festspielhaus* has never lost its power to impress both performers and audiences, an ideal acoustical balance between singers and orchestra was not achieved automatically from the outset. Heinrich Porges, who was present at the rehearsals for the 1876 première of the *Ring* cycle at Bayreuth, noted that it was far from plain sailing and also made a remark on the drama-versus-symphony question that flies in the face of Newman's assertion quoted earlier:

The stage rehearsals of the *Ring* brought home the imperative need to moderate dynamic expression-marks, convert fortissimos into fortes, fortes into mezzo-fortes etc., in order to ensure that the singers' words and inflections make their proper impact. We must never be allowed to forget that we are attending a dramatic performance which seeks to imitate reality; we are not listening to a purely symphonic work … Wagner declared that the orchestra should support the singer as the sea does a boat, rocking but never upsetting or swamping – he employed that image over and over again.[51]

In *Actors and Singers* Wagner provided his own potted history of singing (at least in the 250 years of opera that had preceded him). He was scathing of the earliest form, giving rise to the recitative, the tedium of which led to the singer's reward of opportunities for vocal fireworks with no dramatic significance (divorced from the text), spawning a kind of specialisation eventually to become the domain of the castrati. Such things were not for the Germans and remained foreign even when skilfully handled by German masters. Even Gluck's celebrated reform of opera 'had no permanent result in the formation of a healthy German-operatic style'. To redeem the German singer of his day from bad habits Wagner's 'compulsorily simple plan was to make him really and distinctly speak in singing, whilst I brought the lines of musical curvature [*die Linien der Gesangsbewegung*] to his consciousness by getting him to take in one breath, with perfectly even intonation, the calmer, lengthier periods on which he formerly had expended a number of gusty respirations'.[52] This sounds like the exact opposite of what became known, soon after Wagner's death, as the 'Bayreuth bark', as it advocates the sustained line and accurate intonation of bel canto and eschews the bursts of emphatic declamation verging on shouting, characteristic of the 'bark'. His singers would have

---

[51] Heinrich Porges, *Wagner Rehearsing the 'Ring': An Eye-Witness Account of the Stage Rehearsals of the First Bayreuth Festival*, trans. Robert L. Jacobs (Cambridge University Press, 1983; originally published in German as *Die Bühnenproben zu den Bayreuther Festspielen des Jahres 1876*, in instalments in *Bayreuther Blätter*, 1881–1896): 12–13.

[52] Wagner, *Actors and Singers*: 201–4.

instinctively applied portamento (and vibrato too) in the time-honoured way that their training required them to do. Wagner occasionally indicated both vibrato and portamento and these would mean in addition to what would come naturally to the singers. He continued to advocate traditional vocal technique and meticulous attention to its expression, and although there is no room for substantial singerly additions Wagner clearly expected the customary trills, mordents and appoggiaturas that singers would expect to apply. Lotte Lehmann famously recalled how her teacher Mathilde Mallinger (the first Eva of *Die Meistersinger von Nürnberg* in 1868) had introduced a trill during rehearsals. Wagner's reaction was far from indignant at this liberty with his score: 'Let her have her fun. We'll keep the trill since Mallinger likes it so much.'[53]

If the art of Wagnerian singing, especially in *Tristan* and the *Ring* cycle, brought problems to the singers and frustration to the composer, its subsequent history was no less controversial. David Breckbill tentatively suggests a four-part division, starting with the period within the composer's own lifetime, continuing with the period after his death up to the years between the two world wars, then the interwar years themselves, and finally the period since 1940, viewed by Breckbill as 'a prolonged, gradual, but decisive decline'.[54] Breckbill questions first the assumption that the first period must have been of the finest quality for the two reasons that Wagner himself was able to supervise the preparation of roles and the singers he assembled were uniformly fine: 'While Wagner was alive, the diversity of the singers he chose went largely unnoticed.'[55] Wagner's experience with Georg Unger was not untypical: the crucial role of Siegfried in the 1876 Bayreuth première of the *Ring* cycle was given to Unger, of whom Wagner (desperate to find a new Schnorr) had great hopes following the tenor's lessons with Julius Hey (even to the extent of floating the idea of an Unger Tristan the following year) but Unger was deemed not to be a success and the Unger Tristan never materialised.[56] The evidence of recordings is the obvious means of assessing what Wagnerian singing has sounded like over its 150 or so years, and we have recordings of five singers who sang in the 1876 and 1882 Bayreuth Festivals: Lilli Lehmann, Marianne Brandt (one of three Kundrys in 1882), Hermann Winkelmann

---

[53] Lotte Lehmann, *Wings of Song* (London, 1938): 77.
[54] David Breckbill, 'Wagner on Record: Re-evaluating Singing in the Early Years', in Millington and Spencer, *Wagner in Performance*: 156.
[55] Ibid.: 162.
[56] Wagner's letter to Unger of 1 January 1876 in *Selected Letters of Richard Wagner*, trans. Stewart Spencer and Barry Millington (New York: Norton, 1987): 851–2.

(the first of three Parsifals in 1882), Luise Belce and Adolf von Hübbenet. There are also recordings of Gustav Walter who sang under Wagner in 1862, and Julius Lieban who seems to have impressed him; these singers were, of course, well past their prime.[57]

Wagner never did discover another Schnorr von Carolsfeld, but perhaps more importantly he did find a kindred spirit in the singing teacher and coach Julius Hey. Hey was a cultivated man who had studied art and was never himself a performer, but he understood, as few of Wagner's acquaintances seemed to, that there was nothing incompatible between the fundamentals of traditional Italian technique and Wagner's ideas of a dramatic declamation articulated by beautiful singing. Hey became the chief coach of Wagner's singers until the composer's death in 1883, and the decline (as many would see it) in Wagner singing can be dated to Cosima Wagner appointing Julius Kniese as Hey's replacement. Kniese, appointed by Cosima as head of her new opera school in 1892, was largely responsible for the distortion of Wagner's ideal, later referred to as *Sprechgesang* (speech-song), into the much-maligned Bayreuth style at the end of the century.[58] Hey was a major interpreter of Wagnerian singing, not just through his association with the composer from 1864 and his involvement as singing adviser in the first Bayreuth festival, but also through his primer on German singing and memoirs of Wagner covering that period.[59]

The primer may have illustrated Wagner's perception of a difference between the Italian and German styles, but it never desisted from emphasising the importance of bel canto and even claimed that there was no aspect of Italian technique that could not be developed by the German school. Assuming that Wagner would not have approved of these developments at Bayreuth seems borne out by reports that he predicted the

[57] See Breckbill, 'Wagner on Record' 157ff.; Lilli Lehmann (no connection with the aforementioned Lotte Lehmann) had a close personal relationship with Wagner. She was the daughter of Marie Löwe, a harp player and singer, who was also 'an old flame of his Leipzig days' (Gutman, *Richard Wagner*: 90). Löwe worked with Wagner during his time at Magdeburg and Königsberg in the 1830s. Wagner later met her and the teenage Lilli in Prague in 1863 and showed the kind of interest in the girl, to the point of suggesting adoption, all too familiar to her more knowing mother (ibid.:324). The fact that both mother and daughter were Jewish should not escape mention (ibid.: 578).

[58] Jens Malte Fischer, '*Sprechgesang* or Bel Canto: Toward a History of Singing Wagner', trans. Michael Tanner in Ulrich Müller and Peter Wapnewski (eds.), *Wagner Handbook* (Cambridge, MA: Harvard University Press, 1992): 527–8.

[59] (*Deutscher Gesangs-Unterricht*, 3 vols. Mainz, 1884; *Richard Wagner als Vortragsmeister, 1864–1876: Erinnerungen*, Leipzig, 1911). The condensed version of Hey's treatise *Die Kunst des Sprechens* (The Art of Speaking), known as *Der kleine Hey*, was first published in 1900. The current (Mainz: Schott & Co., 1997) edition is still used as the basis of much German singing teaching.

decline to Julius Hey in 1875, remarking that the ideal of speech-song would become perverted into intensified speech, moreover to lose in the unequal combat with the orchestra. Some singers went down the Kniese route: Pelagie Greef-Andriessen, Anton van Rooy and Theodor Bertram, a singularly powerful baritone, sacrificed legato to emphatic enunciation of each consonant and syllable, but the tenor Leo Slezak (also known as a Mozart singer) complained that both Cosima Wagner and Julius Kniese expected the Bayreuth singers to sing with full voice at every rehearsal, until their voices were exhausted. Away from Bayreuth there was genuine Wagner singing to be heard, from Johanna Gadski, the contralto Ernestine Schumann-Heink, Leo Slezak and Jacques Urlus.

The beginnings of the so-called Bayreuth bark ('bell' canto from the German *bellen* to bark) can be traced firmly to the composer's widow and her vocal coach, both of whom either misunderstood or wilfully misrepresented Wagner's vocal vision. We should remember that all of Wagner's singers were traditionally trained, and had to sing the standard repertoire in the traditional way, so they could not afford to sing in ways that might harm their voices; the concept of the dedicated Heldentenor would not exist until well into the next century. Erik Schmedes and Ernest van Dyck were two tenors who felt unhappy at the coaching given to them by Kniese (though both returned for more). The letters from Cosima Wagner to Ernest van Dyck in connection with his proposed engagement at Bayreuth are especially illuminating. In 1888, having heard him in Karlsruhe, she writes:

Concerning the language ... we cannot make the slightest concession at Bayreuth. Our stage differs from all other operatic stages in Germany in having drama as the centre of all the performances that are there given. We look upon music as the means, not the end. Drama is the end, and the organ of drama is language. In Vienna an impeded pronunciation, absence of freedom in expression, will not only not harm you but, up to a certain point, will obtain you the good graces of a public which still goes to the theatre retaining the old habits and traditions of the opera, a public which above all else wishes to hear singing. Here, our main preoccupation is to show the action, to make it as clear as possible by free and assured speech, and, if there must be sacrifice at all, to sacrifice rather the music (singing) to the poem than the poem (language) to the music.[60]

Later in the same letter she even suggests a performance of Parsifal without any music at all. Poor van Dyck, who only wanted to sing ...

---

[60] Henri de Curzon, 'Cosima Wagner and Bayreuth', *Musical Times*, 71:1051 (1930): 794–6.

NEW SINGING, ANCIENT TRADITION

The dichotomy experienced by Wagner's singers – having to give themselves over to a new kind of declamation that was still defining itself, while still maintaining their 'Italian' technique – is not visible in the pedagogical literature until much later. But by the end of the century the singer's world was far removed from the brilliant but uncertain era of the late baroque. Idiosyncratic virtuosity had been largely replaced by conventions that owed more to the requirements of the composer than to the creativity of the singer. Music was less often written with specific singers in mind, and more with an eye to a more generic kind of performance and the maximum number of repetitions: the role was becoming more significant than the singer who performed it, and the essential aspects of each role were transferable from performer to performer and did not require rewriting to accommodate singerly whim or vocal idiosyncrasy. There was a profession to which singers could aspire, and it was underpinned by an institutionalised pedagogy. With so much that was new compared with what we know of the singing of a hundred years before, we might reasonably expect to see significant changes in teaching regimes and published pedagogical material, yet much of the technical information found in treatises throughout the century is broadly similar. The nature and degree of *messa di voce*, portamento and rubato changed with fashion and taste, and we can never be completely sure of the meaning of these key terms at any given point before we can actually hear them. Explanations become more detailed in the nineteenth century: singers and teachers are more interested in *why* things work, and not just *how*.

By the end of the century there were still examples to be found of the old master–apprentice pedagogy, and of successful singers who had no teacher at all. There was still a role for the serious amateur, who could hold his or her own at a soirée alongside the most famous stars, and if any of them read a singing treatise they would probably recognise many of the same basic principles as their forebears: there was an accepted way to train. As we enter the twentieth century, however, there is an increasing disconnection between the training of singers and the music they might expect to sing. Eighteenth-century teaching (as exemplified by Porpora's legendary single page of exercises) equipped a singer to sing the most complex music then imaginable. At the end of the nineteenth century singers were still expected to sing anything, but a large slice of the traditionally taught skill-set bore very little relationship to the music fashionable composers were expecting them to sing. Teachers in particular, especially the increasing numbers of those who had retired from semi-successful careers, could not let go of the notion that they were responsible for maintaining a great and mysterious art legitimised by a glorious past, and increasingly ignored the music of the present (a tendency that is still with us today). It must have seemed very strange to conservatoire students or interested amateurs to spend all day practising scales and agility exercises as a preparation for performing Puccini, Wagner, Mahler or Schoenberg. Nevertheless, the professional teacher with perceived connections to the great tradition was increasingly commonplace and in demand.

Albert Bach, a bass-baritone who taught singing in Edinburgh for many years, is a good example. Bach (born Bak, in Hungary in 1844) had had some success as an opera singer in Italy and Hungary and as a recitalist in Britain; he specialised in the songs of Löwe, which he edited and translated. Like his predecessors he commends the great singers of the past whose singing he hopes his students will emulate: Jenny Lind, Mara, Pisaroni, Grisi, Persiani, Catalani, Sontag, Patti, Rubini, Donzelli and Tamburini and others. These were all virtuosi whose main claim to fame was the velocity of their divisions. He gave a series of lectures between 1880 and 1882 in which he locates these singers firmly in the tradition of Bernacchi and Tosi. He defines portamento as:

a mutual, intimate, connection of two notes in tone, each of the notes having a syllable of its own assigned to it. It is brought about by anticipating the note of the second syllable while continuing with the vowel of the first.[61]

and devotes a whole chapter to it. He makes it clear that as late as the fifth edition (1898) the basic elements of portamento, *messa di voce* and the joining of registers were still fundamental to good singing, and that science simply confirms and explains this:

modern science has merely established theoretically what the old Italian school sought and found in an empirical way ... There is no new art of singing ... There is no new *portamento*, or *legato*, no new *messa di voce*, no new shake.[62]

His science is sometimes muddled but in many respects he links a profound understanding of 'the old Italian school' with a knowledge of current vocal acoustics. He is one of the first to realise that 'only the cavity of the mouth ... is to be considered resonant' and that vowels are formed by modification of the supralaryngeal tract rather than by the

---

[61] Albert Bach, *Musical Education and Vocal Culture* (5th edn, London: Kegan Paul, 1898): 136. The complete lecture (133–71) also deals comprehensively with legato, shakes and recitative.
[62] Bach, *Musical Education*: viii.

cords themselves.[63] He proves by a series of experiments that there is no acoustic resonance in the head (and that therefore the term 'head register' is a misnomer).[64] He defines a register succinctly as 'a succession of notes produced by the employment of one and the same vibrating mechanism', and considers Garcia's early five-register disposition confusing, acknowledging only two.[65] He fully understands diaphragmatic breathing and the basic division of tone into clear and sombre. Bach's worry (despite the optimistic tone of much of his writing) is that refined singing is being replaced by stentorian bawling. This he puts down to the lack of individual attention given to students, who now tend to learn at the hands of schoolteachers who at best will be organists rather than professional singers ('superior artistes').

Bach's book is one of a number of detailed singing reference books that appear towards the end of the nineteenth century in Europe and the USA. The market for such publications is competitive, and writers tend to emphasise both the depth of their knowledge and the extent to which it relates to traditional methods. This is doubly fortunate for historians of singing as for the first time we can actually hear the singing that they talk about. Reading these didactic writings in conjunction with listening to the earliest recordings gives us aural clues to a tradition that is by then several hundred years old. One final silent example from Norris Croker's *Handbook for Singers* (1895) for those who aspired to become singers, 'whether for the drawing room, the concert-hall, or the stage', may stand for a summary of the state of the art immediately before the first surviving examples that we can actually hear.[66] It is dedicated to his teacher, the Anglo-Italian Albert Visetti who coached and taught Adelina Patti (for whom he composed the song 'La Diva') and who was for many years a professor of singing at the Royal College of Music. Croker's writings, then, are within the establishment tradition and probably represent a broad mainstream of opinion. His examples are detailed and comprehensive, almost as though the cumulative attempts over several hundred years to describe the unhearable have forced a certain sophistication in the description of things aural (or perhaps he is aware that recording technology is about to enable people to hear what he is talking about

---

[63] Which he writes as 'chords', an early example of this misspelling.
[64] Bach, *Musical Education*: 58.   [65] Ibid.: 67.
[66] Norris Croker, *Handbook for Singers* (London: Augener, 1895), from his prefatory remarks 'To the Student'. The three genres recall those of the seventeenth century, with the difference that the concert hall has replaced the church. The *Handbook* continued to be read well into the twentieth century and is among those recommended by Roland Foster in a letter to *Musical Times*, 16:1003 (September 1926): 834–6.

so it is important for him to be as precise as possible). He says that most students will have at best one or two lessons a week, and claims not to be imparting any new knowledge but to be presenting traditional teaching in a user-friendly way. It is ideal for use by a student who will be having a weekly lesson: there are 255 numbered paragraphs, cross-referenced and indexed, with particular difficulties flagged up by the warning 'note this well'. At every point he explains 'the sensations to be felt'.

The manual's modern-ness is further signalled by the opening chapter on physiology, which is concise and reasonably accurate; Croker then deals with breath management and the role of the diaphragm, so the student immediately begins to understand the workings of the voice and its power supply. He then talks about the classification of voices, not by range as would be traditional, but by voice quality, which means that in discussing registers he does not specify the highest possible notes of each voice. He numbers the registers (1–3), which still need to be joined, and insists that the larynx should be kept low at all times, understanding the importance of maximum supralaryngeal acoustic space. The traditional elements are covered later, once the student has a thorough understanding of the mechanisms. There are separate chapters on portamento, *messa di voce* and ornamentation. This last has none of the elaborate roulades of the French treatises and is confined to basic appoggiaturas and trills (which should only be used when indicated in the score).[67] The traditional mainstays of technique are still essential, however:

Slur (*portamento*) and legato

Slur defined: To slur is to carry the voice, either quickly or slowly, from one note to another – whatever may be the interval. The intervening notes are heard, but faintly and indistinctly. This means that the tones between the notes that are connected by a slur are not to be heard as when the voice sings a scale, but as when a violinist slides his finger up the string, to gain the same effect. It is an ornament that must be only occasionally employed, as its frequent use (a great and common fault, especially with sopranos) is very worrying to the listener; it gives an impression of dragging, and an air of sick sentimentality to the singing. It is useful in exercises for blending the registers and removing inequalities of tone.[68]

He follows his basic definition with a warning about the fact that the same sign is used for a phrase mark, a bind (what we now call a tie) and a slur (his preferred term for portamento) and that the student has to use 'careful judgement' as to which is which. He reminds students that

[67] Croker, *Handbook*: 105.   [68] Ibid.: 89.

slurring uses a lot of breath so good breath control is essential and he then gives instruction for practising portamento. His musical examples are very like those of Vaccai but he first prints them without a slur, so that the student makes the anticipatory leap cleanly.

For the next stage Croker is even more precise, explaining with text and music how to apply the slur artistically once the basic intervals have been mastered without it. Control of this is achieved by a diminuendo out of the lower note as one slides upwards, then a crescendo during the anticipatory phase of the new note; descending dispenses with the crescendo, though there need not always be anticipation or diminuendo, and it need not always be subtle (his Verdi example is of a heavily marked cadence sung with full voice). He goes on to say that one of the uses for an unanticipated slur is to join two phrases, especially between the end of the middle section and the repeat of a da capo aria. This is something we will hear clearly in the Patti and Melba recordings of Mozart within a few years of Croker's publication. Finally, Croker explains what true legato singing is. He does not use the same textual device as Vaccai but he does make it clear that that 'no cessation of tone occurs in the slightest – no slur being heard whatsoever. This means that the sound of one note must not cease until the following note is sounded.'[69] Portamento, then, is clearly still a significant aspect of singing style, and we would expect to hear plenty of it when we encounter the first recorded singers. Croker is less enthusiastic about *messa di voce*, which is the subject of his next chapter. He stresses that 'the control of the breath is the secret of success in this ornament'.[70] Significantly, though, he refers to it as an ornament, whereas earlier writings imply that it is a basic technique as well as fundamental to good style. He says that it is over-used and students should not use it unless marked (which it rarely is); nevertheless, his instructions are clear and comprehensive.

Very little is known about the life of Norris Croker. His book is not a particularly original work and he may or may not have been a good teacher, but in his pedantic way he does set out as clearly as we could wish the basic principles of good singing at the end of the nineteenth century. There are clear echoes of the tradition of which Vaccai and Garcia were a part. It is significant that the *Handbook* was still available in the 1920s: Garcia's works were reprinted well into the twentieth century and are now reprinted in modern editions; Vaccai's English edition has never been out of print since its first publication. These are puzzling statistics,

[69] Ibid.: 92.   [70] Ibid.: 96.

given the fact that portamento and *messa di voce*, two of the techniques on which these three authorities predicated the essence of good singing, are relatively rare in modern singing. Immediately before the first recordings, though, it is quite clear that it was normal for singers to employ a nuanced mixture of pitch and rhythmic inflection when they needed to be particularly expressive. It is also clear that by now exaggeration is a commonplace and a sure sign of bad taste. Croker's is one of the last treatises to offer both comprehensive instructions and written performance practice examples: future writers and teachers would be able to refer readers to recordings; instruction manuals, especially those by famous singers, would need relatively little written explanation and would focus more on technique than style.

PART III

Recorded voices

CHAPTER 6

A Great Tradition: singing through history – history through singing

The focus of this chapter is the classical music of the Indian subcontinent, especially the Hindustani tradition of the northern two-thirds. We have decided on this as the topic of a whole chapter because it is probably the best Eastern counterpart to the Western traditions (principally of art music) that fill much of this book, and it also has special importance to the history of singing. There is probably no tradition on earth that places such emphasis on singing as Indian music, even if its instrumental manifestations are probably far better known around the world. The concept of 'Great Tradition' was prevalent in anthropology some fifty years ago and used to describe literate, mainly urban traditions practised and received by an elite minority (as opposed to the 'Little Traditions' of rural peoples). Though not much used today, the concept survives and can be mapped on to long histories, and perhaps a long future. The 'Great' and the 'Little' are by no means entirely separate but they incorporate elements of each other's practices. Indian civilisation was cited as a prime example of this polarity, for good reason: in music it has a clearly delineated Great Tradition and also a plethora of Little Traditions and the two have intermingled over the centuries; the same can be said of Europe and what is loosely termed Western music. Among the many problems in the 'great–little' opposition is the tendency to keep 'great' for so-called classical traditions and 'little' for everything else. This duplicates the separation of Western classical music from World Music (also folk music, pop music, jazz and so on) and can also invidiously separate literate traditions from oral ones. Ingrained in us are several assumptions that must be questioned: 'literate' is superior to 'illiterate' (as it suggests education versus the lack thereof); long traditions are superior to newer, less tested ones; musical training is formalised and usually happens in conservatoires. Indian classical music does rest on a very long tradition and depends on rigorous training (hardly ever received in institutions) but not on the literacy of the practising musicians. Although a vast body of theoretical treatises exists most musicians do not (even cannot) read such texts. Similarly, a simple notation system has been devised for the music with which musicians will be familiar but probably never use, and certainly never in performance.

Terms like 'Sanskritisation' or 'Sanskritic Hinduism' alert us both to the idealisation of an ancient golden age, in which modern Indian culture was thought to be born, and to the tension between a perceived indigenous Hindu culture and a more recent (if already thousand years old) Muslim civilisation, which has had a comparably profound influence on modern India. The first Indian monument to come to most minds will be the seventeenth-century Taj Mahal, a tomb erected by the Mughal emperor Shah Jahan. By the time of his reign the influence of the Mughals and their Muslim predecessors of the Delhi Sultanate had risen to prominence, not only in architecture but also painting and music. Shah Jahan's grandfather, the greatest of the Mughals, Akbar, had espoused not only a Hindu princess but also a whole agenda of religious inclusion and tolerance, at the heart of modern India, patronising Hindu artists and commissioning the translation of Sanskrit treatises. Inevitably perhaps, a prevailing view of Indian history, and certainly one found in music history, involves a rather simplistic polarisation, at least in the northern part of the subcontinent, between Hindu (and Sanskrit) and Muslim (and Arabic, Turkish and Persian) influences. At its best is the recognition that both elements have enriched the culture; at its worst are partisanship and exclusivity. Beyond controversy, the notion of a Great Tradition is far from monolithic and comprises at least two Great Traditions, plus countless other ones that feed them: 'because India had a "primary" or "indigenous" civilization which had been fashioned out of pre-existing folk and regional cultures, its Great Tradition was culturally continuous with the Little Traditions to be found in its diverse regions, villages, castes and tribes'.[1]

If the invidious comparisons implied by 'great' and 'little' are less acceptable in the present age, why preserve outmoded concepts? The stark oppositions of the adjectives remain problematic, especially under scrutiny in the Indian context. 'Great' versus 'little' has little or nothing to do with urban versus rural, notated versus orally transmitted, or ancient versus modern,

[1] Milton Singer, *When a Great Tradition Modernizes: an Anthropological Approach to Indian Civilization* (London: Pall Mall Press, 1972): 67. The blurring of Great and Little, as they affect the popularisation of the *bhajan* and other devotional song types, is explored by Peter Manuel in *Cassette Culture: Popular Music and Technology in North India* (University of Chicago Press, 1993).

or complex and virtuosic versus simple and primitive. It is not our task to argue whether or how the classical traditions of the West and India should be called great, other than to make the overridingly important point that this is how they are largely perceived, and that to a large extent they rely on this perception to survive. The two moreover seem to have a special mutual respect and enjoy a high degree of homogeneity, lending themselves to clear definitions and understanding, as well as being dispersed over a huge geographical area (and historical development). Defining Indian classical music is probably easier than defining the classical music of other traditions: it is based on a tradition of *raga*[2] (melody) and *tala*[3] (rhythmic cycle) stretching back well over a thousand years. The defining function of raga is so strong that the music is often simply referred to as *ragdar*[4] (having raga) because all classical music must have a raga, whereas tala need not (and most probably will not) be present at all times.

To find a tradition with which to compare their own and on which to bestow anything approaching the respect in which they hold it, Indian musicians always cite Western music, imagining a kind of aristocracy of music, led by their own 'classical' tradition and that of the West. Indian music should not, in their opinion, be denigrated as merely another type of 'World Music'. This kind of elitism has been around for a long time and in fact we can refine our earlier definition of Great Tradition to one that is not just practised and received by an elite minority but to some extent invented by it. Why this should be has much to do with colonial inter-action and rivalries. Even before the British Raj several discrepancies were observed. A persistent example was the discrepancy between the written theory of an educated elite and the actual performance practice of musicians perceived to be not only illiterate but also degenerate. Hence there existed (and exists) a disdain for contemporary practice and nostalgia for a golden age in Sanskritic antiquity, or at least in the age preceding the current one. This in turn led to an elevation in status of genres and traditions which seemed to come closest to that ideal. Thus some vocal styles

---

[2] At their first appearance in this chapter Indian terms are italicised and are thereafter written without italics in a less consistent but more accessible orthography. A more accurate and consistent transliteration of vowels is provided in the notes, if significantly different from the orthography used in the body of the text, thus *rāga* for this term. The purpose is less to do with scholarly presentation than offering aids to pronunciation. Indian words are frequently transliterated into the Roman alphabet rather haphazardly, so a word like *gīta* (song) may appear as 'geeta' where the equivalent of the letter i does not appear. Written without the diacritical marking ('gita', or in its modern spoken version 'git') would lead to an unfortunate mispronunciation. *Rāga* (spelt 'raga' in this chapter) is often seen as 'raaga' to ensure that the first a is not pronounced as a short vowel, giving a pronunciation like 'rugger'.

[3] *Tāla.*   [4] *Rāgdār.*

discussed later still enjoy a much higher status than others, while many commentators, including North Indian musicians, often hold the South Indian tradition to be 'purer' than that of the north. This tenet is usually based on the assumption that the South Indian tradition better maintains the ancient Hindu tradition, free of the Muslim influence which dominated the north for more than five hundred years. Another factor is that the South Indian tradition was systematised and governed by theoretical models, suggesting not only organisation and theoretical coherence but also enhanced richness of repertoire. Systems, written theory, extensive repertoire from which a canon may be constructed, are all pointers towards a 'classical' music, under which heading this Indian music is always proudly revealed.

During the British Raj, especially in its last fifty years, British and Indian intellectuals and educated, literate musicians colluded in this idealised view of an ancient art surviving while in need of protection from degenerate and ignorant musicians and modernisers bringing such incongruities as the European harmonium into the music. The musicians themselves pursued various strategies to elevate their status: restricting marriage, prioritising their sons and close, talented pupils (generally, and tellingly, referred to as 'disciples') and joining, by various means, musical clans through which they could assume, or aspire towards, a kind of musical pedigree. Great importance was therefore placed on having a combined musical and blood line, and the further it stretched back the better – if possible to the legendary sixteenth-century treasure of Akbar's court, Miya Tansen (*c.* 1500–1589). These clans or schools were usually fostered under court patronage, so when the princely states were disbanded following Independence in 1947 the hereditary system met a major challenge from a confident, educated middle class of largely non-hereditary, high-caste Hindu musicians, typified by the most famous Indian musician of recent times (at least in the West), Ravi Shankar. He did not mince his words in his effort to distance Indian music not only from the drug culture and pop generation of the 1960s (despite owing his worldwide success in large part to this very generation) but also from just about any other non-Western music:

I am chagrined even today to see that there are still people who categorize it [Indian music] in the same way as music from Java, Bali, Borneo or Africa; that is as 'ethnic' music, and – though this is found more in the USA – put it under the classification of Ethnomusicology.

This reminds me of something which happened a few years ago at a music seminar in Madras. A very learned Indian scholar of music got up and suggested that 'from here on we should term Western classical music as "ethnic music" because in India what we really consider classical music is our own'. This resentment goes to show how strongly and proud we feel about our music. I personally feel that the only two 'classical' forms of music are the 'Western' and the 'Indian' because of their roots and development which have never stopped up to date.[5]

The criteria of roots and development are unfortunately weak, simply because they are universal. The most striking word, perhaps, is 'resentment'. Of course this impassioned opinion stems from the perception, mentioned earlier and which is as widespread as it is absurd, of Western classical music as a single impregnable entity, forcing just about all other music on earth into the huge 'World Music' cauldron, from which many, like Ravi Shankar, are at great pains to opt out. He was, in fact, subscribing to the classicising, idealising agenda already discussed. The danger of being perceived as a pop musician (the Beatles' guru) was counteracted, in part, by his composing sitar concertos – an overt move to thoroughly classical genres, even if the two 'classical' musics involved (Indian and Western) mix no better than oil and water. This debate and effort to construct twin towers of classical music is not, however, the main reason for this chapter, although it inevitably takes up a position by making the link between Indian and Western *classical* music. The main reason, far more pressing than any other, is that Indian music is unsurpassed in its dependence on singing, so a focus on it for one chapter could be paradigmatic of the whole study.

CARRIERS OF TRADITION

There remains an interesting tension between that which helps define the Indian music under investigation as 'classical' and that which captures its essence as an enduring oral tradition. How and why a music should be termed classical is perhaps less important than the fact that Westerners use the word for one of their major traditions and Indians do likewise. Shared criteria include a long, documented history and belief in a canonic immortality. The documentation of the tradition is crucial. It is synonymous with a written theory, which validates the tradition and enhances its status (and helps put it out of reach of the mass of the population). That in turn throws up another obstacle: the relationship

---

[5] In Peggy Holroyde, *Indian Music: a Vast Ocean of Promise* (London: George Allen and Unwin, 1972): 9.

of theory to performance practice and the danger of assuming that they are conjoined. In the case of India the two can neatly be captured by two terms at the very heart of the tradition: *shastriya sangita*[6] and *guru-shishya-parampara*.[7] The former means music recorded in treatises, nearly always in Sanskrit, the ancient language of learning which automatically elevates what it is used to describe, conferring on it both long tradition and almost religious status. Such respectability also abundantly applies to guru-shishya-parampara, which has a much more immediate relevance to the practice of Indian music. It means the master–pupil succession, conjuring up possible resonances with royalty (and indeed the first-born son is most likely to be regarded as the principal successor). The fact that a guru is more than a master and something also of a spiritual guide and the pupil is usually described as a disciple imparts a quasi-religious element to the relationship. The guru shows the way that the disciple must follow. The two are bound in a lifelong relationship – literally bound, as the unison is symbolised in a ceremony, known as *ganda-bandhan*,[8] not unlike a marriage, in which threads are tied around wrists to give a visible sign of the ties that bind. The guru has the responsibility of teaching and guiding the student, traditionally offering complete care including food and lodging. The pupil reciprocates by serving and obeying the guru in every way, never questioning or ignoring the teaching given, and has the responsibility to look after the guru in old age.

This is the essence of the parampara but no less important to add is the fact that it is an oral tradition. Typically the guru sings or plays a phrase and the pupil repeats it – over and over as necessary – until the guru is satisfied. It is therefore the teaching of music through music, without a reliance on verbal discourse. (This method not only captures the essence of the exchange but can also be advantageous to a foreigner who may not share a language with the guru but is able to understand purely in terms of listening and imitating the music itself.) The use of the present tense is deliberate. While the guru-shishya-parampara has changed in modern times and been threatened by social mobility, political pressures, the growth of music schools and colleges, recording and broadcasting technologies, and other major changes of the last century, its survival and the importance attached to it are indicative of its resilience. No major professional musician will omit an acknowledgement of his or her guru and the long and deep teaching experience. The fact is emphasised relentlessly that

[6] *Śāstrīyā saṅgīta.*
[7] *Guru-śishya paramparā.* Another word commonly used to refer to the pupil is *shāgird.*
[8] *Gaṇḍā-bandhan.*

music cannot be learned from books (which thus includes the hallowed *sastras*)[9] or, nowadays, recordings, and should not be gleaned piecemeal through a kind of promiscuity with many different teachers, but must be learnt gradually through a relationship with a guru lasting many years. The rigidly authoritarian feel to all of this can be mitigated by other realities. Many musicians – in fact the majority – have more than one guru in their lives. This may be because they need training in another style or on another instrument, or because the first guru may die or no longer be able to teach for whatever reason. Not all gurus expect the same loyalty; indeed many will actively encourage the student to listen to as many other musicians as possible.

As Indian music not only rests on a long oral tradition but is also predominantly a hereditary profession, musicians tend to learn from their fathers or other close relatives. As mentioned, they may be actively encouraged by the first guru to go out and seek instruction from others, and stories abound of aspiring artists journeying far and wide to study, sometimes eavesdropping on the practice or performance of those from whom they wish to learn. The exceptions, however, prove the rule that there will be one central guru and inspiration. Manifestations of the strength of the guru-shishya-parampara can very often be seen on the concert stage. If the guru is present the disciple will not only acknowledge his or her presence by the familiar joined palms greeting but also by touching the guru's feet with the hand. The guru's permission and blessings will be sought before the performance may begin (actually these marks of respect can be shown to any senior and respected person). Musicians often accompany a mention of their guru, or any legendary musician of the past from whom they claim musical descent, by the beautifully expressive gesture of raising a hand and cupping it over one ear, or gently tugging at the earlobe. As hands touching feet is a gesture acknowledging seniority and higher status, so the touching of one's ear symbolises that through the teaching of the guru has passed the art of music. When an established guru is him/herself the soloist it is common to find one or more shishya involved in the performance as *tambura*[10] (drone instrument) players, and it will be expected that the guru will occasionally give the shishyas opportunities to show their own vocal prowess in short interludes.

The discussion so far, describing the nature and importance of tradition in Indian music, is also a basis for understanding the history of singing.

---

[9] *Śāstra*. The familiar plural marker 's' at the end is not Indian and is added for convenience to English readers.
[10] *Tambūrā*.

One can surmise that the guru-shishya-parampara has many concomitants. Its strength and authority led to clearly distinguished styles and the maintenance of these styles and the demand for loyalty led to a culture of rivalry and secrecy. With the growth of broadcasts, recordings and the modern concert stage much of the secrecy evaporated, though the spirit of rivalry persists as strongly as ever. Since a guru would be likely to attract far more students than those in his or her immediate family a style would develop around the guru, sometimes taking his name (the practice seems to be reserved for male teachers) but more likely from the place of residence. In nearly every case that place was the location of the court in which the guru served. Until relatively recently (the time of Indian Independence in 1947) Indian classical music could also be defined as an art of the royal courts. A further tension will be discussed later: that between court and temple or royal sovereign and the ultimate divine authority. For now the focus is on the courts which had such a significant influence on the history of Indian music, and especially singing.

ORIGINS AND PRIORITIES

The word most commonly given for music is the Sanskrit *sangita*,[11] a rather more complex term comprising three main elements: vocal music, instrumental music and dance. Arnold Bake showed how the three have been linked throughout Indian music history and why vocal music is placed first:

It seems that at the time when these theories were first formulated the function of the vocal chords [*sic*] was unknown. Thus it is easily understandable that the miracle of the change from silent life-breath (*prâṇa*) into sounds of meaning and beauty, without the aid of any visible or perceptible agent, came to be considered as a spontaneous manifestation of sound itself, basically different from the sound produced by a man-made instrument.[12]

It is widely believed in India that the Vedic chants of the early Hindus are the source from which Indian music flowed. They are referred to as the *yoni* of music: the womb, or, rather more precisely, the birth canal. Yet, however pure the water at the river's source, the same could not be said of the water at the other end, as the river picks up tributaries and extraneous elements along the way. The ragas of Indian classical music are not mentioned in treatises until the eighth or ninth century, some two thousand

[11] *Sangīta*.
[12] Arnold Bake, 'The Music of India', in Egon Wellesz (ed.), *New Oxford History of Music*, vol. 1. (Oxford University Press, 1957): 197.

years after the development of Vedic chant. The connection is not unlike the proposition that Western music originated in Gregorian chant. In both cases the emphasis is on a revered canon of religious music and the influence of folk music and even of foreign accretions is overlooked. But the resilience of the sacred chants cannot be denied, as both types are still very much practised to this day, while all manner of genres, styles and repertoires coming much later have long since fallen by the wayside. Thus the ancient and medieval types of singing examined later are all modern as well, as they continue to thrive in the present day.

Once we step outside the Western world we run into conflicts with what we assume history to be, thinking that our chronological apprehension is the only one and unable to grasp other views. Worse still, we are liable to dismiss these views as a lack of historical sense or even a lack of history altogether. As A. H. Fox Strangways, one of the earliest and most thorough of Western commentators on Indian music, forthrightly put it:

The Indian does not make or read histories, and does not appreciate the value of chronological record. It is the custom to smile at this; but it would be well to understand his point of view first. A whole people is not generally mistaken about its real needs.[13]

The crucial and wisest part of this statement is the last sentence. India's real needs are not the same as ours, and its music is not the same either. This book cannot avoid huge omissions and will doubtless make mistakes, but the one it cannot afford to make is to assume an absolute and universal understanding of history. The point is also made if we consider the current preoccupation in the West with what used to be called 'authenticity' and, when that was accepted to be almost meaningless, what is now more coyly referred to as 'historically informed performance'. It logically rests on the premise that continuity was disrupted by conflicting styles, so there is a need to strip them away, like additions of varnish to a painting, in order to recover a lost performance practice. The disruption of continuity is another way of saying that there is a lack of an unbroken oral tradition. We will reproduce what the previous generation did, overlooking the changes that accrued through many generations. One could say that exactly the same thing happens in India, so modern singing is no closer to that of the distant past than is the case in the West. The important distinction is that the Indian tradition is an oral one and, yet more important, that is how it is perceived. Thus performers can be oblivious

[13] A. H. Fox Strangways, *The Music of Hindostan* (1914: Oxford: Clarendon Press, 1965): 73.

to concerns such as 'historically informed performance' because the consciousness of the oral tradition, sustained by the guru-shishya-parampara, makes the concept redundant and, rightly or wrongly, they will not be led to think that their tradition was in any way disrupted. Such, again, are differing notions of history.

Without entering into a discussion of the distinctions between myth, legend and history, we should note that all have enduring value even in the most rational and enlightened cultures. Indian music history is as much hagiography as hard fact. Key figures emerge around whom are as many legends as historical facts, yet we are in no position to reject them for lack of concrete evidence as to do so would be to undermine a belief system that underpins the tradition. The strongest theme in the Indian perception of history is twofold: antiquity and spirituality. The former can be stretched without regard to particular dates while the latter accounts for the tendency already noted towards a kind of hagiography. The singers of Hindu mythology were celestial musicians – the Gandharvas with their female companions the dancing Apsarasas – and mystics. Among the Gandharvas was Tumburu, described by Fox Strangways as 'the first singer', who also is credited with expanding the scale of the Sama Veda (or *samaveda*)[14] from five notes to six or seven,[15] a development given great importance in the history of Indian music and supposedly leading to the eventual formation of the ragas. Indian mythology and the Sanskrit treatises abound with examples of good and bad singing. Fox Strangways provided a varied selection, including the tale of the captured fairies who refused to sing for a king, fearing that any imperfection in their song would incite anger. When he commanded that they be killed and cooked for his meal they explained why they had refused and offered examples of their art, earning the king's reprieve and their freedom.[16] Perhaps the most famous among the fables is the one about the anchorite Narada who thought he had mastered music. To teach him the extent of his arrogance, Vishnu took him to the gods' abode where many mutilated men and women were lamenting their sorry state. When asked the reason for their distress they replied that they were the melodies that Narada had sung incorrectly, and only a singer truly expert in music would be able to restore them.[17]

On the basis of more superficial comparisons, chant may sound as simple as the word suggests, yet it is important to note that the Sanskrit word *gana*[18] can mean both singing and chanting. Much Vedic chant

[14] *Sāmaveda.* [15] Fox Strangways, *Music of Hindostan*, 75.
[16] Ibid.: 81. [17] Ibid.: 75. [18] *Gāna.*

uses just a few notes, often only three, while a classical raga must have at least five, distributed over the whole octave (in other words, the notes cannot be all bunched together at one end of the scale). As intimated earlier, the Sama Veda stands out among the four Vedas (the others being the Rig Veda, Yajur Veda and Atharva Veda) for its greater melodic scope. The musical potential of the other groups should not be discounted. Vedic chant not only tends to use a more limited set of notes but also relies far less on the vocal skills required for classical music. It does, however, depend on oral tradition and feats of memorisation and sometimes uses a variation technique of which a modern counterpart forms a cornerstone of raga improvisation. Even within the three or four notes of many Vedic chants may be found the practice of *vikriti*: a kind of variation achieved through a fragmentation of the text by exploring the combinations of the available syllables and notes. Around 800 years ago, the system of *khandameru*, or *merukhanda*, known to every musician today (usually as *mirkhand*),[19] was established.[20] It is a good example of another facet of the Hindu mind that should never be underestimated and which counterbalances the facile notion of historical vagueness: the propensity to create systems and codifications, sometimes based on the Indian genius for mathematics, hence precision (we see this precision in many ways in musical practice: a great concern for subtle variations of intonation, as well as the most demanding accuracy in the most complex of rhythmic structures). In mirkhand a selection of notes may be combined and permutated in a wide variety of kaleidoscopic patterns and at any speed. Usually just a few notes are explored in this way, as already a large number of possibilities are offered. The basic number of combinations for three notes is 6, for four is 24 and for five is 120 – already more than enough – though which patterns may be selected is governed by the shape of the particular raga.

So, far from being purely mathematical the mirkhand technique of combining notes in patterns derived from their combinations is directly relevant to Indian musical practice. It may be comparable to change bell-ringing but is otherwise alien to the Western classical mind. It is one facet of Indian music which demonstrates a genius for elaborating a small amount of material. Thus we often hear how a great musician improvised for an hour or more on just two or three notes, but another vital means of

[19] *Mīrkhand*; also known as *svaraprastāra*.

[20] The workings of this system are examined by Nazir Ali Jairazbhoy in his article 'Svaraprastāra in North Indian Classical Music', *Bulletin of the School of Oriental and African Studies*, 24: 2 (1961): 307–25.

elaboration and variety is the much more familiar concept of ornamentation. While the word tends to mean what it says in Western music, in Indian music it is something of a misnomer: singing (and playing) without ornamentation could actually render the music incoherent. Not only is ornamentation part of every phrase but it is also an essential feature, in precisely taught ways, of many ragas, so to sing them without the ornaments or the wrong ones would destroy them (in much the way described in the legend of Narada, recounted above). As we shall see, specific ornamentations are distinguishing features of vocal genres and may not be randomly mixed. The word ornamentation is thus woefully inadequate to describe the range of slides, shakes, turns, slow and fast vibratos and so on which permeate Indian singing and without which a raga could be distorted or even destroyed. Closely connected with this is the question of intonation, but this is a vast and somewhat controversial topic. Suffice it to say that intonation is another essential element in the expression and differentiation of ragas. Indian musicians readily accept the premise that the voice is the most versatile and expressive 'instrument', capable of producing all the 'ornaments' and subtle shades of intonation. Instruments are judged largely by the extent to which they can imitate the voice.[21]

CARNATIC MUSIC

Indian classical music is divided into two strands: the northern or Hindustani and the southern or Carnatic (also spelt with an initial k replacing the c, and Karnatak).[22] Carnatic music predominates in the Indian states of Andhra Pradesh, Karnataka, Tamil Nadu and Kerala, and also Sri Lanka. Hindustani music is distributed across the wider area north of these states, including Pakistan and Bangladesh (part of India prior to Partition in 1947). Although it covers a smaller area and smaller proportion of the total population Carnatic music is no less important and cannot be ignored in a discussion of Indian music. The distinction between the two systems is not as much a matter of modern political states as older languages: the Hindustani system prevails in the region

---

[21] The British tenor Nigel Rogers studied Indian vocal technique, especially that of the great singer Bhimsen Joshi, as part of a quest for historically informed performance (we might more fittingly call it 'geographically enhanced performance'). In this case he was paying close attention to Joshi's fluent and virtuosic ornamentation in order to enrich his own repertoire in the performance of Monteverdi and other composers of 'early music'.

[22] Karnatak (Karṇāṭak) is the more likely spelling nowadays. The older 'Carnatic' is used not only because it was used for so long but also because it does not draw attention to the modern state of Karnataka, at the expense of Tamil Nadu and the other states where the music flourishes.

of Indo-European languages (nowadays dominated by Hindi, even promoted as the national language) while Carnatic music covers the region of the Dravidian group of languages. The highly venerated ancient literary language of Sanskrit, while being Indo-European, is a strong influence too on the Dravidian group, especially Malayalam (spoken in the state of Kerala) and many Carnatic song texts are in Sanskrit, as are most of the important treatises on Indian music. It is also a language written in metric verse, rather than prose, which is another significant influence on music. Hindustani and Carnatic singing sound different in large part because they mostly use very different modern, spoken languages. Turning to Carnatic music before Hindustani is a way of emphasising not only its parity but also its widely perceived role in the preservation of ancient Hindu civilisation. Placing initial emphasis on Carnatic music, even if the vast topic cannot be accorded the depth it merits, not only reveals a whole tradition based on singers and a vast repertoire of songs but also pays lip service to the idea that the tradition represents the oldest Indian music, for the simplistic reason that the south largely escaped the foreign accretions brought by the Muslim invaders to the north from around the thirteenth century. The fact that the cornerstone of the Carnatic repertoire rests on a 'Trinity' of singer-saint-composers, all roughly contemporary with Beethoven, and has continued to be fed by nineteenth- and twentieth-century compositions, is but one fact that militates against such a simple assumption. The truth is that both traditions had significantly moved on from what was recorded in treatises a matter of two or three hundred years before the rift became formally recognised. Debates on claims to be the longer tradition are therefore as futile as they are rife, as are claims for the superiority of one tradition over the other. We are fortunately more likely to find mutual respect and admiration, translated into borrowings from one another, and even duets simultaneously displaying both styles and repertoires. While two singers, one from the north and the other from the south, may sing the same raga (albeit by different names) and same tala (again by different names, often conveniently fitting together in a 2:1 ratio, somewhat like our 2/4 and 4/4) they will be distinguishable not only in the languages used for speech and singing but also in the ways of using the voice. The actual singing thus varies markedly between the two main traditions, not just what is sung, in which case different repertoires of ragas, talas, compositions and improvisation techniques are principal determinants.

Risking generalisation and simplification, perhaps the best way to recognise instantly one or the other is through ornamentation, which is even more persistent in Carnatic singing than Hindustani. The latter has its arsenal of ornamentation and many types and terms are shared (usually via Sanskrit, for example *gamaka*)[23] with the south, but notes are often held for long breaths without any wavering, whereas in Carnatic singing it seems that hardly a note is sung without some kind of ornament. Even in a simple demonstration of a raga outline the Carnatic singer will include what sound like wide vibratos to many of the notes, or oscillations between two notes, not as optional ornamentations but as the very life of the notes. (The Hindustani singer will include any obligatory ornaments but is likely to apply them to fewer notes.) Here the Indian word *svara* has far richer meanings than merely 'note'. It might more accurately be translated as 'noteness' as it does not always indicate an exact, steady pitch but may be used for notes that, to the untutored ear, 'wobble' quite markedly, yet are meticulously controlled by the singer. Such notes are precisely those which are hardest to replicate on certain instruments (especially the harmonium). Yet they are not optional ornamentations but are required in the particular raga.

The most important argument in favour of common ground rather than difference lies in the fact that before the sixteenth century no systematic distinction was made between Carnatic and Hindustani, despite clear signs of divergence in the centuries leading up to that point. In a Sanskrit treatise (the usual way of documenting Indian music in writing), entitled *Svaramelakalanidhi*[24] – *Treasury of Melas* – (by Ramamatya, *c.* 1550) a clear pointer was given to the *mela* (scale) system which is a principal distinguishing feature of Carnatic music. (A comparable classificatory system for Hindustani ragas was not adopted until the twentieth century, and ten such scales were proposed, in contrast to the seventy-two of Carnatic music.) By the sixteenth century it is clear that the two major traditions had assumed separate identities, and the period corresponded to the lives of iconic musicians in each tradition. Purandara (or Purunthara) Das (1484–1564) is so important that he is nicknamed the 'grandsire' of Carnatic music. He did not start out as the typical singer-saint of Carnatic music but was born near Poona (nowadays more in the Hindustani area) to a family of bankers and also became wealthy as a money lender. It is said that an act of kindness by his wife towards a beggar showed him the error of his ways, which he abandoned in favour of study with a

---

[23] In northern languages, most notably Hindi, it is common to omit the short 'a' at the end (sometimes also in the middle) of Sanskrit words, so gamaka becomes gamak, raga becomes rag, tala becomes tal, svara becomes svar, and so on.

[24] *Svaramelakalānidhi.*

famous singer named Vyasaraya. He also took the name by which he is now known, signifying his devotion to Krishna. His enormous output of songs, put at 475,000 (only a fraction of which have survived), therefore shows a leaning towards praise of this god, with the associated mixture of eroticism and devotion. He also composed songs for beginners, which are still used today. Not only that, but he is also respected as a seminal theorist of Carnatic music, laying the foundations of the modern classificatory systems of raga and tala, as well as of the song form *kriti*, which is at the heart of the modern orally transmitted Carnatic repertoire.

The modern kriti has three parts: *pallavi-anupallavi-caranam*[25] (and the pallavi will also be reprised before and after the caranam). If sung straight through it might only take a few minutes and a recital could contain several kritis as well as examples of other Carnatic song types of similar length. The kriti, however, can be greatly extended in a variety of ways: there could be a long *alapana*[26] (improvised unfolding of the raga without text) at the start of the performance; this prelude could even become a kind of double alapana, as it is common to have one performed by the main artist followed by another performed by the melodic accompanist, who in Carnatic music is most likely to be a violinist. The sections of the kriti proper may also be augmented by *svara kalpana* (melodic and rhythmic improvisation sung to the note-names) and improvisations on lines from the kriti. Near the end there could be a solo by the accompanying *mridangam* drum and any other percussion taking part, such as the *kanjira* (tambourine) or *ghatam* (clay pot beaten with the bare hands).

At least as revered as Purandara Das were the much later *trimurti*[27] (Trinity) of singer-saints, who were heavily influenced by him. They were all Brahmins (the highest Hindu caste), came from the Tanjore (Thanjavur) district of modern Tamil Nadu and were close contemporaries. Probably the greatest of them all was Tyagaraja (1767–1847), often known as Swami Tyagaraja, the son of a Brahmin scholar and musical mother. He is renowned for his matchless output of kritis, many of which are in praise of Rama, the deity to whom he dedicated his life. So intense was his devotion that he had visions and this is why he is generally regarded as a saint. He also preferred a life of austerity, meditation and begging, rejecting invitations to lucrative employment in the courts. Hardly a lesser figure was Muttuswami Dikshitar (1775/6–1835), who was one of the most adventurous and innovative of Carnatic composers. He

---

[25] The last word of the three is pronounced more like 'charanum'.
[26] *Ālāpana.*   [27] *Trimūrti.*

spent a period of five years in the north, in the holy city of Varanasi, which allowed some Hindustani influences into his music, and he also showed an interest in the music of the British rulers, even composing words for their national anthem in Sanskrit (unusually his preferred language for song texts). But his contribution of some 461 compositions was firmly rooted in the tradition of his native Tanjore district. Finally, slightly less well-known than the other two, partly because he was less prolific, was Shyama Shastri (1762–1827). As a hereditary priest (rather than coming from a musical family) he spent his time in the Tanjore district. The kritis and other pieces by the Trinity, together numbering more than a thousand, are the most cherished and widely performed song repertoire of Carnatic music. Hardly a concert will pass without a kriti by at least one of them and whole festivals are celebrated annually in their honour.

BIMUSICALITY: WESTERN MUSICIANS CAN MASTER INDIAN MUSIC

This brief survey of Carnatic music concludes somewhat unusually by singling out a singer who was not Indian and came to Indian music in late adolescence rather than early childhood: the American Jon B. Higgins. This is a tribute to a gentle and modest man who caused a sensation at the time through his pioneering achievements and he occupies a special place in the history of singing. He inspired countless others and what he accomplished has been repeated in various ways by other musicians. Had he lived, his career would have gone from strength to strength for at least another twenty years, but he was taken from us in tragic circumstances (a hit-and-run road accident in Connecticut in 1984 when he was only forty-five). His unremarkable name was made special in India by the addition of the honorific *bhagavatar*,[28] a title bestowed on those considered true masters of the art. When Higgins took to Carnatic singing in the 1960s while a student at Wesleyan University (USA) such a venture was extremely rare, but what truly established him as a phenomenon was that he took his newly-acquired skill to India itself and received huge acclaim there (as the title bhagavatar, not given lightly, proves). He studied with the late T. Viswanathan, a Visiting Artist brought to Wesleyan from India by Robert Brown, a former student of Mantle Hood at UCLA. Brown had placed Carnatic music at the forefront of the new World Music programme at Wesleyan, bringing as artists in residence his own teacher, the mridangam

---

[28] *Bhāgavatar.*

player Ranganathan, with his flautist brother Viswanathan, and also their sister, the celebrated Bharata Natyam dancer Balasaraswati. Mantle Hood had pioneered the practice of bringing artists from around the world to teach in America and help realise his dream of a new 'bimusicality'.

Teaching through performance was, in any case, the only way that would have made sense to those artists and it unsurprisingly proved very popular with the students – and also spectacularly effective, as the example of Higgins showed. His immersion in Indian music slightly pre-dated the 'Great Sitar Explosion'[29] of the mid-1960s, when count-less pop and even classical musicians turned to Indian music and mysti-cism following the example of the Beatles (especially George Harrison, who studied with Ravi Shankar). Their gravitation tended to be towards Hindustani instrumental music rather than Carnatic singing. Sitar-mania aside, part of the reason is that instrumentalists from one tradition are more likely to gravitate towards instruments in another. Higgins had trained in Western singing before taking up Carnatic music. Not only was he probably the first non-Indian to garner such acclaim in India but also by taking the vocal route he went to the heart of Indian music and also of its Indian listeners, who applauded his ability with their diffi-cult languages as well as vocal techniques. Slight lapses in pronunciation were occasionally remarked upon, which is hardly surprising, and in any case singing in a foreign language demands critical tolerance in any part of the world. The timbre of Higgins's voice may also have sounded rather more American than Indian, but these are petty quibbles and Indian critics were just as understanding and positive, preferring to focus on how well he negotiated the difficulties of Indian voice production, orna-mentation and word expression at a time when it was assumed that no Westerner could manage it to such a professional level. When Hood for-mulated his ideas of 'bimusicality' and put them into practice, followed by Brown, the fact that someone could apply them so successfully helped Higgins stand out. Nowadays 'bimusicality' is so commonplace that there is no longer any need to make as much of the term. A conference in Mumbai (1996) on Indian music and the West featured a series of recitals of Indian classical music (all Hindustani, as it happened) given mostly by American instrumentalists to a discerning audience predom-inantly of Indian musicians and musicologists.[30]

---

[29] Gerry Farrell, *Indian Music and the West* (Oxford University Press, 1997): 171.
[30] As another example, even closer to Hood's experience (as an expert on Javanese music), many have learned the gamelan music of Java, though relatively few (compared to the multitude play-ing gamelan) have seriously attempted to master the vocal styles associated with it. It is beyond

HINDUSTANI MUSIC: *DHRUPAD*

Both North and South India cherish their iconic singer-composers probably more than anywhere else in the world. The northern Hindustani tradition has several figures to compare with Purandara Das, Tyagaraja and Dikshitar in the south and Tansen (*c.* 1500–1589) stands out in a unique way. He became the greatest legend of Hindustani music even during his lifetime and his reputation has never waned since. He is thought to have been born in Gwalior, where he is buried. His tomb is a place of pilgrimage for musicians, partly because of the belief that eating the leaves of the tree that overhangs his resting place will improve their voices. It is widely believed, if not firmly established, that he was originally a Hindu but converted to Islam (something that happened frequently during the Mughal Empire); also that he studied with the Hindu sage Swami Haridas (another revered figure of Hindustani music). A famous story, telling us much about the spiritual priorities of Indian music and chiming with the asceticism of the Carnatic saint-singers, tells how the Emperor Akbar asked Tansen to bring him to hear the great Swami. Akbar was disappointed by the sage's unwillingness to sing, whereupon Tansen remarked that while he sang for his emperor, Swami Haridas sang only for God. There are also stories of the rivalry between Tansen and another Haridas pupil, the singer Baiju Bawra, including a singing competition at Akbar's court when Tansen was actually bettered by his junior.[31] Nevertheless, Tansen was the most celebrated musician of his age and one account in the annals of Akbar's reign (1556–1605), the *Ain-i Akbari* (1597) by Abul Fazl, states that a singer like him had not been heard

---

the scope of this chapter to discuss the reasons for this, beyond pointing out that the notion of vocal music as simply harder will not of itself suffice; some singers have broken through the barrier with outstanding results. By the 1970s the American Laurie Kottmeyer was singing the solo female part (*sindhènan*) in the Mangkunegaran Palace, Solo, Central Java, accompanied by some of the finest Javanese gamelan players, while Martin Hatch and Alex Dea studied Javanese singing, including the solo male *bawa* repertoire. Within the past few years the British singer Esther Wilds has frequently performed *sindhènan* in Java and Europe to great acclaim. These are but a few examples. As with the example of Higgins, the important criteria for critical acceptance within the culture concerned are pronunciation of a difficult language (more than one in the case of Higgins), a vocal timbre which is quite different from Western ones, and the correct rendition of unfamiliar intonation and ornamentation.

[31] A much more lurid account of the rivalry is the subject of the 1952 film *Baiju Bawra* where Tansen even came across as something of a villain. The historical inaccuracies and musical anachronism of a vocal style only prominent since the eighteenth century are countered by the contributions of one of the greatest of all Bollywood 'music directors' (composers), Naushad Ali, and some of the finest classical singers of North India at that time (widely considered a golden age of Hindustani singing).

in India for a thousand years and he was regarded as one of the jewels of the court. His legacy survived both through his blood line (thought to have continued right up to the dhrupad master Dabir Khan in the twentieth century) and, far more so, through the guru-shishya-parampara, with the result that an extraordinary number of musicians claim membership of the Seniya *gharana*[32] (a tradition associated with him), be they singers or instrumentalists. Some famous ragas also bear his name (in fact only the title 'Miya', bestowed on him by Akbar) and he is also credited with perhaps the most revered of all Hindustani ragas, *Darbari*.

The question of what and how Tansen sang cannot be answered conclusively. The assumption is that he was a master of the most respected genre of Hindustani music: dhrupad. Part of the reason for this respect (if not wide appeal) is connected with the twofold theme of Indian historiography remarked on earlier: antiquity and spirituality. Dhrupad is regarded as the oldest major type of North Indian classical music still practised today and its subject is praise of Hindu deities, rather than mundane romantic sentiments or other concession to popular taste. (Such less elevated, occasionally meretricious texts are found in the main vocal genre today: *khyal*.)[33] Tansen was born in a place and at a time when dhrupad is thought to have come to the fore: Gwalior during the reign (1486–1516) of Man Singh Tomar. By the time of Akbar dhrupad had acquired great prestige. The *Ain-i Akbari* distinguished between several types of musicians, from which three types of singer may be singled out: *Dharhi*, who sang Punjabi heroic songs, *Qavval*, associated with qavvali, discussed later, and *Kalavant*, who sang dhrupad and therefore included Tansen among their number. Kalavant has survived to the present as a term to describe solo singers (by no means only of dhrupad) and it therefore conveys considerable prestige. The etymology of the word dhrupad is generally given as *dhruva* (fixed) plus *pada* (verse), from Sanskrit. In fact dhruva songs are discussed as far back as the *Natyashastra*,[34] the first extant Sanskrit treatise dealing with music (dating probably from the early centuries of the Common Era), although the treatise's main subject was drama (natya). The word dhrupad suggests structure, discipline and a relative lack of freedom. In practice there is probably as much improvisation in dhrupad as in any other kind of Indian music, as an important part is the *alap*,[35] which is the slow, mainly improvised unfolding of the raga, mostly without a text, at the start of the performance (like the

---

[32] *Gharānā.*   [33] *Khyāl*. Also frequently written as *khayāl*.
[34] *Nātyaśāstra.*   [35] *Ālāp.*

Carnatic alapana). It may well be far longer than the dhrupad song itself, which is a composition in four sections, called *sthayi, antara, sanchari* and *abhog.* The first two survive as the main sections of other compositions, including those found in khyal and instrumental music, and are characterised by a change of register: sthayi is in the lower and medium ranges; antara focuses more on the upper register. In dhrupad the composition will not only be longer than in other song types but also adhered to more strictly, yet there is still an expectation of impromptu elaboration.

Although eclipsed by the main genre today (khyal) dhrupad survives and has undergone a recent resurgence, even if it remains something of a special interest with none of the wide appeal of khyal and other genres. A reason given for both its survival and restricted appeal is its austere and sober concentration on the detail and 'purity' of raga. One often hears the exhortation to go to a dhrupad singer if one wishes to know how a raga really goes. Great emphasis is placed on alap, as this slow, gradual unfolding of the raga gives the singer time to dwell on the detail – the inner life of the svaras. For this reason, care is taken to produce precise intonation and a concomitant is that dhrupad eschews many of the faster and more exaggerated ornaments of other styles. The question of intonation is mired in controversy, largely because its theoretical discussion goes back as far as the Natyashastra, yet relating theory to modern practice remains difficult. What cannot be doubted is that Indian musicians are meticulous in their attention to intonation. Anyone attending a concert of Indian music will notice how much time is spent tuning up. It is usually the case that a tuning session will have happened in the green room just before the start, and when the musicians come on stage they promptly spend another few minutes tuning all over again. Retuning as necessary during performance is also common and creates none of the anxiety or loss of concentration that would occur, say, in the middle of a concerto movement.

These remarks of course only apply to instruments and there are some paradoxes to explore later in this fascinating and controversial topic. Ancient Indian theory, pre-dating any discussion of raga, indicated twenty-two srutis to the octave, though they were not necessarily equal divisions. In fact, just what the srutis were and how they are still observed in practice is a matter of heated debate. While no singer or instrumentalist will deny their existence their actual realisation becomes problematic and fraught with inconsistency. Part of the respect in which dhrupad singers are held as authorities on the details of ragas rests on their application of sruti, especially as their ability to hold notes steadily for long breaths allows the intonation to be heard more clearly. The distinguished dhrupad master

Zia Mohiuddin Dagar (1929–1990) demonstrated to the author a series of minute differences to just one degree of the scale as they would apply to that note in different ragas. In another personal communication, one of his Indian students related that early voice training would involve holding a note as steadily as possible for as long as possible (a practice reminiscent of Western *messa di voce*). Given the Indian emphasis on assiduous *riyaz*[36] or practice, the students would go about their daily business while continuing to practise this exercise in controlling breath, evenness of sound and utterly steady pitch.[37] The old saying that only the man with the strength of five buffaloes should attempt to sing dhrupad is thus not just about loudness (as much dhrupad singing is very soft and seeks to draw the listener in) but control through all dynamics and registers. The idea of singing just one note for hours on end is typical of the Hindustani approach to musical performance as well as practice. Working on one note at a time, so that the whole palette of the raga is not revealed for several minutes, explains why it can take years to master just one raga and why the slow unfolding of the alap can take an hour or more. Here we are speaking not only of vocal or instrumental ability but also knowledge of raga and proficiency in the techniques of improvisation.

The courtly grandeur, spirituality, austerity and slow pace of dhrupad are conveyed in Mani Kaul's 1982 documentary (entitled simply *Dhrupad*) for the Government of India's Films Division. It opens with the familiar teaching method, whereby the guru (once again, Zia Mohiuddin Dagar) instructs his pupil (his son) by singing phrases for the pupil to replicate (on the plucked *bin*,[38] the principal melodic instrument of dhrupad). This also shows the close link between singing and playing and in fact the guru here could just as easily have played his phrases on the same instrument. Choosing instead to teach through singing, even though both master and pupil are primarily instrumentalists, reinforces what, it has been argued, are Indian priorities.[39] The element of dialogue in Indian music is not

---

[36] *Riyāz.*

[37] Ritwik Sanyal and Richard Widdess (both students in the Dagar tradition) give more detail on this important aspect of voice training, and point out that it applied to holding low notes and very early in the day. They also maintain that it distinguishes dhrupad from other genres, such as khyal. See Ritwik Sanyal and Richard Widdess, *Dhrupad: Tradition and Performance in Indian Music* (Aldershot: Ashgate, 2004): 131.

[38] *Bin*: commonly used abbreviation of *rudra vīṇā.*

[39] When the *sarod* (plucked instrument) maestro Amjad Ali Khan taught at the University of York for a month in 1995 he did so entirely through singing. In 1972, when the author was learning the sarangi (bowed instrument) with the veteran player Abdul Majid Khan, the master usually taught by playing phrases on his sarangi. But when the month of Muharram came he announced that we could not play sarangi during that period of austerity and abstinence

only at the heart of the teaching process but also extends into performance. Duets are common within what is essentially a solo tradition, and
many singers will bring one or more of their students to play the tambura
(drone instrument) and occasionally take turns to sing short sections.
Although an example in the film of a folk song and dance full of call and
response – between solo and group, also men and women – is presented
as a rustic contrast to the urban nobility of dhrupad, this underlying connection of 'folk' and 'classical' deserves mention and reminds us that they
are rarely mutually exclusive categories, not least in India.

KHYAL

Despite the great respect in which it is held and the marked resurgence
of interest in recent times, dhrupad is not the principal vocal form and
style in modern Hindustani music. That position is occupied by khyal.
Dhrupad and khyal are not the only styles, however, as several others
regularly find their way into the concert repertoire and are often sung by
exponents of the two main styles. A slight but significant distinction is
made by which the other song types tend to be grouped together as 'light
classical'. So dhrupad is the most 'classical' and revered, while khyal is
also classical and enjoys greater prominence. The romantic song types
thumri and *ghazal* are usually referred to as 'light classical'.[40] The highly
ornamented *tappa*, also categorised thus, has a more direct link with
(Punjabi) folk song, while the term *dhun* points even more towards folk
song and is another favourite short closing item of a classical recital. *Bhajan*
and *qavvali*[41] both have links to classical music (as they may employ
ragas and be sung by classically trained singers) but they are essentially
devotional songs (Hindu and Sufi Muslim, respectively) and are usually
performed as a group (a kind of call and response rendition) which also
distinguishes them from the essentially solo classical tradition. While

(commemorating the martyrdom of the Prophet's grandson, Husain), yet he wished to continue
the lessons throughout the month. Most interestingly (and challengingly), he insisted that we
sing instead. (In a familiar pattern of modern India, both his sons became khyal singers, preferring that career to the far more precarious one of sarangi player.)
[40] Romantic is a much-used adjective in Indian music, yet can be something of a vague, blanket
term. Thumri not only explores love in its erotic sense but also relates the love and yearning of a
woman for a man (based on Radha's love for the Lord Krishna) to the yearning of humankind
for union with God. It is perhaps also the most visual and acted of the classical song types, as it
is very closely connected to Kathak dance, the principal genre of Hindustani dance. The intense
feelings are portrayed in the dance, while in the purely musical context the meaning of the words
is explored through intensely expressive variations that can move an audience just as much.
[41] *Qavvālī*; often spelt *qawwali*.

bhajans occasionally make their way into classical recitals, qavvalis are highly unlikely to do so, despite being an important influence on khyal in the eighteenth and nineteenth centuries. One item that one would emphatically not expect to feature in a classical concert is a 'Bollywood' film song. Despite the initial reaction 'of course not' – any more than one would expect a pop song to be inserted into a *Lieder* recital – the links are closer than the segregation might imply, and the topic is more appropriately examined elsewhere (see chapter 10 below).

It fits the binary nature partially imposed on the history of Indian music that two main styles of classical singing are generally perceived in Hindustani music. The north–south divide is another example, as is the Hindu–Muslim polarity within Hindustani music. Thus dhrupad is a word derived from Sanskrit (Hindu) and khyal is of Persian/Arabic (Muslim) origin, which supports the assumption that dhrupad is far more ancient and harks back to a Hindu golden age, while khyal came after the Muslim invasion and ensuing Delhi Sultanate (1206–1526) to become established in the latter stages of the Mughal Empire (1526–1858). Yet both are unmistakably Indian and both rely on the two pillars of Indian classical music: raga and tala. The simple binary oppositions do not apply when it comes to the actual singers, as both Hindu and Muslim musicians have for centuries been exponents of all the Hindustani vocal styles mentioned, not only in parallel careers but also intermingling often through marriage and in the guru-shishya relationship. Even if we go back as far as Amir Khusrau or Khusro (1253–1325), the great poet, musician and scholar at a number of courts, most notably of the Delhi Sultans Alauddin Khilji (r. 1296–1316) and Ghiyazuddin Tughluq (r. 1321–1325), who is often credited with the invention of many forms and instruments of modern Hindustani music (including khyal), it is acknowledged that khyal does not have as long a history as dhrupad.

Moreover, the development of khyal does not appear to have gathered real momentum until the eighteenth century with Nyamat Khan 'Sadarang', court musician to the Mughal Emperor Muhammad Shah Rangile (r. 1719–1748).[42] With the waning and eventual collapse of the Mughal Empire in the first half of the following century musicians relied more and more on employment at other courts such as those at Gwalior,

---

[42] Without wishing to make unsustainable comparisons, it is at least interesting to note that the emergence of dhrupad coincided with the era of Palestrina, that of khyal with the age of Bach, while, as already noted, the great 'Trinity' of Carnatic singer-composers were contemporaries of Beethoven. Palestrina is still revered and has long been an iconic, almost mythical figure for composers, yet Bach and Beethoven are of course far better known and loved.

Agra, Jaipur and Rampur. Writing around that time (1834), Captain
N. Augustus Willard observed: 'To a person who understands the language sufficiently, it is enough to hear a few good *Kheals*, to be convinced
of the beauties of Hindoostanee songs, both with regard to the pathos
of the poetry and delicacy of the melody.'[43] This high praise of khyal also
implies that it had come to epitomise Indian singing and supports the
view that khyal was a dominant force, although dhrupad was still placed
first in Willard's discussion. He added an important gender distinction to
the two genres: 'In the *Kheal* the subject generally is a love tale, and the
person supposed to utter it, a female. The style is extremely graceful, and
replete with studied elegance and embellishments.'[44] Contrast that with
his comments on dhrupad:

This may properly be considered as the heroic song of Hindoostan. The subject is frequently the recital of some of the memorable actions of their heroes,
or other didactic theme. It also engrosses love matters, as well as trifling and
frivolous subjects. The style is very masculine, and almost entirely devoid of
studied ornamental flourishes.[45]

Most of Willard's observations still hold good today, with some qualifications. What emerges is the familiar distinction between khyal as
richly ornamented and dhrupad as far less so. 'Studied ornamental flourishes' must be taken to mean ornamentation permitted in khyal but not
in dhrupad, rather than suggesting that dhrupad was totally lacking in
ornamentation. One could argue that an understanding of the language
is less important in khyal than in other kinds of Indian singing, as so
much of the singing makes little or no use of the text. The inclusion of
'love matters, as well as trifling and frivolous subjects' in dhrupad song
texts is less typical of what we know today and would be more typical of
khyal. Regardless of the sentiments and from which gender they emanate,
there is no expectation that a khyal singer be female (though the 'masculine' nature of dhrupad still means that dhrupad singers tend to be
male). The majority of famous khyal singers have been men, especially
Muslim court musicians. Notable exceptions must be mentioned: several talented female singers from the region of Maharashtra learnt from
such men or from their mothers, for example Kesarbai Kerkar, Mogubai
Kurdikar and her daughter Kishori Amonkar, and the recent past has also
seen a number of celebrated Hindu male exponents, such as Omkarnath

[43] Captain N. Augustus Willard, 'A Treatise on the Music of Hindoostan' in S. M. Tagore (ed.),
    Hindu Music from Various Authors (3rd edn, Varanasi: The Chowkhamba Sanskrit Series Office,
    1965): 102–3.
[44] Ibid.: 102.   [45] Ibid.: 101.

Thakur, Bhimsen Joshi and the brothers from the holy city of the Hindus, Varanasi (Benares), Rajan and Sajan Mishra, who have been especially prominent in the UK over the past decade and more. Varanasi is the birthplace of Ravi Shankar and also produced the great shahnai (North Indian oboe) master Bismillah Khan and the (female) khyal and thumri singers Siddheshwari Devi and Girija Devi.

The balance of composition to improvisation is difficult to pinpoint throughout Indian music but in general khyal is regarded as much freer than dhrupad, where the concern is with careful enunciation of the text, limited ornamentation, detail and clarity of notes, which involves careful attention to intonation. The word khyal means thought or imagination and the style allows a wide range of ornamentation and extensive improvisation, especially in extended fast note patterns called *tan*.[46] Whereas in dhrupad we may expect the full composition to be sung this is not always the case in khyal. The emphasis on imagination and improvisation is only part of the reason. Even though the composition will probably have no more than a sthayi and an antara – and sometimes even the antara is omitted – the whole thing might never be sung more than once, in a performance lasting up to an hour or so. There are in fact two types of khyal, usually sung without a break. First comes the *bara* khyal (big khyal), followed by the *chota* khyal (little khyal). As might be expected, the bara khyal takes most of the time and the chota khyal might take as little as a quarter of the performance or less. In one respect, tempo, the difference between the two is enormous. A bara khyal is usually in a long rhythm cycle (tala) of 12, 14 or 16 beats and the tempo is very slow, so that it is common for just one cycle to take around a minute. Thus a sthayi and antra, each taking at least one cycle, would fill a large proportion of the time if subject to repetitions, so that only the last phrase of the sthayi is repeated as a hook between longer improvisations. This also involves a fragmentation of the text and in general the words are less important in khyal than the musical elaboration, often with meaningless syllables replacing words. In the case of the chota khyal, where one cycle of the tala may take five seconds or even less, the whole first cycle of the sthayi will be used as a refrain, thus repeated many times, and the antara may also be repeated a few times. The range of elaborations and improvisations between returns to the composition is extensive. Tans alone come in a variety of articulations: they may be sung to words or syllables from the song text (*bol* tan) or instead use the Indian note names equivalent to our

[46] *Tān.*

do-re-mi etc., (*sargam tan*);[47] most often they are sung to 'ah' (*akar* tan) and occasionally with a vigorous oscillation on each note (*gamak* tan). However articulated, tans are sung with a speed and fluency over wide ranges that most Western singers would be unable to match.

Khyal is historicised primarily through gharanas, which are essentially schools[48] of (khyal) vocalists, although the word is commonly borrowed to apply to instrumentalists. Dhrupad has a comparable tradition, though the word *bani*[49] is used instead of gharana. While dhrupad and khyal are noticeably different, even to an uninitiated listener, they should not be too rigidly demarcated either musically or socially. As we have seen they share many musical traits but even more important is the overlap between the singers themselves. For example, the famous khyal singer Alladiya Khan came from a family of dhrupad singers in Jaipur who abandoned that tradition for the more dynamic khyal, and the Gwalior gharana, one of the most important, was heavily influenced by dhrupad. While the guru-shishya-parampara continues to flourish there is less certainty about the gharanas. In fact, what appears to have happened is that the concept of gharana has become applied more and more to instrumental traditions, of supposed antiquity, rather than to a nineteenth-century taxonomy of khyal singers. The essence of a gharana is that it centres on several generations of a teaching tradition in a city (with a court boasting distinguished musicians) from which the gharana usually took its name. (One sometimes finds gharanas named after their founder or most influential member, as in the Seniya gharana mentioned earlier.) From this lineage the gharana developed its own distinctive style and repertoire, often jealously guarded in the days of court patronage, and strong allegiances resulted.

Wim van der Meer distinguished between those khyal gharanas that were heavily influenced by dhrupad (Gwalior, Agra, Jaipur) and those manifesting a *sarangi* background (Kirana, Delhi, Patiala, Indore).[50] Admitting the danger of oversimplification and unfairness it appears on the whole that the most popular khyal singers of the recent past have come from the latter group just listed. The first half of the twentieth century, especially around the 1930s to 1950s, was a 'golden age' of khyal

---

[47] The seven notes are sa re (or ri) ga ma pa dha ni (corresponding to doh re mi fa soh la ti) and the combination of the first four is what gives the name 'sargam'. While by no means all Western musicians are trained in *solfeggio* all Indian musicians will have a thorough grasp of sargam and, as we have seen, often include it in performances.

[48] Though the root of the term is the Hindi word *ghar*, meaning house or home.

[49] *Bāni*.

[50] Wim Van der Meer, *Hindustani Music in the 20th Century* (The Hague: Martinus Nijhoff, 1980): 58.

singing (owing much of that accolade no doubt to the fact that it corresponded to the advent of sound recording). Still held in the highest esteem are singers like Faiyaz Khan (Agra gharana), Bare Ghulam Ali Khan (Patiala gharana), Alladiya Khan (Jaipur gharana), Abdul Wadid Khan and Abdul Karim Khan (Kirana gharana).[51] The last-named gharana went on to thrive probably more than the others, largely through the postwar legend Bhimsen Joshi (1922–2011). The highly expressive, romantic style associated with that gharana had much to do with its continuing appeal. Another Kirana singer, Pran Nath (1918–1996), made his name in the USA, especially as guru to the minimalist composer Terry Riley and a large number of others. Selecting just a few names and leaving out countless others is bound to seem partial, but the intention is to avoid a set of biographies.

The range of vocal timbres is wide in Indian classical singing, especially khyal, and is often cited as a principal distinguishing feature between gharanas. Vamanrao Deshpande's brief but seminal study tended towards imprecise adjectives rather than scientific analysis to point out some of the contrasts:

In Kirana the voice emerges from a deliberately constricted throat and has a nasal twang. Agra voice is also nasal (*nakki*); in addition it has a gruff, grating quality. In one way or the other both these gharanas have imported artificiality into their voice-production. On the other hand the Jaipur tradition emphasises a natural, free and full-throated voice.[52]

When listening to a khyal singer absorbed in a slow alap or in full flight with dazzling tans (extended fast note patterns) it is essential to remember that the inclusion of what may sound to the uninitiated ear like strange, exaggerated and even unpleasant effects in the range of vocal textures is there for the purpose of expression and to support the singer's creativity. After all, the composed part (sthayi and antara) occupies a relatively small proportion of the performance and the rest is the singer's improvisation. Amy Catlin-Jairazbhoy underlined this important point that the Indian singer has other priorities than just producing an equivalent of bel canto: 'Traditionally, an Indian singer's worth was determined largely by his or her musical ideas as expressed in improvisation, both original as well as those received from the *guru* or *ustad*, not on mere physical tone

[51] The title *Ustād* will usually be given to each of these men. It means something like 'master of the art' and is applied to Muslims. For Hindus the equivalent is *Pandit* (learned man).
[52] Vamanrao Deshpande (trans. S. H. Deshpande), *Indian Musical Traditions: An Aesthetic Study of the Gharanas in Hindustani Music* (Bombay: Popular Prakashan, 1973): 16.

production.'[53] The use of continuous vibrato, which acts as a strong unifying force in Western classical singing, is not present in Indian singing. Instead it is used judiciously where demanded by the raga. Beyond that, different gharanas cultivate different possibilities within the vast range offered in khyal singing, which results in different vocal styles.[54]

One of the most interesting aspects of the gharanas is how they came into being. While being noted for jealously guarding their repertoires and technical secrets they did intermingle, often in unusual ways. It emerges that one gharana was founded on deficient singing while another was built on theft! The founder of the Agra gharana, Ghagghe Khuda Bakhsh, in the first half of the nineteenth century is supposed to have suffered from impeded voice production, so he took himself off to relatively nearby Gwalior to study with khyal singers there. By way of reciprocation he taught some of the Agra dhrupad compositions. He even had to endure death threats from a few Gwalior musicians, who feared that he might appropriate to Agra what he had learned in Gwalior.[55] It is ironic that an even more famous story from Indian music history concerns two of those very same musicians, Haddu Khan and Hassu Khan, usually considered the founders of the Gwalior gharana. During the reign of Jhankoji Rao Scindia (1827–1843) Haddu Khan and Hassu Khan hid behind a curtain and thus undetected were able to copy the technique and compositions of the singer Muhammad Khan, among whose accomplishments were especially difficult and attractive tans.

The mention of impaired vocal production leads to a glimpse of the contrasting worlds of Indian and Western voice training as given in a short article by Mary Grover, relating how she was asked to prescribe a course of therapy for an Indian khyal singer who had severely strained his voice through too much practice. In her introduction to Grover's paper Amy Catlin-Jairazbhoy drew attention to the notoriously lengthy hours spent on *riyaz* (practice) by Indian musicians: 'During that effort, all physical concerns, weariness, stress, and strain are put aside to further the goal of perfecting musical expression.'[56] Grover identified the characteristics of the patient's singing disorder, which included interfering

---

[53] Amy Catlin-Jairazbhoy, introduction to Mary Grover, 'Voice Therapy for a Classical Singer from India: a Case Study Combining Eastern and Western Techniques', in *Seminar on Indian Music and the West* (Mumbai: Sangeet Research Academy, 1996): 210.

[54] More detailed studies of gharanas and individual styles are recommended in the Sources.

[55] Bonnie C. Wade, *Khyāl: Creativity within North India's Classical Music Tradition* (Cambridge University Press, 1984): 83–4.

[56] Catlin-Jairazbhoy, introduction to Grover, 'Voice Therapy': 209.

tension in the jaw, tongue, face, head, neck, larynx and body; high vertical laryngeal position; collapsed pharynx (closed throat); reduced thyro-hyoid space.[57] Indian Ayurvedic remedies and meditation techniques were combined with Western relaxation and breathing exercises to restore the singer's voice and actually improve on its status quo ante.

Good recordings of all the big names, whether or not mentioned in these pages, are not easy to find. Several made it on to LP discs but that meant the performance was abbreviated or that even shorter extracts were transferred from 78 rpm discs. The recording quality was often very poor and some of the great artists recorded were past their prime. It therefore makes sense to focus on the more recent past, when superior recordings could be made and also when the artists' live recitals can still live in the memories of many. For these reasons one singer will be singled out for discussion: Amir Khan (1912–1974),[58] undoubtedly one of the most admired and influential khyal singers of recent times. His singing was generally sober and introspective and maybe what one might have expected more of a singer from the dhrupad-influenced group of gharanas listed above. In fact he came from a sarangi background and learnt that first before concentrating on singing. (By his final years he was almost unable to play the sarangi; he also eschewed it as an accompaniment in favour of the harmonium.) He was influenced by the style of the Kirana gharana (also with a sarangi background) but effectively created his own gharana: the one named after the city of Indore. Once again, the gharana is less important than the name of the individual master, and hardly any other singer has exerted such an influence, not only on other singers but also on instrumentalists. It is an open secret that the incomparable sitar maestro Vilayat Khan (1928–2004) based much of his distinctive and pioneering style on Amir Khan's singing. One characteristic should be singled out: the development of long and complex tans based on the mirkhand idea of note combinations discussed earlier. Whereas other khyal singers, for example Bhimsen Joshi, would sing long melismatic *akar tans* (to the sound 'ah') Amir Khan favoured sargam tans (sung to the note names) with complex mixtures of conjunct and disjunct motion. The author had the great privilege of being allowed to sit in on Amir Khan's daily riyaz (practice) a few years before his tragic death in a traffic accident in Kolkata. With extraordinary humility the great singer would go and sit on his bed, pick up his tambura and

---

[57] Mary Grover, 'Voice Therapy': 212.
[58] To avoid confusion with the British boxer, the reader is advised to conduct any internet search under *Ustād* Amir Khan.

start singing, quite oblivious to the two or three visitors to his Mumbai apartment. The abiding memory is a series of wonderful sargam tans just described, confirming their place as a cornerstone of his art.

The 'golden age' of khyal singing proposed earlier corresponded to a zenith of the gharana fortunes. Though they are still much talked about today several factors have weakened their hold on Hindustani music. Many Indian musicians received their initial training from their fathers (sometimes mothers) and were then sent to learn from distinguished figures of whichever gharana was most favoured within the family. With the rise of the middle classes an increasing number of musicians are coming from families without professional musicians, who are thus sent straight to external gurus, and the same social change has fuelled another significant development: the growth of music schools and colleges. While such institutions are the normal places for training professional musicians in the West, they are regarded more as places for teaching enthusiastic amateurs in India and stand in direct opposition to the gharana-based guru-shishya-parampara (although in fairness they should be welcomed as complementary and a further means of dissemination).

SINGING AND MODERN TECHNOLOGY

Increased mobility and the availability of the widest range of styles through public concerts (rather than the private small gatherings of the old princely courts) and recordings have inevitability led to a mixing of styles to create new ones and a weakening of individual gharana identity. The ease of access through recordings and the widespread practice of copying from them have even led to what has wittily been dubbed the 'Sony gharana', which may be described as at once all gharanas and none. As noted in chapter 1, Indian singers have not always been cooperative in the matter of recording. (The example was cited of some folk singers in Rajasthan who refused to be recorded because they were afraid the microphone would steal their voices.) Fox Strangways, writing in the early days of the recording era, mentioned a similar case:

The singing that appealed to me most was that of Chandra Prabhu at Bhavnagav. She compelled respect at once by refusing on any account to be phonographed; perhaps she thought, amongst other things, that if she committed her soul to a mere piece of wax it might get broken in the train – and my subsequent experience showed that this was only too likely.[59]

---

[59] Fox Strangways, *Music of Hindostan*: 90.

Recording also changed the very structure of recitals, which in the past had had no time limit, and even today concerts can go on all night. One strategy was to excise short extracts from longer recordings, giving the equivalent of Wagnerian 'bleeding chunks'; another was to condense complete khyal performances (typically around an hour in the concert hall) into around twenty minutes to fit on to one side of an LP disc. With the advent of CDs it became possible to represent more closely the concert format (and many are direct transcriptions of live recitals). One way in which recording technology actually rebalanced the structure of a recital was in the 78 rpm era, when a chota khyal could be fitted on to these discs of short duration, thereby bringing it into greater prominence than had hitherto been the case, when it was preferred as a teaching piece.[60] Finally, DVD technology and the internet[61] render easily accessible the visual aspect, a vital element that can be ignored and yet is essential to the communication of Indian singing, even more than an obvious example such as opera.

While singers have the option of refusing to be recorded they will want and need at least to give public concerts. In that context hardly a single Indian musician will perform without amplification. Nowadays there would be an intractable paradox if a singer refused to sing into a microphone for a recording while relying on it for a live performance. The Rajasthani folk musicians and Chandra Prabhu (cited as examples of resistance to recording) did not rely on amplification anyway, so the issue would not have arisen. Today, however, we can be bold enough to claim that every Indian performer will expect amplification in a recital, even for a small audience in a relatively small hall. That suggests that the musicians have become so used to amplification that they rely on it even when it is really not needed. In large halls, very often built for purposes other than music recitals and therefore with poor acoustics, the intimate nature of Indian classical music (essentially a solo recital, or at most chamber music) relies on the boost. Yet even in the traditional gatherings of a few dozen connoisseurs, where performers and audience are seated cross-legged on the floor in close proximity, it is common to find amplification. The main problem is not one of purist horror that a noble tradition of the princely courts has turned into something more like a pop concert, or even a simple Luddite aversion to electronic technology, but that the quality of the amplification is often substandard. Too much generalisation is risky here,

---

[60] The effect of recording on the structure of performances is discussed by Gerry Farrell in chapter 4, 'The Gramophone Comes to India', of *Indian Music and the West*.
[61] YouTube has a huge range, as might be expected.

as superb equipment is available and very often used. What is surprising
is to observe a lengthy sound check a few hours before the performance
(often the only thing resembling a rehearsal) only to see the performers
(main artist and accompanists) disrupt the settings during the performance itself by signalling to the sound technicians for more volume.

Of course amplification does have benefits and they are what performers rely on to justify all the drawbacks. The main defence is that
the minute details of the raga (ornamentation, subtle pitch changes and
slight nuances of vocal colour) can be heard quite easily throughout the
auditorium. Perhaps amplification makes the physical toll of singing
easier to sustain. The fearsome reputation of dhrupad (demanding the
strength of five buffaloes) has been calmed and technology may well have
had something to do with that. While dhrupad (also khyal) singing can
explore extremes of register and dynamics, much of the performance is
a restrained and intimate exploration of svara, sruti and gamaka (note,
microtone, ornamentation) – far from some kind of intimidating stam-
pede. Zia Mohiuddin Dagar, one of the most respected and historically
informed dhrupad masters of recent times, actually had a contact microphone designed for his instrument (*rudra vina*) in order to enhance this
restraint and intimacy. Thus amplification cannot be dismissed simply as
crude and detrimental but can be a means of allowing the voice to relax
and focus on the musical details and expression rather than waste effort
in straining to be heard. The problem is that the snags so often outweigh
the benefits and the persistence of inferior amplification and disrupted
settings can suffocate its potential.

GENDER

It is generally assumed that dhrupad is a male preserve, and this is largely
the case, though some women have taken it up successfully. In the wider
context of Indian singing women have been far from subservient intrud-
ers into a male domain. We can even toy with a type of yin–yang in
Indian music (and the male–female duality was at one time imposed on
its very heart: the raga system). Dhrupad is held to be essentially masculine: it demands physical endurance, powerful singing and uses heavier-
sounding instruments in accompaniment. In the case of khyal (which
is thought to bring together elements from dhrupad and qavvali, both
male traditions) most singers regularly cited as founders and sustainers
of the gharanas have also been men, though khyal is far from being considered a male preserve, nor can it be claimed with any certainty that

most of its exponents have been men. The 'feminine' aspects of khyal have already been noted: it has lighter, more capricious moments than are heard in dhrupad; the *tabla*[62] drums are used in accompaniment and are higher-pitched and nimbler than the *pakhavaj*[63] drum in dhrupad; the bowed *sarangi*[64] is also used in accompaniment and lies more in the female vocal range than the male (despite the fact that tabla and sarangi players have nearly always been exclusively male).[65] Wim van der Meer wrote of contrasting egos in the majority of song texts: masculine for dhrupad and feminine for khyal;[66] yet women chose teachers as much from the dhrupad-influenced as the sarangi-influenced gharanas, in which more delicate and romantic qualities are emphasised. What has tended to inspire singers from outside the gharanas and push one gharana or another to the fore is outstanding individual singers; the name of the singer comes first and is famed, while the gharana may not be universally known and sometimes different gharanas are ascribed to the same singer. Thus gender differences are clouded in khyal, perhaps more than in any other field of Hindustani music.

Apart from the present number of acclaimed female exponents of khyal, the role of women in its early development is even more crucial. While dhrupad singers were often Brahmins (occasionally converting to Islam) and provided the respectable court music associated with iconic singers such as Tansen, the growing preference for khyal was seen as a sign of decadence and decline, especially as it was sung by courtesans. The stigma extended to their accompanists, particularly sarangi players who doubled as their teachers and were occasionally regarded as little more than pimps.[67] The Indian concept of courtesan is difficult to capture in that one word. Pejorative names like *nautch*, used by the Victorians to refer to dancing girls, whom they regarded as prostitutes, and the more commonly accepted and nuanced *bai*, *baiji* or *tawaif* indicate the primary function of singing and dancing. *Bai* is often suffixed to the woman's name, and many of the most famous singers had this suffix. The courtesan's function was not necessarily sexual. Then, as now, many women would have put on a display of singing and dancing as no more than a front for paid sex but the poor quality of the preliminary show and the location in which it was held would have made the true purpose obvious. The real courtesans were above all else expected to be skilled in music and dancing and also polite

[62] *Tablā.* [63] *Pakhāvaj.* [64] *Sārangī.*
[65] More will be said on the subject of accompaniment below.
[66] Van der Meer, *Hindustani Music*: 56.
[67] Farrell, *Indian Music and the West*: 121.

conversation, so that men would be far from ashamed to enjoy their company. In this respect they can be compared to Japanese geishas, as well as to the refined courtesans of Europe.[68] Neuman emphasised the link between courtesans and the art of singing: 'Not all courtesans are vocalists, but until the early part of this [twentieth] century virtually all female vocalists were courtesans.'[69] Since Independence, and even earlier, both singing and dancing have moved outside professional hereditary families and gained a new kind of respectability. It so happens that the first Indian recording stars were courtesans. Farrell recounts the story of Gauhar Jan (*c.* 1875–1930), a tawaif from Calcutta, who in 1902 became the first major Indian recording artist for Gramophone and Typewriter Ltd and whose repertoire was extensive, including khyal, thumri and dhrupad.[70] Another female star, Jankibai, was able to command even greater fees.[71]

An earlier encounter with courtesans occurred at the end of the eighteenth and beginning of the nineteenth centuries, at a time when the British, including their womenfolk, were especially open to Indian culture and even prepared to 'go native' (before the invasion of the British 'memsahebs' and a distancing from Indians and their culture). Quite a vogue for 'Hindostannie Airs' sprang up, both in India and back in Britain. These were Indian songs (generally folk rather than classical) mostly learnt from 'nautch' girls and transcribed into staff notation, often with harpsichord or other keyboard accompaniment. Both informants and collectors tended to be women.[72] While the British performers would often dress in Indian clothes, it is highly unlikely that they adopted an Indian way of singing as they were not trained in it and tended to stick to their Western musical background.

Time and again one hears that women were the repositories of songs, from marriage songs of Rajasthan to khyals of the north and kritis of the south. Part of the reason why this was not more widely acknowledged has to do with the stigma attached to women as performers. It is no coincidence that the baijis and tawaifs of the north and the *devadasis* of the south were regarded as consummate artists but also tainted with prostitution. Singing and dancing went together and often reached the

---

[68] Regula Burckhardt Qureshi, *Master Musicians of India: Hereditary Sarangi Players Speak* (New York: Routledge, 2007): 296.

[69] Daniel M. Neuman *The Life of Music in North India: the Organization of an Artistic Tradition* (Chicago and London: University of Chicago Press, 1990): 100.

[70] Farrell, *Indian Music and the West*: 118.   [71] Ibid.: 119.

[72] This intriguing aspect of East–West musical exchanges is investigated in Ian Woodfield, *Music of the Raj: a Social and Economic History of Music in Late Eighteenth-Century Anglo-Indian Society* (Oxford University Press, 2000).

heights of refinement, as well as plumbing the depths of social rejection, so that the women could teach the men as well as learn from them. The southern devadasis (literally servants of god) were attached to temples and ritually married to the god. As such they were separate from women who married mortals and were often far better educated, as well as being skilled in singing and dancing. They performed not only in the temple but also in the royal courts and their patrons could also fulfil the role of earthly husband. It was when royal patronage declined in the late nineteenth century that many devadasis turned to prostitution as an alternative means of support. Their dance was known as *Dasi Attam* and became *Bharata Natyam*, now probably the most famous of all Indian dance styles. The Victorian opprobrium heaped on 'nautch' girls was replaced by middle-class respectability not only from the change of name (which noticeably removed all connections with the devadasis) but also because the dance was taken up by Brahmin women.

South India also produced the classical singer who can be regarded as probably the most iconic of the past century, M. S. Subbulakshmi (1916–2004). So famous was she that just the initials M. S. were enough to identify her. She was called the nightingale of India and Jawaharlal Nehru famously remarked 'who am I, a mere Prime Minister, before a Queen of Music?', while Mahatma Gandhi is supposed to have said that he would prefer to hear M. S. speak the words of his favourite bhajans than hear anyone else sing them. Although born in Tamil Nadu to a musician father and mother from the devadasi community and initially trained in Carnatic music, she also learned Hindustani singing, which no doubt contributed to her status as a national treasure.[73] A major step in her rise was her appearance in the 1945 hit film *Meera* about another iconic Indian woman: Mira (Meera or Meerabai), a sixteenth-century princess from Rajasthan who dedicated herself to Krishna and composed a large number of bhajans (devotional songs) in his honour. She symbolises feminine creativity and devotion to the extent of a loss of self in ecstatic song. M. S. Subbulakshmi took the part of the saint-poetess in the film, lifting her reputation to dizzying heights and establishing her as a definitive interpreter of bhajans. Mira bhajans are still popular today. Two decades after the film, the queen of film singers Lata Mangeshkar recorded an album in modern musical arrangements by her brother, Hridayanath Mangeshkar.

---

[73] When the author first arrived in India, at Madras (now Chennai) airport in 1971 and was asked the purpose of his visit by the immigration officer, no sooner had music been mentioned than the official asked 'do you know M. S. Subbulakshmi?'

SINGING WITH THE HANDS AND THROUGH
THE INSTRUMENTS

Just as the importance of ornamentation in Indian singing has been emphasised, so too must be the matter of gesture. In fact the two may go hand in hand (or voice in hand): gesture is the physical manifestation of vocal articulation and dates back at least to the Vedic period. Arnold Bake forged a link from these early gestures to the elaborate sign language that is the basis of storytelling through dance, as in the modern classical styles of Bharata Natyam, Kathakali, Kathak and so on.[74] An instrumentalist has his or her hands full with playing, so what of a singer? Although it cannot be claimed that gesticulation applies systematically and all singers rely on it equally, anyone new to the performance practices of Indian music may well think that the singer is somehow enacting a dance at the same time, albeit while sitting on the floor. For a start, there has always been a very close link between music and dance in India (far closer than now exists in the West) and for another thing there are traditions of storytelling through singing and dancing, in which the exponent remains seated. Many would say that the amount of gesticulation in Indian singing is only an extension of everyday activity, as Indians love to gesticulate (allowing for general-isation). Movements of the hands, arms and head serve not only to inten-sify the words but also to give them graphic representation. This happens in singing, where the character of an ornament may be depicted by hand waving, the shape of a note or phrase by an arm tracing a curve, an accent or phrase ending by a flick of the wrist, a long, sustained, usually high note, by a clenching of the fist and tight closing of the eyes, and so on. The listeners too are expected to respond in sound and gestures to indicate their appreciation. Choosing the right moment is a sign of true under-standing and indiscriminate shows of enthusiasm are frowned upon. The responses can include raising an arm to express pleasure at a well-executed phrase and frequent murmurings or even shouts of 'wah' and other words equivalent to 'bravo'. In short, Indian singing should be seen as well as heard to derive maximum enjoyment and appreciation.

HOW SINGING IS ACCOMPANIED

While both traditions, Hindustani and Carnatic, regard singing as the creator and driver equally of the vocal and instrumental repertoires, the

---

[74] Arnold Bake, 'The Music of India', in Egon Wellesz (ed.), *New Oxford History of Music*. Vol. 1: *Ancient and Oriental Music* (Oxford University Press, 1957): 203–4.

relationship is especially close in Carnatic music, where instrumental items are often almost direct replications of composed songs and the greatest names from the past, effectively the founding fathers of the tradition, were noted as singers and composers of devotional songs. Unsurprisingly, therefore, singing and instrumental music have a very close relationship throughout India and classical vocal performances will be supported and enhanced by instrumental accompaniment. The Indian concept of accompaniment needs to be clarified, as we are used to a keyboard instrument accompanying singing and may the more easily assume that the same sort of accompaniment occurs in Indian music. The common word for accompaniment, *sangati*, does convey the meaning of 'going with' and actually more closely realises its essence than its Western equivalent, which generally means a completely separate part. In khyal the tabla drums also provide sangati, consisting mainly of keeping the tala and occasionally improvising, though of course the accompaniment is not melodic. For that purpose the bowed sarangi is the traditional instrument in Hindustani music; in Carnatic music (also occasionally in Hindustani) it is the violin. The harmonium has now emerged as the most likely choice in Hindustani music, but has not similarly threatened the violin in the south.

In an improvising tradition such as Indian music the accompanist will not know what the singer is going to do next and is thus unable to supply a ready-made accompaniment, as would happen in Western music. Three options are thus available, which are all exploited in Indian music:

1   wait until the singer pauses and then get in with one's own improvisation;
2   join in with the singer in unison when pre-composed material is being sung;
3   play what the singer has just sung as a kind of echo or shadowing.

The singer does pause from time to time, either to take a break or think of some new ideas or just to give the accompanist a chance to improvise. The compositions (in whole or in part) are used as refrains and make frequent returns between episodes of improvisation. But the third option is the most interesting and also takes most of the performance. It is a kind of heterophony as the accompanist reproduces as soon as possible what the singer has just sung, creating a kind of blurring and overlap of phrases.[75]

---

[75] The world is full of similar types of heterophonic interplay. Paul Berliner examined a different kind by a single performer in the complex intertwining of vocal and interlocking patterns of *mbira* (sometimes crudely referred to as 'thumb piano') music in Zimbabwe. The singer-player draws inherent pitches together to outline resultant melodies. 'As a result of this sensitive

Here we can take a moment to consider one of the greatest controversies and paradoxes of the tradition: the absorption and rise of the harmonium. At first sight this has nothing to do with singing, yet it turns out to have everything to do with it. Originally an import associated with the nineteenth-century missionaries, the harmonium developed into its small portable version, played, like all Indian concert instruments, seated on the floor. It is now the favourite accompaniment to singing and is to be found in all sorts of music, from the concert stages and film studios of the cities to the villages. The harmonium accompanist engages with all three options listed above but, realising the limitations of the instrument, will not always try to imitate the singer too closely. The advantage is a clearer texture and many singers have preferred this less cluttered sound as well as a more reliable, or at least consistent, intonation than tends to be produced on the sarangi by anyone except the very best players. So despite being a relative newcomer the harmonium has become so popular that it could be described as the most ubiquitous Indian instrument. That is despite the efforts over more than half a century of many leading Indians, led by Rabindranath Tagore, and also of some influential Westerners (for example, the English composer John Foulds and his wife Maud MacCarthy) to have it removed from the subcontinent. It was even banned from All India Radio from the 1940s to the 1970s, but eventually that most important source of patronage accepted its failure to starve the instrument into extinction and relented.

Without entering into the arguments for and against[76] we can use the harmonium to fix one end of a continuum, at the other end of which is the voice. Not a single one of the main vocal ornaments can be correctly reproduced on the harmonium, though many players have found ingenious ways of simulating them fairly convincingly. This is because portamento (*mind*),[77] from the smallest to the longest slides, is at the heart of Indian singing. At various points along the continuum are the melodic instruments of Indian music. Most, especially the stringed and wind

---

interplay between the instrument and the voice, it sometimes seems as if the *mbira* continues to sing a pattern emphasised by a vocalist after the vocalist has stopped singing it': Paul Berliner, *The Soul of Mbira: Music and Traditions of the Shona People of Zimbabwe* (Berkeley, Los Angeles, London: University of California Press, 1978): 117. Berliner identified three basic singing styles: the one already described, which is low in volume and range; a contrasting loud, high pitched singing, incorporating falsetto and yodelling; a refined and demanding style based on poetic texts following the general harmonic movement, ibid.: 115–21. See also p. 290 below.

[76] These were covered in a seminar to review the All India Radio ban, published in the *Journal of the Sangeet Natak Akademi*, 20 (1971).

[77] *Mind.*

instruments, are able to produce portamenti and glissandi, albeit much less effortlessly than the voice and often involving a degree of pain and disfigurement to the fingers. For example, on the (plucked) sitar the metal string is pulled along the frets, while on the (bowed) sarangi the fingernails slide along the string, and on both instruments many consecutive notes are played with the same finger, further facilitating the seamless joining of notes. The other crucial drawback of the harmonium is its restriction to twelve divisions of the octave, whereas Indian theory recognises twenty-two srutis (discussed earlier in this chapter). Maud MacCarthy (1882–1967) was credited by no less an authority than Fox Strangways with an ability to sing all twenty-two srutis up and down the octave.[78] This curious feat was observed during her pioneering series of lectures around England soon after her return from a first stay in India (*c.* 1908–9). Her sensitivity to intonation (she was also a celebrated concert violinist) was another reason for her passionate hatred of the harmonium.

Ornamentation can not only be the main criterion of 'vocal-ness' (the ideal of Indian music) but also serve as a principal distinguishing feature between vocal styles. In the West we are at least conversant with the vocal ideal: keyboard players are exhorted to 'sing' almost as much as their Indian counterparts and 'cantabile' is a favourite marking in instrumental scores. We also associate certain kinds of ornamentation with different genres: quick 'scoops' from one note to another above are common in folk song and quite prevalent in stage musicals, but the same mannerisms might sound comical in classical singing, where they would generally conflict with the notation. Even portamento goes in and out of fashion so, once again, it might sound like a comical and incongruous mannerism. At the same time, a degree of freedom is afforded to the singer, who is guided by taste and personal preference as much as by teaching, genre and sense of tradition, so the matter of ornamentation is neither as systematised nor central to its tradition as is the case with Indian singing (where ornamentation is really too vital to be given that somewhat *laissez-faire* title).

TOWARDS VOCAL AND INSTRUMENTAL PARITY

Finally, let us return to the notion of singing as the basis of all Indian music. While affirming that it is nowhere truer than in India certain

---

[78] Neil Sorrell, 'From "harm-omnium" to harmonia omnium', *Journal of the Indian Musicological Society* 40 (2009–10): 123.

qualifications must be admitted. It might be pointed out, for a start, that the Hindu deities stand out more as instrumentalists than singers: Krishna with his flute; Shiva with his drum; Saraswati with her *vina*.[79] In earthly music instruments have, throughout history, fulfilled one role as an accompaniment to singing. Even when played solo a large part of their repertoire is derived from singing. This is particularly noticeable in Carnatic music, where instruments reproduce entire vocal compositions, with even the song texts given in announcements, CD insert notes and so on. A similar process, if less detailed and pervasive, applies in Hindustani music, where vocal compositions are frequently employed by instrumentalists. Making the connection clear has become quite fashionable, especially since the time that the late sitar maestro Vilayat Khan pioneered the *gayki*[80] (singing) style. By exploiting his unrivalled control when pulling the wire of the main playing string he could imitate the intricate vocal ornaments. He also made a feature of singing the compositions as well as playing them, to make the connection abundantly clear and also to demonstrate how faithfully he could follow his own singing in his playing.[81] In an interview with the author (1997) Vilayat Khan underplayed his part in the creation of the gayki style, suggesting that it had been part of Indian music all along. He preferred to celebrate his application of the mirkhand principle (discussed earlier in this chapter) to elicit unusual and expressive patterns in the raga.

Ram Narayan (b. 1927), the most famous player of the sarangi (often regarded as the most vocal of Indian instruments) expressed an ambivalence towards singers as temperamental artists rather than to the importance of vocal music, which he always followed in his playing. He started his career in the way of all sarangi players by accompanying singers. His frustration at being denied his own expression and frequently finding himself more competent than the singer led him to abandon this role and strike out (in the 1950s) on an unchartered career as a soloist exclusively. This meant that he took his vocal expertise with him but was free to develop the sarangi's individual capabilities and create his own distinctive style. Finding ways of getting the best of both worlds is also the concern of many younger sarangi players, for example the soloist Dhruba Ghosh (*b.* 1957) who has focused on adapting the sarangi to the modern world,

---

[79] *Vinā.*   [80] *Gāyki.*

[81] This is systematically demonstrated by the sarangi virtuoso Ram Narayan on the cassette accompanying Neil Sorrell and Ram Narayan, *Indian Music in Performance: A Practical Introduction* (Manchester University Press, 1980). First he sings a composition and then plays

treating it as an instrument in its own right rather than a second-best to singing. The following remark makes it clear that he considers the replication of vocal music no longer to be the way forward for instruments:

And even today, a sarangi player thinks that following vocal is his religion. I mean, his performance religion! What has happened is that when a sarangi recital takes place, what a sarangi player does is reflect the vocal recital.[82]

Ghosh pointed out that by studying singing the sarangi players 'used to be called "125 percent singer" (*sawai gawayya*, literally "one-and-a-quarter singer")'.[83] At the present time, therefore, not everyone is paying lip service to the supremacy of vocal music, with instruments treated as a poor second in their attempts to imitate the voice. The recent history of Indian music if anything suggests the opposite, as the most famous and widely travelled artists since the heyday of Ravi Shankar have been instrumentalists, and their virtuosity has shone in its own right. Dhruba Ghosh is challenging a very protracted status quo and warning that an acceptance of the primacy of singing without critical inquiry would be to iron out the many interesting creases in Indian musical history. His proposed fusion of instrument-specific patterns with the vocal style as a way forward for the beleaguered sarangi[84] does not take into account that comparable fusions may have been going on throughout history and there is also evidence to suggest that instruments were less obviously 'vocal' in the past. Nor should we overlook the role reversal, whereby singers imitate instruments. This does not happen very often but is a feature of dhrupad singing and is probably most familiar in tabla solos when the player vocalises the drum sounds.[85] The primacy of singing has been emphasised in this chapter, not only to fit the agenda of the whole book but also to reflect what has evidently happened throughout Indian history. Yet to keep instrumental music firmly behind singing, as in the definition of sangita (music) given near the start of the chapter, would be to ignore other riches of Indian music. Instrumental techniques and styles develop away from singing as

---

it on the sarangi, extending that rendition with a series of tans to turn it into a small-scale performance.

[82] In Qureshi, *Master Musicians of India*: 147.
[83] Ibid.: 149.   [84] Ibid.: 148.
[85] Beyond the Indian classical experience a simple reason for imitating instruments is that they may be lacking or even banned, while the voice is always there (except during illness) and is therefore a means of preserving the memory of instrumental repertoires. Courlander noted that during a period when drums were banned in Haiti their music was often reproduced by men who could imitate their tones and rhythms vocally: Harold Courlander, *Haiti Singing* (University of North Carolina Press, 1939; repr. New York: Cooper Square Publishers, 1973): 184.

well as in conjunction with it. While the voice is regarded as uniquely versatile, instruments can do things beyond its capability and if instrumental music had been restricted to following the voice at all times it simply would not have evolved into the dazzlingly virtuosic music that has travelled the world so successfully and could conceivably threaten the primacy of singing.

CHAPTER 7

Classical singing in the twentieth century: recording and retrenchment

THE GRAMOPHONE AND THE END OF INNOCENCE

The history of singing (though not yet the singing itself) changed fundamentally and for ever at the end of the nineteenth century with the serendipitous series of technological breakthroughs that led to machines being able to capture the sound of the human voice. This turned out to be a revolution, ultimately leading to vocal immortality for all who would like it (and some who would not), but the story of its faltering beginnings is one of bizarre ironies and what seem in hindsight to have been wasted opportunities. Thomas Edison was an extraordinarily creative inventor and entrepreneur but was easily side-tracked from whatever his current enthusiasm happened to be. This divergence occurred at two important points in the gramophone's history. The original recording machines which famously repeated Edison's 'hullo' and subsequently spouted 'Mary had a little lamb' were a byproduct of his attempts to speed up transmission of telegraph messages through the transatlantic cable. In the 1870s he was working on a means of transcribing Morse code telegrams on to paper tape. The indentations produced could be read and repeated at much higher speeds for onward transmission or storage. The sound of this whirring paper tape happened to remind the increasingly deaf inventor of a human voice. This sound, which actually had nothing at all to do with voices but was simply caused by fast-running paper tape with dents in it, inspired the imaginative leap in Edison which resulted in his applying the same principle to the vibrations produced by a voice. He first made a machine which would record the vibrations of speech on to paraffin paper, and then in 1877 he asked his assistant John Kruesi to build a device which used a needle and tin foil to reproduce its inventor's celebrated nursery rhyme recitation. The new process was greeted as something almost magical by those who heard the first phonographs, but it turned out to have a short life.

It is important to remember (before we start blaming him for not recording Jenny Lind and other voices lost to history) that Edison did not set out to invent the recording process as we now know it. Unlike the Frenchman Charles Cros, who at about the same time devised (but did not make) a similar machine (the paleophone) that he imagined might store the voices of loved ones, Edison's mercurial mind was far more interested in the process itself than in the uses to which it might be put. The immediate result was a series of exhibition talking machines, which gave public performances in several languages and could repeat human and animal noises apparently at will. Edison did make a number of prophetic announcements about the future of such machines, but the novelty value of the talking machines soon wore off; with no obvious purpose behind further development production came to a halt as Edison moved on to contemplating the electric light.

This is the difficult bit for historians of the early gramophone: it was a further eight years before a patent was granted to Chichester Bell and Charles Tainter for their 'graphophone', a machine which was in essence an improved version of Edison's machine using wax cylinders instead of foil. The rival patents spurred Edison (who had by now perfected his light bulb) to return to the phonograph, though even as late as the 1890s he was adamant that his invention was a business machine, closer to what we would call a dictaphone rather than what became the jukebox. In the late 1880s things moved quickly; the patents issue was resolved and the fledgeling industry capitalised sufficiently for commercial production to begin in 1890. The new technology was so novel and so magical that consumers were happy to put up with its deficiencies. Reproduction was poor and only two minutes' worth of material could be stored on each cylinder. There were two major problems for the manufacturer: each cylinder had to be individually recorded as they could not be duplicated, and the frequency spectrum that could be captured by the horns was very limited. A singer might be captured on three machines whereas a brass band was loud enough to register on ten, after which the cylinders would be changed and the performance repeated as many times as the musicians could manage in a three-hour session.

Sousa marches quickly became the best-selling cylinders in the USA, but very few divas would submit themselves to the indignity of multiple repeat performances or would wish to be in the same catalogue as John Y. AtLee, the artistic whistler, and street entertainer George Graham's imitations of a cat and dog fight. The evolving technology did not move in a simple straight line. Edison's cylinder machines were powered by electric batteries which proved too cumbersome for domestic use and were eventually replaced by clockwork, a retrogressive step that was later reversed. Edison also considered the flat disc as an alternative to the cylinder, opting for the latter as it produced better acoustic results. The flat disc eventually replaced the cylinder, and in the form developed by Émile Berliner became amenable to mass production. During the 1880s Berliner had been working on an alternative kind of phonograph which he called a gramophone. Berliner had no illusions about where his potential market lay: his machine was exclusively for home entertainment, and he foresaw mass production with payment of royalties to artists. Although Edison-type cylinders continued to be produced until the late 1920s, the ease of duplication and storage finally won the day for the rival medium.

On the face of it, it is an extraordinary thing to research an aural phenomenon using only written and iconographic materials (it is hard to imagine a history of art in purely aural terms). Perhaps because people took it for granted for so long that we would never be able to hear the music of the past, we have been able to give free rein to our thoughts on what it might actually have been like. Scholars have, on the whole, continued to do this well into the age of recording and it is only around the beginning of the twenty-first century that we see the first 'revisionist' histories of musical style that take into account the evidence of the first recordings. The impossibility of ever encountering an aural historical truth left us plenty of room to interpret the documents and pictures in whatever way we like, and this creative freedom is something that is not easily given up. Perhaps, then, it is not so surprising that it has taken a hundred years for many scholars and musicians to become aware of the historical significance of old recordings. The singing we hear on transfers from the first cylinders is rather a shock, and very different from the kind of singing that anyone now living is likely to have experienced. It is not only different from our received ideas of what singing is, but in many respects it is also not what our study of the silent written sources pre-gramophone would predict. We instinctively envisage history as progressing more or less chronologically while at the same time looking backwards through the filter of our own experiences.

THE SONG REPERTOIRE AND THE CREATION OF ART SONG

An encounter with early recordings brings us instantly closer to the past, and has particular resonance and relevance for those interested in the history of singing or 'historically informed' performance. The early music movement which began in the 1970s looked for things which were thought to be absent from the current mainstream and assumed to be present in the classical period and earlier; it favoured small-scale voices that could tune properly (and in a number of temperaments) and articulate accurately. This was in many ways a reaction to the 'big singing' prevalent in the earlier part of the century, which appeared to marginalise any singer not inclined towards opera. The twentieth century was also the great age of institutionalisation, and the need to explain and rationalise the musical past (especially since we write musical history in terms of great composers) has undoubtedly coloured our perception of it. The evolution of the concept of the art song is a case in point. The development of the song repertoire parallels the enormous changes in music conception and consumption between the mid-nineteenth century and the present. Every culture has an equivalent of a popular song tradition, a common pool of songs that have an appeal that crosses class boundaries. European composers have used popular tunes since the medieval period, and the song form itself evolved as a form of domestic entertainment.

In Germany the success of the Romantic poets in the late eighteenth century inspired many composers to take the *Lied* more seriously, both artistically and commercially. Haydn, Beethoven and Schubert were early examples of shrewd composers who were able to publish songs as a kind of catch crop between their larger, more time-consuming works. The audience for these was the piano-owning and Spanish-guitar-playing middle class, for whom the songs provided domestic entertainment. There is little evidence of professional singers taking to the song repertoire in the nineteenth century as their repertoire even as guests in upper-class drawing-rooms would have consisted almost exclusively of hits from their favourite opera roles. The first performances of much of the early *Lieder* repertoire would have been by cultivated amateurs whose singing probably sounded much like their speech (with its appropriate accent). But the mould was beginning to break: the opera singer Johann Michael Vogl famously sang the songs of Schubert, and Adolphe Nourrit and Franz Liszt popularised Schubert songs outside Germany, though their performances were more often than not at soirées rather than on the concert platform. Many of Schubert's songs were first aired at convivial gatherings of the composer's friends, at which he accompanied himself on the piano. In all European countries foreign songs would have been sung in translation, the sentiments of the text being more important to the bourgeois listener than any musical considerations arising from the unity of words and music. Some of the earliest Schubert

Lieder performances outside the German-speaking countries were heard in French at Parisian salons attended by Nourrit, who was known for his sensitive translations. Singers, critics and composers were increasingly aware of the artistic (as well as the commercial) potential of the song form. William Sterndale Bennett, like a number of English composers, published songs in both English and German, and as the public recital format developed, songs began to appear on concert programmes among the traditional offerings of operatic arias and lighter material.

From the turn of the century onwards enterprising singers (Lilli Lehmann, Lillian Nordica, Marcella Sembrich and Ernestine Schumann-Heink in the 1898–9 and 1899–1900 New York seasons, for example) started to offer recitals from which operatic arias were excluded altogether. The American critic Henry Finck had been among those advocating a more serious consideration of the song repertoire, and his *Songs and Songwriters* of 1900 stands on the cusp of its transition from bourgeois quasi-amateur domestic entertainment to the professional and highly intellectualised art song of the twentieth century. Finck's book is addressed to those amateurs whose taste is determined by the professional singers they hear, and is a plea for more discernment in the selection of repertoire. He understands that professional singers want (still) to show off how well they can sing but urges them to consider the beauty intrinsic to the song. He knows that foreign songs are usually sung in translation but hopes that singers will attempt the original language, castigating the flowery re-creations of most translators.

There are very few *Lieder* among the first crop of recordings, and songs are generally absent from the pedagogical literature until well into the twentieth century, the focus for the student still being the demands of the fast-disappearing virtuosic operatic repertoire of Rossini and his contemporaries. This was not to everyone's taste, of course. The eighty-nine-year old Manuel Garcia in his 1894 *Hints on Singing* ruefully comments that traditional virtuosic singing has been almost universally replaced by 'declamation', apart from the works of Handel. Despite the lack of pedagogical assistance, the generation of singers between the two world wars in effect reinvented the *Lied* as an art form. The core nineteenth-century repertoire of German and French song was consolidated and canonised, and the public perception and professional treatment of it changed out of all recognition. The singing had no virtuosity requirement but was still in large measure as much *about* the singing as the music; it retained the long sustained lines of the nineteenth-century professional, a style that even a cultivated amateur would find difficult to sustain. Opera singers found that they could reach an appreciative audience via the dedicated song recital. The consumer was still the middle class, as it had been a hundred years before, but instead of making the music themselves at home, people experienced it in public, sung by specialists in the new art. Amateur music lovers in effect forwent the pleasures of singing the repertoire for fun, in favour of silently appreciating it as great art.

By mid-century successful practitioners such as Elisabeth Schumann or Lotte Lehmann could fill the pedagogical gap with accounts of their own artistic interpretations, which aspired to be transcendent, acknowledging the genius of the composer. The new performing/listening model was reinforced by conservatories throughout Europe and America, which could offer classes in German, French and English song. The repertoire eventually left the realm of the amateur altogether; the stylistic and technical craft required was beyond the reach of all but the most highly trained professional performers. After World War II the genre reinvented itself for the second time, discovering more declamatory ways to relate the text to the music and incorporating English, American and other European song into the canon. The influence of Dietrich Fischer-Dieskau and Kathleen Ferrier was crucial here, both singers representing a reinvigorated style derived from meticulous articulation of the text (if necessary at the expense of the musical line). By the end of the twentieth-century this style had carried all before it, and as the market in live song recitals dried up, performances once again returned to the domestic environment, this time through recordings, often consumed in multiple versions, all of which were the product of prolonged study and coaching. *Lieder*, since World War II, have been about 'artistic transformation' or the opportunity to experience metamorphosis, as Elly Ameling put it.[1]

The change in production and consumption between the invention of recording and the present inevitably meant changes in sound, style and technique, all of which can be discerned in the history of the song repertoire during this period. There is a frustrating gap of some seventy years between the deaths of Schubert and Bellini and the first surviving recordings of their music (though much less for Rossini and Donizetti). Although this is only the average length of one human lifetime, the shift in the musical and cultural terrain that took place during this particular generation would probably have been unimaginable to the young mid-century composer. As the nineteenth century drew to its close the contexts in which the songs were performed had widened to include the

[1] Deborah Stein and Robert Spillman, *Poetry into Song: the Performance and Analysis of Lieder* (Oxford University Press, 1996), foreword by Elly Ameling.

public (and commercial), and the voices for these new arenas had been formed during some of the most radical changes in vocal production that Western music had seen. The shift to what we would recognise as modern, low-larynx technique was already in train during Schubert's lifetime, but perhaps not in the drawing-rooms with which he was familiar, where the singing would always have been a mixture of the professional and amateur. Private performances still continued at the end of the century and beyond, but evolving styles and techniques eventually change the nature of the voices that sing them, and perceptions of what exactly a *Lied* was were beginning to change beyond anything the composer would probably have recognised. Between the first recordings and the present day all of those processes have accelerated; the then new technology (to us primitive contraptions of wire, tin foil and wax) would begin a process that would take song beyond the solar system (something that might have amused Mozart and Schubert, had they been able to think the thought).[2] The time elapsed between us and the earliest recordings, and between those performances and the late Classical and early Romantic periods, can seem tantalisingly small in historical terms. We can revive Monteverdi or Josquin Desprez and be reasonably confident that even after four or five hundred years we have a fairly accurate idea of what their performances may have sounded like. Confidence is perhaps the key word here – we can have no actual knowledge of the sounds of Renaissance music so there is always room to doubt one's detractors: with plenty of circumstantial evidence but no proof, there can be argument either way. But if it works for Monteverdi, it should work with Schubert, many of whose contemporaries were still alive when the first recordings of his music were made.

INTERPRETING THE FIRST RECORDINGS

The oldest voice on record is that of Danish baritone Peder Schram, who recorded some extracts from *Don Giovanni* during his retirement party from the Royal Danish Opera in 1888. His surviving vocal remnants are in Danish and without accompaniment. It takes a while to recognise the tunes, and Schram, though successful in his day, may not have been a typical Mozart singer. Nevertheless it is a shock to hear what we think of as great music treated in a way that can best be described as informal.

---

[2] The Voyager spacecraft launched in 1977 contained recordings of Bach, Mozart and Beethoven. Western art music singing was represented by 'Der Hölle Rache kocht in meinem Herzen' from Mozart's *Die Zauberflöte*.

To paraphrase Borges 'In listening to this ... the thing we apprehend in one great leap ... is the limitation of our own thought, the stark impossibility of imagining *that*'.[3] Listening to Schram makes subsequent experience of the first recordings easier on the ear. The young English contralto Edith Clegg made one of the earliest *Lieder* recordings in 1898 (some eight years before her début at Covent Garden), a truncated version of Schubert's 'Ave Maria'. The didactic literature at this period is still almost exclusively concerned with operatic repertoire so it is no surprise that written examples of Schubert performance practice are non-existent. It is instructive to listen to early *Lieder* recordings therefore, and we find many notions about how *Lieder* should be sung. Fred Gaisberg had arrived in London from the USA in July 1898 and the following month set up his Émile Berliner machine in a hotel basement in Maiden Lane. His first successful subject was a bar maid, and he would happily record anyone with a voice big enough to register on the machine. Edith Clegg's second visit, on 11 October, resulted in the Schubert. She had been a pupil in London of Herman Klein, critic and singing teacher, who had himself been a pupil of the younger Garcia.

If Edith Clegg was young, dynamic and relatively inexperienced, the tenor Gustav Walter is an early example of the many older and well-established figures to commit their voices to posterity. He was born in 1834, six years after the death of Schubert, and many who heard him sing at the Vienna Opera had known the composer well. He left the opera house in 1887, but came out of retirement in 1904 to record three cylinders at the age of 71. All the usual caveats about early recording need to be borne in mind when listening to these performances and we should be wary of drawing too many hard and fast conclusions; but by listening to both old and young singers performing *Lieder* at roughly the same date we can note what broadly characterises the actual singing. We cannot really deduce much about their technique – too many frequencies are simply not there; singing into the horn was a bizarre business and far removed from any sense of live performance.

Most modern listeners would not suspect that Walter was more than twice the age of Clegg when they made their recordings. The singers in the two recordings have certain basic traits in common which they do not share with most modern singers. Both have a fairly flexible attitude to tempo (neither singer seems to worry about synchronising precisely with

[3] Quoted by Michel Foucault in his preface to *The Order of Things* (New York: Random House, 1973): xv.

the accompaniment) and their sense of pitch is not quite what we are used to. Walter appears to be slightly under the note for much of the time but he has a clear, almost limpid sense of line. He uses relatively little vibrato, unlike Clegg, who has a steady wobble. There are many examples of portamento in both directions (Walter's are bigger events, Clegg is a little more restrained). The words of both singers are perfectly clear but never so articulate as to destroy the legato. In Walter's 'Feldeinsamkeit' (Brahms) and 'Leb wohl aus' (Thomas) he takes more risks and threatens to break into *Sprechgesang* but both singers give the impression of being completely in control of what they are doing. The most obvious similarity is the way they get from note to note; there is none of the textual energy that one would expect from a modern performance. This legato style is very characteristic of early recordings: extraordinarily, after reading so many references to legato singing over a period of hundreds of years, we can now actually hear it.

Perhaps the most famous diva of the second half of the nineteenth century was Adelina Patti. She was born in 1843, just after her mother, the soprano Caterina Barilli, had sung Norma in Madrid. Her father, tenor and impresario Salvatore Patti, took the family to New York, where Patti made her concert début at the age of eight. The *Mirror* described La Petite Prima Donna Adelina Patti as 'a perfect miniature Lind or Malibran' who 'astonished the audience by her ease, self-possession, and power' and the prophetic *Musical Times* concluded that 'she will yet merit the honourable appellation of the great cantatrice of the Western world'.[4] She was shrewdly managed by her sister's husband, the sometime Giuditta Pasta pupil Maurice Strakosch, who exploited her precocious talent, allowing her voice to develop at its own pace and passing on what he had learned from Pasta. In 1861 he took her to London, and secured the contract that began her twenty-five years at Covent Garden. Patti was a superstar; more than that, she was an industry. She was the first singer to have a career on both sides of the Atlantic created and crafted by managers, agents and promoters. The public obsession with her singing was such that she and those who looked after her made enormous sums of money. The impresario 'Colonel' Mapleson recalled the 1882 season in his *Memoirs* of 1888 awaiting the arrival from Europe of his investment – at 4.30 in the morning:

There was the usual crowd on the wharf all night awaiting the ship's arrival. I had left orders for a telegram to be sent to me as soon as the vessel passed

4 Vera Brodsky Lawrence, *Strong on Music: the New York Music Scene in the Days of George Templeton Strong* vol. II (University of Chicago Press, 1995): 214–15.

Fire Island in order that I might be in time to dress and go down to one of the specially chartered steamers … military bands, fireworks etc. …We steamed up alongside … Our band struck up God save the Queen and everyone bared his head…most of those present from admiration of the lyric queen who had come for another reign to the delighted people of New York. Handshaking and greetings followed. After we had got Patti through the Custom House she was placed in a carriage and taken to the Windsor Hotel, the room being piled up with telegrams, cards and bouquets. There was also a large set piece with the word 'Welcome' embroidered on it in roses. In the evening there was a midnight serenade in front of the Windsor Hotel, and ultimately *La diva* had to appear at the window, when orchestra and chorus, who were outside, performed the grand prayer from *Lombardi*. After three hearty cheers for Adelina Patti people went home and she was left in peace.[5]

She had the inevitable huge triumph, and so fabulous was her coloratura that people took bets on how many notes she sang, and calculated the increase in the value of her diamonds as they poured out.

  She was not young when she entrusted her voice to the horn, and this has often been held against her by her critics. Patti's recordings are of crucial significance as her relative old age means that her historical pedigree may reveal evidence of vocalism from earlier in the nineteenth century, or perhaps suggest ways of interpreting the literature. To many modern listeners her singing sounds utterly bizarre: the 1905 recording of Mozart's 'Voi che sapete' at the age of sixty-two (ten years after her Covent Garden farewell performances) features extreme register changes, inaccurate pitching, rampant portamento and radical tempo changes that are not marked in the score, not to mention appoggiaturas put in where not marked and left out where Mozart put them in. Is this the work of a performer past her prime, or are we listening to the remains of a dynamic style and technique that may have had its origins a generation or two earlier? Not all divas were happy when they heard their own voice for the first time, but Patti was enraptured, remarking that it was no wonder she was who she was: 'Maintenant je comprends pourquoi je suis Patti … Quelle Voix! Quelle artiste!'[6] Throughout, Patti alternates between a smooth legato and portamento of varying degrees. Over the course of 'Voi che sapete' almost all of the music is sung at some point without significant portamento, demonstrating her control of the basic legato line. This suggests that when she wants to slide between notes it might have more to do with artistic decision-making than failing technique. Many of the glides

[5] Harold Rosenthal (ed.), *The Mapleson Memoirs: the Career of an Operatic Impresario 1858–1888* (London: Putnam, 1966): 157.
[6] Landon Ronald, *Variations on a Personal Theme* (London: Hodder and Stoughton, 1922): 103–4.

are associated with word stress and expressive tempo manipulation, often with initial crescendi and exiting decrescendi, remnants of *messa di voce*, perhaps. The problem for modern listeners is the substantial nature of her glides, which appear to be excessive compared with any other singer of the period.

However, transcribed *à la* Garcia, her performances would not look very different from the great teacher's Crescentini or Cimarosa realisations (see page 128 above). If that did turn out to be the case, then what we are listening to has more to do with the fact that Patti learned her trade some fifty years earlier. There is a strong argument that her performances represent an earlier tradition, perhaps overlaid with a patina of familiarity and over-use which produces the occasional 'abuse'; Albert Bach heard Patti's performances twenty-three years earlier and he seems to confirm this: 'The most expressive and sympathetic portamento that I have ever heard is that of the darling of gods and men, Adelina Patti … The greatest *cantatrice* of our times … has not her equal in *coloratura* or ornamental style.'[7] This could have been a description of Banti a hundred years earlier. Michael Scott, in his *Record of Singing*, reminds us of the potential significance of the Patti–Strakosch connection: as Giuditta Pasta's accompanist Strakosch worked with a soprano who had created roles for Donizetti and Bellini, and had sung Zerlina in London within twenty-five years of Mozart's death.[8] What might seem to us wayward and strange may actually owe something to a performing tradition that Mozart himself might have recognised.

PORTAMENTO AS A DEFINING CRITERION OF
GOOD SINGING

Patti's distinctive use of portamento is one of the reasons why modern singers are reluctant to engage with it. The history of early twentieth-century singing could be written entirely in terms of the rise and fall of portamento as a criterion for good singing, as it is the single most significant aspect that commentators complain about. It also reveals the tension (or at least the time lag) between performance, pedagogy and criticism. Patti's most illustrious successor was Nellie Melba, who recorded 'Voi che sapete' at least twice. Both 1907 and 1910 versions have less portamento than Patti, but there is still plenty of it. The one at the

---

[7] Albert Bach, *Musical Education and Vocal Culture* (5th edn, London: Kegan Paul, 1898): 137 and 150.
[8] Michael Scott, *The Record of Singing*, 2 vols. (London: Duckworth, 1977): 23.

return of the opening music is important enough for her to join the two sections at the expense of a kind of musical coherence, which means she has to breathe after 'Voi', breaking the sense. She does this in both recordings which means it must have been more important for Melba to link the two sections with a portamento than to get the breathing right. This is something advocated by Norris Croker; he calls it 'Slur for binding two phrases' and says that it is particularly effective in returning to the opening phrase of an aria after a contrasting middle section. This is a clear example of evidence from recordings confirming what the literature seems to be saying.[9] Like almost all singers of the period Melba is quite free with the tempo; she also improves the ending with a one-note cadenza plus downward glissando, a really creative yet subtle ornament. Melba's thoughts on singing are summarised in her *Method* of 1926, which has a series of 'Exercises on Intervals' for joining different intervals and she cautions that these should be sung without portamento, which 'is an ornament and must at all times be used very sparingly. *It must not be used at all by beginners.*'[10] Her portamento exercises are fairly basic; there are no instructions. The student could by then have heard plenty of Melba on record if not in live performances but even in an age where it was ubiquitous there is no attempt to teach portamento via the book: the reader still needs a teacher to explain how it works.

Melba's teacher, Mathilde Marchesi, first published her vocal method in German in 1886 having learned with Garcia and subsequently set up her own singing schools in Vienna and Paris. The cover of the English version of her manual (dating from around 1903) contains the legitimising legend 'Teacher of Melba and Calvé, successor to Garcia'.[11] She has the usual exercises for agility and crossing the registers, and two pages each of preliminary slurring and portamento exercises which are later developed in seven pages of portamento vocalises. There is very little in the way of supporting text, again confirming that a personalised rather than a generalised approach is required. The exercises are extrapolations on Garcia, and we can hear the results in the recordings of her daughter Blanche's 1906 recording of Bach's 'Bist du bei mir'. Marchesi's singing confirms the integration of rhythmic and tonal inflection. Phrases mostly start cleanly, with portamento employed at key textual moments. There are several examples of pitch glides over a third (up and down) and two

[9] Norris Croker, *Handbook for Singers* (London: Augener, 1895): 91.
[10] Nellie Melba, *Melba Method* (London, 1926): 23.
[11] Mathilde Marchesi, *Bel canto: a Theoretical and Practical Vocal Method* (New York, n.d. [1903]?, rpr. New York: Dover 1970 with an introduction by Philip Miller).

important downward fifths all of which could come straight from the exercises of Lind or Mathilde. The opening two bars are sung cleanly, with the first portamento occurring between 'geh' and 'ich'. This is more or less in time, perhaps because the tempo still needs to be established near the beginning of the piece. The third phrase 'zum Sterben und zu meiner Ruh' is also sung relatively strictly apart from a small glide between 'zu' and 'meiner'; the singing until this point has been a text-book example of legato. From the repeat of the text the performance takes on a different character, almost all of the portamenti consisting of a controlled glide that delays the onset of the succeeding note. The 'zum sterben' section is repeated a fifth higher and there is a dramatic slowing on 'Ster' and on 'mein', enabling Marchesi to control the shape of the text by varying her rate of glide. This is exactly the kind of interpretation that could be predicted from the exercises in her mother's book and clearly shows the difference between the rigorous smoothness of legato and the expressive unpredictability of portamento.

Portamento was not exclusively an affectation of opera singers. Though almost all Garcia's examples are from operas, it must be remembered that successful singers sang operatic arias in concerts alongside non-operatic material and that all vocal music, of whatever period or style, was sung in broadly the same way. The language of George Dodds, a teacher and choirmaster from the north of England, would be recognisable to any singer living in the 1920s:

[Portamento] … may … indicate a gliding from one note to another, similar to the *glissando* performed by a violinist when sliding his finger-tip up or down the string of his instrument. The pitch rises or falls continuously until the second note is reached, but as no stop has occurred, no definite note is heard between the first and second tones …

It should be clearly understood that … the portamento is not a necessity of voice production, but an artistic resource … its employment must be for artistic reasons alone, and the singer who achieves a top note by means of a 'scoop' is guilty of an abominable abuse of a beautiful vocal effect.[12]

This confirms what we can increasingly hear: artistic sliding is tasteful, but there is a line which can only be crossed at some risk to the reputation of the singer. At the beginning of the century writings and recordings come into a kind of interpretative alignment: we can hear what Marchesi, Melba and Dodds mean by listening to recordings. From this point onwards there is no doubt about what portamento actually *is*, as recorded (as opposed to

[12] George Dodds, *Practical Hints for Singers* (London, 1927): 33–4.

live) performances become most people's normative experience; the question remaining is about taste: how often and how much should it be used. Two years after Dodds, Gregory Hast is far more vitriolic:

Then, the pernicious use of portamento. What an epidemic of this disease is raging at the moment! Some singers appear to be incapable of singing a descending interval without a horrible slur. It is the cheapest and easiest performed stunt in the repertoire and will reduce temperament to a gush. No good singer should indulge in it except as an embellishment – never as a habit. Once, when discussing this, Sims Reeves laid down this rule, 'One portamento in a song, never more.' When I told Santley that, he said, in his usual gruff manner, 'And that's once too often.'[13]

Presumably these two grand old pros were expressing general distaste rather than actually prescribing a specific number of slides per piece, but Hast's gleeful quoting of these two famous stars does suggest that there was a very wide spectrum of taste.

At about the same time Henry Wood published his little-known but comprehensive singing manual. He had a lifetime's experience of a huge number of singers and is well aware that portamento has to be treated carefully:

notation alone is unable to symbolise the very fine shades of a singer's portamento. The ear alone must be the judge. Both teacher and pupil should give the greatest attention to vocal slurs. In a large building they occasionally assume huge proportions: a keen ear can almost discover the chromatic semitones in one of the vocal scoops perpetrated too frequently.[14]

Herman Klein, a former Garcia pupil and by now the distinguished critic of *The Gramophone*, is still insistent upon its proper employment:

One attribute of the art of phrasing that immediately distinguishes the accomplished vocalist is the correct employment of the portamento, both in the upward and downward movement of the voice.[15]

Klein was a perceptive connoisseur of singers over a very long period. His *Gramophone* articles include several comparisons of acoustic and electric

[13] H. Gregory Hast, 'Vocal and Unvocal', *Music & Letters* 10:3 (1929): 252. Santley was the most successful nineteenth-century British bass, having studied with Gaetano Nava in Italy and Garcia in London. He was nevertheless far from being one of the great voices of the period, as his surviving recordings demonstrate. He certainly used portamento sparingly on the ten recordings made in 1903–4 at the age of seventy (*Santley & Lloyd: The Complete Recordings*, Cheyne Records CHE 44372–3), but none has as few as two examples and he frequently uses controlled glides to signal rallentandi when approaching cadences. His portamenti tend to be descending, and it may be that it was the ascending variety that he took exception to.
[14] Henry Wood, *The Gentle Art of Singing* (London: Milford 1927/30): 35.
[15] *Herman Klein and the Gramophone*, ed. William R. Moran (Portland, OR, Amadeus Press: 1991): May 1932, 347–8.

recording. The latter came in from 1925 onwards and was a major change in the process of recording, which over time may have initiated changes in attitude towards key elements of vocal style. It is hard for us to hear obvious differences: electrical recording is still relatively primitive compared with what we have become used to. But Klein and other critics writing in the 1930s can compare the two processes in similar terms to our own evaluation of LP versus CD. It may be that the microphone, in enabling a much more subtle sort of performance (unlike the horn, you did not have to scream into it), had a democratising effect on the process. The legitimisation of jazz and blues eventually brought all the slides and glides of the crooner into the recorded domain. These were far more directly speech-related than the stylised portamento used by 'classical' singers. Perhaps this less discriminate use of portamento began to be thought vulgar, as popular stars began to steal the clothes of trained singers. The electrical recordings made by Bing Crosby between 1927 and 1934 reveal him to be a fine light tenor-baritone. He is obviously making very little effort to project, but in many respects, especially when he sings ballads rather than novelty numbers, his delivery is an exaggeration of that of a 'classical' singer: there is vibrato, portamento and rubato, much of which is elegantly applied to popular tunes. The portamenti, however, tend to be frequent and indiscriminate, with little of the finesse and logic that are evident in *Lieder* and opera singers.[16]

THE WAR YEARS AND AFTER: 'STÄNDCHEN' AS A BAROMETER OF TASTE

Changes in the aesthetics of singing, in style and technique, have almost always taken place over a period of time and only come into focus some time after the events that characterised them. The Second World War, however, does represent a turning point in singing history. The war years were catastrophically disruptive of professional and educational infrastructure, and although concerts continued to happen it was almost as though history was suspended, with musicians having little sense of a viable future. Many of the characteristics of pre-war singing came to be viewed as extravagant, or even decadent, with little connection to the uncertain reality of many people's lives. Portamento is a key marker of the changing aesthetic, and it came to be associated with self-indulgence and a certain sloppiness with regard to pitch. Richard Tauber recorded Schubert's 'Ständchen' several times, and seems to have varied his

---

[16] As, for example, on the CD reissue *I Surrender, Dear*, Patricia Records ApS CD 23106.

portamento according to context. His self-accompanied rendering in the filmed version of *Lilac Time* is a drawing-room performance in which he slides into and out of almost every note, recomposing and ornamenting the ending.[17] The slightly later film *Blossom Time* has him performing the same piece in a recital; this is a much more serious affair with no ornaments and portamenti. Tauber appears to be adjusting his singing style according to the expectations of his audience. These versions may demonstrate a degree of self-parody, but what it certainly suggests is that 'popular' singers slide more, and it is the association of sliding with popular music that increasingly becomes a factor in portamento criticism. Tauber's wartime recordings, perhaps subconsciously due to the seriousness of the times (and, perhaps, his Austrian origins), show much less frequent use than either of his film versions.

The opposite is true for the American tenor Richard Crooks, who in effect brought art music to the allied forces as entertainment. Crooks had a reputation during the 1930s for Verdi, Wagner and Mozart, but the virtual monopoly on recordings of this repertoire by European tenors meant that record companies steered him in the direction of lighter repertoire. He uses a great deal of portamento (there are thirty-nine examples in his 'Ständchen' recording) and is a rare example of a singer whose upward slides outnumber the downward (24:15). It would be wrong to think of Crooks's rendering as pandering to the mass market. He sings in English with a consistent, liquid tone and exquisite diction. The piano introduction starts at just under sixty (a slowish tempo compared with most) which Crooks takes up on his entry 'Through the leaves', but he uses an upward portamento on the first syllable of 'moving' (as in 'The night winds moving') to slow down quite dramatically. The approach from below signals to the pianist exactly how Crooks intends the tempo to change; by using such a rhetorical device on the way up Crooks does not need to do a downward portamento at a point where few can resist. This is an extraordinarily sophisticated effect, as the word 'moving' is completed without any attempt at additional word painting and the music appears briefly to be almost stationary, drawing the listener into the performance rather than emphasising the obvious. He only sings one strophe, each line meticulously crafted and with his usual penchant for upward glides with associated rubato. There is one more major tempo change: towards the end of the B section on the repeat of the words 'To thy dreaming heart', he again brings the music almost to a standstill with an upward portamento

---

[17] *The Art of Singing*, Warner Music Vision DVD 0630–15898–2.

on 'dream-' before sliding down on to the second syllable; more conventional word painting perhaps, but no less effective for that. On the repeat of this music before the final coda to the words 'bid it, love, be still' he does a similar upward slide into 'love' but omits the downward, finishing the song in a soft *mezza voce* more or less strictly and absolutely cleanly.

Crooks was one of the most prolific portamento users, and the effect was such an integral part of his style that the moments he chose not to use it (where others might) are equally effective. As a child he had a remarkable treble voice, and sang in Elijah alongside Ernestine Schumann-Heink in 1910 at the age of ten.[18] This early exposure to great singing from the beginning of the century surely connected his own future singing to that of a much earlier period, where clarity of text was enabled by vocal devices that were integral to the technique rather than extraneous to it: text delivery via the unbroken legato line. Yet in the bleak cultural mood during and after the war it is not surprising that a performing style that appeared to be extravagant or even decadent would be increasingly disparaged. In the 1930s and 1940s we rarely read about dragging and sliding in the Tosian sense, and references become increasingly pejorative, with 'crooning' and 'scooping' becoming the abuse of choice:

Another terrible disease is that of which the virulent form is crooning, but has many stages before that is reached. It begins with an emotional slither, a passionate portamento, the mildest form of which, rising to the note, is sometimes called scooping. A famous prima donna was given to this failing. She happened to be also a great actress, and felt that it aided the expression of dramatic emotion. When she made her debut in New York the audience, startled at the unusual sight of a singer who could act, roared its approval. The next day one of the newspapers splashed the headline: 'She scoops to conquer.' For some mysterious reason the downward portamento sounds less offensive – or is it that it has become so common that we notice it less?[19]

By the time we get to Bairstow and Plunkett Greene there are calls for much less frequent use, and it is clear that the appropriation of portamento by singers of popular music has reduced its value, potentially terminally:

The portamento, or slur, needs special attention, for many singers seem to think that its use depends upon the words: they will slur any syllables easy to slur, such as those separated by the continuant consonants *l, r, m* and *n* [gives examples in

[18] Roland Vernon (1997), liner notes to *Richard Crooks in Songs & Ballads*, Nimbus NI 7888.
[19] Edwin Evans, 'The Art of Singing in Decline', *Musical Times* (1943): 202. His article is a passionate indictment of the state of singing, especially the over-use of vibrato and portamento.

English from Schubert and Stanford]. To slur frequently ... is a common habit
and a bad one. It should be used as infrequently as it is by good string players ...
It will be found that many people who slur in speech are usually insincere, for
instance, the beggar who comes to the door with a false tale and tries hard to
enlist sympathy. It has exactly the same effect in song; it gives an unconvincing
sound, as if the singer did not really feel the music but was trying hard to make
you believe that he did. The street singer slurs *ad nauseam*.[20]

Taste has clearly moved on from Garcia's day, when portamento was considered an aid to sincerity.

In the renewal that followed the exhaustion of war it is possible that
old paradigms were lost, and that this failure of legitimacy fuelled the
impression of decadence that came to be associated with extravagant
vocal gestures. The process can be seen in the experience of Dietrich
Fischer-Dieskau, a singer who not merely entertained troops but had
actually fought as a soldier. Fischer-Dieskau's 'Ständchen' is the performance of a singing actor in which consistency of tone is replaced by wide
variations in vocal colour together with extreme dynamic range from full
voice to an intense piano. He only once sings a truly bel canto legato
line: this occurs on 'mit der Töne süssen Klagen flehen sie fur mich' and
is presumably deliberate (or even ironic). Instead of using glides to indicate tempo fluctuation Fischer-Dieskau controls word shapes by varying the rate of dynamic expansion or contraction. The text is articulated
with great clarity and with little thought for the traditional smoothness
of line, and already present is the trademark Fischer-Dieskau late final
unvoiced consonant (on 'nicht' and 'mich'), something that makes the
word unmistakably clear but which a conventional *Lieder* singer of the
period would consider a violation of line. It is a remarkable performance
that records a radical change in singing style. The text of 'Ständchen' is
a fairly trivial one even by Schubert's variable standards, and very few
of the earlier twentieth-century interpreters were able to use the song as
a creative opportunity. In Fischer-Dieskau's performance, however, it is
immediately obvious that there is more than mere singing going on. In
the more serious songs from the same sessions you can almost hear the
fully mature singer living the music in a way that does not occur in any
previous recordings.

Many famous pre-war singers were still making major recordings
(Lehmann and Björling, for example, were still in their prime) but among

---

[20] Edward C. Bairstow and Harry Plunkett Greene, *Singing Learned from Speech* (London, 1945):
66–7.

younger artists a revolution was occurring. In the hands of the great specialist *Lieder* singers such as Elisabeth Schumann, Elena Gerhardt and Lotte Lehmann, the *Lied* had transformed itself from domestic entertainment and become great art, but it was an art form legitimised by history and a certain bourgeois usage that reached back to an age which had been fatally compromised. The extraordinary circumstances of his childhood and early adulthood enabled Dietrich Fischer-Dieskau to find something in this music that managed to transcend the history that he was himself a part of. The singer himself seems, though, to be unaware of this:

It is remarkable when people say how different I am from earlier singers because I overlapped with singers like Heinrich Schlusnus and Erna Berger and I was not conscious of being different in approach. On the contrary, I tried to be like them, to be as perfect as I thought they were.[21]

No one would guess from listening to them today that these two singers were Fischer-Dieskau's models, but it is possible to identify qualities in their singing which he may have appreciated. Both recorded 'Ständchen' (Schlusnus at least four times). Berger's is an elegant rendering and her portamenti demonstrate small upward glides on the liquid starts to 'Lieder' and 'Liebchen', indicating a care for textual detail. Schlusnus was a Verdi baritone and *Lieder* singer who had a successful career at the Berlin State Opera; he made a big high-energy sound and it may have been this that appealed to the young Fischer-Dieskau. His 1927 and 1948 'Ständchen' recordings have the falling portamenti on 'flehen', 'stillen' and 'Mondes' and he occasionally permits himself a rising glide (into 'flehen', 'stillen' and 'Mondes') and he does the usual climactic portamento on the 'Holde' cadence, but in the B section he employs an energised legato at several points (such as the descending arpeggio figure on 'Busens Sehnen') where many singers would add portamenti. This tensioned restraint is something that becomes axiomatic in postwar singing and is characteristic of Fischer-Dieskau's work.

His autobiography stresses not the singers that may have informed his musical development but his awareness of literature, the theatre and the social and cultural tensions of growing up in Nazi Germany. He was a sensitive teenager with an intellectual streak that led him towards German poetry, discovering the joys of reading poetry aloud many years before his adult singing voice developed; it seems to have been a feel for spoken poetic declamation that led him towards song rather than opera. He was conscripted into the German army, where he was wounded by a grenade and spent several months starving in the Italian countryside before being taken prisoner by the Americans. He makes clear in his memoirs that his childhood love of music and poetry sustained him during the traumatic years which saw his first performances. For the precocious intellectual soldier music was essentially text, something in the mind that would only be performed in extreme conditions.[22] His lack of exposure to conventional models was certainly a factor in the lack of convention in his song realisations. Unlike most aspiring performers he did not see the singing as an end in itself. His lack of acknowledgement of the Italianate bel canto tradition is striking; he credits Hermann Weissenborn with being his teacher and mentions in passing that he used Garcia's exercises but he does not place himself within any sort of vocal tradition: 'The great singers I have encountered surely did not acquire their greatness from those we customarily call teachers.'[23] This was a music-centred approach rather than one founded on personal ambition, giving primacy to music and poetry, with singing as the means of realising it. There are few precedents for this and none at all for the conditions under which he took his first steps as a performer. Fischer-Dieskau's performances show a textual energy derived from the shape of the words themselves. They do join up, but each word has its own shape and space.[24] Pre-Fischer-Dieskau, the line was more important than the language. The result was the creation of an entirely new performance rhetoric which owed very little to his illustrious predecessors.

The scale of the changes implied by the new singing is confirmed by comparing Fischer-Dieskau's 'Ständchen' recordings of the 1950s with almost any of his successful contemporaries. Lotte Lehmann broadcast 'Ständchen' in one of her *Standard Hour* programmes in 1950. This is the performance of a German former patriot who became an American resident, and on whom recent history has made no impact. It is singing in all its old-fashioned extravagance, with copious portamenti that display the voice rather than the text. Gérard Souzay numbered Lehmann among his teachers but was more inspired by the sensitivity of Pierre Bernac. His 1955 recording is elegant and restrained but is singing in its purest form: absolute

[22] His first *Winterreise* at the age of eighteen (and while still a student) was famously interrupted by an air raid on Berlin. Dietrich Fischer-Dieskau, *Reverberations: the Memoirs of Dietrich Fischer-Dieskau*, trans. Ruth Hein (New York: Fromm International, 1989): 45.
[23] Ibid.:75.
[24] A byproduct of this method of text delivery is an over-production of consonants, a fact which may have made Dieskau particularly appealing to singers brought up in the English choral tradition.

smoothness of line and consistency of tone. He was five years older than Fischer-Dieskau but managed to avoid the war, making his début in Paris in 1945. His singing is the antithesis of what Alan Blyth has called 'the interventionist style' of Fischer-Dieskau.[25] The text is admirably clear and much of his portamento use coincides with the 'tasteful' disyllable use, but his legato line represents not only an older style but an older world view altogether. By the time we arrive at the 1950s those singers who continued with the older tradition sounded extremely mannered compared with their younger contemporaries. Pedagogical literature from the 1960s confirms that sliding around had no place in the new singing; as Husler and Rodd-Marling put it, 'the exaggerated portamento … so popular with natural singers, is scrupulously avoided as "ugly and vulgar" by the professional artist'.[26] Very few teachers would now encourage singers to slide between intervals, even if the historical evidence is pointed out to them.

PORTAMENTO AND CURRENT PERFORMANCE PRACTICE

Portamento in its pre-war incarnation has never entirely disappeared in opera singers, particularly those whose initial training was in the conservatories of the old Eastern Europe and in the many opera companies from the former Soviet Union that now try to make a living touring the West.[27] The singing of these performers is often relatively untouched by postwar Western influences and is only heard on CD when an exceptional star emerges, such as Angela Gheorghiu, who graduated from the Bucharest Music Academy in 1990. Her portamento use is in line with current teaching in conservatories in the Balkan countries, the Baltic states and the southern ex-Soviet states. Many would consider it excessive, compared with that of her Western-educated predecessors and contemporaries such as Kiri te Kanawa, and the more snobbish might think it vulgar in comparison with the more restrained singing that we have become used to.[28]

The cultivation of ever larger voices has perhaps been a factor in the diminishing number of recordings of *Lieder* by opera singers (Bryn Terfel is relatively rare in being equally at home in Wagner and Schubert). *Lieder*

---

[25] Alan Blyth, liner notes to *Gerard Souzay sings Schubert Lieder*, Testament SBT 1313 (2003).
[26] Frederick Husler and Yvonne Rodd-Marling, *Singing: the Physical Nature of the Vocal Organ* (London: Faber and Faber, 1965, rev. 1976): 89.
[27] The Chesinau national opera from Moldova, among others.
[28] Compare, for example, her 'Vissi d'arte' (EMI 7243 5 57955 0 2) with that of Kiri te Kanawa (*Puccini: Great Opera Arias*, Sony SBK89286).

recordings at the beginning of the twenty-first century are now largely the province of young singers or specialists. Michael Volle's is typical of performances to be heard today in Germany, adding nothing to the notes that are in the score (which is the Neue Schubert Ausgabe), with the text energised in a way that recalls the young Fischer-Dieskau. His articulation is so accurate that the listener may perceive no portamento at all. It is perhaps influenced most of all by the early music *Zeitgeist*, although in this instance he is accompanied by a modern piano. There are now several recordings of singers accompanied by fortepiano, and presumably aimed at the market for historically informed performance. Like the 'modern' performance of Volle, however, they tend to find no place for portamento. This is oddly transgressive: the early music movement has been nothing if not iconoclastic and one would expect radical differences between 'uninformed' and historically informed practice recordings, yet it is quite normal for early music singers to use no portamento at all.

Listening to the first recordings opens the lid on an extraordinarily diverse vocal universe which has receded so far and so fast that we can hardly grasp it at all. We now expect our sopranos to sound like sopranos, not like people with individual voices. Our overly literal respect for pre-twentieth-century composers' scores is something that neither original composer nor performer would recognise. We can cope with a score – a controlled environment, standardised and quantifiable. What Schubert actually heard would probably have been none of these things. Schubert was inspired by the performances of Vogl, whereas we tend to prefer measurable excellence to the randomness of inspiration. It is very hard to judge how excellent these old singers were without a common standard to apply.

FROM PARADIGM TO PERFORMANCE: PERFORMERS, TEACHERS AND THEIR MODELS

The evolution of the classical style that the foregoing study of portamento has illustrated runs like a thread through the singing of the entire century. The causes of change are difficult to pin down, but it is possible to identify key factors which drive the process of change. Perhaps the most important is the availability of recordings, especially from the era of the LP onwards. Before 1900 or so nobody had a clear idea of what a soprano or a tenor was supposed to sound like: they all presented very individual vocal personae, and audiences responded to them as individuals. When everyone is listening to the same singers on record, common ideas of what good singing is are bound to coalesce, and market forces will take care of the consequences. The age of recording also coincided with the death of opera as the living engine of vocal creativity, with the creation of new repertoire slowing almost to a standstill, and singers' function reduced to the interpretation of existing roles (and only those roles that their teacher considers within their *Fach*). Even had this not been the case, recording would on its own have brought to an end the thousand years of singerly creativity: when you play a recording, the singer performs in exactly the same way as last time; not only do audiences get to agree on what a voice should sound like, they expect the way the music goes to be the same every time. The century produced many fine singers, as every other century has presumably done, and we have the luxury of keeping their voices alive indefinitely. Nobody would wish to be without the singing of Flagstad, Schwarzkopf, Callas, Sutherland or Victoria de los Angeles, Franco Corelli or Placido Domingo. But the repertoire we require them to sing even from beyond the grave, though potentially vast, focuses on a very small amount of music which has hardly changed in a hundred years. Choice, the famous engine of capitalism, means that we can choose to listen to a large number of excellent singers all performing broadly the same thing.

This situation is not helped by the conservatoire system, which, rather than explore creative singing of all types, cares only for a narrow definition of singing, confined to a very small repertoire. The system also produces far more singers than the profession can absorb, which creates a vicious circle of competition with more and more singers chasing fewer opportunities to sing a very small amount of music. Music colleges have become ends in themselves and have only recently felt the need to change with the times. It is perfectly possibly for singers who studied at a conservatory forty years ago to return to their school and find the same repertoire being taught in the same way. By maintaining the status quo so successfully, Western institutionalised pedagogy must surely be sacrificing long-term survival for short-term gain. There will come a time when the system is no longer financially viable, and audiences in a generation or two's time may find that their music has become atrophied, a high-status niche music like Chinese opera or Japanese Kabuki. It is already the case that the importance of singing in some of the most elaborate operatic productions is secondary to that of the production itself.

CHAPTER 8

Post-classical: beyond the mainstream

This chapter looks at varieties of singing that have been of considerable significance in terms of performances, recordings and critical acclaim, but remained apart from the mainstream of classical vocal culture. Early music and the extended vocal techniques of the avant-garde are essentially post-World War II phenomena, and are seen to be 'classical' yet distinctly other; Jewish singing has a much longer historical pedigree but has also changed radically in the second half of the twentieth century and remains a mystery to many lovers of classical singing. We also consider the fragmentation of taste and style, and the weakening sense of genre that is characteristic of the early twenty-first century, and the growing tendency for classically trained singers to collaborate as ensembles, rather than compete as soloists.

It may seem odd to start a post-classical chapter with some thoughts on Jewish singing, which has a far longer history than Western classical or popular music and has at several points interacted with both. But for many non-Jews the rich and troubled heritage of Jewish music is hardly known at all, and yet it has produced some of the most spectacular singing of the twentieth century. Much of the singing described in previous chapters is secular; the performance of Renaissance sacred music is secularised by the modern concert hall, and even composers such as Arvo Pärt, for whom music is primarily a means of spiritual expression, write for the concert platform rather than for the liturgy. But the classical singing of Europe (and subsequently much of the Americas and the wider English-speaking world) can be described as having Christian roots. The secular variety developed initially within the church and then became professionalised via the court, opera house, concert hall and beyond; secular and non-secular singing therefore share many of the same characteristics at any given point in history. In modern multicultural Western countries there are many other varieties of singing to be found, and where these exhibit what might be thought of as classical characteristics they are also often influenced by religious custom.[1] There is no equivalent to classical singing in Islam – the muezzin who issues the *Azan* (call to prayer) and leads the five daily prayers is appointed for religious, not musical reasons. Although the voice of the reader of the Qur'ān may be inspirational, the chanting in most mosques is a form of recitation rather than singing. Disagreement among Muslim scholars over the extent to which singing should be used in worship has perhaps inhibited the development of singing in a formal religious context, although there are many traditions of Muslim secular singing.

Among ethnic singing varieties within Western culture but also separate from it, Jewish singing has the longest history, sometimes interacting with Christian music but more often completely isolated from it and with a unique history of its own. In the very distant past the two religions may have shared much of the same music (see chapter 2 above) in the form of monophonic chants which in the Western tradition eventually gave rise to church polyphony. The two religions also shared a proscription on the use of instruments in religious worship for much of their respective histories, and the exclusion of women from ritual music-making; in both cultures singing flourished, though very much as a male activity until the twentieth century when reformist movements in both traditions sought a more equal role for both sexes. The Jewish diaspora and the historic alienation of exiled Jewish culture from much of European society made it impossible for a uniform variety of singing to develop, and Jewish singing remained essentially oral and monophonic for many hundreds of years.

The singing in the synagogue is traditionally led by a *chazzan* or cantor, whose task is to motivate and inspire the congregation to a greater spiritual union with God. The office of cantor is an ancient one and its origins within an oral culture are not easy to determine, but it may have assumed a greater importance after the destruction of the Temple in Jerusalem in CE 70. As the diaspora began, Jewish worship devolved to the more localised and flexible synagogue with its emphasis on expressive prayer as opposed to the more elaborate and centralised ritual of the Temple and its associated panoply of instruments and singers. The fixed elements in Jewish prayer were clearly important in a culture that had lost its homeland and was condemned to surviving within other, alien societies, but this formality was balanced by the improvisation (often idiosyncratically creative) that the *chazzan* would bring to his task. The structure of the

---

[1] There is also a reverse process in some twenty-first-century evangelical churches, which have adopted musical ideas and singing styles from pop music.

liturgy was set by rabbinic authority but regionally standardised musical modes and themes guided the recitation of the text. From the medieval period onwards the *chazzan* was elected by the community and his specialist knowledge was passed from singer to singer, often with the senior figure taking in a number of *meshorerim* (pupils who might become *chazzanim*) in a master–apprentice relationship reminiscent of that found in Italian opera singing. This remained the case until the nineteenth century, when a number of cantors in German-speaking Europe began to consider more rigorous training, especially where they had been exposed to Western art music. Later in the century cantors in the Austro-Hungarian Empire formed professional associations to promote more consistent standards and to preserve certain improvisational formulae which were written down for the first time. The greatest *chazzanim* were still very individual vocally gifted charismatic prayer leaders and performers, however, and there was no equivalent to the Western conservatoire tradition until schools began to be established in the USA and Israel after the Second World War.

In an oral tradition no performance can ever be the same as any other, even if the singers tended to return to improvisatory patterns that they were familiar with as the cycle of prayer was repeated. At the heart of cantorial singing is the link between singing and spirituality: the singing is never intended as an end in itself but always as a means to spiritual engagement. A *chazzan* is required to be an upright member of the community with a knowledge of the appropriate texts and an ability to move listeners through singing, and throughout history (as far as we can tell) it is the latter quality that has often been a sine qua non. There are relatively few formal restraints on the cantorial art, which means that *chazzanim* can allow themselves to be entirely subsumed in the process of creating a sung prayer, using whatever rhetorical means they are gifted with. The diaspora, by its very nature, has itself shaped several key aspects of Jewish singing. Unlike the centralising Christian papacy, there could be no single authority or structure, but many dispersed communities preserving what they could of a common tradition. There has always been concern for the Jewishness of Jewish music (never more so than when it was exposed to Christian influences) and the distinctive Oriental modality, with its imprecise microtonal inflections and improvised passages without formal rhythm, is a reminder that the psychology of Jewish exile requires an underlying belief in a return to the East. The singing of the *chazzan* is often suffused with a mordant sense of longing, and this is perhaps driven not just by the desire for a closer union with God, but also for an end to persecution and exile.

Despite the institutional anti-Semitism of the medieval Catholic Church there were instances of cross-fertilisation between the two cultures, and by the seventeenth century we can see evidence of an uneasy but improving understanding between the two musical communities. It is unlikely that Christian singers were influenced by Jewish singers, as Jews were discriminated against as a minority culture (required in much of Europe to live in ghettos from the sixteenth century until emancipation at the very end of the eighteenth granted them basic human rights). It was relatively rare for Christians to attend synagogues, although on grand occasions or at carnival time the ruling families of Italian city states would attend one of the synagogues of their Jewish subjects. The Christian composers Orazio Vecchi (1550–1605) and Adriano Banchieri (1568–1634) were familiar enough with Jewish cantillation to satirise it in their madrigal comedies, so there must have been some mutual understanding. Churches, on the other hand, were meeting places in a wider sense, and from the Renaissance period onwards services at the wealthier European establishments were often more like public concerts (and in some cities Jews were compelled to listen to Christian sermons). There were, perforce, many opportunities for Jewish singers to be influenced by Christian singing, and even to have lessons from non-Jewish teachers.

Salamone Rossi (*c.* 1570–*c.* 1628) was employed by the Gonzaga dukes in Mantua, and is thought to be the first Jewish composer to work within the context of Western art music while still maintaining his own culture and religion. Like Christian composers of the time he wrote madrigals, setting some of the most fashionable Italian poets of the day, including Guarini and Rinuccini. More significantly, he wrote settings of the psalms in Hebrew, *HaShirim asher L'Shlomo*, often translated as 'Songs of Solomon', but more likely a pun on the composer's own name. We know nothing of the context in which these were performed, but if they were sung in the synagogue they would be one of the earliest examples of Jewish engagement with Western art music. Not the least of Rossi's problems was how to reconcile Western notation, which reads from left to right, with Hebrew texts which read from right to left. He wrote the texts backwards on the grounds that it would be less confusing for the singers, who he thought would need to pay more attention to the notes than the words.

Despite their enforced separation the two singing traditions had certain similarities. Although church music required notation, singers were expected to improvise and embellish: the written notes were a framework which could be elaborated (see chapter 3 above). Jewish music did not have notation in the Western sense (there are rhetorical cantillation signs but these do not indicate pitch) and the highest forms of cantorial singing required considerable improvisatory skill. A discerning Christian listener in the eighteenth century might not like what he heard in the synagogue but there would be certain elements that he would be able to appreciate, given the growing liberality of the Enlightenment aesthetic. Charles Burney, on his tours of Europe undertaken to research the first history of music, visited both churches and synagogues purely out of musical curiosity; he notes after a visit to a German synagogue in Amsterdam that three 'sweet singers of Israel' also had a following among the Gentile community. He finds the 'confused clamour' of the congregation difficult to understand and he does not really like the voices, but he does appreciate the virtuosity of one of the soloists, who 'forced his voice very frequently in an outrageous manner' yet 'had certainly heard good music and good singing'.[2] Burney does not comment on the music itself (likely to have been semi-improvised) but his encounter confirms that the solo singing is similar in many respects to the church singing that he is used to; the essential difference is the much more highly charged emotional commitment on the part of both soloists and congregants, which he finds distasteful but which is entirely idiomatic.

The rhetorical and emotional engagement of the *chazzan* is viewed in a more positive light by Isaak Lachmann, who described hearing the great Latvian-born cantor Yoel Dovid Levinsohn officiating in 1849:

Never again in my life did I hear such a voice, such a performance, such a holy spirit expressed in worship. I never again in my life heard such a coloratura, which seemed [like] living garlands of pearls coming from his mouth, and flying in the air of the Synagogue. His voice was a lyric tenor, rather weak, for he was greatly worn, and more spirit than body. It was a year before his death. He seemed to stand before the pulpit entranced, oblivious of his environment, swaying in the higher spheres. His singing was without effort. He hardly moved his lips even. It was more an exhalation of soul than a sounding of voice.[3]

The questioning of cultural and institutional values that drove the philosophy of the Enlightenment generated schism and reform in the church, with a corresponding weakening of religious values. The liberalising of thought and aesthetics had a parallel effect on Judaism, with many eighteenth-century intellectuals either forsaking the faith (for the much more straightforward Christian church) or demanding reform of Jewish ritual to make it less Asiatic and medieval, more appropriate for

[2] *The Present State of Music in Germany, the Netherlands and United Provinces* (London, 1773): 298–30.
[3] Quoted in Abraham Z. Idelsohn, *Jewish Music in its Historical Development* (New York: Holt & Co., 1929; repr. Schocken, 1967): 301.

the contemporary European environment. In the nineteenth century, influenced by Christian reforms in Germany, reformist Jews began to introduce Protestant hymn tunes into Jewish ritual (sometimes notated backwards to accommodate Hebrew texts) and for the first time since Rossi there is renewed engagement with the (Christian) mainstream. A key figure in this regenerative process was Salomon Sulzer, an Austrian cantor admired by Meyerbeer, Liszt and Schubert (whose songs he sang) who became chief cantor in Vienna in 1826. Between 1838 and 1866, Sulzer published *Schir Zion*, the earliest collection of synagogue music for cantor and choir, heavily influenced by Viennese paradigms (notably Haydn and Schubert). This was a period when Western composers were increasingly thinking in terms of the ownership of their compositions, and Sulzer's determination to instil discipline and rid cantorial singing of its more extravagant flights of fancy was in keeping with the times. Idelsohn quotes a mid-century English Christian traveller, who may well have heard *chazzanim* singing in a manner that was not far removed from the opera singing of his day:

It has often excited our wonder that in the principal capitals of Europe, wherever there is a synagogue we have generally found a vocal performer or two who sang in the Italian manner and in exquisite taste ... so it was in Paris, Amsterdam, Milan, Venice, Rome, Naples, and we have had instances at home of exquisite Hebrew singing in our own country.[4]

Sulzer's disciple Louis Lewandowski added Mendelssohn to the growing number of non-Jewish *contrafacta* resources available to cantors, and in France the reformer Samuel Naumbourg (who resurrected Rossi's works, which had been preserved in a collection of the Rothschild family) was responsible for adding Meyerbeer to a list of influences that included Bizet, Halévy, Flotow and Verdi. Sometimes the influence went in the other direction: in a conversation with Herman Klein in 1891, Arthur Sullivan revealed that part of 'Rebecca's Song' in *Ivanhoe* was not strictly his:

When I was the Mendelssohn Scholar and living in Leipzig I went once or twice to the old Jewish synagogue, and amongst the many Eastern melodies chanted by the minister, this quaint progression in the minor occurred so frequently that I have never forgotten it.[5]

Just as Jewish musicians adapted to elements of European culture, Jews in the USA experienced even greater tolerance and freedom, and an

---

[4] Ibid.: 243.
[5] Herman Klein, *Thirty Years of Musical Life in London 1870–1900* (New York: Century, 1903): 336. Klein also gives the musical example.

enculturation that welcomed both change and integration. The wave of German, Polish and Russian migration towards the end of the nineteenth century brought with it not only a vast increase in the Jewish population but a keener interest in the role of the *chazzan*, who became more of a focal point among the existing disparate congregations. Many were influenced by Sulzer, and what Idelsohn called 'the German Protestant style with operatic flavor',[6] and many found a competitive market where the best could become celebrities. By the last decades of the century great cantors in both Europe and America were using a style of delivery that showed they had absorbed much of the style and technique of opera singing. In some respects they were living repositories of eighteenth-century singing techniques: the bravura passage work and enormous range, with tenor *chazzanim* in particular able to extend into falsetto. This 'bicultural' singing inevitably produced singers who in purely vocal terms would be able to function as either opera singers or cantors.[7]

The most famous early twentieth-century cantor was Yossele Rosenblatt. Born in the Ukraine in 1882, Rosenblatt was a child prodigy who learned his art from his cantor father and seems to have had no formal training. As an adult he became a tenor, but was often credited with having three or four voices, able to extend his range down into the bass register and upwards into a very high soprano falsetto. After positions in Hungary, Slovakia and Germany, in 1912 he emigrated to the USA where he became something of a sensation in both Jewish and Gentile communities. He was one of the earliest cantors to make recordings and, like his older contemporary Caruso, was at his peak at a time when the demand for recordings was growing exponentially. In 1918 his concert in Chicago was attended by Cleofonte Campanini, director of the Chicago opera, who offered him the role of Eleazar in Halévy's *La Juive*. To tempt him, Campanini promised $1000 a performance, only Jewish female co-stars, kosher food, no Sabbath appearances and the retaining of his own beard. Rosenblatt, who was devout and without operatic experience, turned him down. A few days later he sang on the steps of the New York Public Library in aid of the War Savings Stamp campaign to an audience of tens of thousands. His son Samuel recounts how Enrico Caruso was so moved by Rosenblatt's rendering of 'Eili Eili' (which was among the cantor's most popular recordings)

---

[6] Idelsohn, *Jewish Music*: 325.

[7] 'Bicultural' is Mark Slobin's term. See Mark Slobin, *Chosen Voices: the Story of the American Cantorate* (University of Illinois Press, 1989): 76 n3. Jan Peerce and Richard Tucker are examples of tenors who were at home in both cultures (see John Potter, *Tenor: History of a Voice* (Yale University Press, 2009): 111–13.

that he came up and kissed him.[8] Rosenblatt went on to make his Carnegie Hall debut having learned Italian opera arias in just three weeks, and his 1927 appearance in *The Jazz Singer* (the first 'talkie') confirmed his reputation as one of the great singers of the age.

Rosenblatt was the first and most successful of the *émigré* East European *chazzanim* who were responsible for what many consider to be a golden age of cantorial performance in the USA. Their impassioned virtuosity and musical risk taking was often in marked contrast to the beautiful but bland offerings of the opera house, and the greatest stars had reputations well beyond the synagogue, often assisted by lucrative record contracts. In England Herman Klein began reviewing new Jewish vocal records for the *Gramophone* in 1928 in response to the successful marketing of Jewish singers by companies such as Brunswick and Columbia. Klein had been a student of Manuel Garcia in his youth (he was born in 1856) and was familiar with the greatest opera singers of the period. He understood the uniqueness of Jewish singing, and although he did not like the *voix nasillarde* (as he put it) of the secular material, he appreciated the virtuosity and passion of cantors such as Gershon Sirota and Mordecai Hershman, whose recordings he clearly placed on the same level as the best opera singers. Sirota first became a cantor in Vilnius, and had remained in Europe, but he too was successful in the USA and sold out Carnegie Hall. His earliest recordings date from 1903, and through them he became the first cantor to have international success. Sirota's voice was that of a dramatic tenor (Blanche Marchesi compared him to Caruso, yet he appears not to have had any Italian training). Caught in Poland at the outbreak of war, he perished in the Warsaw uprising of 1943. Hershman, a velvet-toned lyric tenor born in Russia, also officiated in Vilnius (then known as Vilna, a major centre of Jewish culture until World War II) and came to the USA in 1920, the same year as the baritone cantor Zavel Kwartin, a fellow Russian, both part of the ferocious displacement of Russian Jews that had begun during the war. Leib Glantz, another Russian child prodigy, arrived in the USA in 1926, the former Leningrad *chazzan* Pierre Pinchik the following year. Glantz had trained as a musician at the Kiev Conservatory and as a scholar and active Zionist hoped to emigrate to Palestine. After recording some of his compositions in the USA he accepted a post in New York, subsequently moving to Los Angeles where he became one of the great stars in the cantorial firmament, finally moving to Israel in

[8] Samuel Rosenblatt, *Yossele Rosenblatt: the Story of his Life as told by his Son* (New York: Farrar, Strauss and Young, 1954): 151.

1954. The sweet-voiced Pinchik (born Pinchas Segal) was educated at the conservatory in Kiev and was drafted into the Red Army, for whom he was asked to write revolutionary communist songs in Yiddish. After emigrating he had particular success in Chicago and developed his singing in both Yiddish and Hebrew. Unusually, he liked to accompany himself on the organ, as can be heard on his surviving recordings.

Moshe Ganchoff, although born in Odessa, was the first of the *émigré* cantors to learn his trade entirely in the United States. A uniquely creative improviser, he was one of the last of the golden age, dying in 1997 at the age of ninety-two. Jewish singers in the USA were insulated from the devastating effects of the Second World War. One of the few East European cantors to survive the war was also considered one of the greatest: Moshe Koussevitzky. Like many of his forebears, Koussevitzky first learned his art in Vilnius, and then succeeded Gershon Sirota in the Warsaw Tlomatska synagogue (then the largest in the world). A singer of great dignity and able to deploy a huge range, he became hugely successful all over Europe. At the outbreak of war he was rescued from the Treblinka concentration camp and spirited to Russia by the Polish underground, eventually becoming principal tenor in the Georgian Tiflis National Opera Company in 1944. He emigrated to America in 1952, by which time he was celebrated as one of the finest cantors of the age.

The voices of Koussevitsky and other cantors of the so-called Golden Age are from the same vocal gene pool as those of opera singers. Beside the obvious differences in musical tradition and repertoire there is a crucial difference in vocal psychology: an opera singer has to convey emotion within the limits of his training; he is both enabled and constrained by his technique and will always work within its natural limits; ultimately, he is acting rather than living the role, and attempting to reproduce a composer's music within the accepted boundaries of his *Fach*. A *chazzan* has a different order of emotional, musical and cultural commitment: there is no core technical armoury that all cantors share, and there are no roles for them to act. The score is a point of departure, and they are free to use any vocal means at their disposal, unhindered by a standardised technique. As well as elaborate ornamentation and freely improvised passages, the singing may feature paralinguistic rhetorical devices such as sobbing, gasping or exaggerated portamento – devices that have largely been eliminated from modern opera singing. There is also an intimacy about cantorial singing, derived from its origin in the synagogue (which is not a concert hall or opera stage); the *chazzan* traditionally *leads* the prayers, he does not 'perform' them. Today, this is often helped by the use of amplification in many cantorial concerts, which enables very quiet singing in a very high tessitura. The distinctive use of falsetto by tenor cantors would be very familiar to eighteenth-century tenors, but has been abandoned by modern singers in favour of the more macho chested top notes.

Golden Ages are constructed retrospectively and generally have as much to do with the present as the past. The golden age of *chazzanut* did mark a spectacular flourishing of a unique vocal art but it is given a traumatic resonance by the genocide that all but destroyed European Jewry in the 1940s. Some escaped the Holocaust and continued to maintain the old tradition. Louis Danto is perhaps the most outstanding example. Born in Poland and a soloist from the age of six, Danto and his family moved to Belarus on the partition of Poland in 1939. After the murder of his entire family he escaped to Minsk, where he studied at the conservatory. After the war he studied in Rome, where his potential was witnessed by Gigli and Schipa (at whose funeral he was to sing many years later). Eventually he moved to Canada, an artist of great stature continually searching for new creative paths, and on his retirement established a library dedicated to Jewish music. Danto was perhaps the greatest among those who maintained the old tradition during the profound changes experienced by the American cantorate in the second half of the twentieth century. The USA found itself the homeland of Jewish music, and set about creating a professionalised cantorate that would maintain the American version of the European tradition. The pursuit of excellence came at a price: as has been the case with Western classical music, the institutionalisation of singing pedagogy has raised standards across the board, but virtually eliminated the charismatic mould-breaker. Would Rosenblatt or Sirota succeed today without having been 'properly' trained? Probably not.

For reasons that are all too understandable the art of the cantor is relatively little known outside the Jewish community, yet all of the twentieth-century cantors discussed above could have had distinguished careers as opera singers. Historically, there have been many points at which Jewish singing has interacted with other varieties. As Alan Bilgora has pointed out, 'Adopting this florid style, often containing Middle Eastern and East European cadences, both enhanced the deeper meaning of the texts and mirrored the melodic invention of the 18th and 19th century opera composers.'[9] In other words, the key characteristics of performative textual exegesis and vocal virtuosity are shared by Jewish *chazzanut*,

---

[9] Alan Bilgora, 'Voices of Prayer and Praise', *Classic Record Collector* (August 2004).

eighteenth-century castrati and many varieties of Middle Eastern singing. In a curious way, elements of early music, world music and opera singing met in a form of synthesis in the best examples of mid-twentieth century *chazzanut*.

STYLISTIC FRAGMENTATION AND DIVERGENCE

The renewal of classical singing represented by Dietrich Fischer-Dieskau was an example of reinvention within the mainstream, but the second half of the twentieth century also saw more radical and experimental forms of vocalism that developed in parallel with conventional classical singing. In a remarkably short time this stylistic plurality led to a breaking down of the pre-war monolithic professional edifice, with some varieties of singing which had previously been minority activities achieving a legitimacy that enabled them to compete seriously with traditional opera and concert singing while remaining apart from them in public perception. The generation of musicians who were teenagers in the late 1950s and 1960s has been well documented; singers who grew up listening to Elvis Presley, the Beatles and Miles Davies as well as Dieskau and Callas were reluctant to be pigeonholed and were increasingly aware of a potential malleability of genre. A new confidence could be felt in a number of areas as singers began to explore alternatives to the traditional conservatoire route, often forming small ensembles rather than aiming at professional success as a soloist. There were two specific sorts of music in which this phenomenon led to completely new developments, the forward-looking avant-garde and the retrospective early music movement, both of which involved attempts to find dynamic alternatives to received ideas of what singing was. These new areas, initially on the margins of professional musical life, were open for all to explore; they were non-institutional and, at least to begin with, admitted of no pedagogy. The vocal production and the musical aims had little to do with the singerly certainties of the pre-war period: it seemed to many at the time that there were no limits on what the human voice might do.

THE EARLY MUSIC MOVEMENT

There has probably been no time in history when singers have ignored the music of the past, but there are no obvious precedents for the attempts to integrate versions of the past into the culture of the early twenty-first century. The reference by the medieval scribe known as Anonymous IV to the music of Leonin and Perotin is an early example of musicians valuing their predecessors, and although music was constantly in a state of renewal, by the seventeenth century it was common for English cathedral choirs to retain repertoire from earlier generations. Secular antiquarian collectors such as Samuel Pepys sometimes acquired considerable holdings of older material. The overwhelming influence of Handel on English music of the mid-eighteenth century ensured the survival of his music beyond his lifetime, and *Messiah* in particular was one of the earliest vocal works to become embedded in the musical culture as part of a permanent canon of significant works. In Europe, Bach quickly followed, the appreciation of his music very much driven by composers of succeeding generations such as Mendelssohn; the homage paid to Mozart by Haydn and Schubert among others was a similarly important factor in Mozart's canonisation.

This reification of 'the work' was a historicism of the head rather than a look back at historical reality: although the mastery of the composer was recognised, before Wagner the musical score was still treated as source material to be used by performers in whatever ways they wished. The music was still in a very real sense owned by the performers at the moment of delivery, and there was no attempt to realise it in a way that might have been meaningful to the original composer. Thus Pepys, on his roof of a summer evening in the 1660s, may have played fragments of fifteenth-century vocal polyphony on his viol; the Handel Commemoration of 1784 saw *Messiah* and other works performed in the context of the continuing fashion for ever-larger choirs, and Mendelssohn had no qualms about cutting and re-orchestrating Bach's *Matthäuspassion* in 1829. The later nineteenth century also saw the beginnings of historical musicology, which resulted in enormous numbers of medieval and Renaissance compositions being edited and published in modern editions. In the early twentieth century this appreciation of the past shifted towards an understanding of the idea of the work as a historical artefact which should be treated as such, rather than considered in the same way as contemporary music. This gained considerable currency after 1945, in part because postwar performers began to seek refuge in the idea of a more distant past that would erase the trauma of the more immediate present.

For instrumentalists there were new sounds, textures and techniques to be discovered: keyboards, wind and stringed instruments could be reconstructed from surviving originals or iconographical evidence and new sound worlds revealed as a result. It was different for singers: human larynxes had not changed in any way at all for thousands of years (what changes is the usage of the vocal tract) and it is perhaps not surprising that the voice could not be subjected to such minute analysis without threatening singers' sense of who they were. There was plenty of experiment in early vocal music, but it was largely about applying a musicology of the composer rather than considering the sound itself. In the revivals of the 1950s and 1960s it was the *idea* of the past that was important, as was composerly authority. The editor assumed the function of pseudo-composer, with the same protective attitude to the score as most modernist composers. Performance was required to be faithful to what were thought to be the composer's intentions in terms of the notes sung, and performances were expected to be refined, precise and on a small scale.

In England the counter-tenor Alfred Deller came to be identified with the early music *Zeitgeist*: his ethereal voice was like nothing in the present, and it came to symbolise what a voice from the past might be like. Male altos had been a feature of English cathedrals for hundreds of years, and Oxford and Cambridge colleges produced a succession of increasingly successful counter-tenors legitimised by the Deller experience. In time counter-tenors from Europe and the USA would revolutionise the sound and technique of the falsetto voice, elevating it to a position of distinction that it rarely occupied historically and enabling revivals of baroque opera roles composed for castrati.

It was not only the otherworldly high male voice that came to define the early music voice. Almost all of the singers working in Britain in the nascent early music scene in the 1960s and 1970s were formed by the English choral tradition: they had learned the trade in university or cathedral choirs, a way of working that goes back to the reform of cathedral music at the end of the nineteenth century. This involves a uniquely disciplined approach to singing derived in part from the practical realities of running choirs containing a lot of children. Every singer from such a background is taught to attack notes cleanly and accurately and to sing with minimal vibrato and maximum consideration for the overall blend that this facilitates. Not hitting a note cleanly is regarded as a sign of incompetence and has probably not been tolerated by any English choirmaster in living memory. The style was the very antithesis of the soloistic singing to be heard in opera: portamento was absolutely forbidden and vibrato discouraged, something to laugh at when caricaturing old fashioned singers. This is not a style rooted in any consideration of historical performance practice but is a living tradition based on a certain sort of musical discipline; for most choristers it is the only 'proper' way to sing. The discipline also encourages a good ear for rhythm and tuning, and both of these skills have had effects on modern ideas of what early music should sound like. Singing should be rhythmic and together, and a good ear enables questions of temperament to be addressed with some precision.

The post-Deller trajectory in Britain was continued by a number of entrepreneurial conductors and ensembles. David Munrow's Early Music Consort of London was founded in 1967 and featured the counter-tenor James Bowman. The initial focus of the group was on Munrow's remarkable skills as a self-taught performer on reconstructed instruments. His friendship with a number of singers was one of the factors that led him into vocal music towards the end of his short life. His performances of medieval and Renaissance music using singers from the London cathedral choirs and Oxford and Cambridge colleges, like those of Deller before him, created a very plausible ancient sound world and established an ethos that continues into the twenty-first century. The combination of an 'authentic' sounding instrumental ensemble and a choir of ex-choral scholars was enough to satisfy most audience's ideas of what old music should sound like, and fared rather better commercially than the more experimental approach of the other significant ensemble of the period, Musica Reservata. This group, led by Michael Morrow, was the first to realise that the *sound* of medieval singing might have more to do with untrained (and possibly un-English) voices than Oxbridge choral scholars. The singing of soprano Jantina Noorman was loud, even raucous, owing something to European folk musics and very little to the English choral tradition. The sound proved too deviant from the imaginary norms of the new medieval sound world, and the ensemble had relatively little commercial success.

The Early Music Consort was phenomenally successful worldwide thanks to its recordings, which greatly benefited from the evolving technology of the LP. High fidelity sound became an end in itself, enabled by advances across the entire recording technology from microphone to speaker. By the early 1970s vast amounts of the classical canon were available on LP, and early music offered not only the possibility of entirely new music that was easy to listen to, but also the chance to market newly fashioned 'authentic' versions of pieces consumers already owned. For the recording companies there was the prospect of quick profits compared with opera recordings (which were the industry's long term big money spinner, being expensive to produce but selling consistently over many years). In England many choirs were founded specifically to perform and record the 'new' Renaissance and early baroque repertoire. John Eliot Gardiner's Monteverdi Choir and Roger Norrington's Schütz Choir were among the first professional choirs not directly attached to a university or cathedral establishment. The steady stream of singers generated by the Oxbridge system potentially added some thirty singers a year to the pool available for choirs and ensemble work. For many of them there was the chance to try their luck as professional singers, using skills that had been second nature to them since childhood before deciding whether to risk the freelance life or opt for a permanent job outside music. The effect on the choirs was profound, producing a synthesis of much that was good about the English choral tradition and raising standards to new heights.

New choirs continued to be founded (Andrew Parrott's Taverner Choir and its associated Consort was a particularly original example) but more significantly, singers began looking for other ways in which exploiting their choral skills would bring them greater control over their own musical and professional lives. A succession of vocal groups formed from the mid-1970s onwards and established their own distinctive profile within the early music movement, despite often singing very similar repertoire. Gothic Voices was an early success, the inspiration of Christopher Page, an Oxford (and subsequently Cambridge) academic specialising in medieval French literature; Page's vision of early vocal music was entirely different from that of the Munrow generation: he reasoned that a lack of text did not of itself imply instrumental performance, and that singing was essentially a cappella, thereby at a stroke rendering many of the instrument-orientated ensembles obsolete. What Howard Mayer Brown termed 'the English *a cappella* heresy' was a helpful boost for vocal performance and English groups flourished as never before.[10] Page believed that the Gothic Voices sound was actually representative of the medieval period, whereas Peter Philips, director of the Tallis Scholars, never claimed that an 'authentic' sound was either possible or desirable. The democratically run Hilliard Ensemble did not even claim to be an early music group; they had a broad knowledge of the relevant source material but often chose to ignore it, using the gaps in their knowledge as a creative opportunity.

After the first rush of inspirational performers the movement began to concern itself with 'authenticity' and composers' intentions. Record magazines such as *The Gramophone* began hiring specialist early music reviewers and singers had to make sure that their musicological credentials

---

[10] See Christopher Page, 'The English *a cappella* heresy', in Tess Knighton and David Fallows (eds.), *Companion to Medieval and Renaissance Music* (London: Dent, 1992; repr. University of California Press, 2011): 23–9.

were in order if they were to retain academic and commercial credibility. A considerable gap began to open up between musicologists and professional performers, and during the 1990s the concept of authenticity gave way to the idea of performances being 'historically informed'. The disciplined, modernist aesthetic of musicology is in many ways incompatible with the instincts of the creative singer, and the looser ideology made it easier for performers to be creative. It has often been amateur groups who have found ways to collaborate with musicologists; professional performers cannot avoid the demands of a market in which they need to be seen to be musically self-sufficient.

A significant part of the early music agenda was to strip away the vulgarity, excess and perceived incompetence associated with stylistic quirks such as portamento and vibrato, and the ensembles that came to be marketed as early music groups did this very artistically. The clean, one voice to a part approach not only fitted the modern aesthetic but also enabled efficient application of musicology where the singers were prepare to engage with it: chords could be tuned appropriately, issues of *musica ficta* resolved according to ancient treatises. Often it is only in their acknowledgement and occasional use of historical musicology that the groups have some claim to be thought of as 'early music' ensembles in a historical sense. The use of single voices for what was originally choral music (most fifteenth-century polyphony, for example) is an entirely modern phenomenon, as is the basic sound of the singers. As we have seen, modern singing dates from the nineteenth century, when singing changed from a high larynx position which produced a more speech-like vocal persona to a low larynx position and its concomitant concerns with tone colour and breathing technique.

Singers tend not to address this question. There is no avoiding the fact that no medieval or Renaissance singer used anything like a modern technique, and the evidence for the baroque period suggests a concern for flexible virtuosity and textual clarity, rather than tone colour and rhythmic precision. The pioneers of the revival were able to present a convincing – and commercially successful – case for a kind of singing that was in principle the same as people were already familiar with: a conventional modern technique but reduced in scale. Singers such as Emma Kirkby, who became a model and an inspiration for women singers in much the same way as Alfred Deller and James Bowman were for counter-tenors, were taught by conventional teachers and generally learned a generic singing technique. Although there were many complaints that conservatories and universities did not take early music seriously (early music singers

were not thought to be 'proper singers') within a short time conservatories began to offer courses of study. While this had obvious benefits for
singers, it inevitably perpetuated the use of a modern technique in early
music singing. The benefits include the ability to cope with a wide variety
of singing styles both within and outside early music, but the downside
was that the singers never developed a community of practice in the same
way that instrumentalists did. During the last quarter of the century
early lutenists and string players in particular developed a living tradition,
owing something to the past but rather more to their way of exploring
it in the present. Singers never needed to do this, as the 'opera singing
light' technique precluded debate about the actual vocal practice of the
pre-twentieth century (and what singers could learn of it from old recordings did not encourage them to explore further). It would have taken a
very brave student indeed to dispense with the advantages of a modern
technique and attempt Renaissance or baroque music according to the
principles outlined in chapter 2 above. The resulting basic sound would
probably be closer to a modern rock or folk singer, which would make
their own expensively acquired skills largely irrelevant.

The forays into early music by rock singers such as Jeff Buckley and
Sting reveal the potential of a speech technique to illuminate the poetry
of the text and the redundancy of much early music singing pedagogy.
It has taken a long time and the vision of rock singers to take this step.
There is a further step that could be taken, should a pop singer have the
courage and curiosity to do so. Sting's singing of Dowland informs us
about one of the central aspects of seventeenth-century singing: clarity
of text. The other key characteristic is virtuosity. It is particularly hard
for modern singers to conceive of Bach sung without the full rigour of
a modern technique; there is no evidence that Bach's singers had such a
technique, but no professional singer has yet been bold enough to attempt
his music without one. In the meantime, the number of highly trained
early music singers sound increasingly generic, preferring technical excellence to inspired risk-taking.

THE VOCAL AVANT-GARDE

Many of those involved in early music also experimented with the avant-
garde. The group dynamic flourished in a similar manner, with many
singers steering clear of the mainstream and experimenting with both
old and new music. Like the early music movement, the avant-garde had
roots in musical events earlier in the century and grew out of attempts to

extend or bypass conventional singing. Standardised conservatoire training and the ubiquity of recordings meant that by the beginning of the
twenty-first century many listeners shared for the first time a common
perception of what professional singing should be. This sense of a singing establishment eventually required new forms of vocal expression, and
these would inevitably be drawn either from speech itself or the paralinguistic gestures and sounds that are associated with it.

The connection between singing and speech had become much less
obvious as the lower larynx technique became widely accepted towards
the end of the nineteenth century. There were alternatives to both straight
theatre and opera in the form of the German *Singspiel* or melodrama, both
of which incorporated spoken dialogue, but despite significant works by
Mozart, Benda and others, the inexorable rise of the all-sung stage work
tended to overshadow the hybrid genres (although in England, where vernacular opera never quite achieved the same musical cohesion as imported
products, there had been a tradition of spoken dialogue since the semi-
operas of Purcell and his contemporaries that extended through the ballad opera tradition of John Gay and others to the operettas of Gilbert and
Sullivan). It was in Germany that the first significant attempts to extend
speech into song occurred, and it was an extrapolation on the melodrama
that provided Schoenberg with the vehicle for his *Pierrot Lunaire* settings of
1912. He composed the cycle for Albertine Zehme, a *diseuse* more at home
in cabaret, requiring the pitches to be spoken, not sung. What he meant
by this was never entirely clear but the piece captured the imagination of
performers, audiences and composers, and the controversy over the use of
Sprechgesang generated a wider interest in the musical use of speech.

It is only a short step from melodrama to cabaret, and the Dada and
Futurist movements used the less formal venues that these genres required
to create performance art that crossed a number of boundaries between
speech, song, poetry and drama. The two movements represented very
different political ideologies (Dada being anti-war, the Futurists eventually becoming associated with fascism) but both had a liberating effect
on the performing arts. Filippo Marinetti's 'Zang Tumb Tumb' of 1914
was an early example of *parole in libertà* in which the typeface itself (as
well as the onomatopoeic text) assumed expressive potential, requiring a
performance rather than a mere reading. Sound poetry reached its most
effective expression in Kurt Schwitters's *Ursonate*, a phonetic celebration
of expressive and virtuosic vocalism. Although it does have a visual aesthetic value the work makes little sense unless it is performed. Schwitters
began work on it in 1922 at about the same time James Joyce published

Ulysses. Ursonate was finally published in 1932, by which time (after many experimental performances by its creator) it had become a kind of phonetic map, suggesting a colourful sound structure but leaving the choice of pitches and rhythms to the performer. Unlike Joyce's stream of consciousness it is constructed according to formal principles (a very elaborate version of sonata form). Both works would have a significant effect on composers and performers later in the century, the colour and structure of phonemes offering composers a way forward that might bypass the structural rigour of serialism, and providing endless creative performative material for singers.

Schwitters was not a trained singer, and the Dada movement was an anti-establishment entity during the lifetime of most of its adherents. For 'non-classical' singing to gain a wider acceptance there needed to be some acknowledgement by professional singers that there were possibilities beyond the comfort zone of their classical technique. The Second World War inevitably caused a hiatus in the performing arts, and it was not until the 1950s that the next significant developments in vocal performance emerged. The performative freedoms gained by the Dadaists and Futurists then resurfaced in the works of Mauricio Kagel, György Ligeti, Luciano Berio and John Cage. Kagel's *Anagrama* (1957–8) for four solo voices, speaking chorus, and instruments, was first performed in Cologne in 1960. It is constructed out of the phonetic elements of an elaborate palindrome (sometimes attributed to Dante),

In girum imus nocte et consumimur igni

(referring to moths or butterflies, meaning 'we circle in the night and are consumed by fire'). The phonemes in turn generate new words in four languages which often combine together to make absurd sentences. The work impressed Ligeti, who came late to phonetic poetry, only discovering Schwitters after he moved to Vienna following the Hungarian uprising of 1956. His *Aventures* and *Nouvelles Aventures* use meaningless texts (devised according to a logic that the composer took with him to the grave) to explore the emotive power of vocal gesture.

Kagel's and Ligeti's pieces could only have been written if the composers could call on singers willing to experiment and go beyond the techniques that were familiar to them, and from the 1960s onwards an increasing number of dedicated performers put themselves at the disposal of composers, generating an enormous number of new works. Creative singers of the period included Jane Manning and Mary Thomas (both of whom were associated with the works of Peter Maxwell Davies and many others), but the *doyenne* of them all was Cathy Berberian. Berberian trained as an opera singer, but had a flexible voice and insatiable musical and intellectual curiosity which made her a perfect exponent of new music (and unlike the early practitioners of the early music revival she was never in danger of being told that she could not sing). Berio referred to her as his *studio di fonologia* and she was, in effect, co-composer of many of his vocal works.[11] *Sequenza III*, to 'a few words' by Markus Kutter, was created entirely around Berberian's technical repertoire (which included a dental trill, an effect which at the time only she could do). More importantly, the collaboration showed how a classically trained singer could transcend her original training and extend the possibilities into the vocal unknown. Like the *Ursonate* and the works of Kagel and Ligeti, the *Sequenza* assumes a theatrical presentation; like Renaissance music it requires the clear declamation of the text, and like baroque music it demands a virtuosity that impresses for its own sake: the work is a vocal *tour de force*.

Berio had begun his exploration of Berberian's voice in *Tema (Omaggio a Joyce)* in 1958 (in which he electronically modified her reading of Chapter 11 of Joyce's *Ulysses*), and it was hearing her recitation that inspired John Cage to write his *Aria* for her the following year. *Aria* is also an exploration of the technical armoury of Cathy Berberian, but instead of reifying technical effects in notation, Cage produced a multicoloured graphic score with instructions for the performer to assume a number of personae, each associated with specific symbols. Like the *Ursonate*, this too has no fixed pitches or rhythms, and cannot exist unless it is realised in performance. Many of Cage's later works also use expressive speech and give the performer considerable freedom, but it was Berio who forced the pace in the artistic exploration of the voice, and always in collaboration with specific performers, most notably with the Swingle Singers, for whom he wrote *Sinfonia* and the eight-voice version of *A-Ronne*. *Sinfonia* (1967–9) places the amplified singers in the pit as an extension of a symphony orchestra. The relationship between voices and instruments is a subtle one: the singers should not dominate, and the multiple quotations (from Claude Lévi-Strauss and others) should be only just heard above the orchestra (to the chagrin of many a sound engineer). Ward Swingle's original group were jazz singers, and the fifth movement features very fast scatting in unison with an orchestra of up to a hundred instruments, a feat of vocal virtuosity that few have been able to match. The singers are also required to whisper, shout

---

[11] Luciano Berio, *Two Interviews* (New York: Marion Boyars, 1985/2000): 141.

(and indeed sing) and need to augment their classical technique with an awareness of microphone technique.

Berio explored microphone singing further in *A-Ronne*. In its original 1974 version this was a radio play for five actors (and therefore had no visual dimension at all). He rewrote the piece the following year for the eight voices of Ward Swingle's English group, then called Swingle Two. As the piece was essentially an aural experience, the performance took place in complete blackout apart from the singers' mouths which were individually illuminated by a narrow beam attached to each microphone stand. The lack of light often had unintended effects on audience behaviour. At the first performance in Rome at the Teatro Olimpico in 1975 a fight broke out between those in the stalls who did not like the piece, and those in the balcony who showered those below with insults and missiles. At an Edinburgh Festival performance the following year the singers discovered when the lights came up at the end that the near sell-out hall was virtually empty, many of the audience having slipped away in the dark, unheard above the amplified singing.

The text for *A-Ronne* consists of a collage of quotations assembled by Edoardo Sanguineti from sources as diverse as the Bible, the Communist Manifesto and T. S. Eliot. All are concerned with beginnings, middles and ends, and this agenda determines the overall shape of the piece. The real significance of the work lies in the fact that Berio and Sanguineti take the text fragments through a number of scenes beginning with a party which metamorphoses into a political rally, followed by a bedroom scene, a singing lesson, a confessional, several word games involving considerable verbal dexterity, and other aural landscapes before ending up with coda of 'pure' music and the spoken utterance 'ette, conne, ronne' (the last three letters of an old Italian alphabet, hence A-Ronne = A–Z). By using the same set of text some twenty times in different contexts Berio makes clear what singers may always have known but been reluctant to admit (for fear of jeopardising their status as interpretative artists) that words can mean whatever the performer wants them to mean. The realisation of this fact, obvious though it seems in retrospect, had a profoundly liberating and empowering effect on all who performed the piece. Inspired by their encounters with Berio, four members of Swingle Two left the group in 1978 and formed Electric Phoenix to continue their experiments with amplified voices. As well as continuing to perform Berio, the group took on existing works from the Extended Vocal Techniques Ensemble of San Diego (spectacularly successfully, in the case of *Madrigals* by William Brooks and *Not a Soul but Ourselves* by Roger Marsh). They instigated a vigorous commissioning policy, beginning with Henri Pousseur's *Songs and Tales from the Bible of Hell*, for which they commissioned personal electronic effects boxes from engineer Ian Macintosh.

Other groups and individuals were also experimenting with sound systems and microphones, and developing repertoires of techniques which extended the definition and concept of singing. It was not simply a case of making the voice louder. The microphone became, in effect, an extension of the vocal tract which could be manipulated over a far wider frequency spectrum than was possible in conventional singing. The phonetic richness enjoyed by Schwitters and the sound poets could be experienced in glorious acoustical technicolor. Paralinguistic elements such as sobbing, gasping, whispering and rhetorical breathing, all of which had virtually disappeared from opera singing during the twentieth century, reappeared in exaggerated (sometimes grotesque) form. The breath could become a complex sound source in itself independently of the vocal cords and could produce multiphonics, spectacularly so on the inhale. The mouth cavity could be manipulated to reinforce specific harmonics, and all of this battery of technique could be further modified by electronics.

None of these effects could be standardised as the results were specific to the vocal physiognomy of each individual, and just as Mozart wrote arias based on the unique vocal quirks of individual singers, so twentieth-century composers exploited the sounds that resulted from singers' personal vocal tract disposition. And just as Handel or Mozart would rewrite arias if they were to be performed by new singers, some avant-garde works had to be adapted to the talents of each new performer. The prime example of this is Peter Maxwell Davies's 1969 *Eight Songs for a Mad King*, which the composer created around the unique skills of Roy Hart. Hart died in a car crash in 1975 at the age of forty-nine, and the many virtuoso singers that have sung the *Eight Songs* have had to accommodate the multiphonics to their own vocal tract peculiarities. Hart was one of the most remarkable singers of the century, with a range approximating to that of a piano, and an ability to create multiphonic sounds that resulted in predictable chords rather than random and often unreliable combinations of harmonics. Hart trained as an actor but in 1947 began to have singing lessons with Alfred Wolfsohn. Wolfsohn's approach to singing was grounded in psychotherapy, and he believed not only in the healing power of singing but in the ability of everyone to sing in any range. For Wolfsohn the conventional distinction between the categories of soprano, alto, tenor and bass had no meaning, and his pupils often had ranges of five octaves or more. The sounds the human voice makes at the extremes of its total achievable range have not found a central place in Western art music, but the surviving recordings of Wolfsohn's pupils are quite remarkable. They might be described as technical rather than musical but they are extraordinary examples of how the voice may be extended regardless of gender.[12] Wolfsohn died in 1962, and Hart continued his teaching, eventually forming a company of his own. He went on to create pieces for Henze, Stockhausen and others as well as developing his own repertoire, and the Roy Hart Theatre still flourishes in the house in the south of France in which he lived and worked.

Hart and Wolfsohn's work had a therapeutic, even spiritual dimension to it, and the work of the Roy Hart Theatre today continues to explore the more metaphysical aspects of the voice. Karlheinz Stockhausen similarly believed that singing could access phenomena beyond the merely musical. His *Stimmung*, composed in 1968 for Collegium Vocale Köln, is based entirely on the overtone series for the note B flat. Relatively few professional groups have performed the piece, as a substantial investment of time is needed to be able to identify and tune the harmonics absolutely precisely (Collegium Vocale, Singcircle and the Theatre of Voices, the three groups to record it, include a significant number of early music singers who are familiar with just intonation). It was the composer's only excursion into extended vocal techniques, though *Spiral* for a performer with shortwave radio dates from the same year and has been performed by many singers. In this piece (and its companion pieces *Pole* and *Expo* (1969–70)) the performer receives radio signals (preferably mediated by interference rather than unambiguous musical events) and expands on the source material according to a series of modulation signs. The performer has a great deal of freedom as parameters such as rhythm and pitch are only suggested in very general terms by the signs, and the vocal texture and sound is negotiated between the singer and radio.

The relationship between composers and singers underwent subtle changes towards the end of the twentieth century. For many singers the excitement of the avant-garde began to pall after many years of performing to niche audiences, especially bearing in mind the enormous amount of work involved in learning a new piece. Composers of the so-called New Complexity alienated many performers by expecting them to be strained to the limit at every performance. One of the weaknesses of applying such criteria is that highly skilled performers would often be able to achieve feats previously thought impossible, at which point the tension that was

[12] *Vox Humana: Alfred Wolfsohn's Experiments in Extension of Human Vocal Range*, Folkways FPX 123.

so important for the composer would dissipate. There was also a sense that the new array of speech-related and para-musical techniques had tended to produce works that referenced a limited number of areas (humour and madness, for example), and that composers, many of whom held academic positions and therefore to some extent operated in an artistic vacuum, were slow to respond to the demands from singers for music that was enjoyable to perform and not merely challenging. There was also competition from composer-performers who inhabited a less easily defined world somewhere between new music and pop music. Meredith Monk and Laurie Anderson were creating musical events that were less confrontational and demonstrated a wider emotional range than the old avant-garde seemed to offer. Many of the early music groups which had also included new music in their repertoire began to seek out postmodern composers for whom sheer difficulty was not an end in itself.

As we have seen, the postwar period has been one of retrenchment in classical singing. The mainstream of Western vocal music (and indeed of Jewish singing) remains paralysed by the narrow aims of institutional pedagogy that looks to the past for its cultural integrity. Most conservatories still train large numbers of singers for a very small number of operatic roles, a situation that will surely not be sustainable very far into the new century. Early music has become sufficiently close to the mainstream to be snared by its criterion of bland perfection, and the experimental era of the vocal avant-garde has lost its way as audiences and singers question the need for apparently pointless complexity. But such cultural crisis points can generate unforeseen change, and as the century develops we may be seeing a certain cultural and aesthetic realignment; there is evidence to suggest that what we now think of as the mainstream is contracting, perhaps to become one element (albeit, for the moment, a large one) in a plethora of what Bourdieu called taste markets.[13] The most obvious manifestation of this is the internet, where artistic communities large and small can flourish independently of geography, age, class and conventional professional criteria. Western classical singing may eventually come to be appreciated as one (very significant) variety among countless others. When researchers in a century or two's time look back on the twentieth century they may well be puzzled by our current obsession with maintaining the presence of the past.

[13] Pierre Bourdieu, *Distinction: a Social Critique of the Judgement of Taste* (London: Routledge and Kegan Paul, 1984).

CHAPTER 9

The emancipation of the popular voice

POPULAR CLASSICAL: ASPIRATIONAL IMITATION

The concepts of 'classical' and 'popular' singing have meant different things to different people since the distinction between the two began to appear during the nineteenth century. Before the twentieth century it is perhaps more appropriate to think in terms of private or domestic music and public music. People have always sung for fun, whether in the fields or in the bath, and this informality is also to be found in the earliest public entertainments such as the various gatherings of troubadours or *Minnesänger* in the medieval period, the Italian carnival productions or German drinking songs in the Renaissance. At a more formal level, public opera brought cultivated singing to a wider audience in mid-seventeenth-century Europe, and the movement towards vernacular opera in several European countries from the eighteenth century onwards broadened the class base considerably. Italian opera in particular, for all its rigidly tiered class system (and, in part, because of it – everyone went to the opera to see and be seen), was genuinely popular: Verdi was a national hero, not just among the middle and upper classes. When the only time you could experience music was in the presence of those making it, there was only a vague distinction between what was popular in a vernacular sense and what was not. During the twentieth century 'classical' would come to mean 'unpopular' and the music would lose touch with its mass audience. The term as applied to singing would generally mean one who had been trained (as opposed to a popular singer who just did it). But before such rigid distinctions cut off swathes of music from its potential audience a 'highbrow' operatic aria might be performed to less discerning audiences in the eighteenth-century pleasure gardens or nineteenth-century music hall; the singing might not have been quite as polished as in the opera house, but it was all broadly recognisable as the same singing. Recital programmes from around the turn of the century often seem to be almost

random collections of songs that might include new songs being promoted by publishers, Italian opera arias or folk arrangements by the singers themselves; even the most serious singers would have a lighter encore
or two up their sleeve. The early career of Rosa Ponselle is an example of
how close the vocal requirements for vaudeville and opera could be. Born
Rosa Ponzillo in 1897 to *émigré* Italian parents, she played piano for silent
films as a teenager and became a cinema theatre singer before joining her
older sister Carmela in a highly successful cabaret duo. It was only in
1918 when the two singers decided that the Keith vaudeville circuit was
not paying them enough that Rosa considered opera singing. Singing to
Victor Maurel and Enrico Caruso very quickly led to a contract with the
Metropolitan Opera House. She made her debut opposite Caruso later
that same year as Leonora in Verdi's *La Forza del Destino* having never
sung on an operatic stage before, and went on to become one of the most
famous sopranos of the century.

Public singing aspired to be different (better, or more cultivated) from
private singing and it is this distinction which underlies the relationship between the two genres in the first half of the twentieth century.
There was a sharper distinction between classical and popular singing
by mid-century, partly because the new jazz-influenced, microphone-
assisted idioms were beyond the reach of classical singers (who consequently spurned the 'popular'). Later in the century the distinction
began to blur with the steady legitimisation and sophistication of rock
music and its variants, and the efforts of record companies to find wider
markets by devising 'crossover' strategies for successful opera singers.
Sound and film technology developed on an industrial scale in the USA,
and American music achieved a hegemony over the course of the century
that only began to weaken (apart from a stellar British presence thanks
to the Beatles) with the near collapse of the record industry in the 1990s
and the post-millennium expansion of the internet.

The earliest recordings reveal an extraordinarily eclectic mix of material, much of it consisting of novelty items that are hard to classify in terms
of singing. The heyday of the music hall was past by the time recording
became a viable commercial proposition but many of its successful performers were still treading the boards, often trying to adapt to the advent
of ragtime, revue or whatever the latest craze happened to be (they would
ultimately all succumb to the cinema). Some were reluctant to record,
fearing it would mean that audiences would not want to come and hear
them in the flesh, or because they simply could not grasp the idea of
performing to an absent audience (there would be a similar mistrust of

radio when mass broadcasting got under way in the 1920s). Others saw the new media as an opportunity to broaden their reach, and during the first decade of the century many singers who had made their name in the last quarter of the previous century left examples for us to hear today. Vaudeville and music hall singers were engaging personalities, whose stage act almost always included stand-up routines which depended on interaction with their fans. Telling jokes to a horn cannot have been an easy or exciting experience for any of them, and even stars such as Dan Leno and Little Tich inevitably sound stilted and contrived. Performers and audiences shared a similar basic ambition: everyone was essentially aspirational, seeking to better themselves socially. This can be clearly heard in the earliest recordings, which had to compete with opera arias in a world where everyone recognised 'quality' when they heard it. Even 'professional' cockneys moderated their speech so that listeners would not confuse them with the real thing. This often resulted in a curious hybrid vocal sound, with elements of received pronunciation sometimes hinting at the richer sounds of the trained singer. The Royal Command Variety Performance at the London Palladium in 1912 was the first time the monarchy had acknowledged popular culture, and part of its purpose was to make popular music safe for public consumption. The British patriotic songs of the First World War reinforced the tendency to equate a certain sort of aspirational popular song with the national interest, and in the interwar years a singer such as Noël Coward could find a popular audience despite his middle-class origins. The aspirational style was coincidentally reinforced by the practicalities of projection: to be heard at the back of increasingly large concert halls required the fuller tone that is a consequence of lowering the larynx. This inevitably made popular singers closer in timbre to classical singers than they would be after the invention of amplification.

The first acoustic recordings give some insight into what a pre-gramophone voice sounded like, as the singers still sang as though they were projecting into a theatre. This was partly because they had to in order for the horn to maximise their input, but also because they knew no other way: there was no microphone and therefore no 'mic technique'. Al Jolson, in the many years that he sang without a microphone, had a particularly powerful delivery which was still sufficiently nuanced to captivate his listeners. As Art Klein, Jolson's agent put it, 'In those days you must remember there were no microphones. But this man had the most resonant voice of any human being I ever knew. I stood at the back of the theatre with my hands on the wall – and I could feel the bricks

vibrate.'[1] The disadvantage of the microphone was that it restricted movement: Jolson's act depended on his using as much of the theatrical space
as he could – which might include singing and dancing in the aisles all
the way to the exits. He even performed from a special ramp built into
the audience after trying it out in his 1911 New York Winter Gardens
show – a prophetic effect that would only really come into its own with
the invention of the radio mic towards the end of the century (movement
was so integral to Jolson's singing that he danced way out of range of the
horn during his first Victor recordings).

His popularity was extraordinary, rivalling that of another great singer
who was an early beneficiary of the recording age, Enrico Caruso. The
markets that the two singers appealed to were different but overlapping,
Jolson having a rapport with audiences that Caruso could not reach,
though both had huge mass appeal. Both stood on the cusp of the new
age and would probably have been successful without the new technology, but their ability to embrace it (at least in marketing terms) made
them the first international superstars of the new century. At the end of
World War I there was a charity concert at the Metropolitan Opera in
New York in aid of returning war veterans. Caruso topped the bill in
what was very much his own territory, but Jolson was equally successful with the audience (if not with the critics) and subsequently went on
to do a one man show at the Boston Opera accompanied by the Boston
Symphony Orchestra. This proximity of 'classical' and popular music also
extended to Jolson being sued for plagiarism by the Puccini estate – who
reckoned that Jolson's 'Avalon' was too close to 'E lucevan le stelle' for
comfort. Jolson never developed a mic technique; his highly energised
and robust delivery perhaps compensated in some way for the fact that
in his films and recordings he could not see his audience. By not embracing the performance potential of the microphone he remained associated
with a sub-classical genre that would seem very middle of the road compared with the intimate alternatives offered by jazz singing and crooning. Jolson's 1927 film *The Jazz Singer* was the first to use synchronised
sound for musical numbers and some of the dialogue, mixing the new
Vitaphone recording system with old silent film technology, then projecting the result into theatres via amplified loudspeakers. It was this film
that almost instantly demonstrated that 'The Talkies' were the future of
film, though it was not the talking that did the trick, but the singing. The
film is much more than just a technological marvel, and is a remarkable

[1] Michael Freedland, *Al Jolson* (London: W. H. Allen, 1972): 64.

window on popular song, Jewish cantorial singing and (by default) jazz singing. Jolson is not what we now think of as a jazz singer, but the term clearly meant something much vaguer in the late 1920s, encompassing almost any syncopated popular song. The film shows Jolson's extraordinary versatility, not only in his own popular repertoire but also his rendering of the Yom Kippur 'Kol Nidre' in an appropriately cantorial manner. There is also genuine cantorial singing from Yossele Rosenblatt, one of the most successful cantors of all time, whose services Warner Brothers went to a great deal of trouble to acquire.[2] In his 'jazz' songs Jolson sounds like a light tenor (in his Vitaphone short *Plantation Act* of the previous year he even inserts neat turns and two finely controlled *messa di voce*); the difference between him and operatic tenors of the time is essentially one of repertoire (Jolson's has to be coaxed and played with before it will work, unlike a Puccini aria). But the fact that 'jazz' singing, popular song and Jewish *chazzanut* can all be carried off successfully by the same singer (who might in different circumstances have been a classical tenor) is yet more evidence of the classically influenced popular style that was the norm before the widespread use of microphones.

THE MICROPHONE AND THE INTERNATIONAL PROJECTION OF INTIMACY

Jolson represented a dynamic vocal style that transcended national boundaries in the same way as opera had done in the previous century, but this time the influence was from the USA to Europe rather than the other way round (even if most European cinemas, lacking amplification and speakers, had to show *The Jazz Singer* as a silent). All European countries had distinctive popular singing of their own, but with the exception of British pop music post-Beatles (and the curious case of the Eurovision Song Contest), these tended not to travel well. At the beginning of the century the USA was far from the unified world power that it would later become, and the kaleidoscope of its social and political history produced many rich seams of vernacular song, a synthesis of which would come to dominate Western popular culture from the 1920s onwards and especially after World War II. America too had its bourgeois parlour tradition, heavily influenced by European music and sung in a similar way to the accompaniment of a piano; in vaudeville there was a public entertainment equivalent of the British music hall.

---

[2] See p. 222 above.

North America's multi-faceted history produced local traditions based on ethnicity, geography and class which increasingly formed the essence of its popular song tradition. This process was reinforced by the invention of the microphone after the First World War, which marked a step change in both recording technology and the evolution of radio. It freed singers from the awkwardness of singing into the horn and it offered a considerably improved frequency response and signal-to-noise ratio; crucially, its third use, in live performance, gave singers the revolutionary possibility of singing with amplification. At first using a microphone simply made things louder, but it soon dawned on singers that if the sound system was doing the projecting, they need not try quite so hard themselves. In a very short time it became possible to sing in an intimate, conversational manner and still be heard by the largest audiences. This was a genuinely revolutionary effect: the singer no longer needed to call upon a generic singing technique to project into large spaces, but instead could sing as though whispering into the ear of individual listeners. The big-voiced, acoustically efficient tent show entertainers and blues singers such as Ethel Waters, Ma Rainey and Bessie Smith sold thousands of records but were eventually eclipsed by those who could seduce their listeners rather than batter them. The microphone also offered the possibility for singers to personalise their delivery: relieved of the need to maximise their acoustic potential they were much less likely to sound like generic sopranos, altos, tenors and basses. The microphone created a previously unknown kind of charismatic vocal persona, perfect for the new media of radio, recording and cinema, as well as live performance.

CROONING

Ironically, the singer generally credited with being the first crooner was not American, but spent much of his life in England.[3] Al Bowlly was born in Mozambique in 1898 to Lebanese and Greek parents and was brought up in South Africa before coming to Europe in his twenties. He came to London for the first time in 1928 and sang with a number of English bands. A surviving film clip of him singing 'Melancholy Baby' to a live audience, accompanied by Monia Liter on piano, dating from the early 1930s, shows extremely skilful use of the mic. His voice is that of a light

---

[3] The OED claims nineteenth-century contradictory Scottish origins for the term, none of which seems to relate to its use in 1920s America, where it seems to have referred to the intimate singing of a mother to her baby.

tenor or high baritone, and apart from the lack of physical projection he sings with all the grace and rhetorical elegance of a classical singer. He has a symbiotic relationship with the microphone, which is both his audience and an extension of his voice, and the flexibility that amplification enables also influences the way he understands the song. Jolson sings this song as though it was a music hall piece – milking it for humour that is not really there. Bowlly understands something fundamentally different: he moves closer for more intimate moments and steps back when he wants to use a more conventional singerly style, his phrasing is subtly nuanced and very free, dovetailing in and out of the playing of Liter. This is singing that Caccini would recognise: everything is subservient to the way the text works, nothing is wasted or simply for display. Bowlly can be ornamental, but his bending of notes is a musical means to a rhetorical end. Gene Austin, another voice associated with the earliest crooners, has a similar connection to pre-nineteenth-century singing. In the various film clips of him lip-synching to playback he is rarely shown with a microphone but his technique is completely microphonic, with a nuanced delivery similar to Bowlly's. Both singers avoid the chest register (with its associated power and projection) and opt for a variety of head voice which means they can sing quite high without forcing. In 'Sweet Sue' and 'After you've gone' (and in his 1927 version of 'Melancholy Baby') Austin crosses the break from head voice to falsetto seamlessly – and perhaps gives us an insight into what an eighteenth-century tenor might have sounded like in a similar tessitura.

Jolson, Bowlly and Austin all influenced the young Bing Crosby. Like Al Jolson, Crosby had sung without a microphone at the start of his career (often using a megaphone); although his early recordings with the Whiteman band feature his high head voice and falsetto registers he was (also like Jolson) more of a light baritone than a tenor, and his voice became richer and deeper as he got older. Like Bowlly and Austin he extended the head voice downwards, enriching the tone but not sufficiently to give the illusion of a classical baritone, creating a sound that was very close to his speaking voice. He used the microphone with complete mastery, extending Bowlly's technique into an even more mannered delivery underpinned by consummate breath control. He was one of the first to understand the potential of broadcasting – the microphone not only enabled an intimate performance in the room he was in, but also in the rooms of countless listeners whom he could not see, but who were only a mic-lead away. He also appreciated what the technology could do for singers and invested in reel-to-reel tape technology, becoming one of the first to pre-record his own shows. The radio recordings of Jolson and Crosby duetting show the new and the old techniques clearly differentiated: although they accommodate each other to some extent, the suave Crosby can never be mistaken for the much more forthright Jolson.

In the 1920s and 1930s it was still the norm for singers to turn their voices to whatever music took their fancy, but for the first time we begin to see the emergence of singers who specialised in jazz-orientated music. The origins of jazz are still hotly debated, especially the blending of African, European and white American influences, but its appeal in the early years was primarily to the black community, and it was one of the few areas where black and white musicians could work together relatively easily. In retrospect we do not consider Bing Crosby to have been a jazz singer, but he certainly understood the rhythmic engagement that jazz musicians such as Louis Armstrong brought to their singing, and he applied a similar rhythmic dynamism to his own more middle of the road repertoire. Crosby's melding of the microphonic style of the crooners with the swung delivery of a jazz singer paved the way for other figures such as Frank Sinatra and Ella Fitzgerald who developed the style to its limit in the 1950s.

The biggest influence on Crosby was Louis Armstrong, who in his turn incorporated elements of popular song into jazz singing. Armstrong was a pivotal figure in so many ways – a personality who reached out to black and white audiences, a master of both trumpet and voice respected by all who heard him; he brought a new and sophisticated discipline to the popular voice. The earliest jazz ensembles did not necessarily have rhythm sections but they did have rhythm, and Armstrong (and Crosby) fused the laid back microphonic delivery with a rock solid feel for tempo, creating a vocal version of swing. Swing is that magic that happens between the beats, a fusing of the regularity of the beat with something unmeasurable that goes either side of it. For an instrumentalist this determines articulation, but for the singer it articulates pronunciation. Crosby's speech-like delivery was characterised by an accent that was hard to place geographically (and his English successors would often use a comforting received pronunciation); Armstrong's delivery was also like his speech but he played his African American voice like an instrument, bringing a range of colours that were new to popular singing. He had an uncanny ability to translate his facial expressions into vocal gestures: in the much maligned 'Wonderful World' you can actually hear him smiling.

Crosby and Armstrong were both significant influences on Connee Boswell, the dominant personality of the Boswell Sisters. Connee, wheelchair-bound as a result of childhood polio, was one of the first women to develop a consistent microphone technique. Will Friedwald points to multiple influences on her singing:

Though we hear a considerable amount of Bing Crosby in her work, and something of Bessie Smith and a few of Caruso's techniques, the overwhelming influence is that of Louis Armstrong, and going deeper into the roots of both Boswell and Armstrong, New Orleans itself.[4]

Boswell had that transformative gift that is the hallmark of a great singer: the ability to synthesise influences and create a persona that was greater than the sum of its parts. The ornamental rhetoric of Crosby (with whom she had hit records) allied to the Armstrong sense of swing, plus a wider repertoire that went beyond jazz, ensured her influence on the even more successful subsequent generation of women stars such as Ella Fitzgerald and Doris Day.

VIRTUOSITY, IMPROVISATION AND THE LIMITS OF JAZZ

Armstrong's 1926 recording of 'Heebie Jeebies' was often cited as the first use of scat singing. The actual origins of scat are unknown (and pre-1926 examples are continually coming to light) but Armstrong certainly turned it into an art form. Some remnants of improvisation still survived in opera singing in the 1920s, but composer and conductors would eventually eliminate it altogether from most classical music. From its beginnings jazz had been an oral music, with players often improvising solos and harmony. Singers were more or less stuck with the tune – there was a limit to how far they could stray before the song became unrecognisable. With scat, singers now had the potential to improvise as well as any instrumentalist. This was not just a way of showing how clever you were (though a singer would certainly need to know the harmonic shifts, just as a baroque improviser would) but it meant that emotion could be expressed wordlessly; audiences could reflect on the words during a wordless solo, so the intimate relationship between singer and listener enabled by the microphone was yet further enhanced.

The most virtuosic exponent of scat was Ella Fitzgerald. Her later repertoire covered that slice of popular music history known as 'the great American songbook', her recordings almost having the status of classical music. Before this she was one of the first singers to take up the challenge

---

[4] Will Friedwald, *Jazz Singing* (London: Quartet Books, 1991): 78.

that the extreme virtuosity of Bebop posed for singers. For the first time in history players could routinely accomplish feats that singes were unable to match: the music simply went too fast and was too angular to assimilate. Ella Fitzgerald was capable of extending almost any tune into what seemed like a free-form scatathon, introducing tunes within tunes, on which she would wordlessly extrapolate often at great speed and over several octaves. A close analysis of the recordings reveals an extraordinary musical intelligence at work, a pacing of creativity that works in a similar way to a Dizzy Gillespie solo, combining and expanding cells of material – in ways that links her to the great castrato singers of the eighteenth century.

Scat was not the only means of improvising available to singers, but in the jazz ensembles of the 1920s and early 1930s it was the task of the singer to affirm the tune, in effect providing the source material which the instrumentalists would then embroider. The heart of Louis Armstrong's bands, however impressive his singing, was in the playing. Very few singers had the courage to recompose tunes, as this would have destabilised the band's routine. The exception, and therefore an enormously potent influence on singers of succeeding generations, was Billie Holiday. Holiday was an almost exact contemporary of Ella Fitzgerald (Holiday, born in 1915, was two years older) and had a childhood that was at times traumatic, with no settled family life and an early history of prostitution and drugs. She claimed that her formative musical influences were Bessie Smith and Louis Armstrong, but anything pre-Holiday in her singing is only there as a faint echo. As Linda Dahl put it, her sound 'came through not so much as volume as penetration, a kind of keening intensity that split the air'.[5] Holiday is the first singer whose art seems to spring directly from her life, not from something learned; almost all Holiday songs have a rawness about them, as though she is forming the singing as well as the song. So many of the singers who lived through the Depression saw themselves as a distraction from the real world (it was the entertainment industry, after all): Holiday lived the life, and never allowed anyone to forget it, whether she was singing the heart-rending 'Strange Fruit' or recomposing Gershwin's 'Summertime'. Her apparent inability to stick to a tune at first worked against her – people expected to hear the song as they'd heard it before – but it became identified with the Holiday persona, and took the uniqueness of live performance into new territory. She did work with big bands (Basie and Artie Shaw) but her most creative

---

[5] Linda Dahl, *Stormy Weather: the Music and Lives of a Century of Jazz Women* (New York: Limelight Editions, 1984): 137.

performing was in small ensembles. Her very close listening to sensitive players such as saxophonist Lester Young and trumpeter Buck Clayton gave her phrasing an instrumental fluidity and the improviser's instinct to go either side of the tune. Her personalising of a song had very little to do with her technique, and rather more to do with the direct emotional expression that comes from heightened speech, and it is this quality that later generations would admire (and which showed her to be ahead of her time compared with the musical escapism that her crooner contemporaries often seemed to represent).

THE END OF AN ERA

The high point of the mainstream style that had evolved from Dixieland through the Swing Era was reached with Frank Sinatra. Born in 1915, Sinatra was the son of Italian immigrants from whom he was said to have inherited an instinctive bel canto feel for singing (despite having no training and being unable to read music). He grew up listening to big bands and finally found success in 1939 with the Harry James band and in the following year with Tommy Dorsey. Over the next decade (avoiding the war due to a perforated ear drum) he came to succeed Bing Crosby as the most successful popular singer in the world. Sinatra's voice, and more importantly, the way he used it, had a power and richness that went beyond the elegance of Crosby. He was relaxed and extremely self-confident, and although labelled a crooner had almost nothing in common with his predecessors except an ability to use the microphone to his advantage. Sinatra's technique shows some similarity with the basic principles of classical singing (though he denied any influence): he maintained a consistent tone supported by a systematised breathing technique. We still hear the Crosby rubato and portamento but Sinatra sings straighter and the whole process has been firmed up within the big band environment. It would not have been easy to be subtle over the Dorsey or Nelson Riddle orchestras, and Sinatra revelled in the sheer exuberance and power of all the bands he worked with; at the height of his fame he even sang in classical venues with symphony orchestras. After a dip in his popularity as the 1940s gave way to the 1950s Sinatra reinvented himself as a screen actor, which in turn led to his rehabilitation as a performer. From the 1960s onwards he did some of his best work, while being very critical of Elvis Presley and Rock 'n' Roll.

The 1950s saw some of the most accomplished jazz-orientated pop singing from Sinatra and his 'rat pack' contemporaries, as well as women singers such as Sarah Vaughan, Carmen McRae and Betty Carter – all successful to the point of seeming to lose the sense of creative exploration, even danger, which first drew them to the music and inspired their audiences. Vocal jazz and its offshoots occupied a commercially successful niche which made for comfortingly easy listening. The creative core of instrumental jazz had experienced the epiphany that was Bebop, a development that took virtuosity into such complexity that it left a large slice of its audience behind in much the same way as the classical avant-garde was to do. What could inventive singers do if they were not Ella Fitzgerald? For a brief period the answer seemed to lie in attempting to become instruments. Eddie Jefferson began putting words to instrumental numbers in the 1940s, but the popularisation of vocalese (as the style was known) was due to Clarence Beeks (known as King Pleasure), who had a hit with Jefferson's 'Moody's Mood for Love' in 1952. The most successful exponents were Dave Lambert, Jon Hendricks and Annie Ross, whose eponymous trio recorded *Sing a Song of Basie* in 1957, overdubbing all the instrumental parts. The trio were dazzlingly articulate, but vocalese was almost a parody of jazz instrumental playing, performing a transcription of improvisation which simply added words to existing notes, sacrificing the creativity of improvisation to the exhilaration of sheer speed.

The history of twentieth-century singing is a history of successful recordings. Recordings alone do not give a complete picture, however, and many singers did some of their most representative work on film or in the theatre, particularly on Broadway or in London's West End. As we have seen, singing was what finally persuaded motion picture moguls that the talkies could be a viable proposition, and many actors and actresses who would not normally sing in the theatre found themselves singing on celluloid. Film, as television would become in the second half of the century, is an intimate, close-up medium, for which the microphonic singing of the crooners was ideal: if you had to burst into song in the middle of a love scene you would not want to sound like a Heldentenor or a dramatic soprano. Microphones were not used routinely in theatres until the 1950s, so stage singers needed a completely different technique which recognised what Stephen Banfield aptly called 'the actorly truth of speech and the singerly enchantment of song' while not turning themselves into classical singers.[6] Screen stars such as Ava Gardner, Betty Grable or Jean Harlow could very easily magic their voices into song via a microphone

---

[6] Stephen Banfield, 'Stage and Screen Entertainers in the Twentieth Century', in John Potter (ed.), *The Cambridge Companion to Singing* (Cambridge University Press, 2000): 65.

and then mime to playback; some such as Marilyn Monroe or Sophia Loren were even passably good singers. For the post-Jolson theatre singer there was what has become known as the belt. Ethel Merman is generally credited with being the first belter, but the technique has had several post-Merman definitions based on larynx position and register. Merman was a larger than life Broadway star with an unusually large voice and a Jolson-like twang, and she sang in chest voice (as opposed to something more like head voice used by crooners). The basic belt is a little like a controlled shout – projection is achieved via the chest register but a speech quality is maintained by keeping the larynx relatively high.[7] Versions of this technique are still used in stage musicals, but theatres now use amplification for musical theatre shows. This has had a liberating effect on the singing: in the twenty-first century, musicals, especially the more experimental off-Broadway shows, often feature a variety of singing styles from rock to belting and even classical technique.

ELVIS PRESLEY AND STYLISTIC SYNTHESIS

In a remarkably short time the swing-based musical edifice began to crumble once Elvis Presley appeared on the scene, and the aspirational element with its hint of the classical, a 'better' way to sing which connected the popular style to previous eras, very quickly became anachronistic. Presley's vocal persona brought together a synthesis of singing styles which were integral to American culture but were mostly below the international radar, and reflected a world that was quite different from the post-Depression fantasy world of entertainment. Born in Tupelo, Mississippi, Elvis Presley grew up in Memphis, Tennessee, listening to singers as diverse as country singer Hank Williams and Jimmie Rogers, crooner Dean Martin, opera screen star Mario Lanza, legendary southern blues singers such as Big Bill Broonzy and Art Crudup, and gospel singer Rosetta Tharpe. Many singers grow up listening to a wide range of potential influences, and most eventually decide to aim for the genre for which they feel most suited. The very greatest singers (in any genre) do not do this, but instead find themselves transcending genre and style by fusing an amalgam of influences into something not heard before. Developing such a career is fraught with risks: the talented singer able to succeed in a variety of styles is rarely easy to market, and one who is creating a new

---

[7] For a more elaborate explanation see Gillyanne Kayes, *Singing and the Actor* (2nd edn, London: A. C. Black, 2004): 167–73.

genre even less so. Success often depends on the coming together of seren-dipitous events or personalities elsewhere in the creative process.

Elvis's voice clearly perplexed a number of the promoters for whom he first auditioned. His first private acetate recordings at the studios of Sun Records in 1953/4 were of ballads, but on his fifth visit, at the very end of the session, he launched into Art Crudup's 'That's All Right'. Sun Records's roster of artists consisted primarily of black rhythm and blues singers but Sam Philips, the company's founder, had long been aware that a white singer of this repertoire would have tremendous commercial potential. He realised that Elvis Presley was the singer to achieve this goal and released 'That's All Right' as the schoolboy Elvis's first single, with the bluegrass waltz 'Blue Moon of Kentucky' on the B side. It was not yet the fully formed Elvis but the elegant sliding around (he has an effortless top G) hints at a latent sensuality and contrasts with the more powerful sections derived from blues singing. Many who first heard it could not tell whether Elvis was black or white. The white ballad-singer had made a record of a black blues number, coupled with a rockabilly favourite.

It is from such fusions that new singing emerges, with the pre-existing elements combining to create something that could not have been pre-dicted. African American music has a complicated history, the orality of which obviously pre-dates its documentation, so we can only speculate about its origins. But music born out of physical labour rather than polite drawing-rooms produces a very specific sort of singing. Singing while labouring may be more segmented, effortful and repetitive: the singer has to breathe and will not be able to maintain a constant vocal flow. There may be no intended audience, so the delivery may sound internalised or uncertain, incoherent even. With only a notional listener there is no real need to worry about what it sounds like, and left to its own devices the vocal tract will produce a sound that is acoustically determined by the particular physical make up of the individual, resulting in a sound unique to that person. Suppressed emotion can transcend all this, and there may be outbursts that are closer to shouts than singing. Country music, with its origins in the poor white south, shares a similar disregard for sound, often demonstrating a twangy nasality. The ballad-singer, on the other hand, is telling a story, and the success of his narrative depends on his communicative rhetoric, requiring a more subtle vocalism. Elvis's first attempts at balladeering met with limited success, but his potential was recognised by RCA Records who bought up his Sun contract in 1955. In January the following year they released 'Heartbreak Hotel' which became his first national number one. In 'Heartbreak Hotel' all of the many diverse elements of Elvis's stylistic history come together in a new synthesis: the narrative timing of the ballad-singer melds with the para-linguistic growls and barks, the passion of the blues singer replaces the light tenor of his school days. This was new performance rhetoric, and demonstrated the breadth of style that would make him the first global icon of popular music (in 1973 his TV charity special *Aloha from Elvis* was the first global satellite concert relay, and was said to have reached one-third of the people on the planet).

One further significant change can be charted in the Presley catalogue. His first songs were accompanied by Scotty Moore on guitar and Bill Black on bass. Although drummers were not unknown in jazz and dance combos they were by no means ubiquitous. Elvis's trio eventually added drums, and this quartet of instruments in electric form would become the basic line-up of Rock 'n' roll, and its successor, Rock music. The idea of the bass and drums constituting a rhythm section came from jazz, but the ability to sing on or either side of a consistent beat became a defining char-acteristic of almost all pop singers from the 1960s onwards, giving them a creative and interpretative freedom denied to classical singers who were generally tied to a fixed tempo determined by composer or conductor.

THE SINGER RECLAIMS THE SONG

If Presley released the natural voice, giving singers permission to shout and scream as well as croon, the generation of English singers that began with the Liverpool sound, and in particular that of the Beatles, added a more reflective element which included reclaiming old songs and re-envisioning them in the present. Musical styles are constantly in flux, and changes in fashion locate a performance in any given time period; the parameter that most clearly establishes the temporal *locus* of a song is the vocal delivery itself. In the 1960s few teenagers would have been aware of the Broadway musical *The Music Man*, and fewer still are likely to have enjoyed the versions of its most famous song, 'Till there was you', by Sue Raney (1957), Anita Bryant (1959) or Peggy Lee (1961); such was the speed of the Liverpool-driven revolution that all these versions would have seemed very *passé* by 1963. In that year, however, the song appeared on the Beatles' second album *With the Beatles*, where it shared the vinyl with Rock 'n' roll classics such as the Tamla Motown 'Money' and Chuck Berry's 'Roll Over Beethoven'. Paul McCartney's restrained ballad deliv-ery certainly increased the album's appeal to older audiences who might know the tune, but more importantly it made it safe for teenage listening.

The process of singers' delivery mediating the music they sing has been a constant trope running through the history of popular singing. More recently, the albums of Tom Waits feature classically inspired instrumentation and arrangements that verge on the sentimental. Overlaid by Waits's half-spoken darkly smouldering utterances they gain a power that stems directly from the singer's vocal persona.

Paul McCartney's recording of 'Till there was you' was a cover version. The term was first used in 1966, meaning a song first recorded by someone else. Since the 1960s a thriving genre has evolved in which singers can pay tribute to fellow artists and stamp their own distinctive mark on someone else's song. This can extend to substantial recomposition of the original. Eva Cassidy's 1996 recording of 'Over the Rainbow' is a remaking of the song 'Somewhere over the Rainbow' that in recontextualising it reclaims it for the singer in a manner which calls to mind the performative processes of pre-nineteenth-century classical singing. In Judy Garland's 1939 original recording the music and lyrics are firmly grounded in the original context, the film soundtrack based on *The Wonderful Wizard of Oz* written by Frank Baum in 1900. Baum also wrote the book for the first musical version which appeared 1903 but it was not until the film, with its Harold Arlen songs and lyrics by Yip Harburg, that the *Wizard* became such a powerful symbol of hope, coinciding as it did with the USA beginning to find its way out of the Depression in the late 1930s. The song comes near the beginning of the film, and the Garland character has just been getting in the way and generally causing unintentional mayhem. She begins to fantasise about a place where she will not be told off all the time. There are many later recordings of Judy Garland singing this as an adult; many of those are intensely moving, often in direct proportion to the disintegration of her private life. Judy Garland had very early success in a genre that she completely mastered and from which she never departed. Neither she nor Eva Cassidy wrote their own songs, but each depended on finding material that suited their vocal persona. In Cassidy's case her unique delivery enabled her to sing a wide variety of styles, which made it difficult for record companies to market her (there were several genres that she could have mastered had she decided to specialise). Like many of Billie Holiday's songs, her version of 'Over the Rainbow' leaves the original context far behind, giving audiences space to create their own personal interpretation.

Singers between the wars were supported by an army of songwriters, and in a sense paralleled the process in classical music: songs were created for specific singers. Rock 'n' roll flourished on a mixture of original material and covers, and from the 1960s onwards the professional song-writer went into sharp decline. The morphing of Rock 'n' roll into Rock and its various subgenres was characterised by a huge outpouring of ori-ginal material. The process was given significant impetus by John Lennon and Paul McCartney, who between them wrote some 180 songs. The Beatles' first albums were a mixture of covers and original songs, but from *Rubber Soul* onwards covers were dropped altogether in favour of songs created by the group's members (mostly Lennon and McCartney). The earlier albums in a sense reclaimed the past but looked forward to the future; by writing their own songs the Beatles could also lay claim to the present. The demise of the songwriter, and his replacement with self-penned material, was a revolution in itself, giving pop singers the kind of control over their music not seen since the eighteenth century. Control over the music and lyrics also means control over the singing, which in the post-Beatles world saw text delivery more closely integrated with the singer's vocal persona than ever before.

As the excitement of the 1960s faded, two movements within Rock produced new ways of singing on both sides of the Atlantic. Progressive Rock was an outcome of the sophistication and increased complex-ity of the music, Punk was a reaction to it. From the Ramones' and Sex Pistols' debut albums onwards, Punk often came close to eliminating the 'enchantment' from singing altogether, as its adherents pursued an aggressive simplicity of delivery with exaggerated or distorted working-class accents. Its singers would claim no predecessors, though there were antecedents in the singing of Mick Jagger, who made little attempt to beautify his voice, preferring to keep to an earthy speech-like delivery in the manner of his American blues models. There was also a shouting element to much Punk singing that was not so far away from a Broadway belt or a football chant. The heart-felt call for musical and technological simplicity at the heart of Punk philosophy was an indication of how sophisticated Rock music had become: Progressive Rock had become a *de facto* classical music. From the beginning of the gramophone era popular music had been inextricably bound up with the fate of classical music; as the century progressed, the legitimisation of American and anglophone popular music and their increasingly global hegemonic status paralleled a consumer reluctance to embrace the music of modernism and the avant-garde. The end point of the composer-as-genius scenario turned out to be music which did not have to acknowledge the listener at all, creating a vacuum in middle-class consumer demand which was filled by increas-ingly sophisticated popular music.

The Progressive Rock movement of the 1970s represented the peak of this phenomenon, with many consumers able to find in the music of bands such as King Crimson, Genesis and Yes, or the more esoteric creations of Frank Zappa and Brian Eno, the kind of satisfaction that in another era might have been found in Elgar, Vaughan Williams or Copland and which they could not get from Stockhausen or Ferneyhough. The Progressive Rock movement produced singers who employed speechsong with increasing sophistication. Foremost among these was Phil Collins, first with the band Genesis and then as a solo artist. Collins had been a successful child actor and joined Genesis as a drummer. These two attributes contributed to a delivery that perhaps comes closest to the ideal of speaking in song. His acting experience left him with a profound understanding of the rhetoric of text delivery – he is a supreme storyteller. As one of the leading Rock drummers of his time, he had a faultless sense of rhythm; his rhythmic sense is not in itself obvious from his singing, but it provides a musical foundation for his rhetoric in the same way that a jazz singer maintains a tempo while singing on either side of it. He very rarely employed artificial tone production of any sort: his singing is simply heightened speech. These musical, vocal and narrative skills enabled him to deliver any lyric with conviction (however banal). Almost all pop singers nuance their singing, either as a conscious or unconscious way of personalising their sound or because some awkwardness in their delivery creates idiosyncratic vocal quirks; Phil Collins rarely resorts to this. The progressive movement and related complex pop music threw up many singers with a narrative intelligence: Collins, Freddie Mercury, Peter Gabriel, Jon Anderson and Sting were among the most sophisticated singers of their age.

HIP-HOP: A GLOBAL SUBCULTURE

The 1970s also gave birth to Hip-hop and its musical incarnation, Rap. Declaiming poetry in rhythm has a history that goes back to the Viking sagas and ancient Greek epic, and the emergence of such a style in 1970s Bronx took the musical world at first by surprise and later by storm. In its early 'old school' phase Rap was party music which developed out of DJs isolating and repeating beat patterns on LPs, then sampling musical cells or riffs and creating repeated or evolving patterns over which an MC would recite. As the genre developed, public attention was inevitably drawn to the rapping of the MC rather than the virtuosity of the turntablist, and rappers began to broaden their subject matter, some of it becoming violent and sexist, much of it lyrical and poetic. Rap succeeded where Punk had failed, by giving performers the means to personalise their delivery, something that is fundamental to popular singing. Simplicity is not sufficient as an end in itself, and Rap has blossomed into a global phenomenon because of its adaptability – anyone can do it to some degree, and the most virtuosic exponents combine a literary and musical creativity that is unlike any other kind of declamation. Is it singing? Heightened speech as in Schoenberg's *Pierrot Lunaire* or a crooner's intimate relationship with a microphone are recognised as singing because of the musical context. Rap is also microphonic, and manipulating the sound system is part of the rapper's stock in trade, but more than that, nuanced rhythmic speech is music, which means the rapper's speech is singing. Rhythmically Rap moves text declamation yet further from the ternary feel of swing; Rock 'n' roll and Rock were solidly binary, and Rap is even more insistent on a binary downbeat, over which the rapper can do whatever he (usually but not always) likes.

THE END OF THE ANGLOPHONE ERA?

From the first decades of the twentieth century to the first of the twenty-first popular music has undergone a series of dramatic developments. Exploring the earliest recordings we find a lost world of variety, vaudeville, cabaret and novelty songs that belong more to the nineteenth century. Just as classical singing became bigger and richer in part to cope with larger spaces, so public popular singing needed to be loud, exaggerated and fairly unsubtle to be heard at the back of a theatre. The last, and most successful, exponent of this was Al Jolson, seen at his brilliant best in *The Jazz Singer*. The microphone revolutionised singing – at first on radio and in recordings, then, as sound projection developed, in live performance. The age of the crooner was an age of subtlety and sophistication in singing such as may not have been heard since the seventeenth century. A lot of the delicacy was swept away by Rock 'n' roll, which brought a new African American influenced dynamism to popular singing. Liberated from the professional song-writer, Rock 'n' roll matured into Rock, which itself fractured into many subgenres, alongside which non-Rock pop music produced singers as diverse as Kate Bush and Tom Waits. The fragmentation of genres also assisted the global reach of Hip-hop, in which the spoken voice was finally completely integrated into Western popular singing.

Mainstream pop singing (if there is such a thing) has also been increasingly influenced by developments in the music industry. The creation of boy and girl bands can now be achieved according to successful formulae, given sufficient investment, imagination and luck. The singing is often not the most important factor, but one criterion among many defined by marketing requirements. The image-makers' task has been made much easier by the increasing use of auto-tune. This software, developed by Antares Audio Technologies for vocal processing and especially pitch correction, first came to public attention in 1998 with Cher's 'Believe', where it was used to step change whole intervals. The subsequent development of the software following its use by T-Pain, Kanye West, Snoop Dogg and many others brought it within range of any studio. Its use in dance music added a futuristic but also dehumanising effect, reducing the vocal line to a synthesiser that can carry a text (as in Daft Punk's 'Around the World'). Perhaps rather worryingly for singers, it eliminates the need to sing in tune, or indeed to sing at all.

But that is not the end of the story: the big influences on singing in the twenty-first century are cultural and economic as well as vocal and musical. The most immediate are television and the internet, which have radically changed notions of music performance and consumption. Television, with its talent contests and reality shows, allied to extended visual media such as DVD and live concerts streamed to theatres and cinemas, has reinvigorated the visual aspect of singing after half a century of mostly invisible performance on audio recordings. The internet has similarly added a video dimension but, importantly, is a much more democratic and creative tool. The decline of multinational record companies was preceded by the advent of the MP3 player. Personal listening systems such as portable CD and minidisc had been around since the last quarter of the twentieth century, but the internet connectivity of the MP3 player had an enormous impact on music consumption, especially among teenagers and young adults. It was not just the sheer quantity of music which could be downloaded – a factor which would become very important in the reinvention of the concept of live – but computer-assisted ways of organising personal music listening revealed a far more sophisticated sense of genre than most record companies had ever considered. For many people, the assumed categorical distinction between classical and pop, Western or World Music, was simply not very important: consumers often preferred to organise their personal listening according to their own individual categories which might reflect mood rather than genre, and a mood list might well include multiple genres. This fragmentation of taste and weakened sense of genre is very characteristic of early twenty-first-century cultural consumption. One of the consequences for singers is the status of potential models: there are many more instantly available vocal paradigms, so the monolithic model culture of the LP/CD generation becomes diluted, giving singers a much more creative choice of paradigm.

The decline of multinational record companies, which in many respects defined music consumption in the second half of the twentieth century, has had important consequences for singers. In Western pop music there has been a shift from live performance in support of record sales to the sale of recordings to promote live events (and associated merchandising). This also means that there is less money in the system being paid to fewer musicians, which is a stimulus to small-scale creativity. The practice of record companies paying fees to artists has reversed: many musicians now fund their own recordings and then sell the finished product on or market them via the internet, a practice which gives far more editorial control to musicians who wish to use the opportunity. Particularly creative internet marketing solutions have been explored by Radiohead, who have released their own albums on a 'pay what you can' basis (usually following up with a multi-format physical version that dedicated fans will happily pay for). As the twenty-first century gets into its second decade the anglophone hegemony is severely weakened, with no single variety of American or British pop music able to dominate for very long. Singers and audiences are coming to terms with the experience and availability of music from all over the planet.

CHAPTER 10

Sung and unsung: singers and songs of the non-English-speaking world

The moment we step outside the Anglo-American popular music area we are left with a myriad of traditions and stars, some of whom are world famous but a far greater number of whom enjoy fame, even adulation, within their own countries but are now beginning to be appreciated on the world stage. Some of these singers and their traditions are in a state of permanent reinvention (Bollywood, for example), others represent individual strands within a well-established national heritage. Only a small selection can be presented here but the joy of discovery can continue well after reading about this handful (on the whole, the better they are known the less needs to be written about them here). We begin by a brief look at singing in Germany and France, then we examine two major non-European vocal cultures: Egyptian singing as personified by Umm Kulthūm, and the phenomenon of Bollywood. As an indication of the variety of singing to be found across the globe, we have taken two circles of latitude – the 42nd (north) and 22nd (south) parallels – and included brief snapshots of some of the vocal cultures to be found along these imaginary lines which connect Spain to China and Mozambique to Brazil. Part of the discovery is realising that many of the singers in these genres and territories have had a greater worldwide impact than their more circumscribed fame suggests, and this can only increase with the power of the World Wide Web.

On the strength of their musical artistry, poetic gifts and immense charisma it seems strange and unjust that these singers are less well known than a great many inferior anglophone superstars and one is left wondering if it all might come down simply to the matter of language. Yet several other major world languages are involved in the ensuing discussion, including German, French, Spanish, Arabic and Chinese. The small sample, the criteria for selection and the argument that the singers are not as well known as they might be are all somewhat contentious. To argue, for example, that Umm Kulthūm is less well known than Ella Fitzgerald or Édith Piaf, or that Carlos

Gardel is less famous than Bing Crosby, would be unacceptable in the Arab
world or Latin America, but it may hold true for the majority of this book's
readers. In other words, the argument appears to be at once upholding and
deploring what we might refer to as the hegemony of the Western gaze. In
plain terms, not only will the readership be primarily Western but also the
West (primarily the United States) has had a disproportionate influence on
the dissemination of popular music and in the arbitration of taste. We are
not looking in backwaters for interesting vocal traditions (which should be
done, if a definitive study were aimed at) but instead would like to draw
attention to a few important figures and vocal cultures in areas of the world
outside Britain and the USA, in order that a map of world singing should
not be left with too many areas of anglophone white.

GERMANY AND CABARET

Europe, troubled by the physical destruction of two world wars, generally
welcomed the feel-good music from across the Atlantic in the twentieth
century, and it sat more or less comfortably alongside vernacular traditions
of various sorts. Whereas the effects of war led to an exodus of classical
musicians from Europe (with a corresponding effect on classical singing
pedagogy in the USA), in popular music the influence worked in the other
direction, at least up to a point. The vocal culture in mainland Europe
had many traditions of its own and there was often a complex relationship
between genres, but many countries' music absorbed influences from the
American 'other' rather than the national styles of neighbouring states.
Composers such as Kurt Weill and Hanns Eisler wrote elaborately crafted
popular songs between the wars which were sung by cabaret artists whose
prime aim was to reveal their vocal personae through the sophisticated
manipulation of textual rhetoric. Marlene Dietrich and Lotte Lenya were
a generation older than Billie Holiday, but both survived into old age, by
which time their singing had achieved a timeless quality. Both were successful actresses, and had the heavily nuanced speech-like delivery that
characterised German cabaret singers of the 1920s.

It was the performances of the *diseuse* Albertine Zehme that had drawn
Arnold Schoenberg to cabaret. Schoenberg considered himself to be the
embodiment of traditional German hegemonic musical values, but wrote
Pierrot Lunaire for a reciter, bringing the speech culture of the melodrama
and cabaret into the classical sphere. In contrast to this, though still
owing something to the cabaret tradition, were the Dadaists who rejected
mainstream culture altogether, and declaimed sound poetry in ways that

many at the time would not recognise as singing at all. German cabaret was infused with a strong sense of irony, which has characterised much later German popular music and acted as a kind of cultural corrective to the equally strong vein of sentimentality than runs through German popular song. The inescapable fact of Nazism and the Second World War and its consequences opened the country to British and American influences, but from the 1950s onwards mainstream German popular singing was dominated by *Deutsche Schlager* (*Schlager* literally means 'hits') which owe more to the German folk tradition and operetta. Only from the 1970s onwards would German singing find a more original voice in the disembodied music of techno and the Punk-oriented NDW (*Neue Deutsche Welle*). Singing in the German Democratic Republic had a complicated and as yet unwritten history which interacted with politics. Gerhard Gundermann, known as 'the Springsteen of the East', was one of many voices who expressed the complexity of life in the divided Germany, was uncomfortable with reunification and never reached his full potential.

FRANCE AND THE CHANSON TRADITION

In France the popular chanson had developed in the informal and intimate setting of the eighteenth-century café (in contrast to the slightly grander English song and supper rooms of about the same period). By the twentieth century the genre was firmly rooted in French culture. Its key elements were nostalgia, sentiment and an elemental Frenchness inextricably bound up with the French language. Although it flourished in music hall and variety with such singers as Yvette Guilbert, Mistinguett, Maurice Chevalier and the extraordinary African American Josephine Baker, its natural home remained the café, augmented by radio from the 1930 onwards. The microphone was the perfect means for French chanson singers to exploit the rich sonorities of the language. Many achieved fame beyond France, notably Édith Piaf, whose early life (and subsequent lifestyle) was not dissimilar to that of Billie Holiday.

Piaf's iconic status generated a substantial literature, but there were many other great chanson singers who were equally famous in France but who did not achieve Piaf's international reputation. From the French perspective it would be incomprehensible to suggest that she overshadowed three of France's greatest singer-songwriters. It was one of them, Gilbert Bécaud (noted for his flamboyance and lack of false modesty), who is credited with saying 'There are only three great singers from my generation: Brel, Brassens and Bécaud' and many other French people connect the three names. All three lived through the trauma of the occupation during the Second World War; none was originally Parisian; all three survived the radical change of fashion in pop music in the late 1950s and 1960s; all three were finally silenced by cancer. Even the best known of the trio, Jacques Brel (a Belgian, though French speaking and based in Paris for most of his career), did not achieve Piaf's level of fame. The Piaf phenomenon is partly to do with her background of Parisian brothel and gutter, drug addiction, tiny stature and huge voice – one of the most immediately distinctive in living memory. The fact that 'Non, je ne regrette rien' became her famous anthem is remarkable as worldwide fame in popular music has so often depended on English, including translation into it as necessary. (In this respect Brassens suffered the most, as we shall see below.) The emphasis on the letter 'r' has much to do with the need for Piaf's song to be heard in its original French, as her trademark is her gravel-gargling pronunciation of that letter (by no means unique, as Brassens did almost exactly the same thing). It is not a matter of regret that some of the world's most famous songs, sung in English (of course), were originally French but rather that the true composers are hardly known outside France. 'Autumn leaves' is the song 'Les feuilles mortes' by Joseph Kosma with words by Jacques Prévert; 'What now my love' is Gilbert Bécaud's song 'Et maintenant'. These are but two examples and, while the composers are not exactly obscure, it is probably true that their names are not as recognisable as their tunes.

Jacques Brel was the most famous and dashing of this trio of 'B' singers (the irony is intended here, for they were actually among the finest and most influential singer-songwriters of the twentieth century). Many of his songs were successfully covered in English by international names, such as David Bowie ('Amsterdam') and Céline Dion ('Quand on a que l'amour'). The best-known of his songs 'Ne me quitte pas' is far better known in English, under its English title 'If you go away', and it was covered by more artists than can be listed here, including Frank Sinatra, Tom Jones, Ray Charles, Shirley Bassey, Nina Simone, Eartha Kitt, Barbra Streisand and Madonna; also, in a German version, by Marlene Dietrich.

Gilbert Bécaud was born in Toulon in 1927 and died in Paris in 2001. His real name was François Silly – not ideal for a launch into the anglophone world – but the real reason for his taking the name Bécaud was that it was the name of his surrogate father, preferred when his natural one deserted the family. He also acquired the nickname of 'Monsieur 100,000 volts' for his electrifying energy. This followed an incident in the famous Paris venue l'Olympia in 1955 when Bécaud's performance so excited the young audience that they vandalised part of the hall. Before gaining such fame, even notoriety, he was a pianist and film composer. His collaboration with the singer Marie Bizet brought him into contact with Jacques Pills, who became his accompanist for many successful appearances, including a tour of the United States. Pills married Édith Piaf, with whom Bécaud also collaborated. She helped not only his career but also that of another young singer-songwriter who was to enjoy a global success second, perhaps, only to that of Piaf herself: Charles Aznavour. While Bécaud brought a Mediterranean spark and matinée-idol good looks to the stage, Aznavour had a more rugged charm and came from an Armenian background. Very much a cosmopolitan, he espoused causes in France and Armenia and was also a fine film actor. His songs were covered by stars as big as Fred Astaire, Ray Charles and Bing Crosby. Bécaud's most famous song 'Et maintenant' came in 1961 and became a worldwide hit through its English version 'What now my love', sung by the likes of Elvis Presley, Frank Sinatra, Judy Garland and Barbra Streisand. A similar success came to an earlier song 'Je t'appartiens' (1955), which was covered in English (under the title 'Let it be me') by the Everly Brothers, Bob Dylan, Nina Simone and others.

Gilbert Bécaud and Georges Brassens (1921–1981) were southerners by birth and Parisian by adoption. Their southern accents could be heard in many of their songs, more so in the case of Brassens, even when singing of the woods or cemeteries of the Parisian region. Not only was he the least Americanised of the singers mentioned but he never even went on foreign tours. Despite the extravagant claims in many of his songs to all manner of outrageous behaviour and sexual conquests Brassens was rather shy and reclusive. His performances were intimate, even in large halls, and signs of nervousness, or at least diffidence, were often noticeable. He was therefore not a natural showman and certainly not the microphone-hugging, anguished crooner that so appeals to international audiences. His appearance, with his thick moustache and a pipe often added for publicity shots and record covers, was more avuncular than heart-throb and once again made no concessions to the international image of the popular singer. Nor did he stray from his favourite acoustic combination (his own guitar, often a second guitar played by a more competent performer, and a double bass) into the realms of orchestras or rock bands. He did once or twice manifest his love of jazz by allowing a jazz backing but this was the exception that proved the rule. Conquering the United States, or any kind of world tour, were out of the question and he hardly ever left France; strenuous efforts to bring him just across the Channel resulted in no more than a couple of concerts in Cardiff. Covers of his songs exist in

French and a whole show, in the style of a musical, was put on in Paris around his music.[1] Translations have also been made into other major European languages, as well as Hebrew and Esperanto. While certain songs of Brel and Bécaud have become far better known through English covers, Brassens's remain best known in their original versions. Even Jake Thackray's 'Brother Gorilla', a successful version of 'Le gorille' (a hilarious, salacious and mercilessly satirical song about a judge being raped by a well-endowed and rampant gorilla) has not displaced the original. Thackray's cover works so well because the words are not only translated excellently (no easy feat) but also because he presents the song in a parallel fashion to his idol Brassens: accompanying himself on the guitar and not attempting to disguise his regional accent (Yorkshire in his case).

Brassens was a modern troubadour, and even sang of himself in one of his most admired songs ('Supplique pour être enterré à la plage de Sète')[2] as 'moi, l'humble troubadour'. It was an apt description: he was a singer-poet from the south of France, although he did not sing in the regional language of Occitan. He was more troubadour than his fellow southerner Bécaud, because he was celebrated even more as a poet than a singer and he nearly always composed his own lyrics (on a few occasions he did set poems by others, including Victor Hugo, Villon, Lamartine and Banville). Bécaud's two smash hits (covered widely in their English versions) 'Et maintenant' and 'Je t'appartiens' both had lyrics by Pierre Delanoë who also wrote words for Édith Piaf and Charles Aznavour. Like the troubadours, Brassens refused to conform to narrow moralities, and his songs often placed him at odds with the establishment. Sometimes this led to bans imposed by French radio, ostensibly for strong language and pornographic content but also for more subtle affronts to bourgeois French society. Authority, religion, the military, the law and above all petty conformity all fell under his merciless wit. Brassens chose to remain an outsider, so perhaps that must also be his epitaph.

UMM KULTHŪM: THE VOICE OF EGYPT AND THE ARAB WORLD

On the opposite side of the Mediterranean, the Egyptian singer Umm Kulthūm is probably unknown to many readers and even those who

---

[1] 'Le Petit Monde de Georges Brassens', Comédie Musicale, by La Troupe du Phénix (available on DVD by Millennium 3 Project, 2001; the bonus tracks include two covers of Brassens songs in Russian).
[2] 'Plea to be buried on the beach at Sète' (Brassens's birthplace on the Mediterranean coast; also his resting place, though in a cemetery rather than on the beach).

have heard the name may never have heard a single one of her songs. Yet in Egypt and throughout the Arab world she is held in such awe that the word superstar is woefully inadequate to describe her status, and the West has probably never produced a comparable phenomenon. 'Umm Kulthūm was unquestionably the most famous singer in the twentieth-century Arab world.'[3] To start at the end, her funeral in 1975 was a bigger event than President Nasser's. It was attended by an estimated four million mourners (thus vastly more than the huge crowd of around a hundred thousand at Édith Piaf's funeral in Paris in 1963). One criterion of a singer's reputation could be the number attending his or her funeral; a high attendance does imply that such artists were regarded as much on the level of statesmen or royalty as mere singers. Umm Kulthūm was a singer first and foremost but also a leader of her nation, closely linked with Nasser and his revolution after 1952, so her extraordinary funeral reflected far more than just her artistic achievement and gifts as an entertainer. During an unusually long career, lasting from around 1910 to 1973, she recorded about three hundred songs. She was born into a poor rural family and her father was *imam* of the local mosque. He taught religious songs to Umm Kulthūm's brother, which she learnt by overhearing before she gained proper admission to the lessons. Not surprisingly, she learnt Koranic recitation, for which she came to be held in high regard and which had a profound influence on her singing and artistic outlook. 'From her sound and appearance Umm Kulthūm was immediately recognised by her early audiences as *min al-mashāyikh*, reared among the shaykhs' (learned religious people, including her own father).[4] For her earliest performances, singing at weddings and other village celebrations, her father would dress her as a boy to overcome the stigma of presenting a girl in that role. Even when she launched her career in Cairo in the early 1920s she could be seen wearing the Bedouin dress of boys and men.

Virginia Danielson has pointed out a difficulty in categorising Umm Kulthūm's type of music and her argument carries weight not only throughout this section, which considers popular singers primarily outside the Western concept and framework of popular music, but also elsewhere in this book:

---

[3] Virginia Danielson, *The Voice of Egypt: Umm Kulthūm, Arabic Song, and Egyptian Society in the Twentieth Century* (University of Chicago Press, 1997): 1.
[4] Ibid.: 25.

Umm Kulthūm's repertory illustrates the difficulty of applying the Western categories of "art," "popular," or "folk" to non-Western repertories. In particular, her repertory challenges the concepts of the nature of popular culture.[5]

Danielson further untangled the complex strands of Umm Kulthūm's singing and its perception within Egyptian society: 'Words such as *asīl* (authentic), *turāth* (heritage), *klasīkī* (classical), and *mutaṭawwir* (advanced or developed) are used in discussions of Umm Kulthūm's repertory.'[6] Apart from signalling that the popular versus classical polarity is not useful, this analysis helps understand the special nature of Umm Kulthūm's singing and why it succeeded so well within its society and is so hard to comprehend without. An obvious reason – and another thread running through this section – is the language barrier.

While it would be something of a truism to state that the words of a song are important, in the case of Umm Kulthūm they are crucial and one musician remarked to Danielson that 'You can't like this music if you don't understand the words'[7] (which could be said of countless singers of opera, *Lieder*, and many other genres). The counter-argument is that the beauty and expressive power of Umm Kulthūm, or of great opera singers, can convey the emotional essence even when the words are not understood. Another reason for Umm Kulthūm's greatness is that 'She never sang a line the same way twice.'[8] Her songs were often very long, largely because she included a technique of classical Arabic improvisatory singing, also found further East in the *ghazal* and *thumrī* performances and poetry recitations of India and Pakistan. It is based on the repetition of lines or sections to intensify the meaning of the words and explore them in different ways, often by layering different words and imagery on to the original. A poetry recital in the West would consist of a reading of the existing text. In India, a well-received line would be applauded and often the reciter would be encouraged to repeat it, whereupon the singer would recapitulate with added layers rather than a straight repetition. Such elaborations have their musical correlation: phrases can be repeated with different ornamentations, tone colours and melodic extensions (using the modal systems of *raga* in Indian music and *maqām* in Arabic music). With the added power of music and the singing of improvised ornaments and phrases the emotion of the words can be further intensified.[9] Applause and other sounds of encouragement are crucial in

---

[5] Ibid.: 14.   [6] Ibid.
[7] Ibid.: 4.   [8] Ibid.
[9] In India the whole performance can be transported further into the realm of dance and mime, as in the *Kathak* genre of classical dance.

these traditions (including Umm Kulthūm's) so the performer depends on the audience to inspire and lift the rendition, as well as extend a song easily by five or six times its basic length.[10] At the same time, a merely efficient rendition of the words does not make a great singer. At the centre of Umm Kulthūm's art was the all-important element called *ṭarab*, which literally means enchantment and conveys the singer's ability to move the audience deeply (and is comparable to *duende* in the distantly related flamenco tradition of Andalusia). 'The words ... do not contain all the meaning ... *Ṭarab* requires the singing voice.'[11]

Umm Kulthūm's voice had an unusual power throughout its entire range (over two octaves). She also had very well-developed breath control and the stamina required for the long phrases and extended songs. The breath control aided her meticulous phrasing and impeccable enunciation of the text, as did her training in Koranic recitation. An ability to change the colour of her voice was also an essential element of her success:

Indeed, vocal colors could be closely linked to the sound and meaning of the text where melodic invention was viewed as devoid of meaning or textual connection. For Egyptian listeners this distinction separated text oriented Egyptian singing from the more melodically motivated Turkish style or European bel canto, and linked Umm Kulthūm's singing to that of the *mashāyikh*.[12]

Other attributes of Umm Kulthūm's singing included two Arabic criteria for good voices: *baḥḥa* and *ghunna*. *Baḥḥa* ('hoarseness') could overtake a weak or strained voice but Umm Kulthūm used it to expressive effect, allowing her voice to break on a high pitch to enhance the emotion of the text. *Ghunna* involved a simultaneous resonating in the mouth and nose, never becoming what critics would disparage as singing through the nose. Thus it also required careful control.

BOLLYWOOD

There are at least two problems with the word 'Bollywood'. One is that it is out of date: in the Bombay + Hollywood portmanteau the former has changed its name to Mumbai, so we should nowadays strictly be speaking of 'Mollywood'. The other is that it focuses on one place, albeit the major location of the Indian film industry, thereby excluding Chennai (formerly Madras), Kolkata (formerly Calcutta) and all the other

---

[10] Danielson analysed some of Umm Kulthūm's techniques of elaboration and extension in the section of her book subtitled 'She never sang a line the same way twice' (Danielson, *The Voice of Egypt*: 146–58).
[11] Ibid.: 12.   [12] Ibid.: 93.

significant contributors to that industry. In fact, Mumbai's share declined from around 40 per cent in the 1950s to around 20 per cent in the 1990s. The outpourings from the Mumbai studios should more strictly be termed Hindi cinema (in Chennai the principal language is Tamil and in Kolkata it is Bengali). While the popular films from Chennai sit reasonably comfortably under the Bollywood label, the 'art' films of Satyajit Ray, Shyam Benegal and others emphatically do not, so we must not confuse Bollywood with Indian cinema at large.

The songs that grace every 'Bollywood' film, and are taken out of their cinematic context to assume an independent existence as hit singles, could also be referred to by a more precise Indian term *filmi gīt* (pronounced 'geet'), which literally means 'film song'. Bearing in mind the distinctions between art and popular, Mumbai and the rest of India, 'Bollywood' serves conveniently as an instantly recognisable generic description for the popular Indian cinema which not only continues to be widely used but will also fit our purposes. The inescapable fact is that 'Bollywood' is a global phenomenon and the word has entered the musical lexicon (so it can be used hereinafter without quotation marks). Its distinctive sound world, typified by an unmistakable vocal sound and instrumental combinations, especially ones dominated by high, screeching strings, may lead to the perception of Bollywood music as one style, whereas it is a blend as lavish and exaggerated as anything seen on screen. Before 1987, the (erroneous) supposed date for the coining of the term 'World Music' it was often informally observed that the wildly eclectic music of the Indian film industry could be described as the true world music. As a blend of global influences and no less through its global popularity (not just within the Indian diaspora) Bollywood music can be described as a true world music long before that problematic term was coined. Jazz, Rock 'n' roll, Disco, Latin and Reggae influences creep in according to the dramatic context. Sometimes popular Western songs are covered, and the development of the large studio orchestra owes almost everything to Hollywood. That such a mixture sounds so distinctively Bollywood is all the more remarkable. While the instrumentation varies drastically (sometimes from Indian classical and folk to the latest Western pop) to accompany different locations and dramatic situations, the distinctive Bollywood vocal timbre stays remarkably constant.

As the film industry does not have a long history, it is possible to summarise key developments quite briefly. The cinema came to India through the Lumière brothers' private screenings at Watson's Hotel, Bombay in 1896, but it was not until 1913 that Dhundiraj Govind Phalke started the

Indian film industry with *Raja Harishchandra*. As language was not an issue in the early silent films the stars were often Anglo-Indian or Jewish. As in the West, the silent films were accompanied by live music: usually a small band of both Indian and Western instruments rather than the familiar piano of Western cinemas. The first sound film was *Alam Ara* in 1931 and it had seven songs. As in the early Hollywood movies these additions to the films were thus considered indispensable from the out-set, and the 1930s were the heyday of singing actors such as Shanta Apte, Kanan Devi and Jahan Ara Kajjan. This period also saw the beginnings of added simple harmonisations, the birth of the 'playback' singer (dis-cussed below) and the lifting of film songs from their original context to a contemporary recording format (78 rpm discs), gaining wider dissem-ination as pop songs. The development of pop songs from the cinema is by no means restricted to India, though it is there that we have the most striking and enduring example. Peter Manuel pointed out that 'In many other cultures, pop music has evolved in close connection with its use in cinema; Indonesian *dang-dut* [itself heavily influenced by Bollywood], Argentine tango, and modern Egyptian urban music all matured in the context of cinematic musicals.'[13]

Recording technology also had an influence in reducing the length of Bollywood songs, as the theatre songs from which they were derived were longer, sometimes up to twenty minutes. The pendulum would swing the other way by the 1970s: recording technology had long since moved on but also the instrumental interludes, permitting dance routines and slices of action, became far longer and often outstripped the vocal sections (with-out diminishing their central importance).[14] By taking the songs from their cinematic context this practice not only increased the number of lis-teners – affordability of recordings was not an issue as Bollywood songs could be heard from loudspeakers in almost any street – but often assured the songs' survival. While songs and films are closely linked they do not always enjoy equal success, so this separation allowed hit songs to thrive away from film flops and sometimes the financial gains of the former could offset the losses of the latter. Such was the appeal of the independent film songs that All India Radio banned them for a while in the 1950s, fearing they would pollute traditional Indian culture. Listeners simply retuned to stations like Radio Ceylon, forcing All India Radio to rescind its ban.[15]

---

[13] Peter Manuel, *Popular Musics of the Non-Western World: an Introductory Survey* (Oxford University Press, 1988): 172.
[14] Anna Morcom, *Hindi Film Songs and the Cinema* (Aldershot: Ashgate, 2007): 64.
[15] Ibid.: 5.

In the early days of sound the actors also had to sing as the cameras could only record sound and image simultaneously. This meant a wide disparity of singing styles and abilities. The sound tended to be loud and coarse, partly a reflection on the restricted technology of the time, and also another legacy of the theatre traditions from which Bollywood grew, including the singing of the *tawaifs* (courtesans). A more standardised vocal sound came about through the crooning style of Kundan Lal Saigal (1904–1946), usually considered Bollywood's first superstar, who continued the tradition of actor-cum-singer. The next generation of famous crooners (offscreen) such as Mohammad Rafi (1924–1980) and Kishore Kumar (1929–1987) demonstrated Saigal's enduring influence and consolidated the Bollywood male singing style. The tradition of the playback singer commenced within a few years of the coming of sound. The actors no longer sang but were instead lip-synched to the song which had been recorded separately. For this reason Bollywood singers are referred to as 'playback' singers and the practice has become a defining characteristic of Bollywood film making. Apart from allowing actors to pursue all kinds of activities incompatible with singing the technique made it possible for a handful of specialist singers to provide the songs for a wide variety of actors.

Restricting the numbers actually singing in the films thus helps explain why the most famous playback singer of them all, Lata Mangeshkar (born in 1929), entered the *Guinness Book of Records*, with an almost unbelievable output of at least 25,000 songs[16] spanning around forty years. The relatively small number of singers also advantaged the recording industry: 'the tendency toward stylistic homogeneity is even more clear, and affords its producers the advantages ... of offering a standardised product to a mass audience rather than catering to smaller, specialized markets.'[17] Becoming an icon as a playback singer is the more remarkable for Lata Mangeshkar as she had to struggle at the start of her career in the late 1940s to get the playback singer even named in recordings. Once established she dominated Indian film singing (thereby also becoming a pop superstar) until the 1980s, managing to sound like a young girl throughout her career. By the late 1980s other defining voices, such as those of Mohammad Rafi and Kishore Kumar, had gone and the music directors were finding new blood in singers like Anuradha Paudwal and Kavita Krishnamurthy.

[16] The figure is debatable and often put far higher. For example, Manuel gives it as more than 30,000 (*Popular Musics*: 179); see also Peter Manuel, *Cassette Culture: Popular Music and Technology in North India* (University of Chicago Press, 1993): 51.

[17] Manuel, *Cassette Culture*: 51.

The links between stage and screen are as close in India as elsewhere, but a parallel history of Indian theatre would go back thousands of years and lie well beyond our scope. Nevertheless, the link is especially important in the Indian context as theatre tends to include an essential rather than incidental musical element. The roots of Bollywood can be found in the Bengali Jatra (as the industry was based in Kolkata before moving to Mumbai) as well as in forms of classical and folk dance drama. For example, in the Kathakali dance drama of Kerala (south-west India) the actor mimes (and dances) while a different singer (accompanied by percussion) produces the music from the side, visibly yet quasi-off-stage. Thus, when actor and singer became separated in the films it could be said that the practice was already rooted in ancient Indian tradition (as well as several others in Asia). But probably the greatest theatrical influence came from Marathi theatre (spoken in the language of Maharashtra, in which state Mumbai lies), which had had a relatively short gestation (going back to 1843)[18] before nurturing key figures in the Mumbai film industry. Bollywood films are musicals, relying heavily on singing, dancing and a wide range of instrumental backings. Marathi theatre also relies heavily on music and most of its actor-singers were trained in vocal music by classical masters. Bal Gandharva (1889–1975) was famous for female impersonation (in dress and singing)[19] and his normal singing had a high tessitura (a likely influence on what was to become the trademark Bollywood style). Not only singers but also composers (known as music directors) started out as theatre musicians, including some of the famous duos: Kalyanji–Anandji; Lakshmikant–Pyarelal; Shankar–Jaikishan. Dinanath Mangeshkar, the father of Lata Mangeshkar and Asha Bhosle, probably the greatest female names in the history of Bollywood singing, was also a star of the Marathi theatre, so his daughters were raised in the tradition. It is hardly surprising, therefore, that the music directors brought existing theatre songs to the films, or similar songs mixing classical and folk idioms,[20] or that the singing style of the theatre initially dominated that of the cinema.

A significant part of theatrical training was Indian classical singing, which has also played a pivotal role in Indian cinema, both of the popular and 'art' varieties. Firmly in the latter category – even leading it – are the (Bengali) films of Satyajit Ray, who had a passion for Indian classical music

[18] Janaki Bakhle, *Two Men and Music: Nationalism in the Making of an Indian Classical Tradition* (Oxford University Press, 2005): 83.
[19] Ibid.: 89.   [20] Morcom, *Hindi Film Songs*: 4.

and gave it prominence in many of his greatest films: *Jalsaghar* (*The Music Room*) is even a film *about* music. His preference was for Hindustani classical music, the type for which Kolkata is regarded as a leading centre, and he collaborated with Ravi Shankar in his celebrated film *Pather Panchali* (1955). Shyam Benegal also used music by one of India's leading composers: Vanraj Bhatia (a pupil of Nadia Boulanger). A classical-pop opposition does not, of itself, distinguish these art (= classical music) films from the Bollywood (= pop) torrent, as Hindustani classical music has featured in many smash hits of Indian cinema. No less of an enthusiast for that tradition than Satyajit Ray was the music director Naushad Ali (1919–2006), often known simply as Naushad. He came from Lucknow, one of the most important centres of music and poetry. There he learnt Hindustani music, listened to qavvali (devotional songs of the Sufi Muslims) and spent hours in the cinema sowing the seeds for his later career in Mumbai. He was also very interested in the inexhaustible riches of Indian folk music and in Western classical music, so his songs included harmonisations and orchestrations more from the West than from India.

His principal mission was to integrate Hindustani music with the traditional Indian values expressed in the films, especially in the drive towards national unity and postcolonial identity following Independence in 1947. Thus many of his greatest songs use ragas. The 1952 film *Baiju Bawra* did this in a kind of self-conscious way, as the subject matter concerned a rivalry between two classical singers. Although they sang in more modern styles and repertoires than the sixteenth-century setting warranted, the music was typically classical and the more usual Bollywood song style would have been ludicrous. Naushad took his job extremely seriously and brought in two of the top names in Indian classical singing at the time, Amir Khan and D. V. Paluskar (as well as two ubiquitous stalwarts of Bollywood singing, Lata Mangeshkar and Mohammad Rafi). This resulted in an interesting mixture of classical singing and the unmistakably Bollywood timbres of Lata Mangeshkar and Mohammad Rafi, also singing classical ragas.

Comparing the sound and technique of the 'filmi' singers with the classical singers brought in for that film gives a useful insight into what makes Bollywood singing quintessentially Indian. While the crooner and high-pitched female sound very different from the classical singers they skilfully use ornamentation, much of which has come from classical singing and which immediately sets them apart from other pop singers. Both classical and 'filmi' singers rely on technology, not just for recording. The former use amplification in live concerts while the playback voices are produced in studios, therefore subject to a wider range of electronic manipulation, including reverberation (not yet tried in classical singing) and auto-tune (though singers are reluctant to talk about the latter). Five years after *Baiju Bawra* came *Mother India* (1957), one of the greatest hits in the history of Indian cinema (with even an Oscar nomination). Without any obvious need for classical music (to come somewhat incongruously from the mouth of a poor woman in a rural setting) Naushad again used ragas to create some of his finest songs. In many ways it could be argued that the dramatic impact and subliminal messages of the classical music were greater than in *Baiju Bawra*, as it was employed in *Mother India* not merely to recreate the imperial court setting of *Baiju Bawra* but to portray the true and simple values of Indian womanhood (again sung by Lata Mangeshkar), free from opulent wealth, corruption or the taint of Westernisation.

The less appealing aspects of Westernisation, specifically the hippie invasion of India and Nepal a decade later, and their power to corrupt Indian society were targeted in *Hare Rama Hare Krishna* (1971), from which the title song (beginning 'Dum maro dum' – meaning to smoke a joint – sung by Lata Mangeshkar's sister Asha Bhosle) became a smash hit and now sounds like a comical, almost 'cheesy' take on 1960s rock. In the film the drug-taking of the Western hippies corrupts innocent and impressionable Indian youth, so it was as much a warning as feel-good entertainment. At any rate, in its wake to be young, Western and casually dressed in India was to attract the cry in every street of 'hippy!' The irony is that while drug-taking and loose morals were attacked, Western rock in this pastiche was embraced almost to become the film's saving grace. 'Dum maro dum' was nearly banned from the film, not on musical grounds but because its message was seen as mixed: while supposed to satirise hippie drug-taking it also appeared to be encouraging it.[21]

Not so far from this kind of decadence, gangsters and loose women will be accompanied by Western popular styles and uninhibited dancing, while traditional Indian virtues and values are underlined by something that at least suggests traditional Indian music and dance, even if reclothed in the glitter of Bollywood. Apart from the musical style and blatant references (often actual covers of Western songs) the contrast is far more in the instrumentation than in the singing. Players of the sitar, sarangi, tabla and other instruments will be brought in to supply the Indian music, while other session musicians, or entire bands, will take care of

[21] Asha Bhosle, interviewed by Jameela Siddiqui, 'World Routes', BBC Radio 3, 15 October 2005.

the Western material. The playback singers, however, tend to remain the same, which helps explain the phenomenally resilient and successful careers of the best among them.

In the same breath inevitably comes the name of Lata Mangeshkar, who epitomises Bollywood singing. She has lived through almost its entire history and has played a major part in creating it. As star of stars among Bollywood playback singers, she developed what is the defining sound of Indian film songs. She also furthered the link between the respected classical tradition and her own, much maligned domain. She learned from Amanat Ali Khan and greatly admired the celebrated khyal singer Amir Khan. In fact the two were neighbours on Mumbai's affluent Peddar Road until Amir Khan's untimely death in 1974. Given the gulf between classical and popular and the different sound of the two singing styles, the idea that the two share such important common ground may seem surprising. Lata Mangeshkar was, however, by no means alone in embracing classical music. Her father had set the example and many famous playback singers had some classical training: for example, Mohammad Rafi learnt from Bade Ghulam Ali Khan and Abdul Wahid Khan, two of the finest classical singers of their generation.

While the classical influence was strong, Alison Arnold has pointed out that the earliest film singers (before the era of the specialist playback singers) came from a variety of backgrounds, some with classical training, and some with no training at all.[22] The early female style had a 'somewhat low-pitched, forceful, often husky voice, a nasal tone and a deliberate, mannered pronunciation of the lyrics'.[23] This sound, so unlike modern singing in Indian films, was tamed by K. L. Saigal and Bengali singers who brought a 'quiet style of crooning, sighing and whispering'.[24] As in the USA, the new style began in the late 1930s, at quite an early stage of the sound era in Indian cinema, and became very popular in the 1940s, a crucial decade in the history of Bollywood singing which also saw the emergence of Lata Mangeshkar. Even with the smoother sound pioneered by K. L. Saigal the legacy of the early singers from a background of professional singing girls and erotic entertainment was not entirely erased. The low register and range (around one octave to an octave plus a fifth for women and almost two octaves for men) remained much the same until the 1950s and the rise of Lata Mangeshkar. By then, as evidenced

---

[22] Alison Arnold, *Hindi filmī gīt: on the History of Commercial Indian Popular Music*, unpublished PhD dissertation, University of Illinois at Urbana-Champaign, 1991, 48.
[23] Ibid.: 49.   [24] Ibid.: 50.

in a film such as *Baiju Bawra* (1952) her characteristic sound was firmly established. At first, however, she had sung in quite a different way, focusing on the lower register in vogue in the 1930s and into the 1940s. She may have raised her voice (in both senses of pitch and intensity) to overcome crude sound reproduction on the gramophone and in cinemas, but Alison Arnold believes the change was influenced by the actress-singer Nurjahan, who had a relatively narrow range and rather 'thin and tense' tone.[25] Lata Mangeshkar's characteristic sound is also 'thin' but higher and with a wider range. She took over from Nurjahan when the latter moved to her new homeland of Pakistan at the time of Partition (1947). Both Lata Mangeshkar's earlier lower-pitched style and her characteristic high-pitched sound can be heard in her songs around this time (the late 1940s).

Anna Morcom summarised some Indian perceptions of why this change of tessitura took place: a search for innocence after the traumas and gloom of war and Partition; a need to distance the sound of the respectable playback singers from their tawaif (courtesan) forebears.[26] This latter notion is highly plausible as the change affected female rather than male singing. The influence of Nurjahan, the changes in recording technology and Lata Mangeshkar's own ideas about singing and how to project her voice no doubt also played their part. Peter Manuel somewhat inverted this argument by suggesting that both artists and audience were manipulated by the film industry itself and the dominance of the one (female) style reflected 'a tendency for common-denominator mass music styles to be created in corporate urban studios and subsequently promoted and superimposed upon a heterogeneous listening audience'.[27] Bollywood singers can only act through their singing as they never appear in the film. Rather than limiting the singers' acting, their absence from the visual action places even greater demands on them. Both directors and singers emphasise the ability to act through singing, mainly because the voices must fit a whole range of characters and emotions, from saint to vamp.[28]

Lata Mangeshkar's sister Asha Bhosle (born 1933) had her own claims to superstardom and there are even claims that she exceeded the number of songs recorded by her sister, due in part to the length and intensity of her professional career, starting at the age of sixteen. While Asha

[25] Ibid.: 145.   [26] Morcom, *Hindi Film Songs*: 66 n. 10.
[27] Manuel, *Popular Musics*: 179.
[28] Asha Bhosle, interviewed by Jameela Siddiqui; Morcom, *Hindi Film Songs*: 49–50.

Bhosle had the same background in Marathi theatre and classical singing as her sister she also became influenced by hearing Carmen Miranda
in her childhood and was attracted to her use of vibrato, which is not
a regular feature of Indian classical singing but is used far more sparingly and according to the prescriptions of the raga. Asha Bhosle not
only copied Carmen Miranda but was further influenced by Bill Haley
and Rock 'n' roll.[29] Her marriage in 1979 to the famous music director
R. D. Burman (1939–1994) brought more pop influences into her singing
and he pushed her technique further. One mannerism he encouraged was
singing punctuated by sharp intakes of breath, which she found particularly difficult. The fact that it was something Lata Mangeshkar did not do
helped distinguish the sisters' otherwise similar sound.[30]

Some idea of this can be heard in one of her most admired numbers,
'Piya tu ab to aaja' ('Lover, come to me now') by R. D. Burman from
the 1971 film *Caravan*. The setting is not far removed from the decadent
Westernised images of *Hare Rama Hare Krishna*, discussed earlier. The
actress-dancer (Helen) is brought down by heavy drinking and loses her
inhibitions (to the extent of starting a striptease, with cuts to the shocked
face of a respectable, correctly clothed Indian woman). The lover in question flits around the set rather ineffectually singing 'Monica, oh my
darling'. The music is the typical Bollywood cocktail (apt word in that
context) with James Bond overtones.

The even more famous R. D. Burman song of the same year, 'Dum
maro dum' (from *Hare Rama Hare Krishna*) references Western rock even
more directly. Both songs are included in the Kronos Quartet's album
'You've Stolen My Heart'.[31] Asha Bhosle's tessitura is lower, because of her
age, but it makes her (and especially the backing female vocalists) much
less strident. ('Dum maro dum' is a minor third lower than in the original
version.) Although the album's homage to R. D. Burman emphasises his
westernised tendencies he was more than just a typical Bollywood eclectic and had firm roots in the Hindustani classical tradition. His teachers
included the great sarod master Ali Akbar Khan and the famous tabla
player Shanta Prasad. R. D. Burman was, moreover, the son of another
successful music director, S. D. Burman (1906–1975), who had resisted
the big Hollywood-style studio orchestras in favour of small ensembles of
Indian instruments. Asha Bhosle was also the subject of the 1997 hit song

[29] Asha Bhosle, interviewed by Jameela Siddiqui.   [30] Ibid.
[31] 'You've Stolen My Heart' – Songs from R. D. Burman's *Bollywood* (Nonesuch 79856–2, 2005);
   the album takes its name from one of its songs: 'Chura Liya Hai Tum Ne'.

'Brimful of Asha' by the British Asian group Cornershop. The song is not only a tribute to her but also makes references to Lata Mangeshkar and Mohammad Rafi, as well as several singers outside Bollywood, including a fleeting reference to a song ('Les amoureux des bancs publics') by Georges Brassens (who is discussed above on pages 265–6).

Another way that Bollywood songs have compounded their popularity, both in India and abroad, is through their 'instrumentalisation'. This transference of vocal repertoires to instrumental renditions is a foundation of Indian classical music, both Carnatic and Hindustani (see chapter 6). Wedding bands reproduce film songs with great gusto (inspiring groups like Bollywood Brass Band in the UK to carry the tradition overseas). The sung version is not needed as the instruments convey it perfectly in their own way. This way of presenting the songs is a stimulus to dance, rather than singing along. The raucous sound of the band, with very loud drumming, drives the wedding guests, especially the men, into exuberant dance steps with arms waving above the head.

The Kronos Quartet album and Andrew Lloyd Webber's production of *Bombay Dreams* (2002) helped Bollywood become 'cool' in the West during the first decade of the twenty-first century. The music of R. D. Burman is featured in the Kronos album, while the talents of A. R. Rahman (born 1966) are showcased in the latter. His compositions enjoyed yet more fame through the success of *Slumdog Millionaire* (the Oscar-winning film of 2008).[32] Growing international acceptance and respect have not quelled the debates that have raged about the quality of Bollywood music, since at least the time of the All India Radio ban in the 1950s. Often the critical reaction has centred on the two obvious polarities of sacred Indian tradition (evinced by the use of classical ragas, instruments, folk styles, bhajans and qavvalis) and a creeping Westernisation which threatens Indian values, as well as being deeply seductive. It is satirised and even vilified, yet the huge amount of imitation can only be seen as some kind of flattery. Perhaps this polarisation was most acute in the years following Independence, when India was establishing its new national identity. More recently, its growing economic and technological importance has created a new kind of confidence and reduced anxieties concerning artistic autonomy. The older styles of film song, with classical elements, still appeal to older generations, while the young, more Westernised urban elite often hold A. R. Rahman as an example of a composer not only to

---

[32] A southerner, based in Chennai, Rahman is strictly speaking not from 'Bollywood' but is still labelled under that ubiquitous term.

have gained significant global recognition but also to have managed to combine ethnic and global strains that are more compatible with Western pop music.[33] Bollywood's new 'cool' cannot quite be described as the modern equivalent of the 1960s craze for Ravi Shankar, the sitar and Indian classical music. In many ways it goes deeper and has a much wider base, including the youth of the Indian diaspora. It may prove just as ephemeral, but it does bring singing to the fore in a way that the earlier craze (aptly known as the 'Great Sitar Explosion')[34] did not.

THE 42ND PARALLEL: A CROSS-SECTION OF THE NORTHERN HEMISPHERE

Bollywood is a rare example of a variety of non-Western singing finding a voice outside its own culture. Most of the varieties in this section have remained specific to their home territory, though many have at some point influenced Western music. We begin our journey across the world on the Atlantic coast.

Fado and Flamenco: the singing soul of the Iberian peninsula

Fado and Flamenco are the national folk musics of Portugal and Spain. The two are entirely separate musics with separate histories but they share certain characteristics, the principal one being a sense of nostalgia which is expressed respectively in the concepts of *saudade* and *duende*. Neither term is precisely definable; 'longing' or 'yearning' are aspects of *saudade*, but the topic of Fado songs can be anything from the sinking of submarines to the death of a footballer from food poisoning.[35] The singer (male or female) is accompanied by the distinctively silvery Portuguese guitar (a double-strung six-course instrument), sometimes with a mellower (single-strung) Spanish guitar to thicken the texture. Historians argue about the true nature of Fado, and there has been much retrospective categorising of this elusive oral music. The Fado we hear today owes much to the international success of Amália Rodrigues, who was largely responsible for the Fado revival that continued after her death in 1999. The origins may be unknown, but most authorities agree that it grew up in bars, often very disreputable ones, which came to be known as Fado houses, the music

---

[33] Morcom, *Hindi Film Songs*: 5.
[34] Gerry Farrell, *Indian Music and the West* (Oxford University Press, 1997): 171.
[35] Paul Vernon, *A History of the Portuguese Fado* (Aldershot: Ashgate, 1998): 1.

experienced with food, drink and a *frisson* of danger (as was jazz or the French chanson). All Fado singers draw their inspiration and their technique from the Portuguese language, and all sound very different from each other, their own vocal persona being dependent on how they put the poetry across. Amália Rodrigues became a worldwide success (not just in Portuguese-speaking territories) as a recording star and film actress, and paved the way for more recent singers such as Mariza. Her small and languid voice swoops and dives, starts and stops, morphs in and out of vibrato, and has the intensity of expression of the singing actress that she was. Her successor Mariza is a much more rounded singer, her *saudade* more forcibly expressed, and with twenty-first-century production values has become the modern international expression of Fado.

Flamenco has a similarly controversial history and has been subjected to considerable academic scrutiny, little of which makes sense to most performers of the music. Little is known about actual performances before the nineteenth century, though a much longer history is often claimed for it. The minimum ingredients were singing and dancing, with rhythmic hand-clapping and foot-stamping, and since the mid to late nineteenth century this has been driven by virtuoso guitar playing. The original flamenco singers may have been gypsies, and the art is strongly rooted in gypsy culture, but the music flourished in the Spanish equivalent of a Fado house, the *café cantante*. As dance is integral to most flamenco performances amplification is problematic, which means that the singing is often loud and aggressive, with male singers in particular sometimes sounding strained and forced. The concept of *duende* which pervades flamenco culture is as elusive as *saudade*; it is the expression of the soul, a feeling of sadness and loss, darkness and melancholy, which is relieved by the passionate interaction of singing and dance. Camarón de la Isla, who died in 1992 aged only forty-one, was a key figure in reviving the genre, and encouraged by his success many performers have brought in elements of jazz, blues and even salsa. Enrique Morente, who died in 2010 at the age of sixty-seven, introduced modern Spanish poets and collaborated with rock musicians, and used the medium to interpret the paintings of Picasso.

Folk polyphony on the 42nd parallel: Corsica, Sardinia, Georgia

Further east along the 42nd parallel we get to the French island of Corsica (and just below it the Italian island of Sardinia). Both these islands have folk traditions of improvised polyphony sung by male ensembles. As with all oral musics the history beyond the twentieth century can only be guessed at, but both traditions are strongly identified with Corsican and Sardinian cultural identity. In Corsica the modern tradition was revived in the 1970s. Groups of between three and nine men, often within families, sing together in three-part harmony. The singers stand very close to each other, and employ a hard, pressed phonation with an ornamental microtonal vibrato. The music may be secular, often about Corsican history, or sacred (there is a strong Holy Week tradition). The soloist is known as the *secunda* (the first voice being an angel and silent); he outlines the tune and text, often with microtonal inflections, and is then joined by the *terza* who will generally sing a third above, and the *bassa* who will provide the bass or a drone. The music draws obliquely on French and Italian harmony, which is sometimes used functionally but is often wayward as the singers add notes to chords which then suggest a new direction. Secular singing tells of communities, their laments, serenades, weddings, funerals and harvests in Corsican, but the equally strong sacred tradition is in Latin. Today polyphony is still sung in villages, but it is more often performance as entertainment rather than a socially essential activity. Corsican groups such as Barbara Furtuna, whose performances retain something of the original improvised randomness (especially in the sacred repertoire), have taken the music to international success. Those who succeed outside Corsica tend to have the rough edges edited out of them, and are more likely to get together because they have matching voices rather than similar day jobs.

The Sardinian tradition is similarly grounded in the everyday life of village communities, but has a very different musical structure and vocal production. The singing is known as *cantu a tenore* (singing in ensemble) and has several subgenres – love songs, lullabies, religious themes and so on – but the form is always the same. The tune is outlined by the soloist, the *boghe* (literally 'mouth'), who is then joined by three other singers, the *bassu*, who normally sings the tonic, the *contra* who takes the fifth, and the *mesa boghe* who usually sings descant around a tempered third above the *boghe*. The backing singers may stagger their entries to build up a chord using formulaic nonsense syllables which then generate a rhythmic chordal backing. The soloist has a great deal of freedom, and like his Corsican counterpart can use microtonal inflections and ornamentation. His phonation is consciously different from the harmony singers, often sounding more like those on the North African coast. The lower voices may sing entirely on one note, using a high-tension resonance that emphasises the upper harmonics and gives a unique colour to the vowels. In 2005 Unesco proclaimed *cantu a tenore* a masterpiece of the oral and intangible heritage of humanity, which has probably helped the commercially successful groups such as Tenores de Oniferi and Tenores de Bitti to maintain their very strong vocal and cultural identity.

The use of nonsense syllables combined with reinforced harmonics may have originated in the calls Sardinian shepherds used in the mountains to round up their flocks. A similar vocal technique is found further along the 42nd parallel among Mongolian horse farmers, as we shall see below. Nonsense syllables are also found in the Genoese *tralala* found on the Italian mainland, however (perhaps brought there by sailors from the islands). This is also a male tradition in which singers use onomatopoeic syllables to give rhythmic impulse to their imitations of instruments. The mainland Italian folk tradition has been almost subsumed by modern urban music, and while we may lament its disappearance we should be glad that the suffering much of the singing was intended to relieve is a thing of the past too. There was until fairly recently a unique tradition of work songs, sung in improvised polyphony, among the women rice workers of the Po valley. Jonathan Keates, passing through the rice fields of Piedmont, heard the gangs of female weeders' call and response:

they slopped and shuffled through the mud, singing strange, haunting chants whose pitch and rhythm was given by a leader and answered by the grunting chorus. All that is left of the *mondine* [weeders] is … a folk memory of exhaustion and poverty and the squalor of life as a migrant worker … an incubus of misery that haunts their resolve to work harder, save more and get away into the city.[36]

There is a similar (but unrelated) tradition in the former Soviet Republic of Georgia. Like the island traditions it features male voices, often organised on family or village lines. The songs are extended pieces, usually between one and three voices over a movable drone which gets filled in with chords at significant moments. The vocal quality is quite different from the Mediterranean timbre, more relaxed and sometimes resorting to very quiet falsetto. Much has been made in the previous chapter about the significance of recording, and its use revolutionised researchers' fieldwork in the early twentieth century. The earliest fieldtrips were actually for commercial reasons, and in 1909 the Gramophone Company sent the German recording engineer Franz Hampe on a trip to the Caucasus with his Berliner machine. He crossed the 42nd parallel a number of times, and his recordings of polyphony from what are now Georgia and Armenia confirm the authenticity of the current Georgian tradition.[37]

[36] Jonathan Keates, *Italian Journeys* (London: Heinemann, 1991): 78–9.
[37] *Before the Revolution*, CD and text compiled by Will Prentice from the British Library National Sound Archive TSCD921.

Bulgaria

Countries of the old Soviet bloc often benefited from the state's inclination to preserve folk or minority culture (within certain limits). From the nineteenth century onwards research into Bulgarian folk music had recorded a rich variety of genres, many of which flourished under communism (there is also a Bulgarian epic genre similar to that of Serbia and Croatia). The Bulgarian State Television Female Vocal Choir was founded in 1952 and was making recordings of folk-inspired music from 1957 onwards. Unlike state funded choirs in the West (such as the BBC Singers) it preserved the traditional vocal technique. The singers are drawn from village communities and bring their own repertoires so the tradition is continually refreshed. They sing in a forcefully projected chest register with a range limited to about an octave, creating a particularly effective choral sound with a narrow harmonic compass which directs the attention to the vocal texture. The Swiss ethnomusicologist Marcel Cellier recorded the choir as *Le Mystère des Voix Bulgares* in 1975 on his own label and it was subsequently released on an English label in 1986. The sound of massed chest voices was an international hit, resulting in members of the choir collaborating with Western musicians and the growth of Bulgarian singing workshops outside the country.

Mongolia

The *chömei* tradition (literally 'guttural') of Tuva and Mongolia, like the lower voices of Sardinian polyphony, uses a very different technique from the phonation used in almost all other varieties of singing today. The basic principle stems from a fundamentally different concept of singing: the voice as polyphonic instrument rather than carrier of text. Most of the varieties referred to in this book use a similar phonation – the vocal cords (or folds) are excited by the air from the lungs, creating a raw sound which is then turned into what we perceive as singing by the manipulation of resonance in the vocal tract. *Chömei*, or overtone singing, also works in this way, but employs the false vocal cords to generate an extra, flute-like note, which can then be controlled by using the tongue and soft palate to change the pitch. It is a high-pressure process which can, after prolonged use, sometimes damage health, but it enables a singer to duet with him- or her-self, creating melodies over a drone. There are subgenres which use slight variations of method, but the technique is found all over the region (a less pressurised version is used by

Tibetan monks simply to drone and reinforce specific harmonics). The process has also been used in Western art music, notably Stockhausen's *Stimmung*. Modern ensembles such as Huun-Huur-tu combine this with modern instruments and have created a curious Tuvan–Rock–Country hybrid. The texts reflect the distant origins of the music, and are almost always about horses.

China, Korea, Japan

China, Japan and Korea have something akin to the equivalent of the Western classical tradition: a stylised, courtly music that is not folk song. Despite the huge variety of sung dramas around the world, the only common use of the term 'opera' beyond the familiar genre that originated in late sixteenth-century Italy is applied to Chinese opera (also popularly known as Peking or Beijing Opera). In theatrical traditions around the world we often find the use of the voice to be far more strictly codified and stylised than in the West. This becomes imperative when one person is responsible for all the characters and clear vocal distinctions are essential. Another reason, of direct significance to the twists and turns in the history of singing, is the widespread occurrence of cross-gender impersonation (familiar to us from Shakespeare plays and some castrato roles, and still seen in pantomimes). In Japan it is a feature of Noh and Kabuki plays. The emphasis is on men imitating women, which is most obviously achieved vocally through falsetto. Of course this is not to say that the use of falsetto is only for imitating women or even for 'feminising' the male voice (it is likely that men will at least unconsciously remember that as boys they once had voices almost indistinguishable from those of the opposite sex anyway). Male pop singers routinely use it without any reflection on their masculinity; Indian classical singers employ it freely to extend their range.[38] A tantalising prospect is gender A imitating gender B imitating gender A, as used to happen in Chinese opera, where troupes were originally all-male. Certain actors would impersonate women by singing falsetto; as recently as the start of the twentieth century, when women took over the female roles, they imitated the male falsetto, producing the special 'squeezed' sound that so characterises Chinese opera today.[39] We can

---

[38] In Haiti falsetto is used to demonstrate vocal prowess, without aspersions: 'Men often use falsetto; it is considered an accomplishment for a man to be able to sing well "like a woman."' Harold Courlander, *Haiti Singing* (University of North Carolina Press, 1939; repr. New York: Cooper Square Publishers, 1973): 184.

[39] Peter Fletcher, *World Musics in Context: a Comprehensive Survey of the World's Major Musical Cultures* (Oxford University Press, 2001): 367–8.

also hear in Chinese opera, and in Japanese folk song, the special alternation between singing and stylised speech that sounds strange to Western ears and still makes its equivalent in the *Sprechgesang* of Schoenberg's *Pierrot Lunaire* sound almost outrageously modern a hundred years after its composition. In Chinese opera the words are delivered according to a number of different language levels (whether spoken or sung). The most stylised is classical Chinese (*wenyan wen*), which is the ancient written language of Chinese literature. Each word was represented by a single written character, which becomes a single spoken or sung syllable carrying the meaning of a whole word. It is this process which accounts for the hyper-stylised delivery: the singer is conveying sequential units of meaning rather than the joined-up phrases of everyday speech. The vernacular is used too (mostly *putonghua* or Mandarin), depending on the status of the character. Each level has further subdivisions which are determined by the poetic genre at any given point in the play.

Singing is only one of the elements that combine to make a Chinese stage performance (the others being speech, dancing/acting and combat/acrobatics). Japanese *Kabuki* is a similarly multifaceted genre: the word is a compound meaning 'singing-dancing-skill'. Now an all-male genre (women have been banned for several hundred years), female roles are played using a mixture of head voice and falsetto. The singing is heavily stylised, again based on ancient forms of language, and singers are not immune from throat problems caused by putting too much stress on the larynx. In *Bunraku*, the Japanese puppet theatre, the singers also have to be very careful with their voices. The solo chanter, or *tayu*, sits at the side of the stage and narrates the entire story, including the characters in their appropriate voices, accompanied by a shamisen player. His task is to invest the puppets with emotion, both by his facial expressions and the vocal acting that accompanies them. In the Korean *P'ansori* tradition the singer, the *kwangdae*, is also responsible for the whole narrative, but accompanied only by a drummer. *P'ansori* ('song sung on a stage') developed from shamanism in the distant Korean past and has now become a globally exported national music. It is sung by both men and women with a huge range of vocal dynamics and gestures. Unlike *Kabuki* and Chinese opera characters, *Bunraku* and *P'ansori* singers never stop (except when interrupted by applause), and consequently develop vast reserves of vocal stamina.

THE 22ND PARALLEL

For our slice of singing south of the equator we will visit latitude 22, which connects the continents of South America, Africa and Australia.

These vast territories all have multiple singing traditions, and this whistle-stop tour will only give a tiny insight into the infinite vocal possibilities that further exploration will reveal.

Chile, Bolivia and Argentina

The South American countries share histories of pre-Columban music and colonial genres, in much the same way as the African countries tend to produce a singing synthesis of indigenous and imported music. Chile, Bolivia and Argentina are Andean countries and share the indigenous music of the Quechua and Aymara peoples who lived in the mountains before the Spaniards arrived. The mountain air seems to favour high, penetrating voices, whether male or female, frequently combined with panpipes. From the 1960s onwards they have also shared *Nueva Canción* ('new song'), a left-wing cultural and musical protest movement. In Chile the movement was known as *Nueva Canción Chilena*, and one of its most eloquent singer-songwriters was Victor Jara. Jara's songs to the guitar were often gently expressed if forthright in political intent. In 1973 he was one of the victims of the Pinochet regime's cull of its opponents, tortured and shot in the stadium that now bears his name. His songs have since been recorded by Sting, Peter Gabriel and Robert Wyatt, among others. The movement did not really take off in Bolivia until the 1980s, when it arrived in the form of *Canto Nuevo*. Emma Junaro's bright, high, delicate voice is typical of the understated *Canto Nuevo*, softly lyrical but as likely to sing of politics as of love.

Argentina is the home of tango and, despite his birth in Toulouse, of Carlos Gardel, the greatest of tango singers. He was born Charles Romuald Gardes in 1890, of an unnamed father (possibly one Paul Lasserre). Partly as a result of the stigma of having an illegitimate child and partly because she had already lived in South America, his mother Berthe Gardes took him to Buenos Aires when he was two years old. So this French boy, later changing his name to Carlos Gardel, was gradually transformed into the greatest musical symbol of Argentina before Astor Piazzolla. The inscription on the monument erected to him in Toulouse describes him as 'créateur du tango chanté qui l'a rendu célèbre dans toute l'Amérique du Sud' (creator of the sung tango which made him famous throughout South America). As well as possessing a rich baritone voice, he composed many of the most famous tango numbers. What established him as the creator of the *tango-canción* (tango song) was 'Mi Noche Triste' (my sad night) which he sang in 1917 and the recording went on to sell 10,000 copies, spreading his name throughout

Latin America. As neither words nor music of that particular song were by him he was not strictly speaking the creator of the genre, but he certainly made it his own through his recordings and his own compositions. He also appeared in several films especially in the last four years of his life. His singing talent and classic good looks made him ideal in that medium. Gardel was killed in a plane crash at Medellín, Colombia. Some mystery still surrounds his death, as it does the precise location and circumstances of his birth (fuelled by Gardel himself, who apparently maintained that he had been born in Uruguay). What is beyond doubt is his iconic status in Argentina to this day.

Paraguay

Paraguay also has its European-influenced music, notably the rhythmically complicated Paraguayan polka and various sorts of rock, but only since 2008 has the country started to liberalise after half a century of dictatorship which prevented either the legitimisation of native musics or the introduction of new or hybrid genres such as we see in postcolonial Africa. For this reason much of the country's music is mysterious and poorly understood. There are still many village communities in which ritual music has a crucial function, with songs for deaths, marriages and births, and the history of the tribe. One such ritual is *anabsoro*, which explains the origins of the world. The singers (all male) utter a series of sustained falsetto cries and whoops, alternating with long notes, projected in a single breath using a chest register. A wordless heterophony ensues, sometimes alighting on a pitch over which a skeleton harmony briefly appears. No outside observers have fully interpreted this music, which the Zamuco tribesmen may have been singing since before they had language, but discovered a need to explain their world.[40]

Brazil

Brazil could hardly be more of a contrast to Paraguay. Now a major world power after generations of instability, Brazil is also one of the great musical melting pots of South America. It also has its pre-Columban musics, but the urbanisation of the culture has produced samba and bossa nova and a plethora of new popular music varieties. Contemporary

---

[40] There is an example on CD1 of *Les Voix du Monde* released by the Centre National de la Recherche Scientifique et du Musée de l'Homme, Paris.

Brazilian singing is perhaps best illustrated by two of its iconic figures, the singer-songwriter Gaetano Veloso and his sometime protégée Virginia Rodrigues. Both singers have a relaxed delivery, in contrast to the often frenetic instrumental dance music that is central to Brazilian culture. Veloso almost speaks into the microphone, and like so many Portuguese singers uses the sonorous complexity of the language to create an emotional narrative. Virginia Rodrigues has a plangent delivery, with a hint of the *saudade* of Fado. Her singing has that very rare quality of being able to move people just by hearing a few bars. She sang in Catholic church choirs in her youth and hoped to become an actress before Veloso recognised her talent and arranged her first recordings.

Africa: Namibia to Madagascar

The 22nd parallel reaches Africa on the Namibian coast and traverses Botswana, Zimbabwe and Mozambique, crossing Madagascar as it heads out over the Indian Ocean. Africa is a country of such diversity and in such a dynamic state of flux that almost anything we can say about contemporary singing on the continent will be out of date by the time you read these words. The speed of change is often driven by a perceived need to update the current genre, whatever it happens to be. It is even something of a generalisation to talk about traditional African music – there are countless traditions, the origins of which are unknowable. As far as we can tell, singing has always been part of the culture, but we can only begin to make sense of it from colonial times. This is not easy either, as the malleable African psyche seems to absorb any music that arrives and then transforms it into a new genre that is distinctly African. Namibia is a sparsely populated country with at least three African ethnic groups and an unforgiving climate, which has been occupied by both Germany and South Africa, finally gaining its independence in 1990. Traditional music is still found at weddings and family gatherings (where you might even hear traditional praise songs) and European and South African influences have resulted in several varieties of fusion that mix European harmonies with African rhythms. The vocal declamation ranges from a sub-American blandness, often in English, to the uninhibited excitement of those who sing in one of the country's twenty-five other languages. Almost all African genres feature drumming. Unusually, the music of the Tswana people of Botswana features a call and response variety which might include shouts of affirmation and a spoken commentary. There are many competing outside influences, including a flourishing Hip-hop scene that competes with imported

South African township music and various European-derived musics such as *Kwasa Kwasa* (an African version of Rumba).

There have been many African international successes, and those that make it have often gone through a tortuous process of mediation between 'pure' African music and the musical cultures that have been absorbed from outside. The Zimbabwean singer Thomas Mapfumo lived in a traditional Shona community until the age of ten; when his family moved to a suburb of Harare he was exposed to anglophone music and by the time he was sixteen he was singing Elvis Presley, Otis Redding and Beatles covers in local bands. In 1972 he joined the Hallelujah Chicken Run Band, the first Zimbabwean band to sing in Shona rather than English and to use traditional music as the inspiration for new material rather than resorting to pop covers. The American guitar sound became transformed into an electric mbira, and Mapfumo's vocal sound also seemed to be influenced by its restless staccato style. As they were singing in Shona the Smith regime had no idea what they were singing about, and very soon the band became associated with the liberation movement. In 1978 Mapfumo formed The Blacks Unlimited, to sing the music he called *Chimurenga* ('struggle'). Mapfumo's vocals are a far cry (literally) from 1960s pop, his delivery shaped by the angularity of the Shona language which he deploys over a wide tessitura. In 1990 he moved to self-imposed exile in Oregon, disillusioned with the Mugabe regime.

Mozambique gained independence in 1975 after five hundred years of Portuguese rule, and almost immediately there was a rush to explore African roots music. One genre to emerge is Tufo, a vigorous women's singing and dancing style accompanied by drums from the Ilha do Moçambique. There is an Arabic influence here, with groups of female dancers singing in two or more parts. The Portuguese influence is still there in *Marrabenta*, the urban salsa-like dance music that reinvented itself after independence using homemade instruments and singing in native languages. Madagascar's history has much shallower colonial roots, the French leaving in 1960 after only sixty-four years, before which the island had been a loose federation of tribes and kingdoms. There is the usual African mix of modified European styles but there is also a huge variety of native genres (which reflects the size of the island – half as big again as California). In the coastal regions, for example, there is a tradition of curing illness by singing. The curing ritual involves summoning up a supernatural entity called *kokolampo*. Women's voices invoke the *kokolampo* in the presence of a male curer, who interprets the medicinal instructions from the singing, shouting, gasping and groaning as the

women are possessed by *kokolampo*. The singing is energetic and virtuosic, call and response onto which is overlaid fast runs and shouts as the
cure evolves.[41]

Australia

The Aborigines have inhabited Australia for at least forty thousand years,
moreover in isolation except for the traumatic past two hundred or so
years. They can therefore claim to be sustaining the oldest surviving
musical culture in the world and, by the same token, the oldest surviving
tradition of singing as well. Another assumption about that enormous
historical span connects the 'primitive' with the 'unchanging': because a
society preserves ancient technologies and subsistence methods (notably
hunter-gathering) the argument is that everything stays the same. Such
a generalisation is less sustainable than others that must occur in such a
brief examination, yet there is evidence that the Aborigines connect with
their very distant past in a special, even unique way. The ethnic, linguistic
and cultural similarities among so many groups dispersed over the huge
area that is Australia also permit the generalised view of the Aborigines
as one people. The islands of Tasmania to the south of Australia and the
Torres Strait to the north have musical cultures different to the northern
and southern practices of the mainland. In the case of Tasmania scholars
must rely on conjecture, as the Tasmanian native peoples became extinct
more than a century ago. A connection with Melanesian music has been
made and in the case of the Torres Strait islands it appears far stronger
than with the Aboriginal music of the mainland.

The first thing that comes to mind with Aboriginal music is probably
the didjeridu, one of a large family of wooden, single-note trumpets found
throughout the region (including the large neighbouring island of New
Guinea). But its use and geographical origin are both limited: to accompany singing and to the northern coastal region of Australia, respectively.
The didjeridu player can also sing while playing. Aboriginal music is first
and foremost singing, and instruments are very limited in variety and role
(the latter primarily as accompanying instruments, such as the didjeridu,
boomerang and wooden clapping sticks). Instrumental performances
without any singing are rare.

Aboriginal history is inextricably linked to the unique creation myth
known as the Dreaming or Dreamtime, when creative powers organised

41 Ibid.

both the physical surface of the earth and its life forms. The timeless past of the Dreaming lives on in the present and music continues to be a process of communication with the mythical powers. This provides evidence not only for an enduring tradition but also for special attitudes to creativity and ritual ownership of songs. Men only can receive and reproduce songs of the Dreaming, which may be received in dreams and trances; the actual creation resides with the powers. Not all music is conceived and executed in the same way. For example, in the northern region of Arnhem Land may be found specialist songmen who own, 'dream' and generally control song performances. This not only departs from the process just described but also encourages innovation and individual expression; sometimes canonic imitation and parallel harmonies result when groups of songmen, perhaps with their assistant singers, perform together.[42] Another intriguing song type is the poison song. Death is thought to be the result of sorcery, which can include singing, so a person may be literally sung to death. The Aborigines also produce rock and cave paintings, both of which are closely associated with music. This accompaniment of painting with music lends credence to Steven Mithen's thesis (discussed earlier in this book) that music and dancing must have existed in prehistoric societies whose cave paintings survive to the present day.[43]

One of the glories of Aboriginal culture is the concept of Songlines, made famous to the outside world through Bruce Chatwin's inspiring book combining fiction and non-fiction.[44] They are also known as Dreaming tracks, connecting them to the Dreaming. Above all, they connect song to the land through which the nomadic Aborigines roamed. In the Dreaming the mythical creative powers walked upon a black and featureless earth and wherever they went they created a feature of the landscape and a series of Dream tracks, preserved in songs that mark individual landscape features in their notes and phrases. If the traveller knew a song cycle he could thus use it like a map or compass and traverse a space hitherto unknown to him.

Trevor Jones noted some features of Aboriginal voice production, including soft 'inward' singing, contrasting with loud, throaty sounds. Some unusual techniques encountered are continuous singing, rather like circular breathing when playing wind instruments, achieved by maintaining vocal cord vibrations even during intakes of breath; 'deliberate

---

[42] Trevor A. Jones, 'The Traditional Music of the Australian Aborigines', in Elizabeth May (ed.), *Musics of Many Cultures: an Introduction* (Berkeley: University of California Press, 1980): 168.
[43] See chapter 1, p. 33.
[44] Bruce Chatwin, *The Songlines* (London: Jonathan Cape, 1987).

"croaking" of two or more pitches at once by allowing the vocal cords to divide into more than one section'; also what he called *polyvocality* by which the singer cultivates different voice qualities to suit the particular song.[45] He also noted an interesting example of polyphony from Arnhem Land, in which two groups simultaneously sing their own ceremonial chants which have different scale structures, melodic ranges and different tempi of stick beating. Where they agree is on the final note of the falling phrases.[46] Melodies tend to start on a high pitch and descend to one much lower, possibly as much as an octave. Ethnomusicologists used to typify 'primitive' singing by this characteristic, and also what they termed 'tiled melodies' when motifs cascade in a sequence of short and narrow phrases on descending pitches.[47] Such melodies are prevalent not only among the Australian Aborigines but also in New Guinea and in the Torres Strait between the two huge islands (of Australia and New Guinea). The rationale is that the voice has the greatest energy at the start of a breath, so the note is high and loud, tailing off in intensity as the melody descends.

Although religion and the arts, including music, are almost entirely male activities Aboriginal women and children have their own music. Women sing lullabies and perform ritual wailings at funerals and initiations. Interestingly, the wailing can extend to discrete versions of the men's chants. This raises the question of female creativity and even the possibility of 'improving' upon male repertoires. If nothing else, it proves than women are not silent even in male-dominated ritualistic cultures, and when they give voice to their creativity they can establish their own distinct repertoires. Children too have their own songs and ceremonies, as well as being expected to imitate adult performances. The disruption to the Aborigines' traditional way of life brought about by the white settlers has resulted in relatively rapid change. Urbanisation and other features of modern life have introduced outside music, including country, reggae and rock, and fusions with traditional Aboriginal music have been created by the bands that have emerged.

We have, in a sense, come almost back to where we started. This has inevitably been a very selective singing history, but we hope we have at least covered a representative chunk. The overall shape of the narrative is obviously limited by not being able to hear any but the most

---

[45] Jones, 'The Traditional Music of the Australian Aborigines': 161.
[46] Ibid.: 163–4.
[47] Cf. Curt Sachs's remarks about pathogenic melodies, quoted in chapter 1, p. 23.

recent history, and the weight of history is firmly in favour of the much documented Western classical variety. Sadly, its greatest achievements occurred before we could record them, and the history of classical singing for the last hundred years or so has been one of stasis – small, frozen repertoires perpetuated by conservative teaching regimes focusing on the abstract pursuit of excellence rather than creativity. Bizarrely, many conservatories are kept afloat by singers from outside the Western tradition wishing to study the art. All classical traditions are by nature conservative, as we have seen in India and also in China and Japan, three other countries with great traditions that may be described as classical. In Japan and China these traditions have been guardians of glorious pasts for much longer than Western opera houses, and however exquisite, however artistic, are ultimately stylised remnants of what was a dynamic living tradition. A similar fate may await institutionalised Western classical singing as it becomes less able to reflect the expressive needs of those who create and consume it.

By far the most dynamic and creative singing at the start of the twenty-first century is to be found outside the tiny classical niche, and much of it makes reference to some of the other varieties of singing that we have looked at here. During the second half of the twentieth century, the breakdown of commercial and academic categories of singing (and the emancipation of almost any genre) legitimised almost any variety of singing as being of potential value. The twentieth century gave Western music the distinction between 'classical' and 'popular'; the twenty-first is replacing that absurd polarity with a plurality of singings.

Sources and references

INTRODUCTION

General surveys of 'World Music' are quite plentiful. Peter Fletcher's *World Musics in Context: a Comprehensive Survey of the World's Major Musical Cultures* (Oxford University Press, 2001) is unusual in being not only single authored but long. Philip V. Bohlman provided a much more succinct, yet no less challenging or satisfying, analysis in his *World Music: a Very Short Introduction* (Oxford University Press, 2002). More recent volumes tend to be collections of essays by individual experts. *The Garland Encyclopedia of World Music* (Routledge) is detailed, as it is presented as one volume per continent or part thereof (searchable at http://glncl.alexanderstreet.com). Single-volume surveys include Simon Broughton, Mark Ellingham, David Muddyman and Richard Trillo (eds.), *World Music: the Rough Guide* (Rough Guides Ltd, 1994, repr. in 2 vols., 2000); Jeff Todd Titon (ed.), *Worlds of Music: an Introduction to the Music of the World's Peoples* (2nd edn, Wadsworth Publishing, 2004); Terry Miller and Andrew Shahriari, *World Music: a Global Journey* (2nd edn, New York: Routledge, 2007).

Alan Lomax had published quite extensively on the Cantometrics project but his classic and most detailed account fills the book entitled *Folk Song Style and Culture* (Washington, DC: American Association for the Advancement of Science, 1968, repr. New Brunswick, Transaction Books, 1968). Further writings by Lomax, as well as some very helpful explanations and appraisals of Cantometrics, with a CD of sound illustrations, are to be found in Ronald D. Cohen (ed.), *Alan Lomax: Selected Writings 1934–1997* (New York: Routledge, 2003), and an important new biography has recently appeared: John Szwed, *The Man Who Recorded the World: a Biography of Alan Lomax* (Portsmouth, NH: William Heinemann, 2010).

Roland Barthes's 'Grain of the Voice' is anthologised in many collections but first appeared as 'Le Grain de la Voix' in *Musique en jeu 9* (1972), translated by Stephen Heath in the collection *Image, Music, Text* (London: Fontana, 1977): 179–89. For comparison, Dietrich Fischer-Dieskau and Charles Panzéra have some overlapping repertoire on Fischer-Dieskau's *French Romantic Songs*, Teldec 4509 and Panzéra's *Mélodies Françaises*, EMI Classics 0777 7 64254 2 9.

1   ORIGINS, MYTHS AND MUSES

Curt Sachs's pioneering work on origins is still relevant today, especially *The Rise of Music in the Ancient World, East and West* (New York: Norton, 1943), *A Short History of World Music* (2nd edn, London: Dennis Dobson, 1956) and *The Wellsprings of Music* (The Hague: Martinus Nijhoff, 1962); similarly Bruno Nettl's *Music in Primitive Culture* (Cambridge, MA: Harvard University Press, 1956); for an earlier approach see Richard Wallaschek, *Primitive Music* (London, Longmans Green, 1893; repr. New York: Da Capo Press, 1970); for more recent work, specifically on singing by early man, see Steven Mithen, *The Singing Neanderthals: The Origins of Music, Language, Mind and Body* (London: Weidenfeld and Nicolson, 2005). *The Origins of Music*, ed. Nils L. Wallin, Björn Merker and Steven Brown (Cambridge, MA: Massachusetts Institute of Technology, 2000), contains informative chapters by Ellen Dissanayake ('Antecedents of the Temporal Arts in Early Mother–Infant Interaction'), Dean Falk ('Hominid Brain Evolution and the Origins of Music'), David W. Frayer and Chris Nicolay ('Fossil Evidence for the Origin of Speech Sounds'), François-Bernard Mâche ('The Necessity of and Problems with a Universal Musicology'), Bruno Nettl ('An Ethnomusicologist Contemplates Universals in Musical Sound and Musical Culture') and Peter J. B. Slater ('Birdsong Repertoires: Their Origins and Use').

There are many studies on specific ethnic communities living in the modern period. These include the classic work of Albert B. Lord on oral epic in the former Yugoslavia, *The Singer of Tales* (Cambridge, MA: Harvard University Press, 1960), Anthony Seeger's monograph on the Brazilian Suyá Indians, *Why Suyá Sing: a Musical Anthropology of an Amazonian People* (Cambridge University Press, 1987), John Blacking's anthropological study of the South African Venda tribe, *How Musical is Man* (London: Faber and Faber, 1976) and Steven Feld, *Sound and Sentiment: Birds, Weeping, Poetics, and Song in Kaluli Expression* (Philadelphia: University of Pennsylvania Press, 1982); see also Merlin Donald, *Origins of the Modern Mind* (Cambridge, MA: Harvard University Press, 1991).

2   THE GENESIS OF THE WESTERN TRADITION
SINGING IN THE ANCIENT WORLD

The Culgi hymns can be found at the *Electronic Text Corpus of Sumerian Literature* web resource (http://etcsl.orinst.ox.ac.uk/index.html#). The ETCSL project (Oriental Institute, University of Oxford) contains some four hundred literary compositions from third- and second-millennium BCE Mesopotamia. For a recent analysis of ancient Egyptian vocal culture, see John Baines, *Visual and Written Culture in Ancient Egypt* (Oxford University Press, 2007): 166–8. Abraham Z. Idelsohn, *Jewish Music in its Historical Development* (New York: Holt, 1929; repr. New York: Schocken Books, 1967) is the earliest comprehensive work on Jewish history and there is a substantial entry on Jewish music in *Grove Music Online* (www.oxfordmusiconline.com).

There are comprehensive surveys of ancient Greek singing in Andrew Barker, *Greek Musical Writings*. Vol. 1: *The Musician and his Art* (Cambridge University Press, 1984) and M. L. West, *Ancient Greek Music* (Oxford: Clarendon Press, 1992), especially chapter 2, 'The Voice': 39–47.

ORAL POETRY AND FORMULAIC EPIC

Milman Parry first proposed his thesis in 'L'épithète traditionnelle dans Homère. Essai sur un problème de style homérique', *Les Belles Lettres* 8 (1928). He intended to apply the theory to Serbian and Croatian epic, and his work was finally completed after his death with Albert B. Lord's *The Singer of Tales* (Cambridge, MA: Harvard University Press, 1960, repr. 1981). A further volume of Lord's writings edited by Mary Louise Lord appeared after his death, *The Singer Resumes the Tale* (Ithaca: Cornell University Press, 1995) with substantial bibliography. Since then there have been further contributions to the literature, including John Miles Foley's *The Singer of Tales in Performance* (Bloomington: Indiana University Press, 1995). A detailed study of the Serbian epic singer Avdo Avdic appears in Kenneth Goldman, *Formulaic Analysis of Serbocroatian Oral Epic Song* (New York: Garland, 1990).

EARLY CHRISTIAN CHANT

Modern chant scholarship begins with Helmut Hucke and Leo Treitler. See Hucke's 'Toward a New Historical View of Gregorian Chant', *Journal of the American Musicological Society* 33:3 (1980): 437–9 for a summary of the 'sacred bridge' model of chant transmission, and the seventeen updated essays by Leo Treitler in his *With Voice and Pen* (Oxford University Press, 2003). The work of James McKinnon on music in the early church is essential reading; see 'Christian Antiquity' in James McKinnon (ed.), *Antiquity and the Middle Ages: from Ancient Greece to the 15th Century* (London: Macmillan, 1990): 68–87 for a brief overview of the relationship between early Christian music and Judaism, and his *Music in Early Christian Literature* (Cambridge University Press, 1987) for a more detailed analysis. The nature of early chant in desert monastic communities is discussed in Joseph Dyer, 'The Desert, the City and Psalmody in the Late Fourth Century' (see especially page 17) and Peter Jeffery, 'Monastic Reading and the Emerging Roman Chant Repertory' (especially pp. 81–3) in Sean Gallagher *et al.* (eds.), *Western Plainchant in the First Millennium* (Aldershot: Ashgate, 2003). Christopher Page's monumental survey *The Christian West and its Singers: the First Thousand Years* (New Haven: Yale University Press, 2010) references almost all singers from the period about whom information survives.

The Treitler–Hucke hypothesis has been criticised by (among others) Peter Jeffrey in his *Re-Envisioning Past Musical Cultures* (University of Chicago Press, 1995). Jeffrey advocated a complementary ethnomusicological approach to chant scholarship in order to account for what he considered weaknesses in the

accepted oral formula theory such as the difficulty of proof and confirmation
and the analogy with text transmission. He also drew attention to the dissimi-
larity between Gregorian chant and Homeric epic, calling for more research into
living oral chant traditions. Recent research into memory in connection with
twelfth-century polyphony does make the case for formulaic learning, however.
See Anna Maria Busse Berger, *Medieval Music and the Art of Memory* (Berkeley:
University of California Press, 2005) especially pp. 128–30.

NOTATION

Guido d'Arezzo's staff notation is outlined in the *Prologus antiphonarii sui*, trans.
Oliver Strunk, *Source Readings in Music History* (London: Faber, 1981): 117–20.
The use of the mnemonic 'Ut queant laxis' is explained in *Epistola de Ignotu
Cantu* (trans. Strunk, ibid.: 121–5).

ICONOGRAPHY

There are many iconographic examples to be found in Edmund A. Bowles, *La
Pratique Musicale au Moyen Age* (Paris: editions Minkoff, 1983) and René Nelli,
Troubadours and Trouvères (Paris: Hachette, 1979). Manuscripts, some illumi-
nated, can be seen online at DIAMM: www.diamm.ac.uk/index.html, the
Digital Imagine Archive of Medieval Music.

MEDIEVAL SINGING

Joseph Dyer, 'The Voice in the Middle Ages' in John Potter (ed.), *The Cambridge
Companion to Singing* (Cambridge University Press, 2000) has an overview of
medieval singing. For a more substantial account and musical examples see
Richard Hoppin, *Medieval Music* (New York: Norton, 1972) and its accompanying anthology of music or Alberto Gallo, *Music of the Middle Ages*. Vols. I
and II (Cambridge University Press, 1985). For the music, the annotated anthology by Thomas Marrocco and Nicholas Sandon (eds.), *Medieval Music* (Oxford
University Press, 1977) contains examples of both chant and polyphony.

CHORAL ESTABLISHMENTS

Craig Wright, *Music at the Court of Burgundy* (Henryville, PA: Institute of
Medieval Music, 1979) has a detailed account of the musical establishments
of Philip the Bold and his successor John the Fearless. For accounts of choirs
in England during the medieval and early Renaissance periods see Kathleen
Edwards, *The English Secular Cathedrals in the Middle Ages* (2nd rev. edn,
Manchester University Press, 1967), Frank Harrison, *Music in Medieval Britain*
(London: Routledge, 1980) and John Morehen (ed.), *English Choral Practice
1400–1650* (Cambridge University Press, 1995).

PERFORMANCE PRACTICE

John Potter, 'Issues in the Modern Performance of Medieval Music', in Mark Everist (ed.), *The Cambridge History of Medieval Music* (Cambridge University Press, forthcoming) discusses the challenges facing the modern performer. Timothy McGee's *The Sound of Medieval Song* (Oxford: Clarendon Press, 1998) is a comprehensive examination of the surviving evidence.

On the medieval understanding of vocal registers see Franz Müller-Heuser, *Vox Humana: Ein Beitrag zur Untersuchung der Stimmästhetik des Mittelalters* (Regensburg: Bosse, 1963): 124ff.; for a modern explication see Johan Sundberg 'Where Does the Sound Come from?', in Potter, *Companion to Singing*: 239.

NOTRE DAME AND THE *MAGNUS LIBER*

For the history of music at Notre Dame in this period see Craig Wright, *Music and Ceremony at Notre Dame of Paris 500–1550* (Cambridge University Press, 1989); the most recent summary of current thought on the relationship between manuscript and memory is Anna Maria Busse Berger, *Medieval Music and the Art of Memory* (Berkeley: University of California Press, 1994).

MEDIEVAL MONOPHONIC REPERTOIRES

On Conrad von Zabern and the singing of monks see Joseph Dyer, 'Singing with Proper Refinement', *Early Music* 6:2 (1978): 207–27 for a parallel translation of relevant sections of the treatise. For background and musical examples of secular monophony see the following:

F. R. P. Akehurst and Judith Davis (eds.), *A Handbook of the Troubadours* (Berkeley: University of California Press, 1995).

Elizabeth Aubrey, *The Music of the Troubadours* (Indiana University Press, 2000).

E. J. Dobson and Frank Harrison (eds.), *Medieval English Songs* (London: Faber, 1979).

Mary O'Neill, *Courtly Love Songs of Medieval France* (Oxford University Press, 2006).

Samuel Rosenberg and Hans Tischler (eds.), *Chanter M'Estuet: Songs of the Trouvères* (London: Faber, 1981).

Ronald Taylor, *The Art of the Minnesinger*, 2 vols. (Cardiff: University of Wales Press, 1968).

Jørn Olav Løset's translation of *Widsith* can be found at home.online. no/~joeolavl/viking/widsith.m#The%20poem%20%22Widsith%22%20 and%20the%20vikings.

3   THE EMERGING SOLOIST AND THE PRIMACY OF TEXT

LATE MEDIEVAL AND RENAISSANCE COURTS AND CHAPELS

There are several studies of music in specific cities or courts, notably:

Eleonora Beck, *Singing in the Garden: Music and Culture in the Tuscan Trecento* (Innsbruck: Studien Verlag, 1998).
Frank Dobbins, *Music in Renaissance Lyons* (Oxford: Clarendon Press, 1992).
Lewis Lockwood, *Music in Renaissance Ferrara 1400–1505* (Cambridge, MA: Harvard University Press, 1992).
Reinhard Strohm, *Music in Late Medieval Bruges* (Oxford: Clarendon Press, 1990).
Craig Wright, *Music at the Court of Burgundy* (Henryville, PA: Institute of Medieval Music, 1979).

All have much to say about singers (Beck on the singing in the *Decameron*, Strohm on Jean Cordier and many others, Lockwood on Pietrobono, for example). For improvised music in Italy see James Haar, *Essays on Italian Poetry and Music in the Renaissance 1350–1600* (Berkeley: University of California Press, 1987), especially chapter 4: *'Improvvisatori* and their Relationship to Sixteenth-Century Music': 76–99.

INTABULATION

Ralf Mattes, in his brief chapter 'Ornamentation and Improvisation after 1300', in Ross Duffin (ed.), *A Performer's Guide to Medieval Music* (Indiana University Press, 2000) explains the Robertsbridge and Buxheimer manuscripts. There is more comprehensive information (especially on Josquin Desprez and intabulation) in Robert Toft, *Aural Images of Lost Traditions* (University of Toronto Press, 1992).

Ralph Maier's 'Assessing Textual Value: Vihuela Intabulations and the Music of Josquin' (www.ralphmaier.com/index_files/Page510.htm) discusses the relationship between instrumental practice and singers.

Jacob Heringman's liner notes to his recording of *Josquin de Prez: Sixteenth Century Lute Settings* (Discipline Global Mobile DGM0006) is an illuminating overview of the Josquin lute intabulations. Pepe Rey's liner notes to Carlos Mena's recording of Victoria choral music arranged for voice and lute or vihuela (*Et Jesum*, Harmonia Mundi HMG 507042) is similarly informative. Both recordings are examples of a performance practice common in the sixteenth and seventeenth centuries which has only rarely been embraced by the early music movement.

ORNAMENTATION AND PERFORMANCE PRACTICE

Extracts from Adrian Coclico's *Compendium*, Finck's *Practica Musica* and Maffei's letter can be found in Carol MacClintock's anthology, *Readings in the History of Music in Performance* (Bloomington: Indiana University Press, 1982) together with passages from Zacconi, Dowland and many others. Zarlino's thoughts on singing are translated in *The Art of Counterpoint: Part Three of Le Istitutioni Harmoniche*, 1558, trans. Guy Marco and Claude Palisca (New York: Norton, 1968).

Vicentino's *L'Antica Musica* is published in an English translation by Maria Rika Maniates as *Ancient Music Adapted for Modern Practice* (Newhaven: Yale University Press, 1996).

Howard Mayer Brown reviews ten key ornamentation treatises in *Embellishing 16th-Century Music* (Oxford University Press, 1976) and there is a comprehensive list of pedagogical sources in Ernest Ferand, 'Didactic Embellishment Literature in the Late Renaissance: a Survey of Sources', in Jan LaRue (ed.), *Aspects of Medieval and Renaissance Music: a Birthday Offering to Gustave Reese* (Oxford University Press, 1967).

There are insightful writings on early vocal technique by Richard Wistreich, 'Reconstructing pre-Romantic Singing Technique', in Potter, *Companion to Singing*: 78–91. This is a basic overview of technical matters, many of which are expanded upon in *Warrior, Courtier, Singer: Giulio Cesare Brancaccio and the Performance of Identity in the Late Renaissance* (Aldershot: Ashgate, 2007). For Monteverdi and singing see his *'La voce e grata assai, ma...:* Monteverdi on Singing', *Early Music* 21 (1994): 7–19; he is also joint editor (with John Whenham) of *The Cambridge Companion to Monteverdi* (Cambridge University Press, 2007).

Murray C. Bradshaw explores the relationship between Conforti's handbook and his compositions in 'Giovanni Luca Conforti and Vocal Embellishment: from Formula to Artful Improvisation', *Performance Practice Review* 8:2 (1995): 5–27.

British Library Egerton MS 2971 is a valuable source of information on Italian practices in England, for which see Mary Cyr, 'A Seventeenth Century Source of Ornamentation for Voice and Viol: British Museum MS. Egerton 2971' *RMA Research Chronicle* 9 (1971): 53–72 and further analysis of two songs by Caccini in John Bass, 'Would Caccini Approve?' *Early Music* 36:1 (2008): 81–93.

The key primary division treatises are:

Giovanni Bassano, *Ricercati, Passaggi et cadentie* (Venice, 1585).
Giovanni Battista Bovicelli, *Regole, passaggi di musica, madrigali et motetti passeggiati* (Venice, 1594).
Giovanni Luca Conforti, *Breve et Facile Maniera...per cantare...*(Venice, 1593).
Girolamo Dalla Casa, *Il Vero Modo di Diminuir* (Venice, 1584).
Francesco Rognoni, *Selva di varii passaggi* (Venice, 1620).

WOMEN SINGERS

The AHRB-funded *Dangerous Graces* project website (Female Musicians at the Courts of Ferrara and Parma, 1565–1589) has sound files, scores and biographies, and links to the ensemble Musica Secreta which is dedicated to the research and performance of music by women musicians of the period (www.soton.ac.uk/~lastras/secreta/dangerous-graces.htm).

Isabelle Emerson, *Five Centuries of Women Singers* (Westport, CT: Praeger, 2005) contains biographies of the leading women singers. The most comprehensive account of the *concerto delle donne* is still Anthony Newcomb, *The Madrigal at Ferrara*, 2 vols. (Princeton University Press, 1980).

The life of Francesco Rasi and his contemporaries is discussed in Warren Kirkendale, *The Court Musicians in Florence during the Principate of the Medici* (Florence: Leo S. Olschki Editore, 1993): 556–603 (with extensive quotes from his letters in Italian). For a discussion of his music see Carol MacClintock, 'The Monodies of Francesco Rasi', *Journal of the American Musicological Society* 14:1 (1961): 31–6.

Key primary sources are:

Giulio Caccini, *Le Nuove Musiche* (Florence, 1602); ed. and trans. H. Wilby Hitchcock (Madison, WI: A-R Editions, 1970).

John Dowland, *Andreas Ornithoparcus His Micrologus or Introduction: Containing the Art of Singing* (1609) (Whitefish, MT: Kessinger Publishing, 2010).

Marin Mersenne, *Harmonie universelle* (1636) (see MacClintock (1979): 170–5.

Michael Praetorius, *Syntagma Musicum*, 3 vols. (Wolfenbüttel, 1619); vol. III trans. and ed. Jeffery Kite-Powell (Oxford University Press, 2004).

4 THE AGE OF THE VIRTUOSO

THE FLORENTINE *INTERMEDI* OF 1589

The British Library has a copy of Bastiano de' Rossi, *Descrizione dell'apparato, e degl'intermedi. Fatti per la commedia rappresentata in Firenze nelle nozze de'serenissimi don Ferdinando Medici, e madama Cristina di Loreno ...* (Florence, 1589). The event is documented in detail (from *trilli* to toilet buckets) in James Saslow, *The Medici Wedding of 1589: Florentine Festival as Theatrum Mundi* (New Haven: Yale University Press, 1996) and Cavalieri's contribution is explored in Warren Kirkendale, *Emilio de'Cavalieri: 'Gentilhuomo Romano'* (Florence: Leo S. Olschki Editore, 2001); the music is available in a modern edition as *Musique des Intermèdes de la Pellegrina* with critical commentary (in French) by Federico Ghisi, D. P. Walker and J. Jacquot. Nina Treadwell, 'She descended on a cloud "from the highest spheres": Florentine Monody "alla Romanina"', *Cambridge Opera Journal* 16/1 (2004): 1–22 discusses Vittoria Archilei's first aria and the distinction between composers and performers. Andrew Parrott and Hugh Keyte created a spectacular television version which was subsequently made available on laser disc and VHS in 1991 but sadly has not been released on DVD. There is a 1993 recording, however: *Una Stravaganza dei Medici: Intermedi (1589) per 'La Pellegrina'* EMI Reflexe CDC 7 47998 2. Details of other recordings can be found on the Medieval Music and Arts Foundation website: www.medieval.org/emfaq/cds/sny63362.htm.

CASTRATI

There are two general histories of the castrato phenomenon: Patrick Barbier, *The World of the Castrati: the History of an Extraordinary Operatic Phenomenon*, trans. Margaret Crossland (London: Souvenir Press, 1996) and Angus Heriot,

The Castrati in Opera (London: Calder, 1960) which includes a chapter on Filippo Balatri, the only castrato to have written an autobiography. There is a concise overview in chapter 2, 'Castrati' in John Rosselli, *Singers of Italian Opera* (Cambridge University Press, 1992). For the early history of the castrati at the Mantuan court see Richard Sher, 'Guglielmo Gonzaga and the Castrati', *Renaissance Quarterly* 33:1 (1980): 33–56. Farinelli and the film of his life are the starting point for Katherine Bergeron, 'The Castrato as History' *Cambridge Opera Journal* 8:2 (1996): 167–84. For the castrato in France, see Lionel Sawkins, 'For and against the Order of Nature: Who Sang the Soprano?', *Early Music* 15: 3 (1987): 315–24. There are many profiles of individual castrati, including Kenneth James, 'Venanzio Rauzzini and the Search for Musical Perfection' *Bath History*, vol. III (Gloucester: Alan Sutton, 1990): 90–113, Daniel Heartz, 'Farinelli Revisited', *Early Music* 18: 3 (1990): 430–43, Nicholas Clapton's 'Carlo Broschi Farinelli: Aspects of his Technique and Performance', *Journal for Eighteenth-Century Studies* 28:3 (2005): 323–38 and *Moreschi: the Last Castrato* (London: Haus Publishing, 2004). The 1902 and 1904 Vatican recordings made by Moreschi are available on Opal CD 9823. On the demise of the castrato see J. Q. Davies, 'Velutti in Speculum', *Cambridge Opera Journal* 17:3 (2005): 271–301.

There are many publications dealing with the wider issues of musical castration and gender, including Roger Freitas, 'The Eroticism of Emasculation: Confronting the Baroque Body of the Castrato', *The Journal of Musicology* 20:2 (2003): 196–249 and Alexandros Constansis, *Hybrid Vocal Personae*, unpublished PhD thesis, University of York, 2009.

SINGERS' BIOGRAPHIES

For contemporary history of singers from castrati to Cuzzoni see chapter 2 of Giambattista Mancini, *Pensieri e Riflessioni Pratiche sopra il Canto Figurato* (Vienna, 1774) trans. Pietro Buzzi as *Practical Reflections on the Figurative Art of Singing* (Boston, 1912). Ellen Clayton gives a nineteenth-century view of thirty-four women singers in *Queens of Song: Being Memoirs of Some of the Most Celebrated Female Vocalists* (New York: Harper Brothers, 1865, facs. Whitefish, MT: Kessinger Publishing, 2005); shorter annotated biographies of women singers including Vittoria Archilei, Francesca Caccini, Barbara Strozzi, Anna Renzi, Gertrude Mara and several nineteenth-century singers can be found in Isabelle Emerson, *Five Centuries of Women Singers* (Westport, CT: Praeger, 2005). There are substantial essays on Margherita Durastanti, Senesino, Cuzzoni and Bordoni in C. Steven LaRue, *Handel and His Singers* (Oxford: Clarendon Press, 1995). Michael Kelly's memoirs are published as *Solo Recital: the Reminiscences of Michael Kelly*, ed. Herbert van Thal (London: Folio Society, 1972). Henry Pleasants, *The Great Singers* (London: Victor Gollancz, 1967) is a well informed and enthusiastically written account of singers from the earliest times to the twentieth century.

The *History* of Charles Burney and the journals from his research trips to Europe are invaluable primary source material; all are available in facsimile either in print or online:

The Present State of Music in France and Italy (London, 1771; facs. Elibron Classics, 2005).

The Present State of Music in Germany, the Netherlands and United Provinces (London, 1773, facs. Travis and Emery, 2003).

A General History of Music, From the Earliest Ages to the Present Period, 4 vols., (London, 1782 and 1789).

ORNAMENTATION AND PEDAGOGY

Luigi Zenobi's *c.* 1600 letter to an as yet unidentified prince, perhaps the most vivid description of the singer's art, is translated with a commentary in Bonnie Blackburn and Edward Lowinsky, 'Luigi Zenobi and his Letter on the Perfect Musician', *Studi Musicali 22* (1993): 61–114; repr. in Bonnie Blackburn, *Composition, Printing and Performance: Studies in Renaissance Music* (Aldershot: Ashgate, 2000).

Key primary sources by country are as follows:

For Italy:

G. Crescentini, *Raccolta di Esercizi per il canto all'uso del vocalizzoi/Recueil d'exercices pour la vocalisation musicale* (Paris, *c.* 1811; facs. *Méthodes and Traités*, Serie ii/1 Paris: Fuzeau, 2005).

Giambattista Mancini, *Pensieri e Riflessioni Pratiche sopra il Canto Figurato* (Vienna, 1774, rev. 1777); English trans. E. Foreman, *Practical Reflections on Figured Singing* (Champaign, IL: Pro Musica Press, 1967).

Patricia Howard, *A Critical Translation from the Italian of Vincenzo Manfredini's Difesa Della Musica Moderna/In Defence of Modern Music* (1788) (New York: Edwin Mellen Press, 2002).

Pier Francesco Tosi, *Opinioni de' cantori antichi e moderni* (Bologna, 1723); English translation J. E. Galliard as *Observations on the Florid Song* (London, 1742); facs. repr. London: Reeves, 1967.

For Germany:

Johann Friedrich Agricola, *Anleitung zur Singkunst* (Leipzig, 1757; facs. rep. Leipzig, 1966/1998); trans. into English as *Introduction to the Art of Singing*, ed. Julie Anne Baird (Cambridge University Press, 1997).

Emily Anderson (ed.), *The Letters of Mozart and his Family*, 3rd edn rev. Stanley Sadie and Fiona Smart (London: Macmillan, 1985).

John Butt, *Music Education and the Art of Performance in the German Baroque* (Cambridge University Press, 1994) also refers to many lesser-known singing treatises in the seventeenth and eighteenth centuries.

Johann Adam Hiller, *Anweisung zum musikalisch-zierlichen Gesange* (1780) ed. and trans. Suzanne J. Beicken as *Treatise on Vocal Performance and Ornamentation* (Cambridge University Press, 2001).

Johann Quantz, *Versuch einer Anweisung die Flöte traversiere zu spielen* (Berlin, 1752); trans. and ed. Edward R. Reilly as *On Playing the Flute* (2nd edn, London: Faber, 2001).

For France:

Bénigne de Bacilly, *Remarques curieuses sur l'art de bien chanter* (1668) (facs. edn. Geneva: Minkoff, 1971); English trans. ed. Austin B. Caswell, *Commentary upon the Art of Proper Singing* (New York, 1968).
Girolamo Crescentini, *Vingt-cinq nouvelles vocalises ou études de l'art du chant* (Paris, 1818–32; facs. *Méthodes et Traités*, Serie II/II Paris: Fuzeau, 2005).
Bernardo Mengozzi *et al.*, *Méthode de chant du Conservatoire de Musique* (Paris, 1804; facs. *Méthodes et Traités*, Serie II/I, Paris: Fuzeau, 2005).
Jean Millet, *La Belle méthode ou l'art de bien chanter* (1666); repr. with intro. by Albert Cohen (New York: Da Capo Press, 1973).

For England:

Domenico Corri, *Singers' Preceptor* (London: 1810 and New York: Garland, 1995).
John Galliard, *Observations on the Florid Song by Pier Francesco Tosi* (London, 1743; facs. London: Reeves, 1967).
Richard Mount Edgcumbe, *Musical Reminiscences of the Earl of Mount Edgcumbe: Containing an Account of the Italian Opera in England from 1773 to 1834* (London, 1834; repr. New York, Da Capo Press, 1973).
Nicola Vaccai, *Metodo Pratico* (1833); trans. and ed. Michael Aspinall (Turin: Giancano Zedde 1999).

MUSICAL EDUCATION

The education of children and orphans is the subject of Jane Baldauf-Berdes, *Women Musicians of Venice: Musical Foundations 1525–1855* (Oxford: Clarendon Press, 1993). The Porpora Project is dedicated to the life and work of the great teacher and composer Nicola Porpora, www.porporaproject.com/nicola_porpora.htm.
Selected secondary literature containing useful insights into performance practice includes:

Clive Brown, *Classical and Romantic Performing Practice 1750–1900* (Oxford University Press, 1999).
Howard Mayer Brown and Stanley Sadie (eds.), *Performance Practice: Music After 1600* (New York: Norton/Grove Handbooks in Music, 1990).
Mary Cyr, 'Eighteenth-Century French and Italian Singing: Rameau's Writing for the Voice', *Music & Letters*, 61/3–4 (1980): 318–37.
Theodore Fenner, *Opera in London: Views of the Press 1785–1830* (Carbondale, IL: Southern Illinois University Press, 1994).

Colin Lawson and Robin Stowell, *The Historical Performance of Music: an Introduction* (Cambridge University Press, 1999).

Leech-Wilkinson, Daniel, '*Portamento* and Musical Meaning', *Journal of Musicological Research* 25 (2006): 233–61.

Daniel Heartz, 'From Garrick to Gluck: the Reform of Theatre and Opera in the Mid-Eighteenth Century', *Proceedings of the Royal Musical Association* (1967–8): 111–27.

On Rossini's singers see Leonella Caprioli, 'Singing Rossini', in Emanuele Senici (ed.), *The Cambridge Companion to Rossini* (Cambridge University Press, 2004); for Bellini and Donizetti, see William Ashbrook, *Donizetti and his Operas* (Cambridge University Press, 1984) and Stelios Galatopoulos, *Bellini: Life, Times, Music* (London: Sanctuary, 2002).

5   THE NINETEENTH-CENTURY REVOLUTION

There are some excellent biographies of individual singers, and at least two good overviews:

Rupert Christiansen, *Prima Donna* (London: Bodley Head, 1984).

Ellen Creathorne Clayton, *Queens of Song: Being Memoirs of Some of the Most Celebrated Female Vocalists* (New York: Harper, 1865; facs. Whitefish, MT: Kessinger Publishing, 2005).

Isabelle Emerson, *Five Centuries of Women Singers* (Westport, CT: Praeger, 2005).

Elizabeth Forbes, *Mario and Grisi: a Biography* (London: Victor Gollancz, 1985).

Charles Neilson Gattey, *Queens of Song* (London: Barrie and Jenkins, 1979).

Barbara Kendall-Davies, *The Life and Work of Pauline Viardot Garcia*. Vol. 1: *The Years of Fame 1836–1863* (Amersham: Cambridge Scholars Press, 2003).

Alan Jefferson, *Lotte Lehmann 1888–1976: a Centenary Biography* (London: Julia MacRae, 1988).

Henry Pleasants, *The Great Singers* (London: Victor Gollancz, 1967).

James Radomski, *Manuel García (1775–1832): Chronicle of the Life of a Bel Canto Tenor at the Dawn of Romanticism* (Oxford University Press, 2000).

John Rosselli, *Singers of Italian Opera: the History of a Profession* (Cambridge University Press, 1992).

Most singers referred to in the text have biographies in *Grove Online*.

Critical appraisal by non-musicians provides essential background to the period. For the London opera seasons to 1834 see Lord Mount Edgcumbe's *Musical Reminiscences of the Earl of Mount Edgcumbe: Containing an Account of the Italian Opera in England from 1773 to 1834* (London, 1834; repr. New York: Da Capo, 1973), and for 1830–60 the writings of Henry Chorley are invaluable: *Thirty Years' Musical Recollections* (New York: Vienna House, 1972). Hermann Klein's *Thirty Years of Musical Life in London* (New York: Century, 1903) is similarly informative, and the anthology of his criticism for *The Gramophone* (Herman Klein, *Herman Klein and the Gramophone*, ed. William R. Moran (Portland,

OR: Amadeus Press, 1990), is essential reading and includes his 1923 essay on bel canto with reference to Mozart (note that he lost one of the n's in his first name between the two publications). Stendhal's *The Life of Rossini*, trans. Richard Coe (London: Calder, 1985) is a readable though somewhat discursive memoir; Edmond Michotte's *Richard Wagner's Visit to Rossini (Paris 1860)* and *An Evening at Rossini's in Beau-Sejour (Passy) in 1858*, trans. Herbert Weinstock (University of Chicago Press, 1968) was written from notes taken many years before the actual events, but is enlightening nevertheless.

Information on Brigida Banti is to be found in Mount Edgcumbe's *Musical Reminiscences, Solo Recital: the Reminiscences of Michael Kelly*, ed. Herbert van Thal (London: Folio Society, 1972) and H. C. Robbins Landon, *Haydn Chronicle and Works: Haydn in England 1791–1795* (London: Thames and Hudson, 1983). See also Austin Caswell, 'Mme Cinti-Damoreau and the Embellishment of Italian Opera in Paris: 1820–1845', *Journal of the American Musicological Society* 28 (1975): 459–92.

FRENCH PRIMARY SOURCES

Editions Fuzeau (Paris) published facsimile editions of all the major Paris Conservatoire singing treatises in seven volumes in the series *Méthodes et Traités* (2005), including:

Girolamo Crescentini, *Raccolta di Esercizi per il canto all'uso del vocalizzo Recueil d'exercises pour la vocalisation musicale* (Paris, c.1811; facs. *Méthodes et Traités*, Serie ii/i, Paris, 2005).
Vingt-cinq nouvelles vocalises ou etudes de l'art du chant (Paris, 1818–32; facs. *Méthodes et Traités*, Serie ii/ii, Paris, 2005).
Manuel Garcia, *Exercises pour la voix* (Paris, c. 1835; facs. *Méthodes et Traités*, Serie ii/iii, Paris, 2005).
Alexis de Garaudé, *Méthode Complète de chant* (Paris, 1841; facs. *Méthodes et Traités*, Serie ii/ii, Paris, 2005).
F.-J. Fétis, *Méthode des Méthodes de chant basée sur les principes des Ecoles les plus célèbres d'Italie et de la France* (Paris and Brussels, 1870; facs. *Méthodes et Traités*, Serie ii/ii, Paris, 2005).
Bernardo Mengozzi et al., *Méthode de chant du Conservatoire de Musique* (Paris, 1804; facs. *Méthodes et Traités*, Serie ii/i, Paris, 2005).

THE GARCIA FAMILY

The elder Garcia's life and career are documented in James Radomski, *Manuel García (1775–1832): Chronicle of the Life of a Bel Canto Tenor at the Dawn of Romanticism* (Oxford University Press, 2000). Garcia's treatise is available in a modern English translation: *Complete Treatise on the Art of Singing*, the editions of 1841 and 1872 collated, edited and translated Donald V. Paschke (New York, 1984); the shorter, later English version is *Garcia's New Treatise on the Art of Singing* (London, 1857, 1870 and n.d. *c.*1915); *Hints on Singing* is available in facsimile from Kessinger Publishing Ltd. There is no recent biography of Garcia; Sterling Mackinlay's *Garcia the Centenarian and his Times* (Edinburgh: Blackwood, 1908) was written soon after his death. The Countess de Merlin's 1840 *Memoirs and Letters of Madame Malibran* is available in facsimile from Kessinger Publishing Ltd, and Barbara Kendall-Davies, *The Life and Work of Pauline Viardot García*, Vol. 1: *The Years of Fame 1836–1863* (Amersham: Cambridge Scholars Press, 2003) is the first of three projected volumes on Viardot. The relationship between Viardot and Turgenev is explored in Robert Dessaix, *Twilight of Love: Travels with Turgenev* (London: Simon and Schuster, 2005) and in Patrick Waddington, 'Henry Chorley, Pauline Viardot and Turgenev: a Musical and Literary Friendship', *Musical Quarterly* 47 (1981): 165–92. The Wikipedia entry on Viardot includes a list of her compositions: en.wikipedia.org/wiki/Pauline_Viardot.

REGISTERS AND VOCAL TECHNIQUE

James Stark has a comprehensive chapter on registers in *Bel Canto: A History of Vocal Pedagogy* (University of Toronto Press, 1999), with much discussion of Garcia.

For an explanation of how formants work see Johan Sundberg, 'Where Does the Sound Come from?' in John Potter (ed.), *The Cambridge Companion to Singing* (Cambridge University Press, 2000), 240–6.

WAGNER

Wagner's own writings are extensive; a good starting point is *Actors and Singers*, trans. William Ashton Ellis (Lincoln: University of Nebraska Press, 1995). Julius Hey's pedagogical works are unfortunately not available in English translation, but are still used in Germany: *Richard Wagner als Vortragsmeister 1864–1876. Erinnerungen von Julius Hey* (Leipzig: Breitkopf and Haertel, 1911) and *Der kleine Hey* (Mainz: Schott Verlag, 1900). The secondary literature is vast, including publications we have drawn on here.

The year 1992 saw a huge increase in Wagner scholarship, with three comprehensive anthologies: the *Wagner Handbook* edited by Ulrich Müller and Peter Wapnewski, trans. John Deathridge (Cambridge, MA and London: Harvard University Press, 1992) contains many key articles, including Oswald Bauer, 'Performance History: a Brief Survey', John Deathridge, 'A Brief History of Wagner Research' and Jens Malte Fischer, '*Sprechgesang* or Bel Canto: Toward a History of Singing Wagner' (524–46).

The Wagner Compendium: A Guide to Wagner's Life and Music London: Thames and Hudson, 1992), edited by Barry Millington, contains similarly informative chapters by David Breckbill on 'Singing' and Stewart Spencer on 'Wagner Literature: Biographies' and 'Reception'.

Wagner in Performance, ed. Barry Millington and Stewart Spencer (New Haven and London: Yale University Press, 1992) includes David Breckbill,

'Wagner on Record: Re-evaluating Singing in the Early Years' (153–67), Clive Brown, 'Performing Practice' (99–119), Christopher Fifield, 'Conducting Wagner: the Search for Melos' (1–14), Joseph Horowitz, 'Anton Seidl and America's Wagner Cult' (168–81) and Desmond Shawe-Taylor, 'Wagner and His Singers' (15–28). We have also drawn on the following:

William Ashbrook, 'The First Singers of *Tristan und Isolde*', *The Opera Quarterly*, 3:4 (1985/6): 11–23.

Henri de Curzon, 'Cosima Wagner and Bayreuth', *Musical Times* 71:1051 (1930): 794–6.

Richard Fricke, *Wagner in Rehearsal 1875–1876: the Diaries of Richard Fricke*, trans. George R. Fricke, ed. James Deaville with Evan Baker (Stuyvesant, NY: Pendragon Press, 1998. Originally *Bayreuth vor dreissig Jahren. Erinnerungen an Wahnfried und aus dem Festspielhause Dresden*, 1906).

Robert Gutman, *Richard Wagner: the Man, His Mind and His Music* (London: Penguin Books, 1971).

Matti Leisma, 'Bel canto ja Richard Wagnerin laulajaihanne' [Bel canto and Richard Wagner's ideal singer], *Musiikki* 22:4 (1992): 25–66 (in Finnish).

Ernest Newman, *Wagner as Man and Artist* (2nd edn, London: Victor Gollancz, 1924 repr. 1963).

Heinrich Porges, *Wagner Rehearsing the 'Ring': an Eye-Witness Account of the Stage Rehearsals of the First Bayreuth Festival*, trans. Robert L. Jacobs (Cambridge University Press, 1983). Originally published in German as *Die Bühnenproben zu den Bayreuther Festspielen des Jahres 1876*, in instalments in *Bayreuther Blätter*, 1881–96.

Stanley Sadie (ed.), *Wagner and his Operas* (London: Macmillan, 2000).

Geoffrey Skelton, *Wagner at Bayreuth: Experiment and Tradition* (London: Barrie and Rockliff, 1965).

Carla Maria Verdino-Süllwold, *We Need a Hero! Heldentenors from Wagner's Time to the Present* (New York: Weiala Press, 1989).

6 A GREAT TRADITION: SINGING THROUGH HISTORY – HISTORY THROUGH SINGING

There are many useful introductions to Indian music and general surveys, but this list will focus on a few titles that more specifically address the vocal traditions. A few are especially noteworthy as they include recordings, so the reader can hear something of what is being written about even if the ratio of sounds to words is low. Such books usually have the even greater advantage of being co-authored by a Western scholar and an Indian performer. The first one was Neil Sorrell and Ram Narayan, *Indian Music in Performance: a Practical Introduction* (Manchester University Press, 1980) but it pre-dated the CD era so the music examples came on a cassette. The book is a general introduction but is also concerned with the closest connection between an instrument and the voice. Also of an introductory nature and primarily a work of reference is Joep Bor (ed.), *The Raga Guide: a Survey of 74 Hindustani Ragas* (Nimbus Records,

1999). The four accompanying CDs illustrate each raga, often with performances by leading singers, so they are an excellent resource for listening to singing styles, ornamentation and a variety of compositions.

Also within the Hindustani tradition are works which include studies of the gharanas. Daniel Neuman, *The Life of Music in North India: the Organization of an Artistic Tradition* (University of Chicago Press, 1990) places them in a social and historical context, while Vamanrao Deshpande, *Indian Musical Traditions: An Aesthetic Study of the Gharanas in Hindustani Music* trans. S. H. Deshpande (Bombay: Popular Prakashan, 1973) attempts a brief discussion of their musical characteristics. More detailed in that respect is Bonnie C. Wade, *Khyāl: Creativity within North India's Classical Music Tradition* (Cambridge University Press, 1984), which was published with a cassette of examples. Among more recent studies of khyal is Deepak Raja, *Khayal Vocalism: Continuity within Change* (New Delhi: D. K. Printword, 2009). Ritwik Sanyal and Richard Widdess, *Dhrupad: Tradition and Performance in Indian Music* (Aldershot: Ashgate, 2004) is a thorough investigation of dhrupad and the ideal book to consult on that topic. It is another co-authored scholar-performer volume with CD examples that enhance its appeal.

Carnatic music is also well represented in the literature. An excellent introduction, again benefiting from co-authorship involving a leading performer and a CD of examples, is T. Viswanathan and Matthew Harp Allen, *Music in South India – the Karṇāṭak Concert Tradition and Beyond: Experiencing Music, Expressing Culture* (Oxford University Press, 2004) which includes quite a detailed analysis of the kriti form. George E. Ruckert, *Music in North India: Experiencing Music, Expressing Culture* (Oxford University Press, 2004) performs a similar function, though more briefly, for Hindustani music, with a CD of diverse examples, Ludwig Pesch, *The Illustrated Companion to South Indian Classical Music* (New Delhi: Oxford University Press, 1999) is a lengthy introduction to Carnatic music, with a useful chapter on voice training.

7 CLASSICAL SINGING IN THE TWENTIETH CENTURY: RECORDING AND RETRENCHMENT

EARLY RECORDING

Oliver Read and Walter Welch, *From Tinfoil to Stereo: Evolution of the Phonograph* (Indianapolis: Howard W. Sams, 1959; rev. edn University of Florida Press, 2006) is still one of the most comprehensive histories. Primary sources include Roland Gelatt, *The Fabulous Phonograph* (London: Cassell, 1956) and Jerrold Northrop Moore, *A Voice in Time: the Gramophone of Fred Gaisberg 1873–1951* (London: Hamish Hamilton, 1976).

For an analysis of the philosophical and aesthetic discourse created by the collision between the arts and technology, see the works of Friedrich Kittler: *Discourse Networks 1800/1900* (Stanford University Press, 1990); *Gramophone, Film, Typewriter*, Stanford University Press, 1999); and *Optical Media* (Cambridge: Polity Press, 2010).

For early recordings mentioned in the text see:
Henry Pleasants, 'Tracking Down the Oldest Singing Voice', *Recorded Sound* 85 (1984): 12–16. The earliest Schubert recordings are discussed in Keith Hardwick's (1997) liner notes to *Schubert Lieder on Record*, vol. I, EMI CHS 5661502. Adeline Patti's recording of 'Voi che sapete' is on Pearl GEMM CD9312. The life of Adelina Patti is one of many singers reviewed in Rupert Christiansen, *Prima Donna* (London: Bodley Head, 1984). See also chapter 4 of *The Mapleson Memoirs: the Career of an Operatic Impresario 1858–1888*, ed. Harold Rosenthal (London: Putnam, 1966).

LIEDER AS ART SONG

The dissemination of Schubert songs in France is discussed in David Tunley, *Salons, Singers and Songs: a Background to Romantic French Song* (Aldershot: Ashgate, 2002). Henry Finck, *Songs and Songwriters* (London: Murray, 1900) is an overview of song at the turn of the century. Early examples of successful singers publishing books on *Lieder* include Lotte Lehmann, *More than Singing: the Interpretation of Songs* (New York: Boosey and Hawkes, 1945; repr. Dover, 1985) and Elizabeth Schumann, *German Song* (London: Max Parrish, 1948). For a late twentieth-century analysis see Deborah Stein and Robert Spillman, *Poetry into Song: the Performance and Analysis of Lieder* (Oxford University Press, 1996).

RECORDINGS

Recordings of Mozart's 'Voi che sapete' have been re-released on CD: Adeline Patti, Pearl GEMM CD9312, and Nellie Melba's 1907 and 1910 versions Romophone 81011–2.

RECORD CRITICISM

The classic work on the history of singers on record is J. B. Steane's *The Grand Tradition* (London: Duckworth, 1974); equally important is Michael Scott's two-volume *The Record of Singing* (London: Duckworth 1977 and 1980) with illustrations from the Stuart-Liff Collection, and its third volume released as a 10 CD set with commentary as *The EMI Record of Singing 1926–1939* (SBT 0132).

8   POST-CLASSICAL: BEYOND THE MAINSTREAM

CANTORIAL SINGING

We have used the spelling *chazzan*, the guttural 'ch' giving the best approximation to the Hebrew pronunciation, but you will also find *chazan*, *chazz'n*, *hazzan* and other variants.

The first scholar to address the history of Jewish music in all its multi-layered complexity was Abraham Z. Idelsohn, who published *Jewish Music in its*

Historical Development in 1929 (repr. New York. Schocken Books, 1967). There is no comprehensive history of cantorial singing, but it is possible to construct one from the biographies of notable *chazzanim*. Many are included in Samuel Vigoda, *Legendary Voices: the Fascinating Lives of the Great Cantors* (M. P. Press, New York, 1981), and Mark Slobin's *Chosen Voices: the Story of the American Cantorate* (University of Illinois Press, 1989) has an excellent summary of the history, before focusing on the American experience up to the end of the twentieth century. For a recent study of the training regime in the modern American cantorate, see Judah M. Cohen, *The Making of a Reform Jewish Cantor: Musical Authority, Cultural Investment* (Indiana University Press, 2009). The two volumes of Sholom Kalib, *The Musical Tradition of the Eastern European Synagogue* (Syracuse University Press, 2002) contain useful definitions of key terms and many musical examples. An overview of the Golden Age with biographical and discographical information is provided by Alan Bilgora in 'Voices of Prayer and Praise', *Classic Record Collector* (August 2004).

The research on Salamone Rossi is summarised in Don Harrán, *Salamone Rossi: Jewish Musician in Late Renaissance Mantua* (Oxford University Press, 1999). Charles Burney's 1773 *The Present State of Music in Germany, the Netherlands and United Provinces* is available in a modern very readable facsimile from Travis and Emery (London, 2003) and Herman Klein's writing on Jewish music is to be found in *Herman Klein and the Gramophone*, ed. William R. Moran (Portland, OR: Amadeus Press, 1990). The information on Yossele Rosenblatt is taken from Samuel Rosenblatt, *Yossele Rosenblatt: the Story of his Life as Told by his Son* (Farrar, Strauss and Young, New York, 1954). There is information on cantorial influence on opera singing in John Potter, *Tenor: History of a Voice* (New Haven: Yale University Press, 2009): 11–113 and in Stephen Banfield, 'Stage and Screen Entertainers in the Twentieth Century', in John Potter (ed.), *The Cambridge Companion to Singing* (Cambridge University Press, 2000): 69–72.

For an ethnological anthropological approach to Jewish music see Philip Bohlman's trilogy *The Land Where Two Streams Flow: Music in the German-Jewish Community of Israel* (Urbana: University of Illinois Press, 1989), *The World Centre for Jewish Music in Palestine 1936–1940: Jewish Musical Life on the Eve of World War II* (Oxford University Press, 1992) and especially *Jewish Music and Modernity* (Oxford University Press, 2008).

ONLINE SOURCES

There are many online sources of information about cantorial singing, often written by cantors. Examples include: www.chazzanut.com/ biographies, techniques, music examples; www.newworldencyclopedia.org/entry/Cantor history, definition, training; chazzanut.org/ in Hebrew; news, articles, biographies; www.operanostalgia.be/html/Greatest_ Cantorial_Voices.htm an introduction to the topic aimed at opera fans; cantorcenter.blogspot.com/ recordings and biographies.

There is a substantial historical overview of Jewish music at *Grove Music Online*, www.oxfordmusiconline.com/public/page/subscriber_services, although it tends to focus on composers (where possible) rather than the outstanding singers who have been the drivers of cantorial song. The Milken Jewish Archive has short biographies and much other information about American cantors at www. milkenarchive.org/.

The most comprehensive sources are the Dartmouth Jewish Sound Archive: www.dartmouth.edu/~djsa, which holds more than 25,000 examples of Jewish music including all the most famous cantors of the twentieth and twenty-first centuries, and the Judaica Sound Archives at Florida Atlantic University: faujsa. fau.edu/jsa/home.php. YouTube also features many video and audio examples of cantorial singing.

There are very few theoretical writings on the evolution of vocal style and technique, but for an example of a three-stage theory of stylistic development which assumes renewal taking place after a period of retrenchment or stagnation, see John Potter, *Vocal Authority* (Cambridge University Press, 1998), especially chapter 10, 'Towards a Theory of Vocal Style': 190–9.

The period of Leonin and Perotin is explored in Craig Wright, *Music and Ceremony at Notre Dame of Paris 500–1550* (Cambridge University Press, 1989) and current ideas on its performance in Anna Maria Busse Berger, *Medieval Music and the Art of Memory* (University of California Press, 2005).

The debate on the nature of early music began with Nicholas Kenyon (ed.), *Authenticity and Early Music* (Oxford University Press, 1988), in which scholars and performers argue for and against 'authenticity'. The complexity of the problem is demonstrated in Laurence Dreyfus, 'Early Music Defended against its Devotees: a Theory of Historical Performance in the 20th Century', *Musical Quarterly* 69 (1983): 297–322, and there is a brief history of the evolution of the movement and its relationship with history in John Potter, 'Past Perfect and Future Fictions', *Basler Jahrbuch für Historische Musikpraxis* (Basel: Amadeus Verlag 2002), a subject first broached in Richard Taruskin, *Text and Act: Essays on Music and Performance* (Oxford University Press, 1995). The current position is summarised in John Butt's 'Authenticity' in *Grove Online* (www.oxfordmusiconline.com/subscriber/).

The debate continues with philosopher Peter Kivy's *Authenticities, Philosophies, and Reflections on Musical Performance* (Ithaca and London: Cornell University Press, 1995), John Butt's *Playing with History: the Historical Approach to Musical Performance* (Cambridge University Press, 2002) and Bruce Haynes's *The End of Early Music* (Oxford University Press, 2007). Daniel Leech-Wilkinson, *The Modern Invention of Medieval Music: Scholarship, Ideology, Performance* (Cambridge University Press, 2002) is the first example of a revisionist history in which a musicologist acknowledges that there is very little evidence to support current ideas of performance practice.

The relationship between performance and musicology is explored in Anna Maria Friman, *Modern Performance of Sacred Medieval Music with Particular Reference to Women's Voices*, unpublished PhD thesis, University of York, 2008; the relationship of modern singing technique to possible historical techniques is the subject of Helena Daffern, *Distinguishing Characteristics of Vocal Techniques in the Specialist Performance of Early Music*, unpublished PhD thesis, University of York, 2008.

Useful sources of information on modern performance practice are:

Benjamin Bagby, '*Beowulf,* the *Edda,* and the Performance of Medieval Epic: Notes from the Workshop of a Reconstructed "Singer of Tales"', in Evelyn Birge Vitz, Nancy Freeman Regalado and Marilyn Lawrence (eds.), *Performing Medieval Narrative* (Cambridge: D. S. Brewer, 2005): 181–92.

Ross Duffin (ed.), *A Performer's Guide to Medieval Music* (Bloomington: Indiana University Press, 2000).

Joseph Dyer, 'The Voice in the Middle Ages', in John Potter (ed.), *The Cambridge Companion to Singing* (Cambridge University Press, 2000).

Martha Elliott, *Singing in Style* (New Haven: Yale University Press, 2006).

David Fallows and Tess Knighton (eds.), *Companion to Medieval and Renaissance Music* (London: Dent, 1992; repr. Oxford University Press, 1998).

Anna Maria Friman, *Modern Performance of Sacred Medieval Music with Particular Reference to Women's Voices*, unpublished PhD thesis, University of York, 2008.

Timothy McGee, *The Sound of Medieval Song* (Oxford: Clarendon Press, 1998).

Timothy McGee (ed.), *Improvisation in the Arts of the Middle Ages and Renaissance* (Kalamazoo: Western Michigan University Press, 2003).

Robin Stowell and Colin Lawson (eds.), *Cambridge History of Musical Performance* (Cambridge University Press, forthcoming).

DADA, FUTURISM

Information about Kurt Schwitters (including a recording of Schwitters performing the Ursonate) can be found at http://ubu.clc.wvu.edu/sound/schwitters. html. Useful background on the two movements can be found in Michael Kirby, *Futurist Performance* (New York, 1971), Hans Richter, *Dada: Art and Anti-art* (London: Thames and Hudson, 1978) and Richard Huelsenbeck, *Memoirs of a Dada Drummer* (Berkeley: University of California Press, 1969).

CATHY BERBERIAN, LUCIANO BERIO

There is comprehensive information about the singer on the official Cathy Berberian website, www.cathyberberian.com/ and an analysis of *Sequenza III* at www.sequenza.me.uk/Berberian_web.htm. Charles Amirkhanian interviews Berberian at her home in Milan here: www.archive.org/details/ CBerberianOTG. Information about Berio's life and works can be found at www.lucianoberio.org/en.

The following books and articles are essential reading on Berberian and Berio:

Istvan Anhalt, *Alternative Voices: Essays on Contemporary Vocal and Choral Composition* (Toronto, London: University of Toronto Press, 1985).
Luciano Berio, *Remembering the Future* (Harvard University Press, 2006).
Joke Dame, 'Voices within the Voices' in Adam Krims (ed.), *Music/Ideology: Resisting the Aesthetic* (Amsterdam: G+B Arts International, 1998): 233–46.
Jean-François Lyotard, 'A Few Words to Sing', in Adam Krims (ed.), *Music/Ideology: Resisting the Aesthetic* (Amsterdam: G+B Arts International, 1998): 15–36.
David Osmond-Smith, '"The Tenth Oscillator": the Work of Cathy Berberian 1958–1966', *Tempo* (2004).
David Osmond-Smith (ed.), *Two Interviews* (New York and London: Marion Boyars, 1985).

EXTENDED VOCAL TECHNIQUE

The two key texts are Michael Edgerton, *The 20th Century Voice* (Oxford University Press, 2004) and Trevor Wishart, *On Sonic Art* (Amsterdam: Harwood, 1996 – also includes CD). There is also useful information on repertoire and performance in Sharon Mabry, *Exploring Twentieth-Century Vocal Music: a Practical Guide to Innovations in Performance and Repertoire* (Oxford University Press, 2002). There is extensive information on Roy Hart at www.roy-hart.com/. For throat singing see Theodore Levin and Michael Edgerton, 'The Throat Singers of Tuva', *Scientific American* (September, 1999).

Most key words and topics (voice types, genres, styles etc) have substantial entries in *Grove Online*.

9   THE EMANCIPATION OF THE POPULAR VOICE

A selection of music hall singers including Dan Leno and Little Tich can be found on *The Golden Age of Music Hall* (Saydisc CD-SDL 380). First World War songs can be heard on *Keep the Home Fires Burning* (Saydisc CDSDL 358). *Rosa Ponselle in Opera and Song* (Nimbus NI 1777) is a three-CD set which demonstrates the breadth of Ponselle's repertoire (and there are several other Ponselle re-releases in the Nimbus catalogue).

The most complete overview of American popular singers of the twentieth century is Henry Pleasants, *The Great American Popular Singers* (New York: Gollancz 1974). Pleasants was a music critic steeped in both classical and jazz traditions, and his two books exploring the divide between genres are uniquely insightful: *Death of a Music? The Decline of the European Tradition and the Rise of Jazz* (London: Victor Gollancz, 1961) and *Classical Music and all that Jazz: an Adventure in Music Criticism* (London: Victor Gollancz, 1969). For the history of women in jazz see Linda Dahl, *Stormy Weather: the Music and Lives of a Century of Jazz Women* (New York: Limelight Editions, 1984).

There is a comprehensive outline of the history of popular music (focusing primarily on Western music) by Richard Middleton in *Grove Online*. Richard

Middleton, *Studying Popular Music* (Milton Keynes: Open University Press, 1990) is the standard work on the topic.

Philip R. Evans, *Al Jolson: a Bio-Discography* (Lanham, MD: Scarecrow Press, 1984) is a mine of information. More immediately approachable is Michael Freedland's *Al Jolson* (London: W. H. Allen, 1972: 8th edn Edgware: Valentine Mitchell, 2007).

The Jazz Singer has been re-released and remastered in an eightieth anniversary edition (DVD Z1 79920) with a bonus CD *The Early Sound Era* and commentary.

For crooners see Michael Pitts and Frank Hoffman, *The Rise of the Crooners* (Lanham, MD: Scarecrow Press, 2001) or Ian Whitcomb's web publication, *The Coming of the Crooners*: www.shsu.edu/~lis_fwh/book/roots_of_rock/support/crooner/EarlyCroonersIntro2.htm.

The standard work on the history of jazz singing (and some related genres) is Will Friedwald's idiosyncratic and prophetic *Jazz Singing* (London: Quartet Books, 1991). See also John Potter, 'Jazz Singing: the First 100 Years', in John Potter (ed.), *The Cambridge Companion to Singing* (Cambridge University Press, 2000).

Bing Crosby's early career is covered in great detail by Gary Giddins, *Bing Crosby: a Pocketful of Dreams – The Early Years 1903–1940* (New York: Back Bay Books, 2002); see also Michael Freedland's, *Bing Crosby: an Illustrated Biography* (London: André Deutsch, 1998) and Crosby's own memoirs, Bing Crosby and Pete Martin, *Call Me Lucky* (New York: Muller, 1953; repr. Da Capo Press, 2001).

There are many biographies of Frank Sinatra; a good starting point is the anthology of writings by Stephen Petrov and Leonard Mustazza (eds.), *The Frank Sinatra Reader* (Oxford University Press, 1997) which included a discography and bibliography.

10   SUNG AND UNSUNG: SINGERS AND SONGS OF THE NON-ENGLISH-SPEAKING WORLD

GERMANY

Two useful biographies are Stephen Bach, *Marlene Dietrich: Life and Legend* (University of Minnesota Press, 2011) and Donald Spoto, *Lenya: a Life* (London: Little, Brown and Company, 1989); Dietrich's autobiography is *Nehmt nur mein Leben* (Munich: Bertelsmann 1979; English translation as *My Life*, London: Weidenfeld and Nicolson 1989). There is a representative selection of singers including Dietrich on the CD *German Cabaret in the Twenties* (EPM 995982).

FRANCE

For the history of French popular music see David Tunley, *Salons, Singers and Songs: a Background to Romantic French Song 1830–1870* (Aldershot: Ashgate, 2002) and Peter Hawkins, *Chanson: the French Singer-songwriter from Bruant to the Present Day* (Aldershot: Ashgate, 2000); for more recent developments see Hugh Dauncy and Steve Cannon, *Popular Music in France from Chanson to Techno: Culture, Identity and Society* (Aldershot: Ashgate, 2003). Studies (in English) of Brel and Brassens include Sara Poole, *Brel and Chanson: a Critical Appreciation* (Dallas, TX: University Press of America, 2004) and Chris Tinker, *Georges Brassens and Jacques Brel: Personal and Social Narratives in Post-war Chanson* (Liverpool University Press, 2005). Two double-CD anthologies give a flavour of the *Chanson: a Portrait of French Café Songs* (Gale 418) and *From France with Love* (Gale 440); there is a DVD of George Brassens, *Le Petit Monde de Georges Brassens*, Comédie Musicale, by La Troupe du Phénix (Millennium 3 Project, 2001) with bonus tracks of two covers of Brassens's songs in Russian. French music hall radio programmes can be found at radiolaworld.wordpress. com/french-music-hall.

EGYPT

We have drawn on the only major study of Umm Kulthūm in English: Virginia Danielson, *The Voice of Egypt: Umm Kulthūm, Arabic Song, and Egyptian Society in the Twentieth Century* (Chicago and London: University of Chicago Press, 1997). There is also an associated VHS tape *Umm Kulthūm: a Voice like Egypt* which brings the singer to life in ways the printed word cannot.

BOLLYWOOD

Indian film music is covered well in the literature. Dinesh Raheja and Jitendra Kothari, *Indian Cinema: the Bollywood Saga* (New Delhi: Roli Books, 2004) is highly informative, and reasonably up to date. Ashsish Rajadhyaksha and Paul Willemen, *Encyclopedia of Indian Cinema* (New Delhi: Oxford University Press, 1994) is a very useful reference work, but only covers films up to 1995, despite a second impression in 2002. A recent scholarly study of Bollywood music in its film context drawn on here is Anna Morcom's *Hindi Film Songs and the Cinema* (Aldershot: Ashgate, 2007). More general books with valuable information on the subject are Peter Manuel, *Popular Musics of the Non-Western World: an Introductory Survey* (Oxford University Press, 1988), which contains a very useful section on Indian film music, and Mark Slobin (ed.), *Global Soundtracks: Worlds of Film Music* (Middletown, Connecticut: Wesleyan University Press, 2008), which not only has useful chapters on Bollywood but also surveys the wider Indian film industry and others in Asia.

THE 42ND PARALLEL

The countries on the parallel are listed here: en.wikipedia.org/wiki/42nd_parallel_north.

Fado

Salwa El-Shawan Castelo-Branco's *Grove* entry is an excellent overview; sources in English are few, but for a more detailed history (with accompanying CD) see Paul Vernon, *A History of the Portuguese Fado* (Aldershot: Ashgate, 1998). Dejavu Retro have produced a double album set of Amália Rodrigues and an anthology of other female fadistas (R2CD 42–07). Ian Biddle's 2003 paper 'Saudade/Duende: Voice and Nostalgia in the Early Recording Era' is available on the web at www.ncl.ac.uk/sacs/POP/papers/mont.pdf.

Mariza's discography currently stands at seven albums, all on EMI or Virgin.

Flamenco

Robin Totton, *Song of the Outcasts: an Introduction to Flamenco* (Hauppauge, NY: Amadeus Press, 2003) focuses on the singing. Jason Webster's *Duende: a Journey in Search of Flamenco* (London: Doubleday, 2003) is an outsider's journey to the inside.

For a representative CD anthology see the *Rough Guide to Flamenco* (World Music Network).

Corsican and Sardinian polyphony

The only study of Corsican song currently available is Caroline Bithell, *Transported by Song: Corsican Voices from Oral Tradition to World Stage* (Scarecrow Press, 2007). An introduction to Corsican music, including information on improvised polyphony and how to perform it, can be found at the Corsica Isula site at www.corsica-isula.com/music.htm#%20%20Introduction. Sardinian music is explained by Ivan Moody in *Sonos: Sounds of Sardinia* at http://ivanmoody.co.uk/articles.sardinia.htm.

There is a *Cantu a tenore* website with information and video clips at http://wn.com/canto_a_tenore

There are many recordings of Sardinian and Corsican polyphony:

Adasgiu, Barbara Furtuna Buda Musique 823002;
Sard Polyphonies, Coro Cantu a Tenores SFO 003;
E Prite Tottu Custu, Tenore San Gavino de Oniferi FY8118;
Sardegna: Antologia della Musica Sarda Antica e Moderna Dejavu Retro R2CD 44–09

The Italian rice workers can be heard on *Donne della Pianura del Po* SFO 001.

Bulgaria

Polygram have released three CDs of *Le Mystère des Voix Bulgares* and there are many other anthologies available. We have been unable to track down Stefan Tschapkanov's bilingual *The Phenomenon of Bulgarian Folksinging*, which appears to be one of the very few books on the subject.

Throat singing

The best introduction is Theodore Levin and Michael Edgerton's 'The Throat Singers of Tuva', *Scientific American* (September 1999). The Friends of Tuva website has many links to sites which explain the history and practice of Tuvan singing: www.fotuva.org/music/theory.html. The classic Huun-Huur-tu album is *Sixty Horses in My Herd: Old Songs and Tunes of Tuva*.

Georgia

There is a recent anthology of writings on Georgian polyphony: Rusudan Tsurtsumia and Joseph Jordania (eds.), *Echoes from Georgia: Seventeen Arguments on Georgian Polyphony* (Nova Science Publishers Inc. 2010) and some information on the Tbilisi State Conservatory website: www.polyphony.ge/index.php?m=555&lng=eng.

There are several recordings available by Georgian choirs and ensembles (*Georgian Polyphony III* JVC VICG-5225–2). The National Sound Archive 1909 anthology is *Before the Revolution* (TSCD921).

Beijing Opera, Korean *P'ansori* and *Kabuki*

Elizabeth Wichmann, *Listening to Theatre: the Aural Dimension of Beijing Opera* (University of Hawaii Press, 1991) focuses on utterance in the context of Chinese Theatre; Marshall Pihl, *The Korean Singer of Tales* (Cambridge, MA: Harvard University Press, 1994) deals specifically with P'ansori singing; Samuel Leiter (ed.), *A Kabuki Reader: History and Performance* (Armonk, NY: M. E. Sharpe, 2001) is a useful collection of essays. There is a comparison of the vocal requirements for Japanese and Indonesian singing in Adeline Hirschfeld-Medalia, 'The Voice in Wayang and Kabuki', *Asian Theatre Journal* 1:2 (1984): 217–22.

THE 22ND PARALLEL

There are many Victor Jara collections. *Antologia Musical* contains re-mastered early tracks from WEA. Emma Junaro's website (in Spanish) is at www.emmajunaro.com/es/ and contains a discography. Simon Collier's *The Life, Music and Times of Carlos Gardel* (University of Pittsburgh Press, 1986) is a rare biography of an Argentinian singer. Caetano Veloso's discography is considerable, and his account of music and politics in Brazil is compelling reading:

Tropical Truth: a Story of Music and Revolution in Brazil (New York: Da Capo, 2003). There are many videos of Virgínia Rodrigues to be found on the web; her album *Nós* (Hannibal HNCD 1448) is a representative example of her plangent singing.

There is no biography of Thomas Mapfumo at the time of writing, but his large discography documents his musical journey. A good starting point from which to work backwards and forwards is *Shumba* STEW22CD. Many native musics are explored in the three-CD set *Les Voix du Monde* released by the Centre National de la Recherche Scientifique et du Musée de l'Homme, Paris.

Apart from a passing reference to Bruce Chatwin's *The Songlines* (London: Jonathan Cape, 1987), a famous but controversial mixture of travelogue and autobiography, the main source used in our brief study of Australian Aboriginal music is Trevor A. Jones' succinct and authoritative survey: 'The Traditional Music of the Australian Aborigines' in Elizabeth May (ed) *Musics of Many Cultures: An Introduction* (Berkeley: University of California Press, 1980). Another important scholar to note is Catherine J. Ellis. Among her many writings may be singled out the substantial monograph *Aboriginal Music, Education for Living: Cross-Cultural Experiences from South Australia* (St. Lucia, Qld.: University of Queensland Press, 1985).

Bibliography

Agricola, Johann Friedrich, *Anleitung zur Singkunst* (Leipzig, 1757; facs. repr. Leipzig, 1966/1998); trans. into English as *Introduction to the Art of Singing*, ed. Julie Anne Baird (Cambridge University Press, 1997).

Akehurst, F. R. P. and Judith Davis (eds.), *A Handbook of the Troubadours* (Berkeley: University of California Press, 1995).

Anderson, Emily (ed.), *The Letters of Mozart and his Family*, 3rd edn rev. Stanley Sadie and Fiona Smart (London: Macmillan, 1985).

Anhalt, Istvan, *Alternative Voices: Essays on Contemporary Vocal and Choral Composition* (University of Toronto Press, 1985).

Aprile, Giuseppe, *The Modern Italian Method of Singing with a Variety of Progressive Examples; and Thirty Six Solfeggi* (London: Broderip and Wilkinson, 1791).

Armstrong, A., 'Gilbert-Louis Duprez and Gustave Roger in the Composition of Meyerbeer's Le Prophète', *Cambridge Opera Journal* 8: 2 (1996): 147–65.

Arnold, Alison, *Hindi filmī gīt: on the History of Commercial Indian Popular Music*, unpublished PhD dissertation, University of Illinois at Urbana-Champaign, 1991.

Ashbrook, William, 'The First Singers of *Tristan und Isolde*', *The Opera Quarterly* 3: 4 (1985/6): 11–23.

Aubrey, Elizabeth, *The Music of the Troubadours* (Indiana University Press, 2000).

Bach, Albert, *Musical Education and Vocal Culture* (5th edn, London: Kegan Paul, 1898).

Bach, Stephen, *Marlene Dietrich: Life and Legend* (University of Minnesota Press, 2011).

Bacilly, Bénigne de, *Remarques Curieuses sur l'Art de Bien Chanter* (1668) (facs. edn Geneva: Minkoff, 1971); English trans. *Commentary upon the Art of Proper Singing*, ed. Austin B. Caswell (New York: Institute of Medieval Music, 1968).

Bagby, Benjamin, '*Beowulf*, the *Edda*, and the Performance of Medieval Epic: Notes from the Workshop of a Reconstructed "Singer of Tales"', in Evelyn Birge Vitz, Nancy Freeman Regalado and Marilyn Lawrence (eds.), *Performing Medieval Narrative* (Cambridge: D. S. Brewer, 2005): 181–92.

Bailey, Derek, *Improvisation: its Nature and Practice in Music* (Ashbourne: Moorland Publishing, 1980).

Baines, John, *Visual and Written Culture in Ancient Egypt* (Oxford University Press, 2007).

Bairstow, Edward C. and Harry Plunket Greene, *Singing Learned from Speech* (London: Macmillan, 1945).

Bake, Arnold, 'The Music of India', in Egon Wellesz (ed.), *New Oxford History of Music*. Vol. 1: *Ancient and Oriental Music* (Oxford University Press, 1957).

Bakhle, Janaki, *Two Men and Music: Nationalism in the Making of an Indian Classical Tradition* (Oxford University Press, 2005).

Baldauf-Berdes, Jane, *Women Musicians of Venice: Musical Foundations 1525–1855* (Oxford: Clarendon Press, 1993).

Banfield, Stephen, 'Stage and Screen Entertainers in the Twentieth Century', in John Potter (ed.), *The Cambridge Companion to Singing* (Cambridge University Press, 2000): 69–72.

Barbier, Patrick, *The World of the Castrati: the History of an Extraordinary Operatic Phenomenon*, trans. Margaret Crossland (London: Souvenir Press, 1996).

Barker, Andrew, *Greek Musical Writings*. Vol. 1: *The Musician and his Art* (Cambridge University Press, 1984).

Barthes, Roland, 'Le Grain de la Voix', *Musique en jeu* 9 (1972), trans. Stephen Heath in *Image, Music, Text* (London: Fontana, 1977): 179–89.

The Responsibility of Forms: Critical Essays on Music, Art and Representation (New York: Hill and Wang, 1985; Berkeley: University of California Press, 1992).

Bass, John, 'Would Caccini Approve?' *Early Music* 36: 1 (2008): 81–93.

Bassano, Giovanni, *Ricercati, Passaggi et cadentie* (Venice, 1585).

Bauer, Oswald, 'Performance History: a Brief Survey', trans. Stewart Spencer in Ulrich Müller and Peter Wapnewski (eds.), *Wagner Handbook* (Cambridge, MA and London, England: Harvard University Press, 1992): 502–23.

Beck, Eleonora, *Singing in the Garden: Music and Culture in the Tuscan Trecento* (Innsbruck: Studien Verlag, 1998).

Becker, Heinz and Gudrun Becker (eds.), *Giacomo Meyerbeer: a Life in Letters* (London: Christopher Helm, 1983).

Bergeron, Katherine, 'The Castrato as History', *Cambridge Opera Journal* 8: 2 (1996): 167–84.

Berio, Luciano, *Two Interviews* (New York: Marion Boyars, 1985/2000).

Remembering the Future (Harvard University Press, 2006).

Berliner, Paul, *The Soul of Mbira: Music and Traditions of the Shona People of Zimbabwe* (Berkeley, Los Angeles, London: University of California Press, 1978).

Berlioz, Hector *The Art of Music and other Essays* (*À Travers Chants*), trans. and ed. Elizabeth Csicsery-Rónay (Bloomington: Indiana University Press, 1994).

Bilgora, Alan, 'Voices of Prayer and Praise', *Classic Record Collector* (August 2004).

Bithell, Caroline, *Transported by Song: Corsican Voices from Oral Tradition to World Stage* (Lanham, MD: Scarecrow Press, 2007).

Blackburn, Bonnie and Edward Lowinsky, 'Luigi Zenobi and his Letter on the Perfect Musician', *Studi musicali*, 22: 1 (1994): 61–114; repr. in Bonnie

Blackburn, *Composition, Printing and Performance: Studies in Renaissance Music* (Aldershot: Ashgate, 2000).

Blacking, John, *How Musical is Man* (London: Faber and Faber, 1976).

Bohlman, Philip V., *The Land Where Two Streams Flow: Music in the German-Jewish Community of Israel* (Urbana: University of Illinois Press, 1989).

The World Centre for Jewish Music in Palestine 1936–1940: Jewish Musical Life on the Eve of World War II (Oxford University Press, 1992).

World Music: a Very Short Introduction (Oxford University Press, 2002).

Jewish Music and Modernity (Oxford University Press, 2008).

Bor, Joep (ed.), *The Raga Guide: a Survey of 74 Hindustani ragas* (Nimbus Records, 1999).

Bourdieu, Pierre, *Distinction: a Social Critique of the Judgement of Taste* (London: Routledge and Kegan Paul, 1984).

Bovicelli, Giovanni Battista, *Regole, passaggi di musica, madrigali et motetti passeggiati* (Venice, 1594).

Bowles, Edmund A., *La Pratique Musicale au Moyen Age* (Paris: Éditions Minkoff, 1983).

Bradshaw, Murry C., 'Giovanni Luca Conforti and Vocal Embellishment: from Formula to Artful Improvisation', *Performance Practice Review* 8: 2 (1995): 5–27.

Breckbill, David, 'Singing', in Barry Millington (ed.), *The Wagner Compendium: a Guide to Wagner's Life and Music* (London: Thames and Hudson, 1992): 354–8.

'Wagner on Record: Re-evaluating Singing in the Early Years', in Barry Millington and Stewart Spencer (eds.), *Wagner in Performance* (New Haven and London: Yale University Press, 1992).

Broughton, Simon, Mark Ellingham, David Muddyman and Richard Trillo (eds.), *World Music: the Rough Guide* (Rough Guides, 1994, repr. in 2 vols. 2000).

Brown, Clive, 'Performing Practice', in Barry Millington and Stewart Spencer (eds.), *Wagner in Performance* (New Haven and London: Yale University Press, 1992): 99–119.

Classical and Romantic Performing Practice 1750–1900 (Oxford University Press, 1999).

Brown, Howard Mayer, *Embellishing 16th-Century Music* (Oxford University Press, 1976).

Brown, Howard Mayer and Stanley Sadie (eds.), *Performance Practice: Music After 1600* (New York: Norton/Grove Handbooks in Music, 1990).

Burney, Charles, *The Present State of Music in France and Italy* (London, 1771; facs. Elibron Classics, 2005).

The Present State of Music in Germany, the Netherlands and United Provinces (London, 1773; facs. Travis and Emery, 2003).

A General History of Music, From the Earliest Ages to the Present Period, 4 vols. (London, 1782 and 1789).

Busse Berger, Anna Maria, *Medieval Music and the Art of Memory* (Berkeley: University of California Press, 2005).

Butt, John, *Music Education and the Art of Performance in the German Baroque* (Cambridge University Press, 1994).

   Playing with History: the Historical Approach to Musical Performance (Cambridge University Press, 2002).

Caccini, Giulio, *Le Nuove Musiche* (Florence, 1602); trans. and ed. H. Wilby Hitchcock (Madison, WI: A-R Editions, 1970).

Cairns, David (ed.), *The Memoirs of Hector Berlioz* (London: Victor Gollancz, 1969).

Caprioli, Leonella, 'Singing Rossini', in Emanuele Senici (ed.), *The Cambridge Companion to Rossini* (Cambridge University Press, 2004).

Caswell, Austin, 'Mme Cinti-Damoreau and the Embellishment of Italian Opera in Paris: 1820–1845', *Journal of the American Musicological Society* 38 (1975): 459–92.

Catlin-Jairazbhoy, Amy, introduction to Mary Grover, 'Voice Therapy for a Classical Singer from India: a Case Study Combining Eastern and Western Techniques', in *Seminar on Indian Music and the West* (Mumbai: Sangeet Research Academy, 1996).

Cattin, G., *Music of the Middle Ages I* (Cambridge University Press, 1984).

Chatwin, Bruce, *The Songlines* (London: Jonathan Cape, 1987).

Chorley, Henry, *Thirty Years' Musical Recollections* (New York: Vienna House, 1972).

Christiansen, Rupert, *Prima Donna* (London: Bodley Head, 1984).

Cinti-Damoreau, Laure, *Méthode de Chant Composée pour ses Classes du Conservatoire* (Paris, 1849); repr. Laure-Cinthie Damoreau, *Classic Bel Canto Technique* (New York: Dover, 1997).

Clapton, Nicholas, *Moreschi: the Last Castrato* (London: Haus Publishing, 2004).

   'Carlo Broschi Farinelli: Aspects of his Technique and Performance', *Journal for Eighteenth-Century Studies* 28: 3 (2005): 323–38.

Clayton, Martin, *Music, Words and Voice: a Reader* (Manchester University Press, 2008).

Cohen, Judah M., *The Making of a Reform Jewish Cantor: Musical Authority, Cultural Investment* (Indiana University Press, 2009).

Cohen, Ronald D. (ed.), *Alan Lomax: Selected Writings 1934–1997* (New York: Routledge, 2003).

Collier, Simon, *The Life, Music and Times of Carlos Gardel* (University of Pittsburgh Press, 1986).

Conforti, Giovanni Luca, *Breve et Facile Maniera ... per cantare ...* (Venice, 1593).

Constansis, Alexandros, *Hybrid Vocal Personae*, unpublished PhD thesis, University of York, 2009.

Corri, Domenico, *Singers' Preceptor* (London, 1810; facs. repr. *Domenico Corri's Treatise on Singing*, ed. Richard Maunder (New York: Garland, 1995)).

Courlander, Harold, *Haiti Singing* (University of North Carolina Press, 1939; repr. New York: Cooper Square Publishers, 1973).

Creathorne Clayton, Ellen, *Queens of Song: Being Memoirs of Some of the Most Celebrated Female Vocalists* (New York: Harper Brothers, 1865; facs. Whitefish, MT: Kessinger Publishing, 2005).

Crescentini, Girolamo, *Raccolta di Esercizi per il canto all'uso del vocalizzo/ Recueil d'exercises pour la vocalisation musicale* (Paris, c. 1811; facs. *Méthodes et Traités*, Serie 11/1, Paris: Fuzeau, 2005).

Vingt-cinq nouvelles vocalises ou études de l'art du chant (Paris, 1818–32; facs. *Méthodes et Traités*, Serie 11/2 Paris: Fuzeau, 2005).

Croker, Norris, *Handbook for Singers* (London: Augener, 1895).

Crosby, Bing and Pete Martin, *Call Me Lucky* (New York: Muller, 1953; repr. Da Capo Press, 2001).

Crutchfield, Will, 'Vocal Ornamentation in Verdi: the Phonographic Evidence', *19th-Century Music* 7: 1 (1983): 3–54.

Curzon, Henry de, 'Cosima Wagner and Bayreuth', *Musical Times* 71: 1051 (1930): 794–6.

Cyr, Mary, 'A Seventeenth Century Source of Ornamentation for Voice and Viol: British Museum MS. Egerton 2971', *RMA Research Chronicle* 9 (1971): 53–72.

'Eighteenth-Century French and Italian Singing: Rameau's Writing for the Voice', *Music & Letters* 61: 3–4 (1980): 318–37.

Daffern, Helena, *Distinguishing Characteristics of Vocal Techniques in the Specialist Performance of Early Music*, unpublished PhD thesis, University of York, 2008.

Dahl, Linda, *Stormy Weather: the Music and Lives of a Century of Jazz Women* (New York: Limelight Editions, 1984).

Dalla Casa, Girolamo, *Il Vero Modo di Diminuir* (Venice, 1584).

Dame, Joke, 'Voices within the Voices', in Adam Krims (ed.), *Music/Ideology: Resisting the Aesthetic* (Amsterdam: G+B Arts International, 1998).

Danielson, Virginia, *The Voice of Egypt: Umm Kulthūm, Arabic Song, and Egyptian Society in the Twentieth Century* (Chicago and London: University of Chicago Press, 1997).

Dauncy, Hugh and Steve Cannon, *Popular Music in France from Chanson to Techno: Culture, Identity and Society* (Aldershot: Ashgate, 2003).

Davies, J. Q., 'Velutti in Speculum', *Cambridge Opera Journal* 17: 3 (2005): 271–301.

Deathridge, John, 'A Brief History of Wagner Research', in Ulrich Müller and Peter Wapnewski (eds.), *Wagner Handbook* (Cambridge, MA and London, England: Harvard University Press, 1992): 202–26.

Denns, Adrian, *Florilegium omnis fere generis cantionum suavissimarum ad testudinis tabulaturam accommodatarum longe iucundissimo* (Cologne, 1594).

Deshpande, Vamanrao, *Indian Musical Traditions: an Aesthetic Study of the Gharanas in Hindustani Music*, trans S. H. Deshpande (Bombay: Popular Prakashan, 1973).

Dessaix, Robert, *Twilight of Love: Travels with Turgenev* (London: Simon and Schuster, 2005).

Dietrich, Marlene, *Nehmt nur mein Leben* (Munich, 1979); English trans. as *My Life* (London: Pan Books, 1991).

Dissanayake, Ellen, 'Antecedents of the Temporal Arts in Early Mother-Infant Interaction', in Nils L. Wallin, Björn Merker and Steven Brown (eds.),

The Origins of Music (Cambridge: Massachusetts Institute of Technology, 2000): 389–410.

Dobbins, Frank, *Music in Renaissance Lyons* (Oxford: Clarendon Press, 1992).

Dobson, E. J. and Frank Harrison (eds.), *Medieval English Songs* (London: Faber, 1979).

Dodds, George, *Practical Hints for Singers* (London, 1927).

Donald, Merlin, *Origins of the Modern Mind* (Cambridge, MA: Harvard University Press, 1991).

Dowland, John, *Andreas Ornithoparcus His Micrologus or Introduction: Containing the Art of Singing* (1609) (Whitefish, MT: Kessinger Publishing, 2010).

Dreyfus, Laurence, 'Early Music Defended against its Devotees: a Theory of Historical Performance in the 20th Century', *Musical Quarterly* 69 (1983): 297–322.

Duffin, Ross (ed.), *A Performer's Guide to Medieval Music* (Bloomington: Indiana University Press, 2000).

Duprez, Gilbert-Louis, *L'Art du Chant* (Paris, 1846).

Dyer, Joseph, 'Singing with Proper Refinement', *Early Music* 6: 2 (1978): 207–27.

'The Voice in the Middle Ages', in John Potter (ed.), *The Cambridge Companion to Singing* (Cambridge University Press, 2000).

'The Desert, the City and Psalmody in the Late Fourth Century', in Sean Gallagher *et al.* (eds.), *Western Plainchant in the First Millennium* (Aldershot: Ashgate, 2003).

Edgerton, Michael, *The 20th Century Voice* (Oxford University Press, 2004).

Edwards, Kathleen, *The English Secular Cathedrals in the Middle Ages* (2nd rev. edn, Manchester University Press, 1967).

Edwards, Viv and Thomas J. Sienkewicz, *Oral Cultures Past and Present: Rappin' and Homer* (Oxford: Basil Blackwell, 1990).

Elliott, Martha, *Singing in Style* (New Haven: Yale University Press, 2006).

Ellis, Catherine J., *Aboriginal Music, Education for Living: Cross-Cultural Experiences from South Australia* (St. Lucia, Qld.: University of Queensland Press, 1985).

Emerson, Isabelle, *Five Centuries of Women Singers* (Westport, CT: Praeger, 2005).

Evans, Edwin, 'The Art of Singing in Decline', *The Musical Times* 84 (July 1943): 201–2.

Evans, Philip R., *Al Jolson: a Bio-Discography* (Lanham, MD: Scarecrow Press, 1984).

Falk, Dean, 'Hominid Brain Evolution and the Origins of Music', in Nils L. Wallin, Björn Merker and Steven Brown (eds.), *The Origins of Music* (Cambridge, MA: Massachusetts Institute of Technology, 2000): 197–216.

Fallows, David and Tess Knighton (eds.), *Companion to Medieval and Renaissance Music* (London: Dent, 1992; repr. Oxford University Press, 1998).

Farrell, Gerry, *Indian Music and the West* (Oxford University Press, 1997).

Feld, Steven, *Sound and Sentiment: Birds, Weeping, Poetics, and Song in Kaluli Expression* (Philadelphia: University of Pennsylvania Press, 1982).

Fenner, Theodore, *Opera in London: Views of the Press 1785–1830* (Carbondale, IL: Southern Illinois University Press, 1994).

Ferand, Ernest, 'Didactic Embellishment Literature in the Late Renaissance: a Survey of Sources', in Jan LaRue (ed.), *Aspects of Medieval and Renaissance Music: a Birthday Offering to Gustave Reese* (Oxford University Press, 1967).

Fétis, F.-J., *Méthode des Méthodes de chant basée sur les principes des Ecoles les plus célèbres d'Italie et de la France* (Paris and Brussels, 1870; facs. *Méthodes et Traités*, Serie II/2, Paris: Fuzeau, 2005).

Biographie Universelle des Musiciens et Bibliographie Générale de la Musique (Paris: Firmin-Didot, 1870).

Fifield, Christopher, 'Conducting Wagner: the Search for Melos', in Barry Millington and Stewart Spencer (eds.), *Wagner in Performance* (New Haven and London: Yale University Press, 1992).

Finck, Henry, *Songs and Songwriters* (London: Murray, 1900).

Fischer, Jens Malte, '*Sprechgesang* or Bel Canto: Toward a History of Singing Wagner', trans. Michael Tanner, in Ulrich Müller and Peter Wapnewski (eds.), *Wagner Handbook* (Cambridge, MA and London, England: Harvard University Press, 1992): 524–46.

Fischer-Dieskau, Dietrich, *Reverberations: the Memoirs of Dietrich Fischer-Dieskau*, trans. Ruth Hein (New York: Fromm International, 1989).

Fletcher, Peter, *World Musics in Context: a Comprehensive Survey of the World's Major Musical Cultures* (Oxford University Press, 2001).

Foley, John Miles, *The Singer of Tales in Performance* (Bloomington: Indiana University Press, 1995).

Forbes, Elizabeth, *Mario and Grisi: a Biography* (London: Victor Gollancz, 1985).

Foucault, Michel, *The Order of Things* (New York: Random House, 1973).

Fox Strangways, A. H., *The Music of Hindustan* (1914; Oxford: Clarendon Press, 1965).

Frayer, David W. and Chris Nicolay, 'Fossil Evidence for the Origin of Speech Sounds', in Nils L. Wallin, Björn Merker and Steven Brown (eds.), *The Origins of Music* (Cambridge: Massachusetts Institute of Technology, 2000): 217–34.

Freedland, Michael, *Bing Crosby: an Illustrated Biography* (London: André Deutsch, 1998).

Al Jolson (London: W. H. Allen, 1972: 8th edn, Edgware: Valentine Mitchell, 2007).

Freeman, D., 'An 18th-Century Singer's Commission of "Baggage" Arias', *Early Music* 20: 3 (1992): 427–33.

Freitas, Roger, 'The Eroticism of Emasculation: Confronting the Baroque Body of the Castrato', *The Journal of Musicology* 20 (2003): 196–249.

Fricke, Richard, *Wagner in Rehearsal 1875–1876: the Diaries of Richard Frick*, trans. by George R. Fricke, ed. James Deaville with Evan Baker (Stuyvesant, NY: Pendragon Press, 1998); originally *Bayreuth vor dreissig Jahren. Erinnerungen an Wahnfried und aus dem Festspielhause Dresden*.

Friedwald, Will, *Jazz Singing* (London: Quartet Books, 1991).

Friman, Anna Maria, *Modern Performance of Sacred Medieval Music with Particular Reference to Women's Voices*, unpublished PhD thesis, University of York, 2008.

Galatopoulos, Stelios, *Bellini: Life, Times, Music* (London: Sanctuary, 2002).

Gallagher, Sean *et al.* (eds.), *Western Plainchant in the First Millennium* (Aldershot: Ashgate, 2003).

Galliard, John, *Observations on the Florid Song by Pier Francesco Tosi* (London, 1743; facs. London: Reeves, 1967).

Gallo, Alberto, *Music of the Middle Ages,* vols. I and II (Cambridge University Press, 1985).

Garaudé, Alexis de, *Méthode Complète de chant* (Paris, 1841; facs. *Méthodes et Traités,* Serie II/2, Paris: Fuzeau, 2005).

Garcia, Manuel, *Exercises pour la voix* (Paris, *c.* 1835; facs. *Méthodes et Traités,* Serie II/3 Paris: Fuzeau, 2005).

   Traité complet de l'art du chant (Paris, 1840, 1847).

   Garcia's New Treatise on the Art of Singing (London, 1857).

Gattey, Charles Neilson, *Queens of Song* (London: Barrie and Jenkins, 1979).

Gelatt, Roland, *The Fabulous Phonograph* (London: Cassell, 1956).

Ghisi, Federico, D. P. Walker and J. Jacquot, *Musique des Intermèdes de la Pellegrina* (Paris: Éditions du Centre National de la Recherche Scientifique, 1986).

Giddins, Gary, *Bing Crosby: a Pocketful of Dreams – The Early Years 1903 – 1940* (New York: Back Bay Books, 2002).

Giustiniani, Vincenzo, *Discorso sopra la musica,* trans. Carol MacClintock (Middleton, WI: American Institute of Musicology, 1962).

Goldman, Kenneth, *Formulaic Analysis of Serbocroatian Oral Epic Song* (New York: Garland, 1990).

Grover, Mary, 'Voice Therapy for a Classical Singer from India: a Case Study Combining Eastern and Western Techniques', in *Seminar on Indian Music and the West* (Mumbai: Sangeet Research Academy, 1996).

Gutman, Robert, *Richard Wagner: the Man, His Mind and His Music* (London: Secker and Warburg, 1968; repr. Penguin Books, 1971).

Haar, James, *Essays on Italian Poetry and Music in the Renaissance 1350–1600* (Berkeley: University of California Press, 1987).

Hardwick, Keith, liner notes to *Schubert Lieder on Record,* vol. I, EMI CHS 5661502 (1997).

Harrán, Don, *Salamone Rossi: Jewish Musician in Late Renaissance Mantua* (Oxford University Press, 1999).

Harris, M., *Porpora's Elements of Singing* (London, 1858).

Harrison, Frank, *Music in Medieval Britain* (London: Routledge, 1980).

Hast, H. Gregory, 'Vocal and Unvocal', *Music & Letters* 10: 3 (1929).

Hawkins, John, *A General History of the Science and Practice of Music* (London, 1776; repr. 1875, facs. 1969).

Hawkins, Peter, *Chanson: the French Singer-songwriter from Bruant to the Present Day* (Aldershot: Ashgate, 2000).

Haynes, Bruce, *The End of Early Music* (Oxford University Press, 2007).

Heartz, Daniel, 'From Garrick to Gluck: the Reform of Theatre and Opera in the Mid-Eighteenth Century', *Proceedings of the Royal Musical Association* (1967–8): 111–27.

'Farinelli Revisited', *Early Music* 18: 3 (1990): 430–43.

Heriot, Angus, *The Castrati in Opera* (London: Calder, 1960).

Hey, Julius, *Der kleine Hey* (Mainz: Schott Verlag, 1900/1997).

Richard Wagner als Vortragsmeister 1864–1876: Erinnerungen von Julius Hey (Leipzig: Breitkopf and Haertel, 1911).

Hiller, Johann Adam, *Anweisung zum musikalisch-zierlichen Gesange* (1780), ed. and trans. Suzanne J. Beicken as *Treatise on Vocal Performance and Ornamentation* (Cambridge University Press, 2001).

Hirschfeld-Medalia, Adeline, 'The Voice in Wayang and Kabuki', *Asian Theatre Journal* 1: 2 (1984): 217–22.

Hogarth, George, *Memoirs of the Opera*, vol. 1 (London: Richard Bentley, 1851; repr. New York: Da Capo, 1972).

Holmstrom, V. M., 'Jenny Lind's Singing Method', *The Musical Quarterly* 3: 4 (1917): 548–51.

Holroyde, Peggy, *Indian Music: a Vast Ocean of Promise* (London: George Allen and Unwin, 1972).

Hoppin, Richard, *Medieval Music* (New York: Norton, 1972).

Horowitz, Joseph, 'Anton Seidl and America's Wagner Cult', in Barry Millington and Stewart Spencer (eds.), *Wagner in Performance* (New Haven: Yale University Press, 1992): 168–81.

Howard, Patricia, *A Critical Translation from the Italian of Vincenzo Manfredini's Difesa Della Musica Moderna/In Defence of Modern Music* (1788) (New York: Edwin Mellen Press, 2002).

Hucke, Helmut, 'Toward a New Historical View of Gregorian Chant', *Journal of the American Musicological Society* 33: 3 (1980): 437–9.

Huelsenbeck, Richard, *Memoirs of a Dada Drummer* (Berkeley: University of California Press, 1969).

Husler, Frederick and Yvonne Rodd-Marling, *Singing: the Physical Nature of the Vocal Organ* (London: Faber and Faber, 1965; rev. 1976).

Idelsohn, Abraham Z., *Jewish Music in its Historical Development* (New York: Holt & Co., 1929; repr. Schocken Books, 1967).

Jairazbhoy, Nazir Ali, 'Svaraprastāra in North Indian Classical Music', *Bulletin of the School of Oriental and African Studies* 24: 2 (1961): 307–25.

James, Kenneth, 'Venanzio Rauzzini and the Search for Musical Perfection', *Bath History* vol. III (Gloucester: Alan Sutton, 1990): 90–113.

Jefferson, Alan, *Lotte Lehmann 1888–1976: a Centenary Biography* (London: Julia MacRae, 1988).

Jeffery, Peter, *Re-Envisioning Past Musical Cultures* (University of Chicago Press, 1995).

'Monastic Reading and the Emerging Roman Chant Repertory', in Sean Gallagher *et al.* (eds.), *Western Plainchant in the First Millennium* (Aldershot: Ashgate, 2003).

Jones, Trevor A., 'The Traditional Music of the Australian Aborigines', in
    Elizabth May (ed.), *Musics of Many Cultures: an Introduction* (Berkeley:
    University of California Press, 1980).
Kalib, Sholom, *The Musical Tradition of the Eastern European Synagogue* (Syracuse
    University Press, 2002).
Kayes, Gillyanne, *Singing and the Actor* (2nd edn, London: A. C. Black, 2004).
Keates, Jonathan, *Italian Journeys* (London: Heinemann, 1991).
Kelly, Michael, *Solo Recital: the Reminiscences of Michael Kelly*, ed. Herbert van
    Thal (London: Folio Society, 1972).
Kendall-Davies, Barbara, *The Life and Work of Pauline Viardot Garcia*. Vol. 1:
    The Years of Fame 1836–1863 (Amersham: Cambridge Scholars Press, 2003).
Kenyon, Nicholas (ed.), *Authenticity and Early Music* (Oxford University Press,
    1988).
Kirby, Michael, *Futurist Performance* (New York: PAJ Publications, 1971).
Kirkendale, Warren, *The Court Musicians in Florence during the Principate of the
    Medici* (Florence: Leo S. Olschki Editore, 1993).
    Emilio de'Cavalieri: Gentilhuomo Romano (Florence: Leo S. Olschki Editore,
    2001).
Kittler, Friedrich, *Discourse Networks 1800/1900* (Stanford University Press, 1990).
    Gramophone, Film, Typewriter (Stanford University Press, 1999).
    Optical Media (Cambridge: Polity Press, 2010).
Kivy, Peter, *Authenticities, Philosophies, and Reflections on Musical Performance*
    (Ithaca and London: Cornell University Press, 1995).
Klein, Hermann, *Thirty Years of Musical Life in London* (New York: Century,
    1903).
    Herman Klein and the Gramophone, ed. William R. Moran (Portland, OR:
    Amadeus Press, 1990).
Knighton, Tess and David Fallows (eds.), *Companion to Medieval and Renaissance
    Music* (Dent 1992; repr. Oxford University Press, 1998).
Krims, Adam (ed.), *Music/Ideology: Resisting the Aesthetic* (Amsterdam: G+B Arts
    International, 1998).
Lablache, Louis, *Méthode Complète du Chant* (Paris, 1840); English trans.
    Lablache's Abridged Method of Singing (Cincinnati, OH: John Church,
    1873).
LaRue, C. Steven, *Handel and His Singers* (Oxford: Clarendon, 1995).
Lawrence, Vera Brodsky, *Strong on Music: the New York Music Scene in the Days
    of George Templeton Strong*, vol. II (University of Chicago Press, 1995).
Lawson, Colin and Robin Stowell, *The Historical Performance of Music: an
    Introduction* (Cambridge University Press, 1999).
Lawson, Colin and Robin Stowell (eds.), *History of Musical Performance*
    (Cambridge University Press, forthcoming).
Leech-Wilkinson, Daniel *The Modern Invention of Medieval Music: Scholarship,
    Ideology, Performance* (Cambridge University Press, 2002)
    'Portamento and Musical Meaning', *Journal of Musicological Research* 25
    (2006): 233–61.

Lehmann, Lotte, *Wings of Song* (London, 1938).
  More than Singing: the Interpretation of Songs (New York: Boosey & Hawkes, 1945; repr. Dover, 1985).
Leisma, Matti, 'Bel canto ja Richard Wagnerin laulajaihanne' (Bel canto and Richard Wagner's ideal singer), *Musiikki* 22: 4 (1992): 25–66 (in Finnish).
Leiter, Samuel (ed.), *A Kabuki Reader: History and Performance* (Armonk, NY: M. E. Sharpe, 2001).
Levin, Theodore and Michael Edgerton, 'The Throat Singers of Tuva', *Scientific American* (September 1999).
Lockwood, Lewis, *Music in Renaissance Ferrara 1400–1505* (Cambridge, MA: Harvard University Press, 1992).
Lomax, Alan, *Folk Song Style and Culture* (Washington, DC: American Association for the Advancement of Science, 1968; repr. New Brunswick: Transaction Books, 1968).
Lord, Albert B., *The Singer of Tales* (Cambridge, MA: Harvard University Press, 1960).
  The Singer Resumes the Tale, ed. Mary Louise Lord (Ithaca, NY: Cornell University Press, 1995).
Lyotard, Jean-François, 'A Few Words to Sing', in Adam Krims (ed.), *Music/Ideology: Resisting the Aesthetic* (Amsterdam: G+B Arts International, 1998).
Mabry, Sharon, *Exploring Twentieth-Century Vocal Music: a Practical Guide to Innovations in Performance and Repertoire* (Oxford University Press, 2002).
MacClintock, Carol, 'The Monodies of Francesco Rasi', *Journal of the American Musicological Society* 14: 1 (1961): 31–6.
  Readings in the History of Music in Performance (Bloomington: Indiana University Press, 1979).
Mâche, François-Bernard, 'The Necessity of and Problems with a Universal Musicology', in Nils L. Wallin, Björn Merker and Steven Brown (eds.), *The Origins of Music* (Cambridge: Massachusetts Institute of Technology, 2000): 473–9.
Mackinlay, Sterling, *Garcia the Centenarian and his Times* (Edinburgh: Blackwood, 1908).
Mancini, Giambattista, *Pensieri e Riflessioni Pratiche sopra il Canto Figurato* (Vienna, 1774, rev. 1777); English trans. E. Foreman, *Practical Reflections on Figured Singing* (Champaign, IL: Pro Musica Press, 1967).
Manuel, Peter, *Popular Musics of the Non-Western World: an Introductory Survey* (Oxford University Press, 1988).
  Cassette Culture: Popular Music and Technology in North India (Chicago and London: University of Chicago Press, 1993).
Marcello, B., 'Il Teatro Alla Moda Part I', *Musical Quarterly* 34: 3 (1948): 371–403.
Marchesi, Mathilde, *Bel Canto: a Theoretical and Practical Vocal Method* (New York: Dover, 1970).
Mattes, Ralf, 'Ornamentation and Improvisation after 1300', in Ross Duffin (ed.), *A Performer's Guide to Medieval Music* (Indiana University Press, 2000).

McGee, Timothy, *Medieval and Renaissance Music: a Performer's Guide* (University of Toronto Press, 1985).

The Sound of Medieval Song (Oxford: Clarendon Press, 1998).

McGee, Timothy (ed.), *Improvisation in the Arts of the Middle Ages and Renaissance* (Kalamazoo: Western Michigan University Press, 2003).

McKinnon, James, *Music in Early Christian Literature* (Cambridge University Press, 1987).

'Christian Antiquity' in James McKinnon (ed.), *Antiquity and the Middle Ages: from Ancient Greece to the 15th Century* (London: Macmillan, 1990): 68–87.

'The Emergence of Gregorian Chant in the Carolingian Era', in James McKinnon (ed.), *Antiquity and the Middle Ages: from Ancient Greece to the 15th Century* (London: Macmillan, 1990).

Melba, Nellie, *Melba Method* (Lodnon, 1926).

Mengozzi, Bernardo *et al.*, *Méthode de chant du Conservatoire de Musique* (Paris, 1804; facs. *Méthodes et Traités*, Serie II/I, Paris: Fuzeau, 2005).

Merlin, Countess de, *Memoirs and Letters of Madame Malibran* (London, 1840).

Mersenne, M., *Harmonie universelle* (Paris: Cramoisy, 1636; facs. Paris: CNRS, 1963).

Michotte, Edmond, *Richard Wagner's Visit to Rossini (Paris 1860) and An Evening at Rossini's in Beau-Séjour (Passy) in 1858*, trans. Herbert Weinstock (University of Chicago Press, 1968).

Middleton, Richard, *Studying Popular Music* (Milton Keynes: Open University Press, 1990).

Miller, Philip, introduction to Mathilde Marchesi, *Method* (New York: Dover, 1970).

Miller, Terry and Andrew Shahriari, *World Music: a Global Journey* (2nd edn, New York: Routledge, 2007).

Millet, Jean, *La Belle méthode ou l'art de bien chanter* (1666), repr. intro. Albert Cohen (New York: Da Capo Press, 1973).

Millington, Barry and Stewart Spencer (eds.), *Wagner in Performance* (New Haven and London: Yale University Press, 1992).

Mithen, Steven, *The Singing Neanderthals: the Origins of Music, Language, Mind and Body* (London: Weidenfeld and Nicolson, 2005).

Moran, William (ed.), *Herman Klein and the Gramophone* (Portland, OR: Amadeus Press, 1991).

Morcom, Anna, *Hindi Film Songs and the Cinema* (Aldershot: Ashgate, 2007).

Morehen, John (ed.), *English Choral Practice 1400–1650* (Cambridge University Press, 1995).

Morley, Thomas A., *A Plain and Easy Introduction to Practical Music* (London: Dent, 1962).

Mount Edgcumbe, Richard, *Musical Reminiscences of the Earl of Mount Edgcumbe: Containing an Account of the Italian Opera in England from 1773 to 1834* (London, 1834; repr. New York: Da Capo, 1973).

Müller, Ulrich and Peter Wapnewski (eds.), trans. John Deathridge, *Wagner Handbook* (Cambridge, MA and London, England: Harvard University Press, 1992).

Müller-Heuser, Franz, *Vox Humana: Ein Beitrag zur Untersuchung der Stimmästhetik des Mittelalters* (Kassel: Bosse, 1963).

Musica Enchiriadis, trans. Raymond Erickson (New Haven: Yale University Press, 1995).

Nelli, René, *Troubadours and Trouvères* (Paris: Hachette, 1979).

Nettl, Bruno, *Music in Primitive Culture* (Cambridge, MA: Harvard University Press, 1956).

'An Ethnomusicologist Contemplates Universals in Musical Sound and Musical Culture', in Nils L. Wallin, Björn Merker and Steven Brown (eds.), *The Origins of Music* (Cambridge, MA: Massachusetts Institute of Technology, 2000): 463–72.

Neuman, Daniel, *The Life of Music in North India: the Organization of an Artistic Tradition* (University of Chicago Press, 1990).

Newcomb, Anthony, *The Madrigal at Ferrara*, 2 vols. (Princeton University Press, 1980).

Newman, Ernest, *Wagner as Man and Artist* (2nd edn, London: Victor Gollancz, 1924; repr. 1963).

Northrop Moore, Jerrold, *A Voice in Time: the Gramophone of Fred Gaisberg 1873–1951* (London: Hamish Hamilton, 1976).

O'Neill, Mary, *Courtly Love Songs of Medieval France* (Oxford University Press, 2006).

Osmond-Smith, David, *Two Interviews* (New York: Marion Boyars,1985).

'"The Tenth Oscillator": the Work of Cathy Berberian 1958–1966', *Tempo* (2004).

Page, Christopher, *The Christian West and its Singers: the First Thousand Years* (New Haven: Yale University Press, 2010).

Palisca, Claude (ed.), *Hucbald, Guido and John on Music: Three Medieval Treatises*, trans. Warren Babb (New Haven: Yale University Press, 1978).

Parry, Milman, 'L'épithète traditionnelle dans Homère. Essai sur un problème de style homérique', *Les Belles Lettres* 8 (1928).

Paton, John Glenn (ed.), *Vaccai: Practical Method of Italian Singing* (New York: Schirmer, 1975).

Pesch, Ludwig, *The Illustrated Companion to South Indian Classical Music* (New Delhi: Oxford University Press, 1999).

Petrov, Stephen and Leonard Mustazza (eds.), *The Frank Sinatra Reader* (Oxford University Press, 1997).

Philip, Robert, *Performing Music in the Age of Recording* (New Haven: Yale University Press, 2004).

Pihl, Marshall, *The Korean Singer of Tales* (Cambridge, MA: Harvard University Press, 1994).

Pitts, Michael and Frank Hoffman, *The Rise of the Crooners* (Lanham, MD: Scarecrow Press, 2001).

Pleasants, Henry, *Death of a Music? The Decline of the European Tradition and the Rise of Jazz* (London: Victor Gollancz, 1961).

The Great Singers (London: Victor Gollancz, 1967).

Classical Music and all that Jazz: an Adventure in Music Criticism (London: Victor Gollancz, 1969).

The Great American Popular Singers (New York: Gollancz, 1974).

'Tracking Down the Oldest Singing Voice', *Recorded Sound* 85 (January 1984): 12–16.

Poole, Sara, *Brel and Chanson: a Critical Appreciation* (Dallas: University Press of America, 2004).

Porges, Heinrich, *Wagner Rehearsing the 'Ring': an Eye-Witness Account of the Stage Rehearsals of the First Bayreuth Festival*, trans. Robert L. Jacobs (Cambridge University Press, 1983); originally published in German as *Die Bühnenproben zu den Bayreuther Festspielen des Jahres 1876*, in instalments in *Bayreuther Blätter*, 1881–1896.

Potter, John, *Vocal Authority* (Cambridge University Press, 1998).

'Jazz Singing: the First 100 Years', in John Potter (ed.), *The Cambridge Companion to Singing* (Cambridge University Press, 2000).

'Beggar at the Door: the Rise and Fall of Portamento in Singing', *Music & Letters* 87: 4 (2006): 523–50.

'The Tenor-castrato Connection', *Early Music* 35: 1 (2007).

Tenor: History of a Voice (New Haven: Yale University Press, 2009).

'The Long Eighteenth Century', in Colin Lawson and Robin Stowell (eds.), *History of Musical Performance* (Cambridge University Press, forthcoming).

'Issues in the Modern Performance of Medieval Music', in Mark Everist (ed.), *The Cambridge History of Medieval Music* (Cambridge University Press, forthcoming).

Potter, John (ed.), *The Cambridge Companion to Singing* (Cambridge University Press, 2000).

Praetorius, Michael, *Syntagma musicum*, 3 vols. (Wolfenbüttel, 1619); vol. III trans. and ed. Jeffery Kite-Powell (Oxford University Press, 2004).

Quantz, Johann, *Versuch einer Anweisung die Flöte traversiere zu spielen* (Berlin, 1752); trans. and ed. Edward R. Reilly as *On Playing the Flute* (2nd edn, London: Faber, 2001).

Qureshi, Regula Burckhardt, *Master Musicians of India: Hereditary Sarangi Players Speak* (New York: Routledge, 2007).

Radomski, James, *Manuel García (1775–1832): Chronicle of the Life of a Bel Canto Tenor at the Dawn of Romanticism* (Oxford University Press, 2000).

Raheja, Dinesh and Jitendra Kothari, *Indian Cinema: the Bollywood Saga* (New Delhi: Roli Books, 2004).

Raja, Deepak, *Khayal Vocalism: Continuity within Change* (New Delhi: D. K. Printword, 2009).

Rajadhyaksha, Ashsish and Paul Willemen, *Encyclopedia of Indian Cinema* (New Delhi: Oxford University Press, 1994).

Rauzzini, Venanzio, *24 Solfeggi or Exercises for the Voice* (Bath, 1808).

Read, Oliver and Walter Welch, *From Tinfoil to Stereo: Evolution of the Phonograph* (Indianapolis: Howard W. Sams, 1959; rev. edn University of Florida Press, 2006).

Rice, J., 'Mozart and his Singers', *Opera Quarterly* 11: 4 (1995): 31–52.

Richter, Hans, *Dada: Art and Anti-art* (London: Thames and Hudson, 1978).

Robbins Landon, H. C., *Haydn Chronicle and Works: Haydn in England 1791–1795* (London: Thames and Hudson, 1983).

Rognoni, Francesco, *Selva di varii passaggi* (Venice, 1620).

Ronald, Landon, *Variations on a Personal Theme* (London: Hodder and Stoughton, 1922).

Rosenberg, Samuel and Hans Tischler (eds.), *Chanter M'Estuet: Songs of the Trouvères* (London: Faber, 1981).

Rosenblatt, Samuel, *Yossele Rosenblatt: the Story of his Life as told by his Son* (New York: Farrar, Strauss and Young, 1954).

Rosenthal, Harold (ed.), *The Mapleson Memoirs: the Career of an Operatic Impresario 1858–1888* (London: Putnam, 1966).

Rosselli, John, *Singers of Italian Opera* (Cambridge University Press, 1992).

Rossi, Bastiano de, *Descrizione dell'apparato, e degl'intermedi. Fatti per la commedia rappresentata in Firenze nelle nozze de'serenissimi don Ferdinando Medici, e madama Cristina di Loreno …* (Florence, 1589).

Ruckert, George E. *Music in North India: Experiencing Music, Expressing Culture* (Oxford University Press, 2004).

Sachs, Curt, *The Rise of Music in the Ancient World, East and West* (New York: Norton and Company, 1943).

A Short History of World Music (2nd edn, London: Dennis Dobson, 1956).

The Wellsprings of Music (The Hague: Martinus Nijhoff, 1962).

Sadie, Stanley (ed.), *Wagner and his Operas* (London: Macmillan, 2000).

Sanyal, Ritwik and Richard Widdess, *Dhrupad: Tradition and Performance in Indian Music* (Aldershot: Ashgate, 2004).

Saslow, James, *The Medici Wedding of 1589: Florentine Festival as Theatrum Mundi* (New Haven: Yale University Press, 1996).

Sawkins, Lionel, 'For and against the Order of Nature: Who Sang Soprano?', *Early Music* 15: 3 (1987): 315–24.

Schneider, Marius, 'Primitive Music', in Egon Wellesz (ed.), *New Oxford Dictionary of Music*, vol. 1 (Oxford University Press, 1957).

Schumann, Elizabeth, *German Song* (London: Max Parrish, 1948).

Scott, Michael, *The Record of Singing*, 2 vols. (London: Duckworth 1977 and 1980) with illustrations from the Stuart-Liff Collection.

Seeger, Anthony, *Why Suyá Sing: a Musical Anthropology of an Amazonian People* (Cambridge University Press, 1987).

Shaw, George Bernard, *Music in London*, vol. 11 (London: Constable, 1932).

Shawe-Taylor, Desmond, 'Wagner and His Singers', in Barry Millington and Stewart Spencer (eds.), *Wagner in Performance* (New Haven: Yale University Press, 1992): 15–28.

Shelmemy, Kay Kaufman, 'Toward an Ethnomusicology of the Early Music Movement: Thoughts on Bridging Discipline and Musical Worlds', *Ethnomusicology* 45 (2001): 1–29.

Sher, Richard, 'Guglielmo Gonzaga and the Castrati', *Renaissance Quarterly* 33: 1 (1980).

Singer, Milton, *When a Great Tradition Modernizes: an Anthropological Approach to Indian Civilization* (London: Pall Mall Press, 1972).

Skelton, Geoffrey, *Wagner at Bayreuth: Experiment and Tradition* (London: Barrie and Rockliff, 1965).

Slater, Peter J. B., 'Birdsong Repertoires: Their Origins and Use', in Nils L. Wallin, Björn Merker and Steven Brown (eds.), *The Origins of Music* (Cambridge: MA: Massachusetts Institute of Technology, 2000): 49–63.

Slobin, Mark, *Chosen Voices: the Story of the American Cantorate* (University of Illinois Press, 1989).

Slobin, Mark (ed.), *Global Soundtracks: Worlds of Film Music* (Middletown, CT: Wesleyan University Press, 2008).

Sorrell, Neil, 'From "harm-omnium" to harmonia omnium', *Journal of the Indian Musicological Society* 40 (2009–2010).

Sorrell, Neil and Ram Narayan, *Indian Music in Performance: a Practical Introduction* (Manchester University Press, 1980).

Spencer, Stewart, 'Wagner Literature: Biographies', in Barry Millington (ed.), *The Wagner Compendium: a Guide to Wagner's Life and Music* (London: Thames and Hudson, 1992).

Spoto, Donald, *Lenya: a Life* (London: Little, Brown and Company, 1989).

Stark, James, *Bel Canto: a History of Vocal Pedagogy* (University of Toronto Press, 1999).

Steane, J. B., *The Grand Tradition* (London: Duckworth, 1974).

Stein, Deborah and Robert Spillman, *Poetry into Song: the Performance and Analysis of Lieder* (Oxford University Press, 1996).

Stendhal (Henri Beyle), *The Life of Rossini*, trans. Richard Coe (London: Calder, 1985).

Stock, Jonathan, *World Sound Matters* (London: Schott Educational Publications, 1996).

Stowell, Robin and Colin Lawson (eds.), *Cambridge History of Musical Performance* (Cambridge University Press, forthcoming).

Strohm, Reinhard, *Music in Late Medieval Bruges* (Oxford: Clarendon Press, 1990).

Strunk, Oliver, *Source Readings in Music History* (London: Faber, 1981).

Sundberg, Johan, *The Science of the Singing Voice* (Dekalb: Northern Illinois University Press, 1987).

'Where Does the Sound Come from?' in John Potter (ed.), *The Cambridge Companion to Singing* (Cambridge University Press, 2000): 240–6.

Szwed, John, *The Man Who Recorded the World: a Biography of Alan Lomax* (Portsmouth, NH: William Heinemann, 2010).

Tagore, S. M. (ed.), *Hindu Music from Various Authors* (3rd edn, Varanasi: The Chowkhamba Sanskrit Series Office, 1965).

Taruskin, Richard, *Text and Act: Essays on Music and Performance* (Oxford University Press, 1995).

'The Pastness of the Present and the Presence of the Past', in Nicholas Kenyon (ed.), *Authenticity and Early Music* (Oxford University Press, 1988).

Taylor, Ronald, *The Art of the Minnesinger*, 2 vols. (Cardiff: University of Wales Pres, 1968).

Tinker, Chris, *Georges Brassens and Jacques Brel: Personal and Social Narratives in Post-war Chanson* (Liverpool University Press, 2005).

Titon, Jeff Todd (ed.), *Worlds of Music: an Introduction to the Music of the World's Peoples* (2nd edn, Florence, KY: Wadsworth Publishing, 2004).

Toft, Robert, *Aural Images of Lost Traditions* (University of Toronto Press, 1992).

Tosi, Pier Francesco, *Opinioni de' cantori antichi e moderni* (Bologna, 1723); English trans. J. E. Galliard as *Observations on the Florid Song* (London, 1742; facs. repr. London: Reeves, 1967).

Totton, Robin, *Song of the Outcasts: an Introduction to Flamenco* (Hauppauge, NY: Amadeus Press, 2003).

Treadwell, Nina, 'She Descended on a Cloud "from the highest spheres": Florentine Monody "alla Romanina"', *Cambridge Opera Journal* 16: 1 (2004): 1–22.

Treitler, Leo, *With Voice and Pen* (Oxford University Press, 2003).

Tsurtsumia, Rusudan and Joseph Jordania (eds.), *Echoes from Georgia: Seventeen Arguments on Georgian Polyphony* (Hauppauge, NY: Nova Science Publishers, 2010).

Tunley, David, *Salons, Singers and Songs: a Background to Romantic French Song 1830–1870* (Aldershot: Ashgate, 2002).

Vaccai, Nicola, *Metodo Pratico di Canto Italiano in 15 Lezioni e un'Appendice…* (1833), trans. and ed. Michael Aspinall (Turin: Giancarlo Zedde, 1999).

Van der Meer, Wim, *Hindustani Music in the 20th Century* (The Hague: Martinus Nijhoff, 1980).

Veloso, Caetano, *Tropical Truth: a Story of Music and Revolution in Brazil* (New York: Da Capo Press, 2003).

Verdino-Süllwold, Carla Maria, *We Need a Hero! Heldentenors from Wagner's Time to the Present* (New York: Weiala Press, 1989).

Vernon, Paul, *A History of the Portuguese Fado* (Aldershot: Ashgate, 1998).

Vicentino, Nicola, *L'Antica Musica: Ridotta alla Moderna Prattica*, trans. Maria Rika Maniates as *Ancient Music Adapted for Modern Practice* (New Haven: Yale University Press, 1996).

Vigoda, Samuel, *Legendary Voices: the Fascinating Lives of the Great Cantors* (New York: M. P. Press, 1981).

Viswanathan, T. and Matthew Harp Allen, *Music in South India: The Karṇāṭak Concert Tradition and Beyond: Experiencing Music, Expressing Culture* (Oxford University Press, 2004).

Waddington, Patrick, 'Henry Chorley, Pauline Viardot and Turgenev: a Musical and Literary Friendship', *Musical Quarterly* 67 (1981): 165–92.

Wade, Bonnie C., *Khyāl: Creativity within North India's Classical Music Tradition* (Cambridge University Press, 1984).

Wagner, Richard, *Selected Letters of Richard Wagner*, trans. Stewart Spencer and Barry Millington (New York: Norton, 1987).
  Actors and Singers, trans. William Ashton Ellis (Lincoln: University of Nebraska Press, 1995).
Wallaschek, Richard, *Primitive Music* (London: Longmans Green, 1893; repr New York: Da Capo Press, 1970).
Wallin, Nils L., Björn Merker and Steven Brown (eds.), *The Origins of Music* (Cambridge, MA: Massachusetts Institute of Technology, 2000).
Webster, Jason, *Duende: a Journey in Search of Flamenco* (London: Doubleday, 2003).
Wellesz, Egon (ed.), *New Oxford History of Music*. Vol. 1: *Ancient and Oriental Music* (Oxford University Press, 1957).
West, M. L., *Ancient Greek Music* (Oxford: Clarendon, 1992).
Wichmann, Elizabeth, *Listening to Theatre: the Aural Dimension of Beijing Opera* (University of Hawaii Press, 1991).
Willard, Captain N. August, 'A Treatise on the Music of Hindoostan', in S. M. Tagore (ed.), *Hindu Music from Various Authors* (3rd edn, Varanasi: The Chowkhamba Sanskrit Series Office, 1965).
Wishart, Trevor, *On Sonic Art* (Amsterdam: Harwood, 1996 – also includes CD).
Wistreich, Richard, '*La voce e grata assai, ma*…: Monteverdi on Singing', *Early Music* 21 (1994): 7–19.
  'Monteverdi in Performance', in John Whenham and Richard Wistreich (eds.), *The Cambridge Companion to Monteverdi* (Cambridge University Press, 2007): 261–79.
  Warrior, Courtier, Singer: Giulio Cesare Brancaccio and the Performance of Identity in the Late Renaissance (Aldershot: Ashgate, 2007).
Wood, Henry, *The Gentle Art of Singing* (London: Milford 1927/1930).
Woodfield, Ian, *Music of the Raj: a Social and Economic History of Music in Late Eighteenth-Century Anglo-Indian Society* (Oxford University Press, 2000).
Wright, Craig, *Music at the Court of Burgundy* (Henryville, PA: Institute of Medieval Music, 1979).
  Music and Ceremony at Notre Dame of Paris 500–1550 (Cambridge University Press, 1989).
Zarlino, Gioseffe, *The Art of Counterpoint: Part Three of Le Istitutioni Harmoniche, 1558*, trans. Guy Marco and Claude Palisca (New York: Norton, 1968).

Index

Printed in the USA
CPSIA information can be obtained
at www.ICGtesting.com
LVHW011120180824
788602LV00008B/607